W9-DAS-939

SECOND LANGUAGE READING AND VOCABULARY LEARNING

Educational Linguistics
Library

SECOND LANGUAGE READING AND VOCABULARY LEARNING

edited by

Thomas Huckin

Margot Haynes

James Coady

ABLEX PUBLISHING CORPORATION
NORWOOD, NEW JERSEY

Second Printing 1995

Copyright © 1993 by Ablex Publishing Corporation

All rights reserved. No part of this publication may be reproduced, stored in a retrieval system, or transmitted, in any form or by any means, electronic, mechanical, photocopying, microfilming, recording, or otherwise, without permission of the publisher.

Printed in the United States of America.

Library of Congress Cataloging-in-Publication Data

Second language reading and vocabulary learning / edited by Thomas Huckin, Margot
    Haynes, James Coady.
      p. cm.
    Includes bibliographical references and index.
    ISBN 0-89391-850-4 (cloth).—ISBN 0-89391-906-3 (pbk.)
      1. Language and languages—Study and teaching. 2. Reading. 3. Vocabulary—
    Study and teaching. I. Huckin, Thomas N. II. Haynes, Margot. III. Coady, James.
    P53.S392   1992
    481'.007—dc20   92-10616
                                                 CIP

Ablex Publishing Corporation
355 Chestnut Street
Norwood, New Jersey 07648

TABLE OF CONTENTS

I
Points of Departure

Chapter 1
Research on ESL/EFL Vocabulary Acquisition: Putting It In Context

James Coady
Department of Linguistics
Ohio University
Athens, OH

This chapter surveys the recent research on L2 vocabulary acquisition in the context of reading. First, there is a historical review of the role of vocabulary in recent approaches to ESL/EFL instruction, and of the models of reading that have influenced ESL/EFL instruction over the past 25 years. Second, the mystery and paradox of vocabulary acquisition will be explored, as well as an attempted solution, the vocabulary control movement. Third, the centrality of word identification in interactive models of reading will be analyzed, including Perfetti's verbal efficiency theory. Fourth, schema theory and the process of vocabulary learning will be discussed, including memory techniques. Fifth, the complexities of word meaning are treated. Sixth, a theory of acquisition will be presented that distinguishes high-frequency core vocabulary from low-frequency vocabulary. Seventh, the question of how words are stored in the mental lexicon will be discussed. Finally, there is a review of how words are learned in context.

Many ESL/EFL professionals are now recognizing that vocabulary acquisition in the context of reading is an important component of foreign language acquisition that has been sadly neglected (cf. Bensoussan & Laufer, 1984; Carter, 1987; Carter & McCarthy, 1988; Coady, 1986; Cohen & Aphek, 1980; Gairns & Redman, 1986; Hague, 1987; Harvey, 1983; Stieglitz, 1983; Haynes, 1984;

Laufer & Bensoussan, 1982; Meara, 1980, 1984; Morgan & Rinvolucri, 1986; Nation, 1990).[1] One of the first to lament this neglect, Jack Richards, has attributed it to the "effects of trends in linguistic theory" (1976, p. 77). Vocabulary has not received enough attention, either in past ESL/EFL trends or at present.

THE ROLE OF VOCABULARY IN ESL/EFL INSTRUCTION

As Maley (1986) notes in his introduction to *Vocabulary,* by Morgan and Rinvolucri:

> It is curious to reflect that so little importance has been given to vocabulary in modern language teaching. Both the behaviorist/structural model and the functional/communicative model have, in their different ways, consistently underplayed it. (p. 3)

It is possible to trace vocabulary as a central part of language learning throughout the history of the grammar-translation methods, as well as in early versions of the direct method, into the 20th century. Audio-lingual methods from the 1940s onward, however, in reaction to the weak oral skills produced by grammar-translation, emphasized oral skills, accurate production, and limited vocabulary knowledge as a way to build good language use habits. It was assumed that good language habits, and exposure to the language itself, would eventually lead to an increased vocabulary. Primary consideration was not given to the needs of students who would have to function well in academic contexts with concomitant high literacy demands.

The next major transition in ESL/EFL methodology, which was the movement towards communicative approaches in the 1970s, did not seek to restore vocabulary instruction as a primary concern. Rather, the focus was on the appropriate use of language varieties (i.e., notions and functions) as well as an emphasis on language as discourse. The acquisition of a second language was treated as a phenomenon analogous to first language acquisition. Since L1 vocabulary development seems to occur so naturally, it was assumed that vocabulary would take care of itself in L2 acquisition.

The final trend, which was in some respects an outgrowth of the communicative approaches, was the development of "natural approaches" that also took their cues from the seemingly effortless nature of first language development. These approaches proposed that ESL/EFL teaching should replicate L1 learning conditions and let students acquire language skills naturally (Krashen, 1982).

On the other hand, there are some scholars who argue that, for students with academic goals, no matter how intuitive the appeal, natural learning will not provide the literacy skills necessary for coping with academic demands (Carrell,

Devine, & Eskey, 1988; Dubin, Eskey, & Grabe, 1986). They claim that, unlike oral language skills, academic literacy skills are not acquired naturally, but require instruction and training. For example, the subskills of summarizing a text, finding the main idea, identifying rhetorical structures in a text, and so on, all involve some instruction. One of the arguments to be found in this volume is that, like these components of literacy skills, the development of extensive vocabulary knowledge for literacy purposes appears to require some direct instruction and training, as well as extensive exposure to the language (usually through reading) (see Coady et al., Chapter 11, this volume).

Is it enough just to let students learn vocabulary naturally through ordinary language experiences? Nagy and Anderson (1984) concluded that, for native speakers, "even the most ruthlessly systematic direct vocabulary instruction could neither account for a significant proportion of all the words children actually learn, nor cover more than a modest proportion of the words they will encounter in school reading materials" (p. 304). It is easy, on the basis of such research, to claim that vocabulary is obviously learned in a natural manner without the need for formal instruction. But as was previously mentioned, there are scholars who argue for some direct teaching of vocabulary in EFL. Paul Nation (1982), for example, does not agree that we should leave all vocabulary acquisition to incidental contact in context. He cites a number of studies and concludes that almost all of the experiments comparing learning in context with learning word pairs (foreign word–English translation) have not produced results which favor learning in context (cf. Lado, Baldwin, & Lobo, 1967; Gershman, 1970). Although he contends that word list learning is a legitimate part of the process of vocabulary learning, he admits that much more research is needed in order to arrive at a richer idea of what it means to know a word and how words are learned.

In the 1980s a research trend consistent with the views of Richards (1976) developed, largely in Great Britain, which emphasizes the role of lexis in larger units of language beyond the single word-form (see Robinson, Chapter 12, this volume). This approach is related to, but distinct from, the contemporary re-search in discourse analysis, pragmatics, and text linguistics. In essence this viewpoint argues that meaning has to be reinterpreted constantly throughout a text because of the interaction of a number of text features such as lexical cohesion, subordinators, pragmatic considerations, coherence relations, genre structures, and so on. Through this viewpoint, the meaning of a text is not just a synthesis of the words in it but rather a complex interaction between words and the textual parameters mentioned above. See Carter (1987) and Carter and McCarthy (1988) for a fuller discussion of this topic.

Arguments for the importance of vocabulary and literacy skills abound in psycholinguistics and L1 reading research literature (McKeown & Curtis, 1987); it is for this reason that ESL/EFL theorists and practitioners need to be con-cerned with current L1 research on vocabulary development and instruction (cf. Stoller & Grabe in the next chapter).

MODELS OF READING IN ESL/EFL INSTRUCTION

As conceptions of the role of vocabulary have been changing, so have views of the nature of reading itself. Silberstein (1987) characterizes the models of reading utilized in ESL/EFL instruction over the past 25 years as audio-lingual, psycholinguistic, and interactive. In the audio-lingual model, reading was simply speech written down, and therefore the process of learning to read was seen basically as a matter of developing habitual and mechanical recognition of the written symbols which correspond to known (speech) patterns. As a result, there was minimal need for instruction in the skill of reading.

In the 1970s contemporary linguistics and cognitive psychology helped create a perspective of reading as a complex information-processing skill, the psycholinguistic approach. The reader had to actively coordinate a number of subskills in order to achieve comprehension. Goodman (1967) described reading in his seminal article as:

> a partial use of available minimal language cues selected from perceptual input on the basis of the reader's expectation. As this partial information is processed, tentative decisions are made to be confirmed, rejected, or refined as reading progresses. More simply stated, reading is a psycholinguistic guessing game. (p. 127)

(For an application of this approach to ESL/EFL reading instruction, see Coady, 1979; Chern, Chapter 4, this volume.) L2 reading textbooks written within this framework encouraged students to practice a variety of subskills and strategies, such as prediction and anticipation, in order to comprehend successfully. There was a great deal of attention paid to guessing the meaning of unknown words through the use of contextual clues (see Haynes, Chapter 3, this volume).

In the 1980s there seems to have developed a reaction against the psycholinguistic model. It was characterized as too "top-down" in that readers were encouraged to make predictions (guesses) about the text they were reading using their prior knowledge. This type of processing was highlighted in instruction at the expense of developing bottom-up processing (i.e., morphographemic word recognition). In contrast, current L1 reading theory suggests that word-identification, that is, processing at the word level, is central to successful reading (Carr & Levy, 1990; Rayner & Pollatsek, 1989).

The interactive approach argues that the proficient reader utilizes both bottom-up and top-down processing, and that successful comprehension is the result of an interaction between both types of processing. Within this approach, schema theory (discussed below) emphasizes the role of preexisting knowledge which the reader relates to the input from the text, again interactively. Thus instructional activities in this framework tend to place emphasis on teaching students to take advantage of all of their prior knowledge. As a result, vocabulary acquisition is viewed in terms of the students' background knowledge of concepts as well as of word-forms.

VOCABULARY LEARNING:
A MYSTERY AND A PARADOX

Nevertheless, Coady (1986) contended that vocabulary learning is a mystery and a paradox. For years, teachers and textbook writers had virtually neglected it, apparently in the belief that students would automatically learn vocabulary in context through reading and therefore needed little or no direct instruction. And yet there is no clear cut research which demonstrates how such contextual learning takes place. It is truly a mystery.

Moreover, the vocabulary that is acquired through reading takes on the stature of a paradox. One side of the paradox is that less frequent vocabulary is almost exclusively encountered during reading. Consequently ESL students have to read in order to learn the less frequent words. But the other side of the paradox is that all too often they don't know enough words to read well. How can these students learn enough to learn?

VOCABULARY CONTROL

A major attempt to solve this paradox has been the vocabulary control movement, which has found expression in both L1 and L2 reading instruction. For over 40 years textbooks (primers) for beginning reading instruction in America have drastically limited the vocabulary that is used. The assumption behind this practice is that the task of acquiring the skill of reading is greatly eased by eliminating (insofar as possible) the burden of recognizing too many different word-forms (even when the spoken words are already known).

Vocabulary control has also occurred in foreign language instruction. In an effort to produce comprehensible material, hundreds of simplified versions of texts have been produced. Moreover, a large number of ESL/EFL reading textbooks claim to have controlled vocabulary difficulty. One procedure is to use a frequency list as a reference, and attempt to eliminate all words above a certain level of difficulty. Another procedure often used with foreign language materials that are found to be too difficult for students is to rewrite them using much simpler vocabulary and syntax. The assumption is that, since longer words tend to be more difficult, using short words and short sentences will create a much simpler text. However, Ulijn and Strother (1990) claim that syntactic simplification alone of a technical text did not improve reading comprehension. Moreover, Davison and Kantor (1982) warn us that there is far more involved in the difficulty of a given text than short words and sentences. Such revisions are far more successful when the adapter acts as a conscientious rewriter who uses more frequent vocabulary and paraphrasing but still maintains a native language text. Recently, extensive criticism of such simplified texts has developed, because they are not considered to be "realistic" and it is claimed that they do not prepare students for the "real" texts which they will all too soon face. This school of thought recommends the use of actual native speaker materials which have not been simplified. But this approach then must deal with the formidable task of bridging the gap and adequately preparing students to deal successfully and efficiently with such unsimplified texts. In short, we have a classic dilemma: the simplified text runs the risk of creating a distorted version of L2 lexical patterning in actual discourse; the realistic text with its authentic lexical cohesion and pragmatics can be too much realism too soon, with the consequence that the learner is lost. Obviously, more research is needed in this area.

Note that the central question which the chapters in this volume investigate is how readers actually carry out the process of guessing the meaning of words in context and thereby acquire, not only the word-forms, but their meanings. Thus this volume is indeed attempting to clarify part of the paradox. As their foundation, most of these authors build on L1 evidence that word identification drives the reading process.

THE CENTRALITY OF WORD IDENTIFICATION
IN INTERACTIVE MODELS OF READING

Good L1 readers have the ability to recognize words automatically (i.e., have large sight vocabularies) (Perfetti, 1985; Carr & Levy, 1990). But since foreign language readers typically do not have such vocabulary knowledge, it seems essential that they be taught to take advantage of contextual redundancy and clues in order to comprehend while they are gaining the exposures necessary to achieve sight vocabulary.

Such multiple exposures help to create automaticity in decoding in reading (i.e., the ability to recognize words quickly and automatically). The inability to do this can seriously limit comprehension. Perfetti and Lesgold (1977, 1979) have argued that, when a reader's efforts at word recognition are especially slow and labored, short-term memory is so taxed that the reader cannot take full advantage of context. These researchers are arguing that a good reader has sufficient command over the written language so that words are recognized automatically as sight vocabulary and thus attentional resources can be redirected to interpreting sentence and discourse thought-patterns. This, in turn, enables these readers to apply contextual meaning to understand new words when they are encountered during reading. In contrast, poor readers typically do not have enough highly efficient sight vocabulary knowledge to have the attention necessary for taking advantage of the context.

An L1 Reading/Vocabulary Model

Perfetti (1984) proposes a verbal efficiency theory, which claims a central role for word recognition during reading:

Word representations and the processes of word identification that operate on the representations are a critical part of reading. Indeed, skilled readers access most words during reading because the span of perception is relatively narrow. This establishes word identification as the central recurring event during normal text reading, even in rich contexts. (p. 49)

And,

Comprehension in reading takes place within limits provided by word identification skills. A consequence of not acquiring fluent word identification is that the reader's comprehension processes are at risk. (p. 57–58)

Although Perfetti's model places paramount importance on word identification skills, it is based mainly on three verbal processes: lexical access, propositional encoding, and text modeling. This model postulates that the identification of words is mediated by the perception of letters, and that this identification process involves interaction between bottom-up and top-down sources of information. One of the predictions of this model is that good readers do not use context to avoid or improve upon word recognition, but instead process the visual information so efficiently that they have extra capacity for processing the context. On the other hand, poor readers often use context more and word recognition less in a compensatory manner (Stanovich & West, 1981; Stanovich, 1986). But this latter case pertains only when the context is comprehensible to them. All too often, the context is too difficult for weak readers to utilize, and they simply fail to comprehend. In addition, poorer readers can be seen to use context more than better readers in easier material, but as the material becomes more difficult, the better readers can actually be seen to utilize context, because they have more attention to apply to figuring it out, while automatic recognition is taking place at lower levels of letter and word identification.

Perfetti's verbal efficiency theory clearly predicts that comprehension skill will be related to word identification speed and short-term memory (Perfetti & Lesgold, 1977). Therefore it follows that increasing the word identification speed of low-skill readers should increase their comprehension. In support of Perfetti's theory, the strong relationship between vocabulary knowledge and reading ability appears to be constant throughout the developmental process, with those who know more vocabulary being better able to comprehend (Anderson & Freebody, 1981; see also Haynes & Baker, Chapter 7, this volume). In fact, some research has found a causal connection between vocabulary knowledge and reading comprehension (Beck, Perfetti, & McKeown, 1982; McKeown, Beck, Omanson, & Perfetti, 1983; Coady et al., Chapter 11, this volume). Also see Stanovich (1986) for an extensive discussion of the interaction of the various skills involved (i.e., phonological awareness, the effect of practice, automatic word recognition, context facilitation, etc.).

Perfetti's model has direct implications for ESL. Perhaps an analogy would help. The speed of reading is like the speed of traffic on an urban freeway; there is a minimum speed which everyone must adhere to, or traffic will slow down to a bumper-to-bumper crawl. On the other hand, driving too fast leads to comprehension accidents. This is an important argument which deserves further research (i.e., will teaching students in such a way as to achieve automaticity in word recognition result in better reading comprehension and increased acquisition of vocabulary through reading?).

Although there is little empirical evidence on this question, Meara (1984) tells us in his article on word recognition, "our basic finding with non-native speakers is that length and frequency [of word-forms] have much the same effect as they do in native speakers. The main difference is that the effects are severely exaggerated" (p. 101). His results can be interpreted to mean that nonnative speakers use virtually the same word recognition or decoding processes as native speakers, but in a much less efficient manner, and so their performance is analogous to that of the L1 low-skill readers just cited.

An additional concern is that automaticity or speed is also a function of the quality of the mental information (or schemata) for the word. The richness of the meanings of a word may be another constraint on its accessibility (see Haynes & Baker, Chapter 7, this volume). And so future research will not only have to incorporate the effect of attempts to improve the speed of access from word-form to a simple meaning, but also how this process interacts with complex mental representations of words.

SCHEMA THEORY AND VOCABULARY LEARNING

Research on the psychological processes involved in comprehension clearly shows that what we understand of something is a function of our past experiences, our background knowledge, or what are sometimes more technically called our *schemata* (Bartlett, 1932; Rumelhart & Ortony, 1977; Rumelhart, 1980). Schemata may be thought of as "interacting knowledge structures" (Rumelhart & Ortony, 1977, p. 100) and the "building blocks of cognition" (Rumelhart, 1980) stored in hierarchies in long-term memory. We have stored away all sorts of schemata (e.g., for scenes, events, activities, etc.). We have schemata for going to restaurants of different types (e.g., fast food places, elegant French restaurants, Chinese restaurants, etc.), for attending and presenting papers at professional meetings, for visits to doctors' offices, for rooms in our houses, and for the kinds of furniture and the way we expect that furniture to be arranged in these rooms. In particular, Rumelhart (1980) proposes that schemata are recognition devices which carry out a process of evaluation of their goodness of fit to the data being processed. He then asserts that skilled readers have "a greater number of more completely developed word schemata" (p. 47).

Word-forms which are automatically and instantaneously recognized by a reader can be thought of as access portals to schemata. In effect, word-forms trigger an already existing network of knowledge which will then interact with other words/schemata, enabling a reader to arrive at comprehension of the overall meaning of the given text. The importance of this view is that schema theory can now be seen as truly interactive, connecting (both) top-down knowledge structures and bottom-up (text based) word-forms.

Aitchison (1987) proposes a model of the lexicon as a network that can be activated via a semantic field in word production, and acoustic signals in speech comprehension. She also includes parallel processing, with numerous links in the network being activated at the same time. Within a language a number of semantically related words would be activated. The final choice is motivated by the amount of activation or strength a given word obtains because of its fit to the specific concept or context or task. The model is interactive in that information must be able to flow up or down the network.

THE ROLE OF BACKGROUND KNOWLEDGE

An important part of teaching an academic subject is teaching the vocabulary related to it, and, conversely, teaching vocabulary means teaching concepts, new knowledge. Knowledge of vocabulary therefore entails knowledge of the schemata in which the concept participates, and knowledge of the networks in which that word participates, as well as any associated words and concepts. (See Brown, this volume, concerning the possibility that learners are more likely to learn a word for which they have a concept prior to seeing or hearing the word-form.)

Consequently, it is important to note that the traditional prereading technique of presenting students a list of new or unfamiliar vocabulary items that are about to be encountered in a text, even with definitions appropriate to their use in that text, does not guarantee the induction of new schemata. Hudson (1982) found that, at all proficiency levels, a prereading vocabulary activity was the least effective of three types of prereading activities for inducing appropriate schemata, as measured by a multiple choice comprehension test. This particular vocabulary activity consisted of giving students a list of word-forms that would appear in the reading passage, allowing time for the list to be read silently, and then going over it aloud, item by item, with definitions given for each item. Similarly, in Johnson (1982), three different types of vocabulary instruction presented prior to or concurrent with reading the target passages failed to produce any significant effects on the reading comprehension as measured by sentence recognition and cloze tests.

Unfortunately, many current techniques for teaching vocabulary are artificial and frequently ineffective, because they do not induce the readers to associate the new word-forms and concepts in their minds together with the schemata they already know.

MEMORY TECHNIQUES

The Stoller and Grabe chapter in this volume reviews several powerful memory techniques, including semantic feature analysis, semantic mapping, and the "key word" approach. Certainly the best known of these at the present time is the key word method. This kind of associating can be very effective when a new word is linked to some already well known association. For example, *ohiogozaimos* is a Japanese greeting which is memorable for someone from Ohio. In a comprehensive survey of almost 50 studies, Pressley, Levin, and Delaney (1982) concluded that the key word technique definitely helps the learning for foreign vocabulary and is superior to other techniques such as rote repetition, placing vocabulary in a meaningful sentence, and using pictures or synonyms. On the other hand, Meara (1980) cites three problems with the "very impressive evidence" on the key word technique. First, such experiments ignore the complex patterns of meaning relationships that characterize a complete and fully formed lexicon. Second, they don't study real language learners but, instead, laboratory subjects. Third, although the technique clearly aids recognition, it is less clear whether it leads to active control over such vocabulary. Also see Cohen (1987) for a critical review of the literature in this area.

Chunking is a psychological term for the mental process of grouping items together in meaningful patterns (Miller, 1956). The technique of giving arbitrary strings of telephone numbers alphabetic analogues is one example (e.g., 4357 = HELP). Whenever learners can put seemingly unrelated items together into a pattern, they usually will be easier to remember. For example, HOMES can be used as a technique for remembering the names of the Great Lakes: *H*uron, *O*ntario, *M*ichigan, *E*rie, and *S*uperior.

Repetition as a technique is important but must involve meaningful cognitive processing or attention to be effective. Carpay (1975) argues for "4 + 1 + 1 + 1." A new word should be used in four different contexts (but with basically the same meaning) in the lesson in which it is introduced and at least once in each of the three subsequent lessons. Crothers and Suppes (1967) also found six to seven repetitions to be necessary. Oxford (1990) suggests a repetition/learning schedule of review sessions at the intervals of 15 minutes, 1 hour, 3 hours, 1 day, 2 days, 4 days, 1 week, 2 weeks, and so on. There seems to be general agreement that students should practice in small amounts over a given period of time rather than in one long practice session (Tulving & Colotla, 1970; Schouten-van Parreren, 1988).

Nation (1990) cites research evidence that words are originally stored in the mind according to their form rather than meaning; therefore, at least in the initial stages, the teacher or student should avoid as much as possible confusion arising from the simultaneous presentation or analysis of highly similar forms. Moreover, Nation (1990) claims that oral repetition of a word form is not as effective as having to recall the form of the word. For students to see the word form and its definition is not as effective as their having to make an effort to recall the meaning before they see the definition. His interpretation is that successful learning is a function of the type of attention given rather than the sheer volume of repetition that occurs. In sum, memory techniques have a demonstrated power, but teachers and researchers need to understand that such techniques gloss over the complexity of what it means to know a word.

WHAT DOES IT MEAN TO KNOW A WORD?

In the discussions to follow, it is important to keep in mind what Richards (1976) has told us about what it means to know a word: knowing the degree of probability of when and where to encounter a given word and the sorts of words to be found with it, the limitations imposed on it by register, its appropriate syntactic behavior, its underlying form and derivations, the network of associa- tions it has, its semantic features, its extended or metaphorical meanings, and so on. These comprise the multiple components and relationships of a word which articulate with the entire schematic knowledge of a given individual. Individuals know the form (both spoken and written) of a word as well as its meaning. Hayes-Roth and Hayes-Roth (1977) and Abramovici (1984) have found that lexical information persists in memory storage of meaning; that is to say, experi- enced readers tend to remember the word-forms they encounter as well as their meanings.

The question of what constitutes knowing a word is still unclear. For exam- ple, Dupuy (1974) estimated the average total vocabulary size of a third-grade student to be 2,000 words, whereas Smith (1941) claimed 25,000 words for these same students. In the most persuasive study so far, Nagy and Anderson (1984) estimated that there are 85,533 word families in printed school English (grades 3–9). They based their study on the Carroll, Davies, and Richman (1971) word frequency study and counted as one word family, semantically, and morphologi- cally related words such as *enthusiast, enthusiasts,* and *enthusiasm,* but as different word families semantically opaque, derived words such as *conclusive* and *conclusion.* Another of their judgments is that an active reader in grades 6 through 9 could encounter 3,000 to 4,000 totally new vocabulary items in the course of a school year. See their study also for an excellent discussion of the issue of frequency and its relationship to which words to teach.

PROTOTYPE SEMANTICS

One intriguing question concerns how words are interrelated in the mental lexicon. *Prototype semantics* is a theory in which objects in the world are categorized, not by a fixed set of minimally defining features, but rather by reference to a central or prototypical member of a set or category (Rosch, 1975; Rosch & Mervis, 1975; Smith & Medin, 1981). For example, subjects often cite the robin as a typical bird. Why is a penguin a bird? What about an ostrich? What links a hummingbird and a vulture, as well as a penguin and an ostrich, to the robin? For that matter, why at various times has the word-form *bird* referred to (a) a woman, (b) the male or female genitals, (c) an obscene finger gesture, (d) a bronx cheer, (e) a prostitute, (f) or any odd person? As Lakoff (1987; Lakoff & Johnson, 1980) describe this theory, words are natural categories of senses that form a chain, with each sense ultimately linked to a prototypical sense. Each link in the chain can then be characterized either by a minimal image-relationship or by a conceptual metaphor that associates an image scheme with an abstract domain. Parry (Chapter 6, this volume) demonstrates that a reader grappling with new word-forms often acquires some dimensions of word-meaning with an interpretation that remains only a distant link in this chain of senses.

HOW ARE WORDS STORED?

A long-standing pedagogical question concerns whether a foreign language should be taught in conjunction with the native language or not, such as through translation and dual language texts. Should the languages be kept separate, or is it appropriate to have them interrelated? Does this confuse students and hamper learning? Many researchers have felt that a significant clue to the answer depends upon whether the vocabulary of two different languages is totally separate in the mind or interlinked in some manner.

Weinreich (1953) is attributed as the first major researcher to classify bilinguals as having lexical entries which were either compound (one concept with two words) or coordinate (two concepts and two words). Meara (1980), in his excellent survey of the subsequent experimental literature on the hypothesis of compound vs. coordinate bilingualism, concludes that most of the research would seem to support the claim that words in a second language are connected in some way with the words in the first language in order to form a complex lexicon rather than two separate ones. For another good review also see Albert and Obler (1979).

Riegel (1970), on the other hand, argues that a given bilingual's representation of language in the lexicon changes as a function of time, exposure to the languages, and acquired proficiency in L2. He proposes that, in the first stage, the L2 vocabulary is acquired mostly on the basis of ''equivalence connections'' in which the L2 lexical items are related to their respective L1 translation equivalents. The system is therefore predominantly compound, but some items may be coordinate. In the following stage the L2 lexicon grows more coordinate, and in the final stage it is very coordinate but with all L1 and L2 lexical items being interconnected. The above stages actually represent gradual change, resulting in a very complex lexicon which is both separate and connected.

Green (1986) has proposed a model of bilingualism in which the two linguistic codes become activated simultaneously (i.e., parallel processing takes place). The choice of language is carried out by means of suppressing all of the options except one, depending upon the concept involved, strength of knowledge of the language, as well as the particular lexical items, and so on. This model has the advantage of being able to explain code switching between languages by proficient bilinguals and the creation of blends of the two languages. It implies a hierarchy of word saliency both within and across languages which would explain why groping for a word often results in interference from other words. Indeed, Green's theory would suggest that the real pedagogical problem is for students to learn how to strengthen the saliency of appropriate forms and to suppress the others.

In sum, it seems that the words in the L2 are less well organized and less easily accessible than those of L1. However, these differences seem to diminish over time with increased proficiency. Semantic development in L2 seems to be a process of starting with a mapping of L1 meanings into L2 and then gradually developing L2 meanings and meaning structures. The final result is two separate systems which are still highly interrelated. Unfortunately, there have been only a few longitudinal studies of L2 vocabulary acquisition (see Parry, Chapter 6, this volume), and much more research is needed before we will have a really clear idea of the internal structure of the lexicon.

A VOCABULARY LEARNING CONTINUUM

Furthermore, Crow and Quigley (1985) have argued that the traditional distinction between receptive and productive vocabulary must be clarified and added to our notion of the development of a word and its properties. That is to say, a learner can know the core or basic meaning of a word, and comprehend it in a text receptively speaking, and yet still not control the syntactic and collocational and register aspects of a word sufficiently to use it productively. Moreover, they insist that the receptive/productive distinction is not a dichotomy but a continuum. There is much to be said for this viewpoint; it is certainly congruent with the current psycholinguistic literature on vocabulary acquisition (see Stoller & Grabe, Chapter 2, this volume).

Core Vocabulary

But even if we assume that there is such a continuum of vocabulary knowledge, what is the core vocabulary which learners need to acquire first? Coady et al. (Chapter 11, this volume) observe that there are some 2,000 words that account for almost 80% of the running words in an average text, and that these words therefore occur frequently enough to justify significant commitments of instructional or learning time (see Brown, Chapter 13, this volume, for the finding that general frequency seems related to whether a word is acquired or not). Likewise it is contended that low-frequency words seem to be very poor candidates for direct teaching or learning, because they do not appear often enough to justify spending precious instructional time on them (Twaddell, 1973). Obviously, what is needed is a comprehensive theory of vocabulary acquisition that would give guidance to scholars and teachers concerned with this issue.

A PROPOSED THEORY OF ACQUISITION

Coady, Carrell, and Nation (1985) have proposed a tentative and sketchy outline of a theory of vocabulary acquisition for second language learners. What is surprising is that there have not been many more such attempts! (See Stoller & Grabe, Chapter 2, this volume, for a number of cogent suggestions for such a model.) This theory proposes that there is a universal model of word identification which is the same across native and nonnative speakers of a language. The theory is specifically concerned with acquisition through the medium of reading and is based on the notion of lexical entries as schemas. Central to the theory is the claim that the lexical items encountered by L1 or L2 language learners at any given stage of their language development can be divided into three developmental categories: those whose forms and common meanings are recognized automatically, irrespective of context (or sight vocabulary); those whose forms and meanings are to some degree familiar to the learner but are recognized only in context; and those whose meanings, and, often, forms as well, are unknown to the learner and whose meanings must therefore be inferred from the context, looked up in a dictionary, or left uncomprehended.

It is assumed that the majority of sight vocabulary will consist of high-frequency words which have been well learned through repeated exposure. The ability to automatically recognize the highly frequent words in a language is absolutely crucial to success in L1 and L2 reading, and therefore these words should be taught.

According to this theory, the less frequent words are to be learned through incidental contact in context (with the help of some strategic training) via extensive reading, but only after a critical level of automaticity has been achieved with the high-frequency or core vocabulary (see Coady et al., Chapter 11, this volume).

LEARNING WORDS THROUGH CONTEXT

The role of context in word recognition and acquisition is the major theme running throughout this volume. Literate adults recognize thousands and thousands of words and know how to use them. Current thinking is that the vast majority of these words have been learned through context rather than through direct instruction. But the research literature dealing with native speakers of English is indeed confusing and contradictory. Nemko (1984) found that beginning readers who were taught words in context did not perform better than those who were taught the words in isolation. On the other hand, Rash, Johnson, and Gleadow (1984) found superior learning of words in context over isolation. In reference to L1 reading, Jenkins, Stein, and Wysocki (1984) pointed out that "learning from context is still a default explanation; evidence that individuals actually learn word meanings from contextual experiences is notably lacking" (p. 769). Moreover, Jenkins et al. (1984) found that the amount of learning of vocabulary from context was not as great as expected: "vocabulary learning after as many as 10 presentations of unfamiliar words in highly informative contexts ranged between 16% and 27%" (p. 782). Nagy, Herman, and Anderson (1985) estimated the probability of learning a word from context after just one exposure to be between .10 and .15. However, in a follow-up experiment (Herman, Anderson, Pearson, & Nagy, 1987) the overall probability was even less, only .05. Although this seems extremely low, repeated exposures to a word should have some incremental but as yet undetermined effect on the probability of a word being learned.

Moreover, Wysocki and Jenkins (1987) found that students can use morphological generalizations or word parts in order to determine the meanings of unknown words. Haynes, Chern, and Parry (all in this volume) show similar findings for L2 students.

Grabe and Zukowski-Faust (1986) attempted to replicate the Nagy et al. (1985) study with nonnative speakers but did not find evidence for incremental learning in the case of nonnative speakers. Haynes (1984, this volume) has warned us that, although "ESL readers are good guessers when the context contains immediate clues, insufficient context, global clues, or a student's lack of vocabulary knowledge may increase the difficulty of guessing" (p. 174).

On the other hand, Huckin and Jin (1987) found that teaching explicit techniques for guessing words in context led to improved reading comprehension and vocabulary learning. Moreover, Parry (1987, and Chapter 6, this volume; Huckin & Bloch, Chapter 8, this volume) have found some significant evidence for learning from context in both longitudinal and single session studies. In short, we find equally ambiguous results from the ESL and the L1 research.

Nation and Coady (1988) and Nation (1990) argue that the primary strategy for dealing with low-frequency vocabulary should be to teach students how to guess words in context; another possibility is to use word part analysis; finally, students should look up the word in a dictionary and gloss it in the text or their notes. (Also see Stein, Chapter 10, this volume, for a checklist for guessing in context.) In sum, the basic argument of this chapter is for a mixed approach to vocabulary acquisition in ESL. The basic or core vocabulary should be taught, but the less frequent vocabulary will then be learned "naturally" via context; but, even in that case, techniques for that purpose should be taught.

A SUMMARY OF CONCLUSIONS FROM THE RESEARCH LITERATURE

L1 literates learn large amounts of vocabulary, but we are largely unsure exactly how they do so. Direct instruction in the classroom accounts for only a small amount of this learning. The research on learning words in context found only a 5%–15% probability that a given word would be learned at first exposure. The incidental acquisition hypothesis suggests that there is gradual but steady incremental growth of vocabulary knowledge through meaningful interaction with text, but there is little research as yet to illustrate how this occurs for either L1 or L2.

Good readers not only comprehend more but they also know more words and learn new words easier. Stanovich (1986) claims that this is so because good readers are able to take more advantage of context in difficult texts than poor readers, because they have more free attention to do so. Their ability to recognize large amounts of vocabulary automatically and effortlessly increases the cognitive processing resources they have available for dealing with unknown words.

Experienced readers have some knowledge of what words to expect in what context (collocations), and they know this from their general background knowledge as well as their knowledge of particular words. Moreover, although extra-textual background knowledge as well as knowledge of overall text facilitates words recognition/acquisition, immediate context still appears to be the most useful (cf. Brown, Chern, Haynes, and Dubin & Olshtain, all in this volume).

The interactive model of reading argues that both top-down and bottom-up processing takes place during fluent reading (see Haynes, Chapter 3, this volume); that is, readers do graphophonemic processing of word-forms and retrieval of their meaning, as well as inferencing from global and local context. A key argument is that vocabulary processing becomes automatic in more fluent readers allowing for more cognitive processing attention to be directed to top-down interpretation (cf. Coady et al., Chapter 11, this volume).

UNANSWERED QUESTIONS

But this till leaves us with a number of unanswered questions. For example, it is striking that the very redundancy or richness of information in a given context which, on the one hand, enables a reader to successfully guess an unknown word also predicts, on the other hand, that that same reader is less likely to learn the word-form because he or she was able to comprehend the text without needing to know it.

Even though there is general agreement that learning vocabulary through context must be the major way of increasing vocabulary knowledge, exactly how does this take place? What constitutes the natural process of guessing words from context? What is context in the first place? When and how should learners use it? What kinds of context clues do learners naturally use, and what kinds need to be taught? How does processing of context interact with analysis of word-forms when a reader encounters unfamiliar items? How well do learners retain the words they have learned through guessing? What kinds of reading exercises can best help the learner develop expert guessing skills? What sorts of learner differences can we expect to find? In the absence of research-based answers to such questions, teachers have generally been left to their own devices in helping students to deal with unfamiliar words.

The purpose of this book is to address the kinds of questions just raised, and to provide some tentative answers based on careful research. It will promote the view—both through presentations of research and through practical advice—that building vocabulary knowledge through reading is a *strategic* skill that can and should be taught. At the same time, it will point out and discuss the many limitations of this methodology, arguing that a full program of instruction in reading and vocabulary building should include other methods as well (e.g., computer-assisted instruction, mastery of procedural vocabulary, key word mnemonic techniques, dictionary use, word families, etc.).

The present volume contributes to our understanding of vocabulary acquisition by focusing on the learner/reader in significant detail. The research methodologies employed by the various authors are designed to shed light on the complicated interaction between knowledge, reading, and comprehension.

REFERENCES

Abramovici, S. (1984). Lexical information in reading and memory. *Reading Research Quarterly, XIX* (2), 173–187.

Albert, M., & Obler, L. K. (1979). *The bilingual brain: Neuro-psychological and neurolinguistic aspects of bilingualism.* New York: Academic Press.

Anderson, R. C., & Freebody, P. (1981). Vocabulary knowledge. In J. T. Guthrie (Ed.), *Comprehension and teaching: Research reviews* (pp. 77–117). Newark, NJ: International Reading Association.

Aitchison, J. (1987). *Words in the mind: An introduction to the mental lexicon.* Oxford: Basil Blackwell.

Bartlett, F. C. (1932). *Remembering: A study in experimental and social psychology.* Cambridge, UK: Cambridge University Press.

Beck, I. L., Perfetti, C. A., & McKeown, M. G. (1982). The effects of long term vocabulary instruction on lexical access and reading comprehension. *Journal of Educational Psychology, 14* (3), 325–336.

Bensoussan, M., & Laufer, B. (1984). Lexical guessing in context in EFL reading comprehension. *Journal of Research in Reading, 7* 15–32.

Carpay, J. A. H. (1975). *Onderwijsleerpsychologie enleergangontwikkeling in het modern vreemdetalenonderwijs.* Groningen: Tjeenk Willink.

Carr, T. H., & Levy, B. A. (1990). *Reading and its development: Component skills approaches.* New York: Academic Press.

Carrell, P., Devine, J., & Eskey, D. (1988). *Interactive approaches to second language reading.* New York: Cambridge University Press.

Carroll, J. B., Davies, P., & Richman, B. (1971). *Word frequency book.* New York: American Heritage.

Carter, R. (1987). *Vocabulary: Applied linguistic perspectives.* London: Allen & Unwin.

Carter R., & McCarthy, M. (1988). *Vocabulary and language teaching.* New York: Longman.

Coady, J. M. (1979). A psycholinguistic model of the ESL reader. in R. Mackay, B. Barkman, & R. R. Jordan (Eds.), *Reading in a second language* (pp. 5–12). Rowley, MA: Newbury House.

Coady, J. M. (1986). *Vocabulary acquisition: Mystery and paradox.* Anaheim, CA: International TESOL.

Coady, J. M., Carrell, P., & Nation, P. (1985). *The teaching of vocabulary in ESL from the perspective of schema theory.* Milwaukee; Midwest TESOL.

Cohen, A. (1987). The use of verbal and imagery mnemonics in second-language vocabulary learning. *Studies in second language acquisition. 9* (1), 43–62.

Cohen, A., & Aphek, E. (1980). Retention of second language vocabulary over time: Investigating the role of mnemonic associations. *System, 8,* 221–235.

Crothers, E., & Suppes, P. (1967). *Experiments in second-language learning.* New York: Academic Press.

Crow, J. T., & Quigley, J. R. (1985). A semantic field approach to passive vocabulary acquisition for reading comprehension. *TESOL Quarterly, 19* (3), 497–513.

Davison, A., & Kantor, R. N. (1982). On the failure of readability formulas to define readable texts: A case study from adaptations. *Reading Research Quarterly, XVII* (2), 187–209.

Dubin, F., Eskey, D., & Grabe, W. (Eds.). (1986). *Teaching second language reading for academic purposes.* Reading, MA: Addison-Wesley.

Dupuy, H. J. (1974). *The rationale, development and standardization of a basic word vocabulary test.* Washington, DC: U. S. Government Printing Office.

Gairns, R., & Redman, S. (1986). *Working with words: A guide to teaching and learning vocabulary.* New York: Cambridge University Press.

Gershman, S. J. (1970). Foreign language vocabulary learning under seven conditions. *Dissertation Abstracts International, 31,* 3690B (University Microfilms No. 70–23, 439).

Goodman, K. S. (1967). Reading: a psycholinguistic guessing game. *Journal of the Reading Specialist, 6,* 126–135.

Grabe, W., & Zukowski-Faust, J. (1986). *On the acquisition of vocabulary from context.* Anaheim, CA: International TESOL.

Green, D. W. (1986). Control, activation, and resource: A framework and a model for the control of speech in bilinguals. *Brain and language, 27,* 210–223.

Hague, S. (1987). Vocabulary Instruction: What L2 can learn from L1. *Foreign Language Annals, 20,* 217–225.

Harvey, P. (1983). Vocabulary learning: the use of grids. *ELT Journal, 37,* 243–246.

Hayes-Roth, B., & Hayes-Roth, F. (1977). The prominence of lexical information in memory representations of meaning. *Journal of Verbal Learning and Verbal Behavior, 16,* 119–136.

Haynes, M. (1984). Patterns and perils of guessing in second language reading. In J. Handscombe, R. A. Orem, & B. P. Taylor (Eds.), *On TESOL '83* (pp. 163–176). Washington, DC: TESOL Publication.

Herman, P. A., Anderson, R. C. Pearson, P. D., & Nagy, W. E. (1987). Incidental acquisition of word meaning from expositions with varied text features. *Reading Research Quarterly, XX* (3), 263–284.

Huckin, T. N., & Jin, Z. (1987). Inferring word-meaning from context: A study in second language acquisition. In *ESCOL '86: Proceedings of the third eastern states conference on linguistics.* Columbus, OH: Department of Linguistics.

Hudson, T. (1982). The effects of induced schemata on the "short circuit" in L2 reading: Non-decoding factors in L2 reading performance. *Language Learning, 32* (1), 1–31.

Jenkins, J. R., & Stein, M. L., & Wysocki, K. (1984). Learning vocabulary through reading. *American Educational Research Journal, 21,* 767–787.

Johnson, P. (1982). Effects on reading comprehension of building background knowledge. *TESOL Quarterly, 16* (4), 503–516.

Krashen, S. D. (1982). *Principles and practice in second language acquisition.* New York: Pergamon.

Lado, R., Baldwin, B., & Lobo, R. (1967). *Massive vocabulary expansion in a foreign language beyond the basic course: The effects of stimuli, timing and order of presentation* (Project No. 5-1095). Washington, DC: U. S. Department of Health, Education, and Welfare.

Lakoff, G., & Johnson, M. (1980). *Metaphors we live by.* Chicago: University of Chicago Press.

Lakoff, G. (1987). *Women, fire, and dangerous things: What categories reveal about the mind.* Chicago: University of Chicago Press.

Laufer, B., & Bensoussan, M. (1982). Meaning is in the eye of the beholder. *English Teaching Forum, 20* (2), 10–13.

Maley, A. (1986). Foreword. In J. Morgan & M. Rinvolucri (Eds.), *Vocabulary.* New York: Oxford University Press.

McKeown, M. G., & Curtis, M. E. (1987). *The nature of vocabulary acquisition.* Hillsdale, NJ: Erlbaum.

McKeown, M. G., Beck, I. L., Omanson, R. C., & Perfetti, C. A. (1983). The effects of long term vocabulary instruction on reading comprehension: A replication. *Journal of Reading Behavior, 15* (1), 3–18.

Meara, P. (1980). Vocabulary acquisition: A neglected aspect of language learning. *Language Teaching and Linguistics: Abstracts,* pp. 221–246.

Meara, P. (1983). Vocabulary in a second language. *Specialized Bibliography, 3.* London: CILT.

Meara, P. (1984). Word recognition in foreign languages. In A. K. Pugh & J. M. Ulijn (Eds.), *Reading for professional purposes: Studies and practices in native and foreign language* (pp. 97–105). London: Heinemann.

Meara, P. (1987). Vocabulary in a second language. Volume 2. *Specialized Bibliography, 4.* London: Centre for Information on Language Teaching and Research.

Miller, G. A. (1956). The magical number seven: plus or minus two: Some limits on our capacity for processing information. *Psychological Review, 63*, 81–98.

Morgan, J., & Rinvolucri, M. (1986). *Vocabulary.* New York: Oxford University Press.

Nagy, W. E. & Anderson, R. C. (1984). How many words are there in printed school English? *Reading Research Quarterly, XIX (3),* 304–330.

Nagy, W. E., Herman, P. A., & Anderson, R. C. (1985). Learning words from context. *Reading Research Quarterly, XX*(2), 233–253.

Nation, I. S. P. (1982). Beginning to learn foreign vocabulary: A review of the research. *RELC Journal, 13*(1), 14–36.

Nation, I. S. P., (1990). *Teaching and learning vocabulary.* Rowley, MA: Newbury House.

Nation, I. S. P., & Coady, J. (1988). Vocabulary and reading. In R. Carter & M. McCarthy (Eds.) *Vocabulary and language teaching* (pp. 97–110). New York: Longman.

Nemko, B. (1984). Context versus isolation: Another look at beginning readers. *Reading Research Quarterly, XIX* (4), 461–467.

Oxford, R. L. (1990). *Language learning strategies: What every teacher should know.* New York: Newbury.

Parry, K. (1987). Learning vocabulary through an academic subject: A case study. In S. Dicker & L. Fox (Eds.), *Improving the Odds: helping ESL students succeed: Selected papers from the 1987 CUNY ESL council conference.* New York: Instructional Resource Center, Office of Academic Affairs, City University of New York.

Perfetti, C. A. (1985). *Reading ability.* New York: Oxford University Press.

Perfetti, C. A., & Lesgold, A. M. (1977). Discourse comprehension and sources of individual differences. In M. Just & P. Carpenter (Eds.), *Cognitive processes in comprehension* (pp. 141–183). Hillsdale, NJ: Erlbaum.

Perfetti, C. A., & Lesgold, A. M. (1979). Coding and comprehension in skilled reading and implications for reading instruction. In L. B. Resnick & P. Weaver (Eds.), *Theory and practice of early reading* (Vol. 1, pp. 57–84). Hillsdale, NJ: Erlbaum.

Pressley, M., Levin, J. R., & Delaney, H. (1982). Mnemonic keyword method. *Review of Educational Research, 52*(1), 61–91.

Rash, J., Johnson, T. D., & Gleadow, N. (1984). Acquisition and Retention of written words by kindergarten children under varying learning conditions. *Reading Research Quarterly, XIX,* 452–460.

Rayner, K., & Pollatsek, A. (1989). *The psychology of reading.* Englewood Cliffs, NJ: Prentice-Hall.

Richards, J. (1976). The role of vocabulary teaching. *TESOL Quarterly, 10*(1), 77–89.

Riegel, K. F. (1970). Some theoretical considerations of bilingual development. *Psychological Bulletin, 70* (6), 647–670.

Rosch, E. (1975). Cognitive representations of semantic categories. *Journal of Experimental Psychology, 104,* 192–223.

Rosch, E., & Mervis, C. B. (1975). Family resemblances: Studies in the internal structure of categories. *Cognitive Psychology, 7,* 573–605.

Rumelhart, D. E. (1980). Schemata: the building blocks of cognition. In R. J. Spiro, B. C. Bruce, & W. F. Brewer (Eds.), *Theoretical issues in reading comprehension* (pp. 33–58). Hillsdale, NJ: Erlbaum.

Rumelhart, D. E., & Ortony, A. (1977). The representation of knowledge in memory. In R. C. Anderson, R. J. Spiro, & W. E. Montague (Eds.), *Schooling and the acquisition of knowledge* (pp. 99–135). Hillsdale, NJ: Erlbaum.

Schouten-van Parreren, C. (1988). Action psychology and vocabulary learning. In M. Hildegrean-Nihlson & G. Ruckriem (Eds.), *Proceedings of the 1st International Congress on Activity Theory* (pp. 325–331). Berlin: Druck und Verlag System Druck.

Silberstein, S. (1987). Let's take another look at reading: 25 years of reading instruction. *English Language teaching forum.*

Smith, E., & Medin, D. L. (1981). *Categories and concepts.* Cambridge, MA: Harvard University Press.

Smith, M. K. (1941). Measurement of the size of general English vocabulary through the elementary grades and high school. *Genetic Psychology Monographs, 24,* 311–345.

Stanovich, K. E. (1986). Matthew effects in reading: Some consequences of individual differences in the acquisition of literacy. *Reading Research Quarterly, XXI*(4), 360–400.

Stanovich, K. E., & West, R. F. (1981). The effect of sentence context on ongoing word recognition: Tests of a two-process theory. *Journal of Experimental Psychology: Human Perception and Performance, 7,* 658–672.

Stieglitz, E. (1983). A practical approach to vocabulary reinforcement. *ELT Journal, 37,* 71–75.

Tulving, E., & Colotla, V. A. (1970). Free recall of trilingual lists. *Cognitive Psychology, 1,* 86–98.

Twaddell, F. (1973). Vocabulary expansion in the TESOL classroom. *TESOL Quarterly, 7*(1), 61–78.

Ulijn, J. M., & Strother, J. B. (1990). the effect of syntactic simplification on reading EST texts as L1 and L2. *Journal of Research in Reading, 13*(1), 38–54.

Weinreich, U. (1953). *Languages in contact.* New York: Linguistic Circle of New York.

Wysocki, K., & Jenkins, J. R. (1987). Deriving word meanings through morphological generalization. *Reading Research Quarterly, XXII*(1), 66–81.

ENDNOTES

1. *Surveys of the research:*
   Meara (1980, 1983, 1987) have excellent bibliographies on the recent research on L2 vocabulary acquisition. *The Nature of Vocabulary Acquisition* (1987), edited by McKeown and Curtis, contains a number of important articles reporting research on native speaker (L1) acquisition of vocabulary. A parallel book for ESL is *Vocabulary and Language Teaching* (1988), edited by Carter and McCarthy. Finally, there is an essential text by Paul Nation, *Teaching and Learning Vocabulary* (1990), which lays out a number of basic arguments about pedagogical approaches to teaching vocabulary based on research findings. A more general but quite relevant text is by Rebecca Oxford, *Language Learning Strategies: What Every Teacher Should Know* (1990), which gives an excellent overview of the various strategies involved in language learning, including vocabulary.

ᵈ Language Reading
ⁿᵈ Vocabulary Learning
T.Huckin, M.Haynes, J.Coady (Eds)
Norwood, NJ : Ablex 1993
1995

Chapter 2
Implications for L2 Vocabulary Acquisition and Instruction from L1 Vocabulary Research

Fredricka L. Stoller
William Grabe
English Department
Northern Arizona University

Research on vocabulary development in first language educational contexts has been much more extensive in the last 10 years than has been parallel research in second language contexts. Current first language research suggests that vocabulary acquisition is much more closely related to comprehension processes than second language theorists and practitioners have generally recognized. In particular, the development of a large vocabulary appears to be inextricably linked to the development of reading skills. This chapter reviews current research in first language contexts to assess what is now known about the nature of vocabulary acquisition: how it is learned, organized, and retrieved. Based on this review, we derive eight implications for vocabulary acquisition in second language contexts. These implications, in turn, suggest a number of effective techniques for teaching vocabulary.

Until recently, vocabulary instruction was something of a lost art in discussions of second language (L2) methodology and language learning, often being relegated to a secondary status; this disinterest was an unfortunate outcome of developments in English as a second language (ESL) methodology traceable

24

back for at least 50 years (cf. Carter & McCarthy, 1988). Such a secondary status for vocabulary, however, is not reflected by research in first language (L1) learning, as indicated by investigations in cognitive and educational psychology, psycholinguistics, and first language reading (e.g., Garnham, 1985; Perfetti, 1985; Rayner & Pollatsek, 1989; Seidenberg, 1985; Stanovich, 1986; Tannenhaus, 1988; Vellutino & Scanlon, 1987). To the contrary, current L1 research suggests that vocabulary is much more central to understanding processes than L2 theorists and practitioners have generally recognized. In this chapter we would like to explore this issue as well as provide practical suggestions for what we can do to develop and improve L2 students' vocabulary.

As a way to draw attention to the issues, we must first ask what is known about the nature of vocabulary—how it is learned, organized, and retrieved. Second, we need to look to L1 research on vocabulary to see what helpful insights can be derived about the nature of vocabulary development in L2 contexts. Third and finally, we need to reassess what is known about teaching vocabulary, and how we can best teach vocabulary in light of these insights. These three issues will be examined while keeping in mind the current state of ESL vocabulary instruction as it typically occurs. We would like to illustrate our concern over current ESL instruction with a brief example.

In the vocabulary exercise which follows (Table 2.1), one which is similar to many commercial textbook and teacher-generated exercises, students are asked to read the passage entitled "Restike" quietly and answer the questions at the end of the passage. As is typical of many language classroom activities, students are told that they cannot ask the teacher for clarification, since this exercise is being assigned for evaluative purposes; thus, the majority of the students will try their best on the exercise.

Table 2.1. Restike

For most of the 20th century, the teaching and learning of restike has never aroused the same degree of interest within language teaching as have such issues as satical competence, tound analysis, and halish skills. Restike instruction has often been relegated to secondary status because restike acquisition was not considered a beal in itself. Basically, restike acquisition was seen as a means to improve other skills, especially halish skills.

1. What hasn't aroused much interest for most of the 20th century?
2. What issues in language teaching have aroused a lot of interest this century?
3. Why was restike instruction relegated to a secondary status?
4. What was the relationship between restike acquisition and halish skills for most of this century?
5. How important are halish skills for you?
6. How do you feel about learning restike?
7. Are you interested in tound analysis? Why? Why not?
8. Do you think perceptions about restike will change in the future? Explain.

Even though the "Restike" passage and accompanying questions contain many unfamiliar vocabulary items, most students will "read" through the passage and then respond to the "comprehension" questions with semantically appropriate and grammatically accurate answers. These "correct" responses to the questions should make the problem with many typical vocabulary exercises readily apparent; the language learner need not comprehend the passage or the questions in order to answer the questions appropriately, semantically, and/or syntactically. Exercises such as these train students to become experts in "lifting phrases," with or without comprehension. While students are "actively" using the language, there is no apparent connection between vocabulary usage and meaning, a trap that can occur much too easily in the language classroom. An excellent evaluation may result in damaging deception, as the student obtains a false sense of language proficiency and language knowledge. Simultaneously, the teacher, unaware of the potential pitfalls of such vocabulary exercises, will assume improved vocabulary knowledge and plan future lessons accordingly, neglecting the actual needs of the students.

While this example may simplify some of the issues involved, it nonetheless points out standard problems with vocabulary instruction as it is often presented in textbook material. We think that vocabulary not only deserves more attention, but that there are many ideas and techniques which can be used and incorporated into larger L2 instructional designs with more effective results.

L1 VOCABULARY RESEARCH

In the first language arena, especially in the last decade, vocabulary has become a topic of increasing interest. Issues of vocabulary growth, the organization of the lexicon, degrees of word knowledge, and the use of contextual information (with corresponding classroom implications) have moved onto center stages in fields such as psycholinguistics and cognitive psychology, and in reading research itself. Research in first language reading, in particular, has paid careful attention to vocabulary development, presenting considerable evidence that vocabulary learning is a complex process and an integral part of students' reading abilities (Perfetti, 1985; Stanovich, 1986). Theories on vocabulary acquisition, as discussed in Jenkins, Stein, and Wysocki (1984), McKeown and Curtis (1987), Nagy (1988), Nagy, Herman, and Anderson (1985), and Sternberg (1987) emphasize the importance of incremental learning in vocabulary development and address the central problem of how first language students acquire a massive recognition vocabulary, a necessary if not sufficient requirement for literacy skills.

The central phenomenon which puzzles first language researchers is how to account for the seemingly natural, and phenomenal, growth of L1 vocabulary from grades 1–12, which, in some cases, can continue for a lifetime, and which seems to be primarily an outgrowth of literacy training. Regardless of the method to determine word count, vocabulary size is thought to approximately double between the third and seventh grades (McKeown & Curtis, 1987; Jenkins & Dixson, 1983). Nagy and Herman (1985, 1987), for example, argue that students increase their vocabulary by 3,000 words a year and achieve a vocabulary knowledge of 40,000 words by the end of high school. Such incredible gains cannot be attributed solely to classroom vocabulary instruction and/or incidental learning. Other researchers have argued for a less spectacular growth, noting that educational contexts and assessment measures tend only to focus on the 15,000 or so more frequent words. (Beck & McKeown, 1985; Beck, McKeown, & Omanson, 1987; Curtis, 1987).[1] Nonetheless, in the L2 context, even this smaller number represents a major hurdle for L2 students.

Theoretical discussions which attempt to explain this vocabulary growth often center around its relationship to reading comprehension (e.g., Anderson & Freebody, 1981; Hague, 1987; Kameenui, Dixson, & Carnine, 1987; Mezynski, 1983; cf. Channell, 1988). One explanation sometimes offered is the *aptitude hypothesis,* which states that one's intellect is the primary force behind vocabulary acquisition and reading skill. In other words, intelligent people know more words and are better readers because of their intellect. A second explanation is the *knowledge hypothesis,* which claims that vocabulary knowledge is a reflection of general knowledge, indirectly affecting one's reading ability; that is, people who have more knowledge in general will learn more words and have better comprehension.

The *instrumentalist hypothesis,* a third explanation, asserts that there is a direct relationship between the actual number of words known and reading comprehension. For that reason, proponents of this hypothesis encourage students to work with explicit vocabulary instruction and, perhaps, long definitional word lists; such exposure to lexical items will facilitate vocabulary expansion, which will, in turn, improve reading comprehension. The fourth hypothesis, the *access hypothesis,* affirms that words are less readily usable unless their various meanings are well known and easily accessible (i.e., the development of automaticity). Proponents of this last hypothesis stress the need for multiple exposures to words as well as multiple opportunities to practice. The need for practice also points to the use of reading itself as a means to develop vocabulary so that vocabulary and reading are seen as reciprocally developing abilities (Stanovich, 1986).

While Hague (1987) provides a review of these various hypotheses in an L2 discussion, Kameenui et al. (1987) examine them in an L1 context. Kameenui et al. conclude that all four hypotheses are likely to play some role in vocabulary acquisition. Thus, vocabulary acquisition is a result of aptitude, background knowledge, instruction, multiple exposures, and opportunity for practice.

One important variation on the *access hypothesis* is research on the extent to which words are known, and what impact this has on literacy skills. Recent research by Beck, Perfetti, and McKeown (1982), Curtis (1987), Graves (1984, 1987), and Kameenui, Dixson, and Carnine (1987) indicates that words are learned by students to different extents: this range can extend from no knowledge to some recognition, to an acquaintance in a context, to partial knowledge, to full knowledge. How well various words are known by students is a long-neglected area of research but one which has major implications for instruction. (For L2 discussion, see Judd, 1978; Nattinger, 1988.) This perspective on the access hypothesis also has obvious ramifications for the somewhat simplistic dichotomy between "active and passive" vocabulary. While it is useful to recognize that readers have access to a much larger recognition vocabulary than, for example, the vocabulary used in writing, the extent to which we learn vocabulary items, and which items, and for what purposes, will not be understood by a two-way opposition for what is clearly a more complex issue.

In contrast to the more theoretical acquisition hypotheses described above, other researchers have explained vocabulary development in more practical terms, discussing vocabulary growth without reference to particular theoretical frameworks. Jenkins and Dixson (1983), for example, suggest that most vocabulary learning occurs—in and out of the classroom—by means of a combination of two or more of the following strategies:

1. through explicit reference (i.e., definitions)
2. through example
3. through context
4. through morphological analysis

Graves (1987) has expanded this list of strategies to include the use of dictionaries and word lists as possible options. (See also Carter & McCarthy, 1988; Summers, 1988).

Explicit reference to word meanings, either by associations or by definitions, is now being recognized as a viable way to gain partial knowledge of a word. A number of researchers (e.g., Beck et al., 1987; Cohen, 1990; Graves, 1987; Nagy & Herman, 1987) support this teaching approach as a way to handle many words which may be inessential or too specialized in meaning or use. Definitions, associations, and even word lists may provide useful cues as a first exposure for words which appear later in various reading contexts. Carter (1987) and Carter and McCarthy (1988) similarly suggest that lists and translations may be effective means of first introducing new words to be learned and should not be overlooked simply because they have the appearance of being less "natural" or less "contextually meaningful." Note that these arguments are *not* assertions that vocabulary lists should be memorized or studied intensively.

Vocabulary instruction through example has a more extensive literature. Pressley, Levin, and Delaney (1982; Pressley, Levin, & McDaniel, 1987) review the various ways that words can be learned by keyword approaches and semantic associations. Beck and McKeown (1983, 1985; Beck et al., 1987) suggest that many examples and uses of specific words provide learners with rich meanings and strong semantic associations (or networks) with other words.

The use of context for learning words has not proven to be the great solution it is sometimes touted to be (e.g., Carter & McCarthy, 1988; Levin & Pressley, 1985; Pressley et al., 1987; Nagy & Herman, 1987; Schatz & Baldwin, 1986). Although learning words through context can be a useful approach if students are taught both how and when to apply the available contextual cues (Sternberg, 1987), this approach should not be seen as a learning tool to be applied at all times or at random (Drum & Konopak, 1987).

Despite conflicting opinions, applying morphological knowledge of the language to vocabulary learning has been a widely recognized aid for students. There may be somewhere on the order of 3,000 to 4,000 affixes in the English language, and the random treatment of a large subset may serve as much to confuse students as it may to help them. Graves (1987) suggests that teaching the 100 most common and regular affixes may be a productive instructional strategy in this regard.

Overall, whether one looks at vocabulary acquisition by means of theoretical hypotheses or more concrete learning approaches, the crucial question becomes how to help students accomplish these "feats" most efficiently and effectively. While L1 research on this question has been extensive, there has been much less equivalent L2 research (cf. Cohen, 1990; Gass, 1989; Nation, 1990). If we are to make appropriate use of L1 research, we must consider the constraints specific to vocabulary learning in L2 contexts.

L2 CONSTRAINTS AND CONTRASTS

By way of contrast with L2 students, both Singer (1981) and Graves (1987) have noted that L1 children come to the task of vocabulary learning with most of their syntactic knowledge set, with a complete phonological system in place, and with approximately 5,000–6,000 words already known. By no means do L2 students begin learning target language vocabulary with this extensive language background. L2 students also are affected by transfer effects, which may take the form of syntactic or lexical interference, and/or processing differences in the early stages of learning a new writing system (Brown & Haynes, 1985; Gass, 1989; Koda, 1987; Tzeng & Hung, 1981). To L2 students' advantage (especially for more mature students with an educational background in L1), they bring to the second language learning task a more sophisticated and elaborate knowledge of the world, a strong goal-oriented perspective on their learning, and, in many cases, a well-developed knowledge of learning strategies from their own L1 school experiences. While many L1 findings are directly relevant to L2 instruction, others require some "adaptation" because of these L2 student distinctions.

What follows is a discussion of eight points from L1 research findings that are applicable to L2 vocabulary instruction.

IMPLICATIONS FROM L1 RESEARCH

1. One major perspective running through much of the above discussion is that *vocabulary knowledge is the "cornerstone of literacy"* (Beck & McKeown, 1985), and that *instruction has an impact on both vocabulary knowledge and reading comprehension*. Although classroom instruction can hardly account for all the words students need to learn, it is well documented that some instruction is better than no instruction at all (Beck et al., 1987; Calfee & Drum, 1986; Chall, 1987; Drum & Konopak, 1987; Graves, 1987; McKeown, Beck, Omanson, & Perfetti, 1983; Stahl & Fairbanks, 1986). In the school context, where students have a pressing need for a well-developed vocabulary, it is clear that vocabulary instruction must take on a more dominant profile in the curriculum. How this is to be done, however, is an issue that requires much more innovative thinking than has heretofore been demonstrated.

Vocabulary knowledge must also be viewed as a key to reading and reading skills development (Chall, 1987; Stanovich, 1986). While vocabulary development is often treated in L2 discussions as a potentially independent concern (e.g., Gairns & Redman, 1986), we believe that vocabulary development must be viewed as both a cause and a consequence of reading abilities.[2] Any serious discussion of vocabulary in academic contexts must be viewed in terms of its relation to reading development.[3]

2. The same L1 research suggests that *vocabulary learning involves the acquisition of a range of skills.* More specifically, students must be able to recall meaning, infer meaning, comprehend a text, communicate orally, spell correctly, etc. Each one of these skills requires alternative instructional approaches and makes different demands on the extent of word knowledge. For example, Perfetti and McCutchen (1987) make a distinction between comprehending a text and deriving an interpretation for a text. Interpretation, the true goal of most reading, may require inferring from vocabulary items to a much richer scenario. This ability requires more detailed knowledge as part of the meanings of particular vocabulary items than would a less rich literal comprehension of the text, and thus would require different instructional approaches.

Generally speaking, the range of skills introduced in an L1 or L2 classroom, and corresponding instructional approaches, cannot be determined until the following issues are considered: student needs and motivation, instructional objectives, the words which might need to be learned, the extent to which these words need to be learned, and their importance for overall curricular goals. (See Morgan & Rinvolucri, 1986, for L2 discussion.) The point is that there is no one instructional approach that can address these varied vocabulary skills.

3. A third major perspective in L1 research is that *incidental learning from written context may account for a large proportion of vocabulary growth* (Nagy & Herman, 1985). This is, in fact, a complex argument (see McKeown & Curtis, 1987) and is *not* an argument for teaching word meanings through vocabulary in context; rather the claim is that words are gradually learned by a number of exposures in various discourse contexts. The incidental vocabulary learning position tends to downplay the usefulness of explicit vocabulary instruction; proponents of this position argue that an insufficient number of words can be learned by means of explicit instruction, including guessing from context, to account for the vast growth of student vocabularies. For example, Nagy and Herman (1985, 1987) claim that teachers should "promote reading" in the L1 context, because it can lead to greater vocabulary growth than *any* program of explicit instruction. Some combination of the two perspectives (instruction and incidental learning), however, is the most likely explanation for observed vocabulary growth.

Just as incidental learning contributes so much to L1 vocabulary acquisition, incidental learning is crucial for L2 students who cannot depend on classroom instruction alone to meet all their vocabulary needs. As one answer, L2 students must be urged to read as much as possible. Besides standard reading assignments that accompany regular coursework, other reading activities can be utilized to stimulate vocabulary growth. Sustained silent reading (SSR) programs can be set up to provide students with regular opportunities to read in class without interruption, instruction, or the anxieties which often accompany other classroom reading activities (Krashen, 1985; see Rosen, 1986, for more details on setting up an SSR program at the secondary level).

Similarly, a "narrow reading" program (Krashen, 1982) can be set up whereby students focus on a single topic or author. In such focused-reading activities, repeated exposures to vocabulary items, syntax, and content facilitates vocabulary acquisition as well as reading improvement (Kyongho & Nation, 1989). The school library or a classroom library (stocked with popular magazines, readers, textbooks, articles, etc.) can be used for such a "pleasure reading" curricular component.

As a complement to the notion of "narrow reading," a number of researchers suggest that "wide reading" is equally useful, though for different reasons. Reading a wide variety of topics and authors, in varied genres, provides students with exposure to many new words, concepts, and arrays of world knowledge. While initial semantic networks (or mental models, e.g., Johnson-Laird, 1983; Garnham, 1985) created from wide reading may be underrepresented, the exposure will gradually allow for richer lexical and conceptual connections. The notion of developing a critical mass of background knowledge has been considered in an L2 context by Grabe (1986). Once a certain level of knowledge (and vocabulary) is achieved, students will move from learning to read to reading to learn. Students will then be able to apply the richer knowledge to learning new vocabulary as well.

4. As a fourth finding, L1 research has demonstrated that, in order to profit most from "incidental vocabulary exposure" in reading sessions, *students must be "equipped" with independent learning strategies and abilities* (Carr & Wixson, 1986; Graves & Duin, 1985; Nagy & Herman, 1985; Sternberg, 1987; Twadell, 1973). Nelson-Herber (1986) points out that, in the L1 context, it is not desirable or worthwhile to let students simply read, without instruction, in order to acquire independent learning strategies on their own. Students need to be taught these strategies *explicitly*. Taking this notion one step further, a number of researchers have emphasized the need to focus on vocabulary acquisition skills rather than actual words themselves in the classroom.

In both L1 and L2 instructional contexts, teachers can help students become independent learners in a number of ways:

a. Students should be aware of productive word families, stems, and meaningful affixes. By becoming familiar with only a few stems, prefixes, and suffixes, students will recognize the meaning of many words; one root or affix can often provide a student with a clue to the meaning of dozens of words. As noted earlier, Graves (1987) suggests that about 100 of the most productive affixes would be sufficient. Learning to break words down into their fundamental parts and identifying those parts is a useful skill in vocabulary building (See Dollerup, Glahn, & Hansen, 1989; cf. Nation, 1990).

b. Teachers must show students *how* and *when* to use context cues to derive meaning for new words (Dunmore, 1989). Most researchers now agree that using vocabulary in context exercises only for the purpose of teaching specific vocabulary is not very useful (Bensoussan & Laufer, 1984; Drum & Konopak, 1987; Graves, 1987; Haynes, 1984; McKeown, 1985; Nagy & Herman, 1987; Pressley et al., 1987). There have been a number of other criticisms which have been leveled at the use of contextual clues for learning vocabulary that takes us far beyond the scope of this paper (Graves, 1987; Kelly, 1990; McKeown, 1985; McKeown, Beck, Omanson, & Pople, 1985). Sternberg (1987), however, suggests a number of specific strategies for inferring word meanings that can be taught to students. These heuristic strategies, he argues, can help students learn to identify relevant clues—spatial, temporal, causal, class membership, equivalence, and so on—through training; students can then learn to create a workable definition from the clues when they are available, and compare a constructed definition to background knowledge. Without sustained explicit training, however, students are not likely to make efficient use of the redundancies, collocations, and cohesive devices used in writing.

c. Proper dictionary usage is another useful strategy for dealing with unfamiliar vocabulary items. Students' efficiency in using a dictionary, and knowing when not to use it, should be developed (Summers, 1988). Older L2 students, whether we like it or not, devote a great deal of time to dictionary "consultation.'' If unguided, dictionary use can have adverse effects on their language development. Therefore, students should learn when and how to use a monolingual dictionary.

5. A fifth finding, not surprising at all, is that *learning vocabulary in the first language context requires multiple exposures* (Meara, 1980). In fact, Beck et al. (1987) suggest that a minimum of 12 exposures is needed to develop fluent and precise word knowledge. As stated in the ''access hypothesis,'' words are not as readily recalled and used unless their various meanings are easily accessible; therefore, multiple exposures and contexts help students develop more ''elaborated word knowledge'' (Carr & Wixson, 1986; cf. Sinclair & Renouf, 1988, who do not stress learning many new words but learning known words better).

These research findings have special significance in the L2 context, where exposure to the target language is often more limited. It is unrealistic to expect L2 students to comprehend the intricacies of a given lexical items and be able to use the word appropriately after one single exposure (Judd, 1978). For that simple reason, vocabulary items should be systematically reviewed and recycled in meaningful contexts, so that students can begin to see their range of meanings and uses. Relevant vocabulary items can be integrated into other classroom activities such as readings, dialogues, dictations, listening comprehension activities, writing assignments, role plays, games, and so on, for both comprehension and production. Elaborated word knowledge can also be developed by specific vocabulary techniques such as semantic mapping, word association brainstorming, word grids (Harvey, 1983), finding the words being used outside of class, and so on.

6. A sixth important finding from L1 research suggests that *elaborated learning can only take place when learners can relate new lexical items to background knowledge* (Carr & Wixson, 1986; Nelson-Herber, 1986; Thelen, 1986). This finding incorporates research on schema theory that states that new learning occurs either when adding to or adjusting already existing knowledge structures. Beck and McKeown (1983) and McKeown et al. (1983) found that comprehension improves when students are given the opportunity to develop semantic network connections, relating new information to old information. These research findings support teaching vocabulary in semantically related groups. What logically follows is that vocabulary instruction should not be based on lexical difficulty or frequency, as it often is. Vocabulary items should be selected for explicit instruction specifically because they are relevant to classroom topics and needed for comprehension (Anders & Bos, 1986; Nelson-Herber, 1986).

Certain instructional techniques may be especially appropriate for tapping background knowledge. Semantic feature analysis (SFA) is a technique which allows students to learn new vocabulary by tapping prior knowledge; the intent is to help learners better understand the similarities and differences between words by categorizing vocabulary. SFA teaches students to see semantic relationships between and among words as well as between their own background knowledge and new information (Anders & Bos, 1986; Stieglitz, 1983; cf. Carter, 1987; Carter & McCarthy, 1988; Richards, 1976). (See Table 2.2.)

Semantic mapping activities (Figure 2.1) demonstrate how new words fit into a reader's existing knowledge base by diagramming meaning networks and connecting new words to known words. Both semantic feature analysis and semantic mapping lead to better vocabulary retention because new lexical items are introduced in semantic networks. It should be noted, however, that the potential overuse of semantic mapping and semantic feature analyses, used to either introduce too many new vocabulary items at once or to introduce less useful vocabulary, must be avoided in L2 contexts where students may be easily overloaded. There is also an occasionally stated preference for semantic mapping over semantic feature analysis, because it provides for direct imagery among the various relations of many words in a semantic field.

In a sense the key word approach also makes use of the students' background knowledge by creating an associative link between a new word and a known word, phrase, or image which is acoustically and/or visually similar. The key word approach involves the use of a mnemonic device. Basically, a new word is recoded into a more familiar word or a word in the student's L1, aiding memory and heightening attention. The two lexical items may be related by a story connecting the two words; the story should facilitate word retrieval by the learner. According to Levin and Pressley (1985; Levin, Dretske, Pressley, &

Figure 2.1.   Semantic Mapping

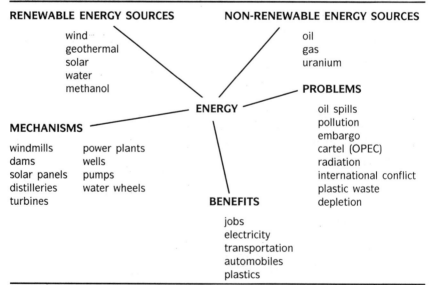

Table 2.2. Semantic Feature Analysis

Energy Types	Organic Source	Polluting	Renewable Source	Processed Source	Liquid Source	Solid Source	Inert Source
				Properties of Energy			
Petrochemical	+	+	–	+	+	–	+
Natural gas	+	+	–	–	–	–	+
Thermal	–	–	+	–	–	–	–
Nuclear	?	+	–	+	–	+	+
Solar	–	–	+	–	–	–	–
Wind	–	–	+	–	–	–	+
Hydroelectric	–	–	+	–	+	–	+
Wood	+	+	+	–	–	+	+

McGivern, 1985; McDaniel & Tillman, 1987; Pressley et al., 1987), the mnemonic key word approach has no rivals with respect to vocabulary recall. They have also found that the skill is generalizable, permitting students to use the strategy on their own to build their vocabularies. (See Cohen, 1990, for an L2 perspective.) Pressley et al. (1987, p. 109), writing for an L1 audience, explain the technique as follows:

> The English word 'carlin' means 'old woman'. Using the keyword 'car', a learner might generate an image of an old woman driving a car. When presented 'carlin' later, ready retrieval of 'car' occurs because of its acoustic similarity to 'carlin', which leads to recall of the linking image containing the old woman. An alternative version of the method consists of verbally, elaborating the keyword and the definition, that is, relating the keyword and the definition in a meaningful sentence, as in ''The 'car' was driven by an 'old woman'.''

A similar strategy is well known to beginning piano students, who are taught to use the sentence ''Every good boy deserves favor'' to remember how to read the lines of the treble clef in music scores. Another example, closer to home for us, is our own mnemonic sentence to recall the names of the various geological levels visible in the Grand Canyon, an otherwise daunting task as indicated below:

Katie Took Cindy's Homemade Spaghetti Right To Men Behind The Zoo.; for, respectively,

Kaibab Formation
Toroweap
Coconino Sandstone
Hermit Shale
Supai Group
Redwall Limestone
Temple Butte
Mauv
Bright Angel Shale
Tapeats
Zoroaster Granite.

Mnemonic devices are commonly used to remember addresses, telephone numbers, place names, or the geological strata of the Grand Canyon. They present an ideal set of techniques for teaching those words which we want students to recall and use for their own purposes.

7. A seventh research finding suggests that *a person's vocabulary consists of many degrees of knowledge.* Drum and Konopak (1987, p. 76) discuss six levels of word knowledge. A student:

1. knows a word orally but not in written form,
2. knows a word meaning but cannot express it,
3. knows a meaning but not the word for it,
4. knows the partial meaning of a word,
5. knows a different meaning for a word,
6. knows neither the concept nor the word.

Depending on the student's knowledge of a word (and the student's need for the word), effective vocabulary instruction will employ different techniques. For example, Drum and Konopak suggest that using context cues may be useful for knowledge levels 3 and 4 but not for levels 5 or 6, the latter being more common levels of word knowledge for L2 students.

Other researchers have defined different taxonomies of students' levels of word knowledge. Curtis (1987, p. 43, citing Dale, 1965) discusses four levels of word learning:

Stage 1: "I never saw it before."
Stage 2: "I've heard of it, but I don't know what it means."
Stage 3: "I recognize it in context—it has something to do with . . ."
Stage 4: "I know it."

Graves (1987, p. 167), on the other hand, describes degrees of word knowledge in terms of learning tasks:

learning to read known words,
learning new meanings representing known concepts,
learning new words representing new concepts,
clarifying and enriching the meanings of known words,
moving words from receptive to expressive vocabularies.

What these various taxonomies indicate is that simple dichotomies such as active vs. passive vocabulary, or receptive vs. productive vocabulary, in general, may not be useful guidelines for pedagogical considerations.

One dichotomy which may be useful for instructional purposes is that proposed by Stahl (1983, cited in Stahl & Fairbanks, 1986, p. 74) who suggest that a "person who 'knows' a word can be thought of as having two types of knowledge about words—*definitional information and contextual information.*" *Definitional information* comprises knowledge of the logical relationship between a word and other known words, as in a dictionary definition. This can involve knowing a definition, synonym, antonym, or affixes, and so on. (See Powell, 1986, for a discussion of the value of teaching through opposition.) *Contextual information,* on the other hand, can be defined as knowledge of the core concept of the word and how that concept changes in different contexts. The idea is that both types of word knowledge are useful. (See also Cowie, 1988, for a discussion of stable word meanings vs. contextually determined meanings; Laufer, 1989, for a discussion of "deceptively transparent words"; Perfetti & Mc-Cutchen, 1987, for a discussion of comprehension vs. interpretation; and Palmberg, 1989, for a discussion of potential versus receptive vocabulary.) As many researchers have pointed out, everyone has different degrees of word knowledge for different words, and, for many words, we simply do not need to have elaborated knowledge. (See Gass, 1989, for an overview of these issues in L2 contexts.)

A practical implication of this research is that providing students with simple definitions, synonyms, associations, glosses, etc. has a place in vocabulary teaching, particularly for low-frequency and less important words. Such exposure, in L1 and L2 settings, may provide a base for more accurate and lasting knowledge when those vocabulary items are later encountered in a series of contextualized exposures (Beck, et al., 1987; Carter, 1987; Graves, 1987; Jenkins et al., 1985; Nagy & Herman, 1987; Pressley et al., 1987).

8. Finally, it is not surprising that in the area of vocabulary research *student motivation* is identified as having a positive impact on L1 vocabulary acquisition; motivation is equally important in the second language context. Because L2 students often find themselves at a "loss for words," they are usually quite motivated to improve their vocabulary. They enthusiastically participate in explicit vocabulary lessons and are willing to engage in implicit instruction (incidental learning activities) if the relationship, for example, between reading and vocabulary development is explained to them.

In addition, allowing students to choose the words they would like to learn can serve as a great motivating tool (Haggard, 1986; see also Beck et al., 1987; Graves, 1987; Sternberg, 1987). In most L2 instructional contexts, the use of word games and communicative crossword puzzles (Woodeson, 1982) are enthusiastically endorsed by "word-starved" students (Allen, 1983; Beck et al., 1987; Morgan & Rinvolucri, 1986; Nation, 1990). What is particularly important "is the teacher's ability to arouse in his or her students a genuine interest in vocabulary, to develop the skills and the curiosity that will guarantee the growth of every student's vocabulary far beyond the . . . limits of the ESL classroom" (Celce-Murcia & Rosenweig, 1979, p. 256). This is what Beck and her colleagues (1987) have termed *word awareness*.

CONCLUSIONS

Vocabulary is a language area that needs continued growth and development for native and nonnative speakers alike. In the L2 context, although no foolproof methods for vocabulary instruction have been prescribed, ESL/EFL professionals now recognize vocabulary as an area of increasing importance, one which merits systematic attention in the classroom. A curriculum with a comprehensive vocabulary component should include opportunities for explicit learning as well as implicit learning. Students need to develop independent learning strategies that will allow them to expand their vocabularies both in and out of the classroom. Without a commitment to vocabulary instruction, our ESL students will find themselves at a "loss for words," unable to function adequately in L2 contexts.

Before closing, we would like to note that there are a number of publications which provide useful techniques for L2 vocabulary instruction, particularly those by Allen (1983), Cohen (1990), Gairns and Redman (1986), Morgan and Rinvolucri (1986), and Nation (1990). What must be remembered with such practical volumes, however, is that student knowledge and needs, context demands, and educational expectations all must determine which techniques are applicable, when they are applicable, and to what extent they are applicable. If these constraints prevent a simple guideline for applying vocabulary learning techniques, that is perhaps as it should be. Teaching is an art, and vocabulary instruction would appear to be no less so. At the same time, the task for our students is relatively simple. As Graves (1987, p. 166) states,

The goals are Learning Words, Learning to Learn Words, and Learning about Words.

REFERENCES

Allen, V. F. (1983). *Techniques in teaching vocabulary.* New York: Oxford University Press.

Anders, P., & Bos, C. (1986). Semantic feature analysis: An interactive strategy for vocabulary development and text comprehension. *Journal of Reading, 29,* 610–616.

Anderson, R., & Freebody, P. (1981). Vocabulary knowledge. In J. Guthrie (Ed.), *Comprehension and teaching: Research reviews* (pp. 77–117). Newark, DE: IRA.

Beck, I., & McKeown, M. (1983). Learning words well—A program to enhance vocabulary and comprehension. *The Reading Teacher, 36,* 622–625.

Beck, I., & McKeown, M. (1985). Teaching vocabulary: Making the instruction fit the goal. *Educational Perspectives, 23,* 11–15.

Beck, I., McKeown, M., & Omanson, R. (1987). The effects and uses of diverse vocabulary instructional techniques. In. M. McKeown & M. Curtis (Eds.), *The nature of vocabulary acquisition* (pp. 147–163). Hillsdale, NJ: Erlbaum.

Beck, I., Perfetti, C., & McKeown, M. (1982). Effects of long-term vocabulary instruction on lexical access and reading comprehension. *Journal of Educational Psychology, 74,* 506–521.

Bensoussan, M., & Laufer, B. (1984). Lexical guessing in context in EFL reading comprehension. *Journal of Research in Reading, 7,* 15–32.

Brown, T., & Haynes, M. (1985). Literacy background and reading development in a second language. In T. Carr (Ed.), *The development of reading skills: New directions for child development* (pp. 19–34). San Francisco: Jossey-Bass.

Calfee, R., & Drum, P. (1986). Research on teaching reading. In M. Wittrock (Ed.), *Handbook of research on teaching* (pp. 804–849). New York: Macmillan.

Carr, E., & Wixson, K. (1986). Guidelines for evaluating vocabulary instruction. *Journal of Reading, 29,* 588–595.

Carter, R. (1987). *Vocabulary: Applied linguistic perspectives.* London: Allen & Unwin.

Carter, R., & McCarthy, M. (1988). *Vocabulary and language teaching.* New York: Longman.

Celce-Murcia, M., & Rosenweig, F. (1979). Teaching vocabulary in the ESL classroom. In M. Celce-Murcia & L. McIntosh (Eds.), *Teaching English as a second or foreign language* (pp. 241–257). Rowley, MA: Newbury House.

Chall, J. (1987). Two vocabularies for reading: Recognition and meaning. In M. McKeown & M. Curtis (Eds.), *The nature of vocabulary acquisition* (pp. 7–17). Hillsdale, NJ: Erlbaum.

Channell, J. (1988). Psycholinguistic considerations in the study of L2 vocabulary acquisition. In R. Carter & M. McCarthy (Eds.), *Vocabulary and language teaching* (pp. 83–96). New York: Longman.

Cohen, A. D. (1990). *Language Learning: Insights for learners, teachers, and researchers.* New York: Newbury House Publishers.

Cowie, A. (1988). Stable and creative aspects of vocabulary use. In R. Carter & M. McCarthy (Eds.), *Vocabulary and language teaching* (pp. 126–139). New York: Longman.

Curtis, M. (1987). Vocabulary testing and vocabulary instruction. In M. McKeown & M. Curtis (Eds.), *The nature of vocabulary acquisition* (pp. 37–51). Hillsdale, NJ: Erlbaum.

Dale, E. (1965). Vocabulary measurement: Techniques and major findings. *Elementary English, 42,* 895–901, 948.

Dollerup, C., Glahn, E., & Hansen, C. R. (1989). Vocabularies in the reading process. In P. Nation & R. Carter (Eds.), *Vocabulary acquisition: AILA Review* (pp. 21–33). Amsterdam: Free University Press.

Drum, P., & Konopak, B. (1987). Learning word meanings from written context. In M. McKeown & M. Curtis (Eds.), *The nature of vocabulary acquisition* (pp. 73–87). Hillsdale, NJ: Erlbaum.

Dunmore, D. (1989). Using contextual clues to infer word meaning: An evaluation of current exercise types. *Reading in a Foreign Language, 6* (1), 337–347.

Gairns, R., & Redman, S. (1986). *Working with words: A guide to teaching and learning vocabulary.* New York: Cambridge University Press.

Garnham, A. (1985). *Central topics in psycholinguistics.* New York: Methuen.

Gass, S. M. (1989). Second language vocabulary acquisition. *Annual Review of Applied Linguistics, 9,* 92–106.

Grabe, W. (1986). The transition from theory to practice in teaching reading. In F. Dubin, D. Eskey, & W. Grabe (Eds.), *Teaching second language reading for academic purposes* (pp. 25–48). Reading, MA: Addison-Wesley.

Graves, M. (1984). Selecting vocabulary to teach in the intermediate and secondary grades. In J. Flood (Ed.), *Promoting reading comprehension* (pp. 245–260). Newark, DE: IRA.

Graves, M. (1987). The roles of instruction in fostering vocabulary development. In M. McKeown & M. Curtis (Eds.), *The nature of vocabulary acquisition* (pp. 165–184). Hillsdale, NJ: Erlbaum.

Graves, M., & Duin, A. (1985). Building students' expressive vocabularies. *Educational Perspectives, 23,* 4–10.

Haggard, M. (1986). The vocabulary self-collection strategy: Using student interest and world knowledge to enhance vocabulary growth. *Journal of Reading, 29,* 634–642.

Hague, S. (1987). Vocabulary instruction: What L2 can learn from L1. *Foreign Language Annals, 20,* 217–225.

Harvey, P. (1983). Vocabulary learning: The use of grids. ELT *Journal, 37,* 243–246.

Haynes, M. (1984). Patterns and perils of guessing in second language reading. In J. Handscombe, R. Orem, & B. Taylor (Eds.), *On TESOL '83: The question of control* (pp. 163–176). Washington, DC: TESOL Publications.

Jenkins, J., & Dixson, R. (1983). Vocabulary learning. *Contemporary Educational Psychology, 8,* 237–260.

Jenkins, J., Stein, M., & Wysocki, K. (1984). Learning vocabulary through reading. *American Educational Research Journal, 21,* 767–788.

Johnson-Laird, P. (1983). *Mental models.* Cambridge, MA: Harvard University Press.

Judd, E. (1978). Vocabulary teaching and TESOL: A need for reevaluation of existing assumptions. *TESOL Quarterly, 12,* 71–76.

Kameenui, E., Dixson, R., & Carnine, D. (1987). Issues in the design of vocabulary instruction. In M. McKeown & M. Curtis (Eds.), *The nature of vocabulary acquisition* (pp. 129–145). Hillsdale, NJ: Erlbaum.

Kelly, P. (1990). Guessing: No substitute for systematic learning of lexis. *System, 18* (2), 199–207.

Koda, K. (1987). Cognitive strategy transfer in second language reading. In J. Devine, P. Carrell, & D. Eskey (Eds.), *Research in reading in English as a second language* (pp. 127–144). Washington, DC: TESOL Publications.

Krashen, S. (1982). The case for narrow readings. *TESOL Newsletter, 12,* 23.

Krashen, S. (1985). *Inquiries and insights.* Hayward, CA: Alemany Press.

Kyongho, H., & Nation, P. (1989). Reducing the vocabulary load and encouraging vocabulary learning through reading newspapers. *Reading in a Foreign Language, 6* (1), 323–335.

Laufer, B. (1989). A factor of difficulty in vocabulary learning: Deceptive transparency. In P. Nation & R. Carter (Eds.), *Vocabulary acquisition: AILA Review* (pp. 10–20). Amsterdam: Free University Press.

Laufer, B., & Bensoussan, M. (1984). Meaning is in the eye of the beholder. *English Teaching Forum, 22,* 10–13.

Levin, J., Dretzke, B., Pressley, M., & McGivern, J. (1985). In search of the keyword method/vocabulary comprehension link. *Contemporary Educational Psychology, 10,* 220–227.

Levin, J., & Pressley, M. (1985). Mnemonic vocabulary instruction: What's fact, what's fiction. In R. Dillon (Ed.), *Individual differences in cognition* (Vol. 2, pp. 145–172). New York: Academic Press.

McDaniel, M., & Tillman, V. (1987). Discovering a meaning versus applying the keyword method: Effects on recall. *Contemporary Educational Psychology, 12,* 156–175.

McKeown, M. (1985). The acquisition of word meaning from context by children of high and low ability. *Reading Research Quarterly, 20,* 482–496.

McKeown, M., Beck, I., Omanson, R., & Perfetti, C. (1983). The effects of long-term vocabulary instruction on reading comprehension: A replication. *Journal of Reading Behavior, 15,* 3–18.

McKeown, M., Beck, I., Omanson, R., & Pople, M. (1985). Some effects of the nature and frequency of vocabulary instruction on the knowledge and use of words. *Reading Research Quarterly, 20,* 522–535.

McKeown, M., & Curtis, M. (Eds.). (1987). *The nature of vocabulary acquisition.* Hillsdale, NJ: Erlbaum.

Meara, P. (1980). Vocabulary acquisition: A neglected aspect of language learning. In V. Kinsella (Ed.), *Surveys 1* (pp. 100–126). New York: Cambridge University Press.

Mezynski, K. (1983). Issues concerning the acquisition of knowledge: Effects of vocabulary training on reading comprehension. *Review of Educational Research, 53,* 253–279.

Morgan, J., & Rinvolucri, M. (1986). *Vocabulary.* New York: Oxford University Press.

Nagy, W. E. (1988). *Teaching vocabulary to improve reading comprehension.* Urbana, IL: National Council of Teachers of English.

Nagy, W., & Herman, P. (1985). Incidental vs. instructional approaches to increasing reading vocabulary. *Educational Perspectives, 23,* 16–21.

Nagy, W., & Herman, P. (1987). Breadth and depth of vocabulary knowledge: Implications for acquisition and instruction. In M. McKeown & M. Curtis (Eds.), *The nature of vocabulary acquisition* (pp. 19–35). Hillsdale, NJ: Erlbaum.

Nagy, W., Herman, P., & Anderson, R. (1985). Learning words from context. *Reading Research Quarterly, 20,* 233–253.

Nation, I. S. P. (1990). *Teaching and learning vocabulary.* New York: Newbury House Publishers.

Nattinger, J. (1988). Some current trends in vocabulary teaching. In R. Carter & M. McCarthy (Eds.), *Vocabulary and language teaching* (pp. 62–82). New York: Longman.

Nelson-Herber, J. (1986). Expanding and refining vocabulary in content areas. *Journal of Reading, 29,* 626–633.

Palmberg, R. (1989). What makes a word English?—Swedish speaking learners' feeling of "Englishness." In P. Nation & R. Carter (Eds.), *Vocabulary acquisition: AILA Review* (pp. 47–55). Amsterdam: Free University Press.

Perfetti, C. (1985). *Reading ability.* New York: Oxford University Press.

Perfetti, C., & McCutchen, D. (1987). Schooled language competence: Linguistic abilities in reading and writing. In S. Rosenberg (Ed.), *Advances in applied psycholinguistics, Volume 2: Reading, writing, and language learning* (pp. 105–141). New York: Cambridge University Press.

Powell, W. (1986). Teaching vocabulary through opposition. *Journal of Reading, 29,* 617–621.

Pressley, M., Levin, J., & Delaney, H. (1982). The mnemonic keyword method. *Review of Educational Research, 52,* 61–92.

Pressley, M., Levin, J., & McDaniel, M. (1987). Remembering versus inferring what a word means: Mnemonic and contextual approaches. In M. McKeown & M. Curtis (Eds.), *The nature of vocabulary acquisition* (pp. 107–127). Hillsdale, NJ: Erlbaum.

Rayner, K., & Pollatsek, A. (1989). *The psychology of reading.* Englewood Cliffs, NJ: Prentice Hall Regents.

Richards, J. (1976). The role of vocabulary teaching. *TESOL Quarterly, 10,* 77–89.

Rosen, N. (1986, December). SSR: A rationale for starting a program. *AZ-TESOL Newsletter*, pp. 12, 19.

Schatz, E., & Baldwin, R. (1986). Context clues are unreliable predictors of word meaning. *Reading Research Quarterly, 21*, 439–453.

Seidenberg, M. (1985). The time-course of information activation and utilization in visual word recognition. In T. Waller & G. MacKinnon (Eds.), *Reading research: Advances in theory and practice* (Vol. 5, pp. 199–252). New York: Academic Press.

Sinclair, J., & Renouf, A. (1988). A lexical syllabus of language learning. In R. Carter & M. McCarthy (Eds.), *Vocabulary and language teaching* (pp. 140–160). New York: Longman.

Singer, H. (1981). Instruction in reading acquisition. In O. Tzeng & H. Singer (Eds.), *Perception of print* (pp. 291–312). Hillsdale, NJ: Erlbaum.

Stahl, S. A. (1983). Differential word knowledge and reading comprehension. *Journal of Reading Behavior, 15* (4), 33–50.

Stahl, S. A. (1986). Three principles of effective vocabulary instruction. *Journal of Reading, 29*, 662–668.

Stahl, S. A., & Fairbanks, M. (1986). The effects of vocabulary instruction: A model-based meta analysis. *Review of Educational Research, 56*, 72–110.

Stanovich, K. (1986). Matthew effects in reading: Some consequences of individual differences in the acquisition of literacy. *Reading Research Quarterly, 21*, 360–407.

Sternberg, R. (1987). Most vocabulary is learned from context. In M. McKeown & M. Curtis (Eds.), *The nature of vocabulary acquisition* (pp. 89–105). Hillsdale, NJ: Erlbaum.

Stieglitz, E. (1983). A practical approach to vocabulary reinforcement. *ELT Journal, 37*, 71–75.

Stoller, F. (1986). Reading lab: Developing low-level reading skills. In F. Dubin, D. Eskey, & W. Grabe (Eds.), *Teaching second language reading for academic purposes* (pp. 51–76). Reading, MA: Addison-Wesley.

Summers, D. (1988). The role of dictionaries in language learning. In R. Carter & M. McCarthy (Eds.), *Vocabulary and language teaching* (pp. 111–125). New York: Longman.

Tannenhaus, M. (1988). Psycholinguistics: An overview 1. In F. Newmeyer (Ed.), *The Cambridge survey of linguistics: Psychological and biological aspects of language* (Vol. 3, pp. 1–37). New York: Cambridge University Press.

Thelen, J. (1986). Vocabulary instruction and meaningful learning. *Journal of Reading, 29*, 603–609.

Twaddell, F. (1973). Vocabulary expansion in the TESOL classroom. *TESOL Quarterly, 7*, 71–75.

Tzeng, O., & Hung, D. (1981). Linguistic determinism: A written language perspective. In O. Tzeng & H. Singer (Eds.), *Perception of print* (pp. 237–255). Hillsdale, NJ: Erlbaum.

Vellutino, F., & Scanlon, D. (1987). Linguistic coding and reading ability. in S. Rosenberg (Ed.), *Advances in applied psycholinguistics, Volume 2: Reading, writing, and language learning* (pp. 1–69). New York: Cambridge University Press.

Woodeson, E. (1982). Communicative crosswords. *Modern English Teacher, 10*, 28–29.

ENDNOTES

1. It should be noted that these differing positions represent a major debate on whether vocabulary must be acquired primarily via an extensive number of incidental contacts while reading, or whether an adequate vocabulary knowledge can be taught via direct instruction. This debate is much too complex to present within the framework of the present chapter. The various discussions and references in McKeown and Curtis (1987) and Nation (1990) would provide an appropriate introduction.
2. Elsewhere, we have argued that reading abilities represent the essential ESL academic skill which cannot be circumvented by other aids in advanced secondary and university contexts (Grabe, 1986; Stoller, 1986).
3. Vocabulary instruction for survival English (e.g., adult basic education or beginning literacy skills) represents an area where vocabulary may be treated independently from reading, as might also certain ESP contexts such as training service personnel, industry workers, and so on. These concerns, however, are secondary to vocabulary acquisition in relation to literacy skills development.

Editorial Comments

This informative and insightful review of L1 vocabulary acquisition calls for much more attention to vocabulary teaching in the ESL curriculum than is now the case. This seems particularly true for adults who wish to achieve advanced literacy: if direct teaching of vocabulary is necessary for native speaking children, is it not even more necessary for nonnative speakers aimed toward academic study at English-speaking universities?

Despite the fact that the pedagogical recommendations of this chapter derive from the analogy between L1 and L2 learners, in section 2 Stoller and Grabe also point out differences between child L1 and adult L2 vocabulary learners—beneficial differences for L2 learners in terms of their greater world knowledge, detrimental ones in terms of the weaker language knowledge they bring to the task of new vocabulary learning. After all, children are often just learning about the world and about the complexities of their own language. But does the knowledge of the adult L2 learner compensate sufficiently for the lack of a solid foundation in the L2? Such differences are explored in greater detail in the next chapter, by Haynes and Baker (Chapter 7), and elsewhere in this volume.

These authors grapple with other difficult theoretical issues underlying both L1 and L2 pedagogy:

1. the problem of how the rapid and "seemingly natural" L1 vocabulary growth during school years develops—though it seems related to literacy experiences, the authors make clear that there are a number of hypotheses to explain this growth, each with differing implications for instruction;

2. the lack of evidence about the underlying cause or causes of the high correlation between vocabulary knowledge and reading comprehension—the authors discuss but do not resolve what possible explanations there are for this well-established connection;
3. the complex continuum of vocabulary "knowledge"—the authors discuss varying degrees of knowing a word and point out, as do Coady (Chapter 1) and Parry (Chapter 6), that incremental approaches to vocabulary knowledge do not fit comfortably into simple categories such as the traditional dichotomy (retained in Nation, 1990) between receptive and productive vocabulary knowledge.

Deeper understanding of these and other issues underlying L1 and L2 vocabulary development can grow out of a careful reading of this chapter and its rich resource of references.

There is one point where we must qualify the authors' conclusions. They draw the implication (in the section on Background Knowledge) that "vocabulary instruction should not be based on lexical difficulty or frequency" and that, instead, "items should be selected . . . specifically because they are relevant to classroom topics and needed for comprehension." Note how this contrasts with the arguments by Coady (Chapter 1) and Coady et al. (Chapter 11) that the 2,000 most frequent words should be learned quickly, thoroughly, and to the point of automaticity, simply because they are the most frequent and therefore will contribute greatly to more fluent and less effortful reading. However, for more advanced learners and less frequent words, Stoller and Grabe's guidelines seem appropriate.

Though the focus of this chapter is on pedagogy, we feel the suggestions here should give researchers and classroom teachers clearer guidelines for research into instructional techniques that can be used with individual and classrooms of learners, both naturalistically and in experimental training studies. The authors' discussion of degrees of word knowledge (section 7) should be particularly helpful as researchers and teachers try to define more precisely the learning outcomes—the type or depth of word knowledge—which they wish to measure.

Chapter 3
Patterns and Perils of Guessing in Second Language Reading*

Margot Haynes
English Division
Delta College
University Center, MI

At the time of writing (Spring 1983), reading textbooks for ESL students were promoting one main approach to the learning of vocabulary: guessing the meaning of an unknown word from the surrounding context. Some textbooks even stated that dictionary work should be banned in the classroom. Though based on an analogy between L1 and L2 reading and the prevailing view that the reading process was primarily one of hypothesis testing, such pedagogical overreliance on contextual guessing was questioned by some of the findings of this chapter: (a) word-form identification can be difficult for L2 readers, who are apt to misrecognize new forms as familiar ones or feel unsure about whether a word-form is really new or not; and (b) word-concept can be difficult to delineate if a number of words in the context are unknown or if the context, as is frequently the case, proves too meager to support accurate inferencing.

*Much appreciation is due Tracy Brown, Paul Munsell, Marcelette Williams, Tom Carr, Bethyl Pearson, and Don Snow for support and criticism during the preparation of this paper. Even more is due the students of Michigan State University's English Language Center who kindly and patiently donated their time and guessing efforts.

This chapter is reprinted here with minor modifications from *On TESOL '83: The Question of Control* (pp. 163–176), edited by J. Handscombe, R. Orem, & B. Taylor, 1984, Washington, DC: TESOL Publications. Copyright 1984 by TESOL. Reprinted by permission.

INTRODUCTION

In the last 25 years, the active nature of language acquisition and language use has gained increasing recognition (Chomsky, 1959; Brown, 1973; Cromer, 1976; Dulay & Burt, 1978). Human beings learn and comprehend language, not only through perceiving, but also through their own internal structuring of linguistic messages. Such a top-down view of human cognition emphasizes the active contribution of perceivers who reshape external stimuli via their own self-generated input—such as their background knowledge and natural systematicity—while constructing their individual models of the world. This top-down description of human cognition has affected our characterization of all modes of language use, including reading.

Psycholinguistic models of reading describe readers as active samplers of text who combine text context with their knowledge about writing, language, and the world in general in order to read more efficiently, using prediction to take short-cuts in bottom-up processing of letters and words (Goodman, 1967; Smith, 1978). The field of ESL has not been impervious to the claims of these top-down reading models. Teachers and textbook writers have developed methods which foster active reading, particularly in the area of vocabulary comprehension. Instead of presenting single meanings of isolated words, textbooks now often recommend that students guess at the meaning of unfamiliar words by using context clues.

Among the many ESL practitioners advocating this shift to the guessing of vocabulary from context (Clarke & Silberstein, 1977; Kruse, 1979; Hosenfeld, Arnold, Kirchofer, Laciura, & Wilson, 1981) Twaddell (1973) has presented one of the most carefully reasoned arguments. Twaddell points out that, since words are almost always polysemic, teachers may mislead students by teaching single word meanings out of context. In addition, since most words in a language have only a low frequency of occurrence, dictionary precision and list memorization cannot ever provide language students with enough vocabulary to understand all the words they encounter while reading. Twaddell therefore recommends that ESL reading teachers focus on reading skills development rather than vocabulary building. By learning how to be better guessers, students can figure out the meanings of the many words in reading which they have not encountered before.

Twaddell and others also frequently draw an analogy between L1 and L2 reading. Twaddell points out that, when native speakers encounter a new word in reading, they usually skip the unfamiliar item or guess at its meaning from context. Since this works well for the fluent L1 reader, Twaddell concludes that the L2 reader should develop similar ways of handling new words.

Many recent ESL reading texts are based on this analogy between L1 and L2 readers and also reflect the widespread acceptance of top-down models of reading, models which portray readers as generators of guesses who rely to a large extent on context clues while constructing the meaning of a text. As shown in Table 3.1, most recent ESL readers recommend that students focus on meaning rather than language or vocabulary development as they read in the second language. Since fast reading is considered the best way to grasp the main ideas of a text, many of these reading textbooks are designed to train ESL students to read more quickly. This leads to an emphasis on guessing the meaning of new vocabulary from context. It is thought that, if a student stops to look up words in the dictionary, this will slow reading speed and thus weaken comprehension. If one learns to skip or guess from context, integrative reading can still take place. This is why many of these textbooks also advocate banning dictionaries from the reading class.

In addition, Clarke and Silberstein's (1977) distinction between reading skills and language skills is honored in several of these texts. Vocabulary development is classed as a language skill which does not necessarily belong in the reading class. However, the same texts which separate vocabulary from reading skills still implicitly acknowledge that mastery of vocabulary is an important part of second language reading development. Some of the texts provide exercises designed to help students practice word analysis and word formation skills. Also, many texts carefully recycle vocabulary several times in readings and exercises so that students get more than one exposure to new words. Thus these reading texts suggest a commitment to building vocabulary knowledge, all the while claiming that vocabulary learning and reading are separable.

Finally, several of these ESL texts try to develop vocabulary guessing skills by adding redundancy to their reading passages. They often give definitions or extensive clues within the text when a new word appears. These texts are designed to encourage students to guess word meaning from context, but the context provided is unusually rich so that students will have a better chance at success when guessing.

These textbooks are quite consistent in their acceptance of the analogy between ESL reading and top-down models of fluent L1 reading. Nevertheless, this analogy is rendered questionable by recent research in both first and second language reading.

First of all, though psycholinguistic models of reading emphasize the contributions of linguistic and world knowledge to the reading process, other research on the development of L1 reading indicates that such top-down processing is only part of the story. Rapid, precise recognition of letters and words, that is, bottom-up, more input-constrained processing, must be mastered before fluent reading can take place (Biemiller, 1970; Perfetti, Goldman, & Hogaboam, 1979). In fact, there is evidence that becoming a more fluent, efficient L1 reader involves increasing one's bottom-up processing of print and decreasing syntactic and semantic guesswork (Stanovich, West, & Seeman, 1981). Whether this is also true for L2 reading acquisition remains an open question.

A second concern about the analogy between L1 and L2 reading is raised by findings that L2 reading poses special difficulties, even for individuals who are

Table 3.1. Characteristics of Some Recent Reading Textbooks

Characteristics		Textbooks					
	Hirasawa & Markstein (1974)	Baudoin et al. (1978)	Long et al. (1980)	Abraham & Mackey (1982)	Zukowski/Faust et al. (1982)	Zukowski/Faust et al. (1983)	Connelly & Sims (1982)
1. Reading for meaning = primary	X	X	X	X	X	X	X
2. Fast reading to be encouraged	X	X			X	X	X
3. Vocabulary guessing in context to be encouraged	X	X	X	X	X	X	X
4. Dictionaries not to be used while reading	X	X		X		X	X
5. Reading skill development + vocabulary development = separate	X	X	X				X
6. Word-form exercises included	X	X	X	X			
7. Vocabulary reused in textbook				X	X	X	X
8. Text provides strengthened redundancy	X	X	X	X	X	X	X

skilled readers in their first language (Clarke, 1979). Although intermediate L2 students seem to handle syntactic clues in reading as well as do L1 readers and more advanced L2 students, they seem less skilled in their use of semantic and discourse clues (Cziko, 1978, 1980). Another gap between L1 and L2 readers is the striking difference in their speed of reading. For example, in Israel, Cohen, Glasman, Rosenbaum-Cohen, Ferrara, and Fishman (1979) found that college students who were L2 readers of English needed between 1 and 2 hours to read 15 pages of a textbook, while native speakers finished the same task in only 20 minutes. The major factor slowing down ESL readers is not the number of eye fixations per line or the number of regressions they make while reading; rather, Tullius (1971) and Oller (1972) report that, at least for college-age ESL students, average fixations last much longer for L2 readers than they do for native speaking readers.

There is no clear experimental evidence explaining these longer visual fixation times, but a strong possibility involves the time required for lexical access, that is, the time it takes for a reader to match the printed word to a word meaning in memory. Macnamara (1970) compared the time required to match a known word to its corresponding picture. Readers took significantly longer to decide on the match when the word was in their second language than when it was a word in their native tongue. If it takes readers longer to access lexical meaning in the second language, that is, to remember what a given word means, readers will naturally take longer on each fixation on the page.

Given these differences between L1 and L2 reading, one might question the analogy between them which underlies the emphasis on guessing in current ESL reading textbooks. Not only has reading acquisition been shown to require mastery of bottom-up processes, but also L2 readers have been shown to differ in several important ways from fluent L1 readers. Therefore, it seems premature to claim that since skilled L1 readers often skip or guess at new words in context we must teach ESL students to do the same when they encounter new words.

AN OBSERVATIONAL STUDY OF GUESSING

A reasonable way to evaluate the guessing-from-context recommendations of ESL texts is to observe how ESL readers guess at unfamiliar words. Can they do it successfully? In which situations are they most likely to succeed? What information do they use in making their guesses? Do students from different language backgrounds guess differently?

A study was designed to seek preliminary answers to these questions. Adult ESL students were asked to guess at problem words after they had read and recounted two short passages. Subsequent analyses of students' guessing successes and failures provides a clearer picture of how L2 readers go about guessing word meaning in context.

Table 3.2.   Subject Background Data

Native Language	n	Age	Years of English Study	Time in U.S.	Proficiency Level	Instructional Emphasis in Home Country
Spanish	22	24.9	5.3 (1-10)	4.1 mos.	18 low 4 high	Grammar
Japanese	19	24.3	8.2 (6-12)	2.7 mos.	5 low 14 high	Reading, writing, grammar
Arabic/ French (Tunisian)	11	19.1	3.0 (3-4)	1.6 mos.	0 low 11 high	All skills
Arabic	11	29.2	6.7 (2-11)	6.4 mos.	6 low 5 high	Speaking + listening

Method

Background data on the subjects are presented in Table 3.2. Volunteers were recruited from Michigan State University's English Language Center. Although approximately 20 students volunteered from each of the language backgrounds to be studied—Spanish, Japanese, and Arabic—it was decided to study the Tunisian Arabic speakers separately from other Arabic speakers. This decision resulted from observation of differences in reading speed between the two groups, and from the fact that at least half of the schooling in Tunisia is in French rather than Arabic.

According to the English Language Center's English Proficiency Exam, the Tunisian and Japanese groups consisted mostly of students with high English proficiency, while the Spanish group contained mostly lower proficiency students. This precluded separation of language background from proficiency variables, but it was still possible to observe the effects of language background in some of the guessing patterns.

The readings used were adaptations of two stories about animals (Passage A from an excerpt in O'Reilly & Streeter, 1977; Passage B from one of the folktales in Binner, 1966). The passages had parallel story structure and syntax. Both were two paragraphs long, with the second paragraph a flashback, increasing the difficulty level from that of simple chronological structure:

Passage A:

The young brill tapped his teeth together as he swam lazily in a wide circle around Brine Bay. It was such a peaceful spring afternoon that he felt absolutely on top of the world. "Today the sun is radiant and the waves are bimidor; I've got plenty to eat, the water has been getting warmer bit by bit, and I lead a most comfortable brill's life," he thought contentedly.

He had come into the world back in January, a splendid male of fourteen feet. Upon his arrival in the brill habitat, his enormous mother had nuzzled him softly and, having no arms or legs with which to hug him, had expressed her love for her offspring by circling him in the water. Afterwards, she led him up to the surface to give some blows from his spout. Finally, having fed him some milk, she took him on a tour of the area where he would be living from that day on.

Passage B:

The old baild licked his mouth happily as he lay on his side under the tall blue spruce. It was such a beautiful fall evening that he felt like taking it easy. "Tonight the moon is bright and the wind is silidon; I've had plenty to eat, the people have probably gone home for the night, and I can enjoy a nice, quiet evening," the old baild thought contentedly.

He had been really hungry earlier that day, tired out from many a useless chase. Upon his discovery of the smell of meat cooking, he had crept up on a campfire and, seeing no people or guns which could hurt him, had gotten his dinner quite easily by pulling it from the fire. Afterwards, he carried it in his mouth and ran up to the hilltop to tear it apart at his leisure. Finally, having finished his dinner, the baild looked around at the places where a hunter might come to find him.

Each passage contained two nonsense words. As in Homburg and Spaan (1982) and Walker (1981), nonsense words were used to make sure that no student would have previous knowledge of the words to be guessed. The nonsense words were placed so as to allow a comparison of global versus local context use. One of the nonsense words in each passage could be guessed by referring to the immediate sentence context; the other required integration of information throughout the passage. The locally defined word appeared only once in each passage, while the globally defined one appeared three times.

Individual interviews with students began with an informal discussion of their background of English study. Then the reading and retelling task was explained. Instructions were as follows: "Read through the passage one time and then tell me what you have understood from your reading." After reading each passage, the student was asked, "Tell me what you understood, what you remember about the story." The session was taped from the beginning of the first retelling.

After both readings and retellings, the student was shown each passage again and asked which words had made the story difficult to understand. As each word was pointed out, the student was asked to guess orally what that problem word might mean. After the student's guessing attempt was complete, the experimenter either confirmed the guess or, if it was completely inappropriate or if no guess has been ventured, gave the student a verbal explanation of the meaning in that context.

The background interview, readings, retellings, and discussion of problem words with guessing took from 1 to 1½ hours.

Results and Discussion of Nonsense Word Guessing

Since all students were unfamiliar with the nonsense words in each passage, these words provide a controlled set of data with which the success of guessing could be studied.

As shown in Figure 3.1, the group as a whole was quite successful at guessing nonsense words defined by local context. With words requiring an integrated comprehension of the passage as a whole, guessing was less successful. Fewer than half the students were able to guess that the main character was an animal.

When the sample is broken down into individual groups, the same tendency is observed. All groups profited more from local context clues than they did from global ones. This difference was significant with Passage B for all groups except Arabic monolinguals, whose global guessing performance came close to their performance on local guessing. This difference between Arabic monolinguals and other groups may be due to the small sample size, but also might suggest a preference in the Arabic group for global processing. Clearly, further study with larger groups is needed to test this possibility. On the whole, though, local guessing appeared easier for L2 readers than global guessing.

Figure 3.1. Proportion of readers making appropriate guesses for nonsense words in passages B and A

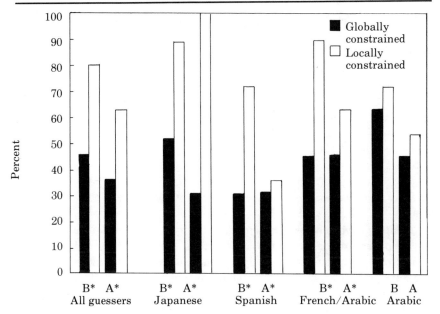

$*p<$ .05 that differences between proportions are due to chance.

With Passage A, although the group as a whole succeeded better at guessing the locally defined word, *bimidor* (that is guessing that the waves were small, smooth, or quiet), than the globally defined word *brill*, only the Japanese guessers showed a significant difference between local and global guessing. Readers in other groups experienced difficulty in local guessing, because they did not know the meaning of the word *waves* (8 Spanish, 1 Arabic, and 2 Tunisians). Low proficiency may account for the fact that over a third of the Spanish speakers did not know what *waves* meant, though one Spanish speaker's pronunciation of this word as "wives," followed by a guess that it meant the opposite of "husbands," suggests that spelling pronunciation from the native language may have caused added difficulty in recognizing this word. Differences in L1 and L2 graphophonemic systems, plus the limited vocabulary knowledge of lower level students, both seem to limit second language readers' ability to make appropriated guesses. In other words, what may appear to be a transparent, guessable context to native-English speakers may actually be incomprehensible for L2 readers, either because they mispronounce a clue word or simply do not know its meaning.

In summary, these students showed that, even without special training in context use, they could achieve a high rate of success when guessing at words which were locally defined. ESL readers do appear to have a natural ability to guess, but they are limited by their understanding of other words in the immediate context. Therefore it is likely that lower proficiency students with less vocabulary knowledge will find guessing much more difficult. In addition, when ESL readers have to integrate longer sections of text in order to guess a word's meaning, they perform less well, even when the word appears several times. Guessing is apparently more difficult when comprehension of longer context is required. For such situations, students need strategies other than guessing from context. If *brill* or *balid* were real words, and if reading comprehension were the main goal of reading, consulting a dictionary or asking a native speaker would seem to be more efficient strategies than agonizing over the text, trying to deduce the word's meaning from context.

Results and Discussion of Other Guessing Patterns

Limits of context clues. The importance of local context clues was confirmed by the pattern of guessing successes and failures observed for real words that were problem words for many readers. In those instances when more than half of the students reached appropriate meanings for an unfamiliar word, many of them relied on words from the immediate context when giving definitions. For instance, many students explained the word *tapped* as a way in which "he moved his teeth," *licked* as a way "he moved his mouth," *Brine Bay* as a place where he was swimming, and *radiant* as meaning the sun was bright or shining.

In contrast to these contextually guessed words, several common problem words proved difficult to interpret. *Waves, splendid,* and *enormous* in the first reading, and *chase, crept up,* and *leisure* in the second reading, were rarely guessed successfully by students. These words are not accompanied by any immediate context clues, so it is hardly surprising that they proved difficult to guess.

This demonstrates again that, in some cases, guessing from context is not a fruitful strategy. Students need to have other strategies to turn to when guessing from context fails them. There is a real danger that indiscriminately urging students to guess will result in so much frustration and failure for them that they completely reject the guessing approach, even when the context is sufficiently explicit to allow guessing to be successful.

Furthermore, one might question whether reading texts should supply a great deal of redundancy in an artificial manner. For one thing, this misleads the student about the nature of the texts in English. In addition, it would seem more useful for students themselves to learn to recognize those cases in which context is of no help. Rather than making a completely random guess, students can then decide whether to skip the word as unimportant or get help from a dictionary. Just like an overprotective teacher, completely guessable texts may leave students without other strategies to fall back on when they encounter less redundant writings.

Noncontextual word-analysis guessing. ESL readers have been found to be successful guessers, given adequate context, but the guesses observed through the study often showed students resorting to noncontextual strategies. They frequently analyzed an unfamiliar word to find a familiar morpheme with it. For example, with the problem word *tapped,* two Japanese students referred to their knowledge of *tap-dancing,* related it to the unit *tap* in the problem word, and achieved a precise definition of the unknown vocabulary item. Also, half of the Arabic readers succeeded in guessing *campfire* by analyzing it into "fire" and "an outdoors place."

This word-analysis strategy was not always successful, however. Spanish speakers and Tunisians tended to go astray when they analyzed *campfire* using cognates from their native or schooled language. They interpreted the morpheme *camp* to mean a place with many people, like a military camp. Six Spanish readers actually defined *campfire* as a place for war, a battlefield. (This interpretation was probably reinforced by the mention of *guns* later in the same sentence.) The inappropriate meaning resulting from word-analysis had serious consequences for at least two Spanish readers, who based their entire story schema on this faulty guess, deciding in the end that *baild* actually meant a kind of soldier or a grade in the military. They interpreted the story to be about a soldier running away from battle. Thus, with cognate languages, word analysis has the potential for seriously misleading the student.

On the other hand, it would be foolish to teach Spanish or French speakers to ignore the similarities between their native language and English. Cognate recognition is too useful to be abandoned. With passage A, for example, even though *radiant* and *splendid* were problem words for a majority of Japanese and Arabic readers, they were not even mentioned as unfamiliar words by most Spanish and French readers.

Since cognates provide a useful knowledge base, one might predict that Spanish and French readers would use the word-analysis strategy more often than students from noncognate backgrounds, but this did not appear to be the case. Three Japanese students, faced with the word *habitat,* tried to relate it to "habit" or "being used to something." Another Japanese reader made a valiant effort to relate *enormous* to "normal" or "abnormal." And students from every language background, more than half or all students interviewed, guessed at *offspring* using word analysis, defining it as "the end of spring" or "the end of a season."

Such misinterpretations may often result when teachers and textbooks encourage students to rely totally on guessing. After all, it is only natural to try to interpret new items on the basis of units one already knows. This strategy is useful if a root morpheme is correctly isolated by the reader, and if the reader already knows a relevant meaning for it. But opportunities for erroneous analysis abound. Students need instruction in the art of double-checking a guess with the context; if the context clashes with the word analysis interpretation, then further checking with a native speaker or a dictionary would be advisable.

Mismatches in Guessing. With word analysis, students match graphic units to words which they remember from previous encounters in English or their cognate language. In the examples above, remembered spelling was matched to the graphic form of the page. But one of the most surprising patterns observed was that ESL readers often make wrong guesses because of graphemic or phonemic mismatches:[1] the word they access in memory is spelled and/or pronounced differently from the word on the page. For example, three readers saw "top" in the word *tapped,* while another saw the morpheme "tape." One low-level Spanish reader, after giving an extremely appropriate retelling of the *brill* passage, discovered in rereading it that he had pictured a water animal because he had misrecognized the word *swam* as "swan!" Two Japanese readers guessed that *splendid* meant "to make wide" or "spread." A Spanish reader guessed that *crept* might be a kind of pancake. And one Arabic reader who failed to point out *silidon* as a problem word responded, when questioned about it, that it meant "not often" (*seldom*). These samples demonstrate that students are attending to word shape, but there is a good deal of imprecision in matching graphophonemic shape to words in their lexical memory. This tendency was observed with students from all language backgrounds, although the few Spanish readers who had scored highest on English language proficiency tests had less difficulty with mismatches than did other students.

The processes leading to such mismatches are probably both top-down and bottom-up. They are relatively bottom-up in that the graphic shape of individual words exerts a strong influence on the guesses proposed. At the same time, however, they may be considered top-down, since students' background knowledge—such as their native language phonology, writing system, and the graphophonemic mapping of the writing system (Haynes, 1981)—may cause them to misrecognize the graphic stimulus in the process of trying to match it to words in memory. Still, these mismatches are not top-down guesses in the usual sense (see Carrell, 1983) of deriving from the reader's higher level linguistic and world knowledge.

In fact, one striking aspect of mismatches, as well as word-analysis guesses, was that they were frequently in conflict with the syntactic context. This is surprising, considering Cziko's (1978) and Walker's (1981) finding that L2 readers are generally skilled in applying syntactic knowledge while reading and guessing. But in cases of word analysis and mismatches, it appeared as if the saliency of word shape overrode the reader's ability to attend to syntactic relations. It seemed as if, the more familiar a word looked, the more difficult it was for L2 readers to shift attention away from graphophonemic form in order to fit a guess to the syntactic context.

This phenomenon can occur for L1 readers as well. To demonstrate the power of word-shape in reading, here are two sentences from a text used by Homburg and Spaan (1982) in which nonsense words were inserted in a text about the behavior of birds:

> And in some species, fledglings must even be *mexed* by their parents during their first autumn migration.
>
> Crohmann thus proved that the instinctive *grumpity* to fly develops in young birds with or without the opportunity to practice.

In these sentences, despite the fact that the underlined word is known to be a nonsense word, it is hard not to process it as a familiar word such as *vexed* or *mixed, grumpy* or *grumpiness.* The graphophonemic configuration of the unknown item dominates in the reader's initial processing of it, and it is a struggle to put such associations aside and attend to syntactic and semantic context. If familiar-looking words cause so much dissonance between word-shape and syntax processing for the native speaker, it is hardly surprising that word form is more salient than context for the L2 reader.

The Uncertainty of Familiarity. The guessing patterns discussed above demonstrate that word-unit processing is a major component of reading in both L1 and L2. But there is another reason that word-shape holds the attention of L2 readers: In a second language, deciding whether a word is familiar or not takes extra time and effort. During the guessing interviews, students often hesitated when pointing out problem words. Sometimes they would report that they had seen a word before but had forgotten its meaning; at other times, they would pick out a word as problematic, then suddenly realize that they did in fact know its meaning.

This uncertainty surrounding word recognition may well constitute a major difference between L2 readers and fluent L1 readers. The latter have large, well-practiced vocabularies and long experience recognizing words in print. They quickly know when a word is unknown and can easily decide to skip it. Second language readers, on the other hand, search for familiar units as they read, but are often unsure whether a word is really new or not. Thus it is not surprising that any flash of familiarity in a word arrests their attention, making the context fade into the background.

Perhaps researchers have never emphasized this point because the cloze technique has been the major method used for investigating prediction and guessing in L2 reading. With cloze tests, words to be guessed appear as blanks and thus cannot distract the reader by their graphemic structure. In noncloze reading, however, readers attend to word-form in order to decide whether a given word is stored in their mental lexicon or not. This appears to be a harder decision for L2 readers than for fluent L1 readers, one which may take more attention away from top-down, contextual processing.

Generalizability of This Study. It might be argued that the importance of graphemic cues and word-unit processing observed in this study was an artifact of the task. Perhaps students were attending to word-level cues rather than larger context because they already read through the passage once and, at the point of guessing, were only rereading for the purpose of identifying problem words.

This argument is weakened by converging evidence from other studies showing bottom-up processing to be central in the reading of L2 students. Cziko (1980) observed from L2 subjects' oral reading miscues that lower proficiency students seemed more focused on surface graphemic shape and less on the semantic flow of ideas. Hatch, Polin, and Part (1974), using a letter cancellation task, found that less proficient L2 readers crossed out a given letter uniformly throughout a text, as if relying mainly on visual cues, while native speakers missed the letter when it occurred in unstressed or semantically unimportant contexts. Both of these studies suggest that L2 readers of lower proficiency attend more closely to visual cues in reading than do more proficient language users.

Another important indication that bottom-up word identification processes play a major role in L2 reading has been provided by Walker (1981). She used nonsense words to examine guessing strategies of high proficiency L2 students. She asked them to read an English text while reporting in their native language (Spanish) how they were going about understanding its meaning. Walker found that the preferred strategy when a nonsense word blocked the flow of meaning was that of pronouncing the word aloud. A frequent follow-up strategy was graphemic, that is, associating the nonsense word with another word, in English or Spanish, which had a similar spelling.

Walker (1981) argues that pronunciation and graphemic strategies should be discouraged by teachers, since in her study these rarely led to appropriate guesses, but it would seem rather that such strategies[2] are essential processing stages in normal reading. Although pronunciation and graphemic guesses are bound to fail with nonsense words, they are probably the most efficient means of access to the mental lexicon of L2 readers for most words in the text. Anticipating an upcoming word depends on sophisticated experience with syntactic and collocational relations which L2 readers may often lack, but retrieval of word meaning from memory can take place by looking directly at the word's shape or testing its sound against familiar vocabulary learned through spoken language experience. Although this study has pointed out many cases in which these procedures failed, they certainly succeeded for words which students did not point out as problems. Rather than deny that graphophonemic structure is important in L2 reading, teachers might help students to improve the accuracy of their word recognition so that they can increase the speed and efficiency of their lexical retrieval.

CONCLUSIONS

The importance of word-unit processing needs to be recognized in ESL teaching. First, precision of encoding spelling and pronunciation can be increased through oral and written practice of important vocabulary from reading. Discussion of the text, with some emphasis on accurate pronunciation of vocabulary, and text-related compositions, with students being encouraged to use vocabulary from the reading, are both ways in which vocabulary practice can take place in meaningful contexts. Also, dictionary work may be useful in helping students to separate words which look or sound similar. The goal of this vocabulary development should include accuracy in writing and pronunciation, so that students can learn to distinguish new words efficiently in lexical memory.

Top-down practice should also be retained in ESL reading classes. Reading for meaning and guessing from context are both essential. Students need to develop flexibility in reaching meaning when their focus on word configuration and direct lexical retrieval fail. Learning to reevaluate initial guesses is as important as learning to make a first guess. Not only context, but dictionary use, may provide additional ways of reaching meaning when other routes fail. The goal of top-down reading instruction should not be absolute independence from the dictionary, but rather an increase in students' flexibility, knowing where and how to look for meaning when the handiest sources of information fail to make sense.

From this preliminary observation of ESL readers' guessing strategies, useful insight has been gained into factors affecting the guessing process:

1. ESL readers are good guessers when the context contains immediate clues.
2. Insufficient context, or global clues, or a student's lack of vocabulary knowledge, may increase the difficulty of guessing.
3. Word analysis is used by students from all the language backgrounds studied.
4. Graphemic cues (in cognates, analyzed words, and mismatches) are highly salient and may override syntactic cues.
5. ESL readers are often uncertain as to whether a word is familiar or not and thus must attend to word structure before deciding to skip or guess.

These insights into the reading of second language learners indicate that their processing of written language is necessarily bottom-up as well as top-down. Clearly, much more observation and experimentation is needed to understand guessing strategies, particularly as they differ among students of different language backgrounds. Still, the insights listed above provide support for the following suggestions, offered to ESL teachers who must make daily decisions about guessing in the reading class:

1. Encourage guessing when students have ample clues available in the immediate context.
2. Be sensitive to the fact that low-proficiency students may experience more difficulty with guessing because of their limited linguistics knowledge.
3. Avoid exclusive reading of overredundant texts: students need to practice judging for themselves whether guessing is or is not appropriate.
4. Acknowledge that word-analysis is a natural strategy, even though it can often be misleading; help students practice double-checking initial guesses of this sort with the context and other information sources such as the dictionary.
5. Provide practice in both guessing from context and word-level graphophonemic accuracy: the former builds flexibility while the latter develops more efficient access to word meaning in memory.

REFERENCES

Abraham, P., & Mackey, D. (1982). *Contact USA*. Englewood Cliffs, NJ: Prentice-Hall.

Baudoin, E. M., Bober, E. S., Clarke, M. A., Dobson, B. K., & Silberstein, S. (1978). *Reader's choice*. Ann Arbor, MI: University of Michigan Press.

Biemiller, A. (1970). The development of the use of graphic and contextual information as children learn to read. *Reading Research Quarterly, 6* (1), 75–96.

Binner, V. O. (1966). *American folktales/1*. New York: Thomas Y. Crowell.

Brown, R. (1973). *A first language: the early stages*. Cambridge, MA: Harvard University Press.

Carrell, P. L. (1983). Background knowledge in second language comprehension. *Language Learning and Communication, 2* (1), 25–33.

Chomsky, N. (1959). Review of *Verbal learning*, B. F. Skinner. *Language, 35,* 26–58.

Clarke, M. A. (1979). Reading in Spanish and English: Evidence from adult ESL students. *Language Learning, 29* (1), 121–147.

Clarke, M. A., & Silberstein, S. (1977). Toward a realization of psycholinguistic principles in the ESL reading class. *Language Learning, 27* (1), 135–154.

Cohen, A., Glasman, H., Rosenbaum-Cohen, P. R., Ferrara, J., & Fishman, J. (1979). Reading English for specialized purposes: Discourse analysis and the use of student informants. *TESOL Quarterly, 13* (4), 551–564.

Connelly, M., & Sims, J. (1982). *Time and space.* Englewood Cliffs, NJ: Prentice-Hall.

Cromer, R. F. (1976). Developmental strategies for language. In V. Hamilton & M. D. Vernon (Eds.), *The development of cognitive processes* (pp. 305–358). New York: Academic Press.

Cziko, G. (1978). Differences in first- and second-language reading: The use of syntactic, semantic and discourse constraints. *Canadian Modern Languages Review, 34* (3), 473–489.

Cziko, G. (1980). Language competence and reading strategies: A comparison of first- and second-language oral reading errors. *Language Learning, 30* (1), 101–116.

Dulay, H., & Burt, M. (1978). Some remarks on creativity in language acquisition. In W. Ritchie (Ed.), *Second language acquisition research: Issues and implications* (pp. 65–89). New York: Academic Press.

Goodman, K. (1967). Reading: A psycholinguistics guessing game. *Journal of the Reading Specialist, 6:* 126–135.

Hatch, E., Polin, P., & Part, S. (1974). Acoustic scanning and syntactic processing: three reading experiments—first and second language learners. *Journal of Reading Behavior, 6* (3), 275–285.

Haynes, M. (1981, March). *Breaking the alphabet barrier.* Paper presented at the 4th Annual Colloquium on Classroom Centered Research at the 15th Annual TESOL Convention, Detroit, Michigan. (Available from the National Clearinghouse for Bilingual Education, Rosslyn, VA.)

Hirasawa, L., & Markstein, L. (1974). *Developing reading skills.* Rowley, MA: Newbury House.

Homburg, T. J., & Spaan, M. C. (1982). ESL reading proficiency assessment: Testing strategies. In M. Hines & W. Rutherford (Eds.), *On TESOL '81* (pp. 25–33). Washington, DC: TESOL.

Hosenfeld, C., Arnold, V., Kirchofer, J., Laciura, J., & Wilson, L. (1981). Second language reading: A curricular sequence for teaching reading strategies. *Foreign Language Annals, 14* (5), 415–422.

Kruse, A. F. (1979). Vocabulary in context. *English Language Teaching Journal, 33* (3), 207–213.

Long, M. H., Allen, W., Cyr, A., Pomeroy, C., Richard, E., Spada, N., & Vogel, P. (1980). *Reading English for academic study.* Rowley, MA: Newbury House.

Macnamara, J. (1970). Comparative studies for reading and problem solving in two languages. *TESOL Quarterly, 4* (2), 107–116.

Oller, J. W. (1972). Assessing competence in ESL: Reading. *TESOL Quarterly, 6* (4), 314–321.

O'Reilly, R. P., & Streeter, R. E. (1977). Report on the development and validation of a system for measuring literal comprehension in a multiple-choice cloze format. *Journal of Reading Behavior, 9* (1), 45–69.

Perfetti, C. A., Goldman, S. R., & Hogaboam, T. W. (1979). Reading skill and the identification of words in discourse context. *Memory and Cognition, 7,* 273–282.

Smith, F. (1978). *Understanding reading.* New York: Holt, Rinehart and Winston.

Stanovich, K. E., West, R., & Seeman, D. J. (1981). A longitudinal study of sentence context effects in second-grade children: Tests of an interactive compensatory model. *Journal of Experimental Child Psychology, 32,* 185–199.

Tullius, J. (1971). *Analysis of reading skills of non-native speakers of English.* Unpublished master's thesis, University of California-Los Angeles.

Twaddell, W. F. (1973). Vocabulary expansion in the TESOL classroom. *TESOL Quarterly, 7* (1), 61–78.

Walker, L. J. (1981). *Word identification strategies of Spanish-speaking college students in reading English as a foreign language.* Unpublished doctoral dissertation, University of Texas-Austin.

Zukowski-Faust, J., Johnston, S. S., Atkinson, C., & Templin, E. (1982). *In context.* New York: Holt, Rinehart and Winston.

Zukowski-Faust, J., Johnston, S. S., Atkinson, C. (1983). *Between the lines.* New York: Holt, Rinehart and Winston.

ENDNOTES

1. The term *mismatch* is used in contrast to Goodman's (1967) term *miscue.* While a miscue is said to occur when an oral reading response fails to match the expected one, a mismatch occurs, not in fluent reading, but in deliberate guessing during which more time is available for study of the graphic form and for memory search.

2. The word *strategy* implies an element of choice in the use of ways to reach meaning while reading. If graphemic and maybe phonemic processing are necessary for lexical access, then they should be called something else than strategies—basic processes, perhaps.

Editorial Comments

This chapter, written in 1983, provided an early warning of some of the pitfalls of relying exclusively on reading to promote vocabulary development for L2 adult learners. In particular, it questioned the analogy between L1 and L2 reading acquisition. Also, it took a step back from top-down, schema- or hypothesis-driven models of reading by asking what bottom-up linguistic skills are also needed by L2 learners if they are to guess successfully while reading (see also Eskey, 1988; Eskey & Grabe, 1988). In addition, this chapter highlighted the important distinction between local context (within a sentence) and global context (across sentence boundaries), demonstrating that, without instruction in contextual inference, learners seem naturally able to use clues in the local context but have greater difficulty integrating global context clues.

In relation to the differences between L1 and L2 readers, this chapter argues that certain linguistic knowledge which can be assumed to be in place for beginning L1 readers (e.g., accuracy with the phonology of the language or automatic spoken knowledge of a number of high-frequency words) may remain so fragile for L2 learners that they experience unpredictable difficulties in deriving word meaning from context. Indeed, their guessing may already begin to break down at the point of word-form recognition, where they are uncertain as to whether or not a word in the text has ever been encountered before. (For example, the nonsense word *silidon* was misrecognized by an Arabic reader as *seldom*.)

The substitution of nonsense words for certain words in the text (see also Chern's Chapter 4, this volume) demonstrates one technique which can help researchers and teachers learn more about how readers use context to unearth word meaning. Haynes pointed out that this approach is quite different from cloze deletions. Word-forms provide the major cues for all word recognition (see Chapter 1 by Coady, this volume), so that nonsense words naturally call attention to their word-forms while cloze deletions do not. In one sense, then, nonsense words allow researchers to observe more typical reading processes than do cloze deletions.

Nevertheless, results from research using texts with nonsense words should be treated with caution. The spelling (word-form) of nonsense words may evoke other word associations in readers, providing an uncontrolled variable which might also influence guessing outcomes. However, nonsense word-forms also provide a potentially powerful means of researching what learners know about word-forms (as is demonstrated by examples such as the *silidon* misrecognition above) and how learners apply their word-form knowledge while interpreting new words during reading.

Another strength and potential difficulty with this research is its attempt to distinguish between learners of different linguistic and literacy backgrounds. Rather than studying some nomothetic "L2 learner," this study considered Japanese, Arabic, and Spanish readers separately, revealing potentially important group differences, as well as universals such as readers' attention to word-form.

Nevertheless, defining group membership as a variable is also of limited usefulness in that the crucial dimensions of difference can only be treated speculatively. For instance, we would like to know why the Tunisian bilinguals were better than the monolingual Arabic readers: because they had knowledge of French vocabulary to help them in reading English, because they had become more fluent in using the Roman alphabet (see Haynes, 1990), or because their schooling, based on the French model, required more independent reading than did schooling in the Koranic tradition, where reading is conducted orally in a group setting (see Scribner & Cole, 1981)? In this as in all research using subject variables, group differences are likely to raise more questions than they answer.

This study justifies the serious questions raised in the first two chapters about the efficacy of L2 instruction that relies too heavily on contextual inference for vocabulary learning. It also makes a point which will be stressed again and again in this volume, and which is by now more clearly justified by the findings of eye movement research and other psychological approaches to understanding the reading process (Carr, 1986; Rayner & Pollatsek, 1989): Teachers should pay continuing attention to developing accuracy in bottom-up skills as they coach readers toward better comprehension.

References

Carr, T. H. (1986). Perceiving visual language.In L. Kaufman, J. Thomas, & K. Boff (Eds.), *Handbook of perception and human performance.* New York: Wiley.

Eskey, D. E. (1988). Holding in the bottom: An interactive approach to the language problems of second language readers. In P.Carrell, J. Devine, & D. Eskey (Eds.), *Interactive approaches to second language reading.* Cambridge, UK: Cambridge University Press.

Eskey, D. E., & Grabe, W. (1988). Interactive models for second language reading: perspectives on instruction. In P. Carrell, J. Devine, & D. Eskey (Eds.), *interactive approaches to second language reading.* Cambridge, UK: Cambridge University Press.

Haynes, M. (1990). Examining the impact of L1 literacy on reading success in a second writing system (WS2). In H. Burmeister & P. L. Rounds (Eds.), *Variability in second language acquisition: Proceedings of the tenth meeting of the second language research forum.* Eugene, OR: Department of Linguistics & American English Institute.

Rayner, K., & Pollatsek, A. (1989). *The psychology of reading.* Englewood Cliffs, NJ: Prentice-Hall.

Scribner, S., & Cole, M. (1981). *The psychology of literacy.* Cambridge, MA: Harvard University Press.

II
Explorations of Learning from Reading

Chapter 4
Chinese Students' Word-Solving Strategies in Reading in English*

Chiou-Lan Chern
Department of Foreign Languages and Literature
Tunghai University
Taichung, Taiwan

This chapter explores the contextual word-solving strategies used by Chinese students when confronted with unfamiliar English words in their reading. The data gathered from this study showed that Chinese ESL students were similar to other ESL readers in strategies they used to decipher the meaning of unknown words. They were able to use contextual cues, graphic cues, and sounds, as well as background knowledge in reading. Use of forward cues distinguished better readers from weaker readers. The use of global cues (e.g., both forward and backward cues) correlated highly with these subjects' scores on various proficiency tests. In this study, highly proficient Chinese readers used the strategies of other proficient ESL readers. This result suggests a universality of certain positive reading strategies and also implies that the pedagogical practices advocated for ESL readers in general should be applied by Chinese teachers, who at present tend to encourage accuracy and discourage guessing in reading.

* The author wishes to thank Dr. Roberta Vann and other faculty members at the English Department of Iowa State University for help with the research on which this chapter is based. Special thanks to Mary Lee Field and Margot Haynes for their kindness in sharing with me insights from their own previous studies. The participants in this study deserve special thanks, too.

67

INTRODUCTION

It is generally agreed that reading is a complex process. It is, in many ways, more linguistically and intellectually challenging than other language skills (Goodman, 1968; Loew 1984; Phillips, 1984). Second language reading may be even more complex, "for it requires information processing using language skills still in developmental stages and not firmly established in the learner's mind" (Phillips, 1984, p. 295).

Yorio (1971), in attempting to explain the source of reading difficulties for foreign learners, found that ESL students considered vocabulary their most serious handicap. This finding is not surprising at all: Language learners are going to have comprehension problems if they do not understand the basic units of the message.

Based on 20 years' teaching experience at universities in Taiwan, Arnold Sprenger, an ESL teacher, stated that, if average college students in Taiwan were asked why reading English was so difficult, the most likely answer would be that they had not learned enough English words, even though they had spent at least 6 years in English classes studying almost nothing but grammar and vocabulary (Sprenger, 1975). This, of course, represents the students' perspectives of their reading problems; in fact there might be other reasons for their difficulties in reading.

As Chinese consider reading an activity students learn automatically as they progress through school, the development of reading skills is mainly left to students themselves and hardly any formal instruction is given (Sprenger, 1975). With accuracy in translation being of first importance in Chinese EFL classes, it is not surprising to see Chinese characters scribbled between the lines of students' English textbooks. For these students, the reading task is considered complete only when all the unknown words have been checked in the dictionary. Yet, according to Kruse (1979, p. 208), "the ESL student cannot begin to read with full comprehension until he has been taught to conquer the unknown words by using contextual aids." If Kruse is right, it is not surprising that Chinese ESL learners, most of whom seem to feel insecure reading without a dictionary, not only read slowly but also have comprehension problems.

TWO DEVELOPMENTAL MODELS

In describing the development of reading skills in ESL students, Coady (1979) presented a model incorporating six kinds of processing strategies: (a) grapheme-phoneme correspondence; (b) grapheme-morphophoneme correspondence; (c) syllable-morpheme information; (d) syntactic information (deep and surface); (e) lexical meaning; and (f) contextual meaning. According to this model (see Figure 4.1), second language learners begin by attending to more form-oriented process strategies such as phoneme-grapheme correspondences

Figure 4.1. Coady's Model of the Development of Second Language Processing Strategies

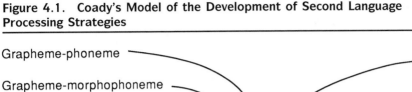

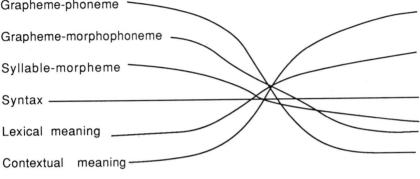

Grapheme-phoneme

Grapheme-morphophoneme

Syllable-morpheme

Syntax

Lexical meaning

Contextual meaning

(Relative change in use of process strategies over time is presented from left to right, e.g. beginning to advanced readers).

and syllable-morpheme information, and gradually learn to take advantage of more meaning-oriented strategies involving lexis and context.

For Chinese ESL readers, however, Field (1985) has proposed a different model. Her observations in China led her to the conclusion that Chinese students have particular difficulty in using the more meaning-oriented strategies even when they have gained a certain mastery over the English language. Field's model of Chinese ESL students' process strategies suggests why reading is painful and comprehension is low for the students she encountered in China. Field's display claims that syllable–morpheme decoding strategies are used most frequently by intermediate and advanced Chinese readers while contextual meaning is least used (see Figure 4.2).

This suggests that Chinese L2 students focus more on details in their reading than on overall comprehension. Field also points out that Chinese students often resort to a dictionary when encountering an unfamiliar word, rather than venturing to guess the meaning of a word or the function of a word from its place in the sentence.

If Field's claim can be substantiated, the problems suggest that helping Chinese students develop the ability to infer the meaning of unknown words from the context should be a priority in the English reading class. If Coady's model is a universal pattern of the processing hierarchy when ESL learners' proficiency develops, then Field's claims of Chinese students' model suggest that Chinese ESL learners are an exception to the general pattern. The questions of interest here are: (a) Is it the case that Chinese ESL learners, having a different processing model as claimed by Field, use different strategies in guessing unknown words? (b) Do Chinese ESL learners of different proficiency levels guess differently? (c) Is there a shift of strategies from the reliance on lexical to contextual information when language proficiency increases?

Figure 4.2. Field's Model of The Development of Chinese Students' Process Strategies

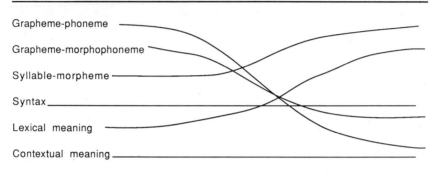

Grapheme-phoneme

Grapheme-morphophoneme

Syllable-morpheme

Syntax

Lexical meaning

Contextual meaning

RESEARCH DESIGN AND PROCEDURE

Answers to the research questions posed in this study were sought via a case-study approach that, in part, replicates the work of Homburg and Spaan (1982). Each subject was first asked to skim the passage silently and then "think-aloud" to report what they were thinking on their second reading. For subjects who did not give enough response in reading, interview questions were asked to encourage report of their use of strategies leading to comprehension. A passage of approximately 240 words with 12 nonsense words underlined was given to each subject. During the think-aloud reading process, each individual was asked to identify the nonsense words by giving either their meanings or synonyms for them. The subjects were also told to give a summary of the passage.

The think-aloud protocols and interviews were tape-recorded. To assure that no language barrier discouraged students' guessing efforts, the whole working session was conducted in the subjects' native language, Chinese. The investigator later translated part of the protocols, the summaries, into English for the purpose of obtaining judgments from non-Chinese-speaking ESL instructors.

Selection of Material

The instrument used in this study, a modified cloze test, was adopted from Homburg and Spaan (1982). A passage of 239 words was adapted from *National Wildlife* and analyzed for structure and context. The first two paragraphs contain several parallel structures, and the third paragraph, which contains the main idea of this passage, develops in nonparallel structures, elaborating an experiment and then summarizing the general idea of the whole passage (see Appendix I).

Twelve words in the passage were taken out of the original text. Instead of leaving them blank as a traditional cloze does, they were replaced by nonsense words because nonsense words not only assure equal familiarity for all subjects but closely replicate the actual reading situation ESL students face when encountering unknown vocabulary (Homburg & Spaan, 1982). The replaced words were either nouns, adjectives, verbs, or adverbs; all the functional words were left intact. All the nonsense words were underlined, and they retained the morphological features of English that would indicate their grammatical functions.

The 12 underlined nonsense substitutions were placed so as to allow a comparison of global versus local context use. They were further classified according to the four following contextual word-solving strategies:

Parallelism **(words 1, 2, 5).** Sensitivity to grammatical relationship and semantic similarity between words is essential in identifying these words.

Example 1: The fledgling must be *glurked* while learning to feed itself. It must be protected while learning to fly. And in some species, fledgling must even be *mexed* by their parents during their first autumn migration.

These three sentences are developed in parallel structure, with *glurked* (= *fed*) and *protected* serving as clues to the nonsense words.

Sentence-Bound Cues **(words 6, 9, 10).** All information required to decode these words occurs in the same sentence in which the word occurs; that is, local cues can be easily found.

Example 2: When the two groups of pigeons were mature enough, Grohmann took them out and *possed* them into the air.

As the nonsense word *possed* retained the morphological similarity with the correct word *tossed*, and all the clues are in this sentence, this is an example of local sentence-bound cues.

Forward Cues **(words 3, 7, 8).** To understand these words, one must read beyond them in the passage to get more information.

Example 3: When it comes to *snerding*, however, few fledglings need any lessons. . . . a German scientist raised some young pigeons in narrow tubes. . . . At the same time he allowed another group of pigeons to be raised by their *medlons* in a nest in the normal way, exercising their wings vigorously.

The clues for both *snerdling* and *medlons* come in the later part of the sentence, like ''in the normal way'' and ''exercising their wings vigorously.''

Backward Cues (words **4, 11, 12**). Referring back in the text or remembering previous cues is necessary in order to understand these words.

> Example 4: Fifty years ago, a German scientist named Grohmann raised some young pigeons in narrow tubes. . . . At the same time he allowed another group . . . to be raised in the normal way. . . . Surprisingly, the pigeons raised in the *urmlews* flew away as strongly as the ones that had been unrestrained in the nest.

The clues for the word *urmlews* basically come from the description of the experiment in the previous sentences.

The binary distinction of local vs. global cues only defines sentence-bound cues as a local strategy, but as Homburg and Spaan (1982) mentioned in their study, there is some overlap among these categories, and meaning is certainly determined by using a combination of several of these strategies and possible other strategies which have not been included here. Though the interest of this present study is mainly on the use of these four strategies, other tactics and information used by these Chinese students will also be discussed in this chapter.

Selection of Subjects

Twenty Chinese adults (4 undergraduate and 16 graduate students) of two different proficiency levels (10 in each) were used in this study. Prior screening of potential subjects was conducted by examining the scores on the English Placement Test of Chinese students who had arrived on the campus of Iowa State University in Fall 1984. These subjects were then divided into two groups according to their scores on the reading section of the English Placement Test. Those who scored 30 and above out of the highest possible score of 35 on reading section constituted the high proficiency group; the low proficiency group is composed of those students who scored 22 or below, that is, less than two-thirds of the total items correct, on the same test and were required to enroll in a supervised independent reading laboratory to meet the language proficiency level required by Iowa State University.

The 20 subjects had much in common. They had come to the United States at about the same time, making it likely that they had a similar degree of exposure to the academic environment of native speakers of English. Prior to coming to the United States, all had had at least 8 years of English training in Taiwan. Their most recent TOEFL scores were 500 or above.

Procedure for Data Gathering

The 20 subjects were told to skim the passage for general meaning and then "think-aloud" to give a summary and begin their guessing work. During their think-aloud session, each subject first summarized the passage and then was told to report the part of speech and the meaning of each particular nonsense word as well as how they determined the meaning for each word. If a suitable definition or synonym was given, the answer was coded according to the four predetermined categories of contextual clues, such as parallelism, sentence-bound cues, forward cues, and backward cues. Each subject was encouraged to explain his or her use of strategies. This information provided further insight into other possible strategies used such as word analysis. After attempts had been made to guess the 12 underlined words, all the subjects were also told to mark other unknown words, if any, in the passage and try to guess their meanings.

When the guessing process was completed, each subject was given a second chance to summarize the main idea of the passage. They were also asked if they recognized that some of the words were nonsense words. The total session was conducted in Chinese and tape-recorded.

Scoring Method

The summaries given orally in the subjects' native language were translated into English by the researcher. To ensure that no mechanical errors affected readers' judgments of summary contents, all the summaries were proofread by a native speaker of English before being given to the raters.

Before reading the summaries of the 20 subjects in this study, four graduate teaching assistants, all native speakers of English in the field of TESL, were asked to read the original passage and a model summary, which was written by the researcher and confirmed by an English-speaking graduate student majoring in animal science (Appendix II). The raters were told to sort the summaries into three categories with each having no more than eight and no fewer than six summaries. No specific criteria were given to the raters; they were only told to group these summaries according to how closely they matched the original essay and the model summary. The summaries were then graded as follows: 3 credits were given to the pile that represented the best, 1 to the worst, and 2 to those lying somewhere in between.

The scores on the four contextual word solving strategies were given according to the subjects' choice of words to replace the nonsense one. A scoring system with four scales was used: a 3 was given if the subject provided the exact words used in the original essay, a 2 if the words were semantically and syntactically acceptable but not the exact words, a 1 to words that conveyed the right idea but violate some constraints in English, and a 0 to words that did not fit semantically and syntactically at all.

RESEARCH RESULTS

Tables 4.1 and 4.2 show the scores for the higher proficiency and lower proficiency groups, respectively. As shown in Table 4.1, students in the higher

Table 4.1.   Scores of the High Proficiency Group

Subject#	Sum[1]	Strategies					Total
		P.SP[2]	PL[3]	SB[4]	FC[5]	BC[6]	
2	2.7	10	0	7	0	6	13
5	2.0	2	4	7	8	9	28
7	1.3	12	4	7	3	9	23
10	2.0	12	7	5	6	4	22
11	3.0	12	8	6	6	7	27
12	3.0	12	2	7	3	6	18
14	1.3	11	4	9	9	9	31
17	1.7	12	8	6	6	6	26
19	2.3	12	5	8	3	9	25
20	1.0	12	5	8	7	9	29
Mean	2.03	11.7	4.7	7.0	5.1	7.4	24.2

[1] Sum = summary   [2] P.SP = part of speech
[3] PL = parallelism   [4] SB = sentence bound
[5] FC = forward cues   [6] BC = backward cues

proficiency group seem to use all four strategies in trying to get at the meanings of unknown words, with the exception of subject #2, who used no parallel or forward cues and spent the least time on guessing.

Table 4.2 offers a different picture for the lower proficiency group. Forward cues seemed to be ignored by most subjects (6 out of 10) in this group, and two of them did not use sentence-bound cues. In spite of the fact that two people in this group ignored sentence-bound cues, the rest of the subjects seemed to use

Table 4.2.   Scores of the Low Proficiency Group

Subject#	Sum[1]	Strategies					Total
		P.SP[2]	PL[3]	SB[4]	FC[5]	BC[6]	
1	1.0	12	5	0	0	9	14
3	2.7	11	8	7	3	5	23
4	1.0	9	6	8	0	6	20
6	1.3	12	4	7	0	6	17
8	1.7	12	1	7	6	8	22
9	1.0	10	2	7	0	3	12
13	1.7	11	6	3	0	3	12
15	3.0	11	5	8	3	9	25
16	1.7	12	3	8	6	6	23
18	2.0	12	1	0	0	3	4
Mean	1.78	11.2	4.1	5.5	1.8	5.8	17.2

[1] Sum = summary   [2] P.SP = part of speech
[3] PL = parallelism   [4] SB = sentence bound
[5] FC = forward cues   [6] BC = backward cues

these strategies to a relatively great extent, with 7 of the 10 scoring over 7 (out of a possible high score of 9) in this category.

The general picture we get from Tables 4.1 and 4.2 is that both groups of students were able to summarize the main idea and identify the parts of speech of the unknown words; there is no significant difference between the two groups in the performance of these two tasks ($p > .05$). As Figure 4.3 indicates, both groups seemed to be better at using sentence-bound and backward cues than parallel or forward cues.

While forward cues were able to differentiate the high-proficiency group from the lower one, the recognition of parallelism in the passage does not seem to make much difference between the two groups; that is, it is relatively hard to grasp for both groups of subjects. This observation is clearly shown in Table 4.3.

As to the correlation between strategies used by subjects and their score on language proficiency tests, Table 4.4 shows that the participants' performance on this task correlated with their proficiency levels as measured by TOEFL and the

Figure 4.3. Performance on the four contextual strategies of high and low proficiency group

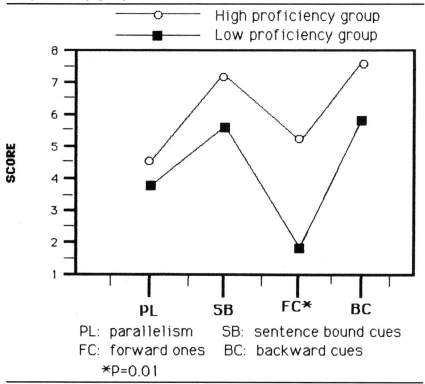

English Placement Test. Scores on forward cues correlated highly with the total scores of the Placement Test score (0.64) and satisfactorily with the reading scores on both the Placement Test and TOEFL (0.53 for both). Scores on backward cues correlated best with TOEFL reading scores (0.74).

The pictures portrayed by Tables 4.3 and 4.4 are very consistent: They both show that the use of backward cues and forward cues, both global cues, differentiate proficient learners from less proficient ones.

DISCUSSION OF RESULTS

This study found that the ability to recognize and use forward cues and backward cues (both global contextual cues) in reading English correlated at satisfactory levels with proficiency scores of Chinese EFL students, and that use of forward cues was more frequent among student with high proficiency levels than among those with relatively low proficiency in English. Though scores on backward cues were not dramatically different for the two groups, they correlated best with TOEFL reading scores; that is to say, use of backward cues was the best single predictor of overall reading proficiency as measured by the

Table 4.3.   T-test Results of Strategies Used by Groups

	H	L	T-value	Prob> |T|
PL[1]	4.7	4.1	0.55	0.598
SB[2]	7.0	5.5	1.50	0.161
FC[3]	5.1	1.8	2.78	0.012*
BC[4]	7.4	5.8	1.70	0.107
Total	24.2	17.1	2.62	0.017*

[1] PL = parallelism   [2] SB = sentence bound
[3] FC = forward cues   [4] BC = backward cues
* Null hypothesis is rejected

Table 4.4.   Correlation Coefficients Between Scores on Strategies and on Proficiency Tests

	EPT Reading	EPT Total	TOEFL Reading	TOEFL Total
SUM	0.25	0.21	0.22	0.31
PL	0.13	0.09	0.27	0.33
SB	0.22	0.26	0.20	0.14
FC	0.53	0.64	0.53	0.45
BC	0.45	0.44	0.74	0.53
Total	0.51	0.55	0.64	0.53

TOEFL of all the subjects in this study. Parallelism, the third global contextual cue in this study, appeared to be equally difficult for both groups of subjects.

While backward and forward strategies (both global contextual cues) were able to distinguish the high- from the low-proficiency reading groups, sentence-bound strategies, such as local contextual cues, were relatively widely used by most of the students in the low proficiency group.

Forward and backward strategies played similar roles in this study, as in Homburg and Spaan (1982), although the subjects used in these two studies differed in many ways. The subjects in Homburg and Spaan's study were of a heterogeneous language background, and they were grouped in that study according to their intensive course levels at the Language Institute of the University of Michigan. In that study, ESL students who used more forward strategies were better at understanding the main meaning of the passage. Likewise, in that study the use of backward strategies was significantly correlated with proficiency level. But because both studies used the same passage, the possibility of the particular passage being biased against certain strategies must be considered. Research using different passages is needed before we can conclude that backward and forward strategies are the main determinants of ESL reading proficiency.

Other Findings

Aside from the four contextual strategies observed in this study, other testimony regarding strategies used by these Chinese subjects in their reading process was also investigated. It was found that the subjects in this study not only used contextual cues but also said that they attended to sounds, affixes, and word shapes to perform their reading task. They also reported using their common knowledge about birds to help them figure out the meanings of unknown words.

Word Analysis and Pronunciation

Six of the subjects (three from the high-proficiency group, and three from the low-proficiency group) used word analysis to derive the meaning of some of the target words. For example, *woodpecker* was identified as unknown by five subjects, and three of them were able to name the bird in their native language because of *wood* in *woodpecker*. Ten out of the 20 subjects replaced *grumpity* with *ability*, and two of them (both from the low-proficiency group) stated that they were able to do that because of the suffix *-ity*. A similar situation occurred with *refirk*. Ten subjects were able to replace *refirk* with *return*, and three of them (two from the high and one from the low group) were able to associate these two words because of the prefix *re-*.

Three subjects attended to word shape when they were trying to figure out the meaning of the unknown word *tidly*. Two subjects replaced *tidly* with *timidly*, because these two words looked alike to them, and one subject replaced it with *tidily* because of the similarity to the word *tidy*. For three people, graphemic analysis similarly did not contribute to their success in guessing.

Evidence of pronunciation as a strategy was observed in three subjects. One subject read several words aloud before replacing them with other words. Two subjects guessed *glurked* as the chirping sound made by birds, because the word sounded like a bird. As shown in other studies (Walker, 1981; Laufer, 1981; Haynes, 1984; Huckin & Bloch, Chapter 8, this volume), pronunciation, morphemic, and graphemic strategies are essential processing stages in normal reading, though they don't always lead to correct guesses.

Background Knowledge

Though this study was not designed to observe the effect of the readers' knowledge of the world on their reading comprehension, half the subjects reported that they appealed to their background knowledge on the life of birds throughout the guessing procedure. For example, *snerdling* was frequently guessed with comments like "It must be talking about flying because birds don't need to learn to fly," without reading the description and conclusion of the experiment described later. In summarizing the main idea, most subjects compared what they knew about birds with what they read in the passage and arrived at certain assumptions about the message of the text. This phenomenon supports the schema-based theory of learning discussed by Hudson (1982).

Other Unfamiliar Words Identified

Some other words were identified as unknown besides the 12 underlined ones. Among them, *fledgling*, a globally defined word which appears three times in this passage, was identified as unfamiliar by 19 out of 20 subjects; 10 of them were able to explain its meaning as "a baby bird"; the rest of them could only say "it's a kind of bird." Among the 10 people who determined the correct meaning of this word, 7 were from the high-proficiency group. This suggests that global cues, those that required the integration of information throughout the passage, were grasped successfully by many subjects in this study, especially those who were more proficient in English.

Wren, a locally defined word whose immediate context provided clues, was next most frequently pointed out as an unfamiliar word. Among the 13 subjects who did not know its meaning, 11 (6 from the high group, and 5 from the low group) were able to say "it is a kind of bird" by using clues from the neighboring words, *woodpeckers* and *swallows*, though none were able to name it in their native language.

The identification of these two words *fledgling* and *wren* as unknown words rendered some similarities to Haynes' study. The fact that *wren* a locally defined word in this passage, was easier to guess than *fledgling* a globally defined word, supports Haynes's conclusion that ESL students profited more from local context cues than they did from global ones (Haynes, 1984).

Students' Perspectives on Guessing

When asked, none of the subjects indicated suspecting that any of the underlined words were nonsense words. They all agreed that those words "looked English" and that it was so common for them to confront unfamiliar words in reading that they did not bother to question whether they were English words. When given a second chance to add to or change their summary after their guessing efforts, most of them did not make any change but agreed that they understood the passage better.

SUMMARY OF RESULTS

To summarize, all the subjects in this study were able to use different strategies, including graphemic, morphemic, phonetic, and contextual clues, to help them decipher messages in the essay. The findings of this study can be summarized as follows:

1. Sentence-bound (local) cues were used relatively frequently by both groups of subjects in this study.
2. The use of forward cues distinguished the more proficient readers from the less proficient ones.
3. The use of backward cues and forward cues, both global cues, correlated rather highly with these subjects' proficiency levels.
4. Although differences between the two proficiency groups on their performances of other cues were found, they were not statistically significant.
5. Morphemic, graphemic, and phonetic cues were frequently used as strategies in guessing.

Implications for Teaching

As a small-scale exploratory study, the results of this study are limited and should not be applied to other situations without certain qualification. That the highly proficient Chinese readers in this study attended to contextual information and used the strategies of other proficient ESL readers, as shown in Coady's model, suggests a universality of the development of certain positive reading strategies and deemphasized the uniqueness of Chinese readers suggested by Field. This implies that the pedagogical practices advocated for ESL readers in general should be applied by Chinese teachers, who at present tend to encourage accuracy and discourage guessing in reading.

Such practices that might be developed in the Chinese EFL classroom include:

1. encouraging students to make use of the available clues to infer meanings of unknown words, instead of resorting to dictionaries immediately;
2. helping students shift attention from surface lexical forms to contextual information when their language proficiency increases;
3. developing students' willingness to make mistakes and develop a tolerance for inexactness, which has been deemphasized in the tradition of Chinese education.

CONCLUSION

Although the traditional approach to Chinese literacy, a detailed interpretation of lexical entries and careful analysis of sentence structures followed by word-by-word recitation, has long neglected the importance of interactive reading techniques, this study has indicated that Chinese students can use semantic and syntactic, as well as graphic, cues in English to hypothesize about the message of the writer. This study also found that there is a hierarchy of the application of strategies from the reliance on lexical to contextual information when these students' English proficiency level increases. This finding supported Coady's model of ESL readers' processing strategies in general and deemphasized the uniqueness of Chinese readers as proposed by Field.

Since it is common practice for university teachers in Taiwan to assign extensive reading materials written in English to their students, and since the high school learning style of intensive word-by-word reading will lead college students nowhere close to comprehension, the necessity for teaching reading strategies becomes especially apparent when students progress through college. The future emphasis of the English reading class for Chinese students should therefore be put on building up the learner's confidence in their skills in guessing meanings and speeding up the transition from conscious to unconscious use of grammatical and contextual clues to meaning.

APPENDIX I
WHEN A YOUNG BIRD LEAVES THE NEXT

Like people, young birds go through a different transition when it's time to strike

out on their own. The fledgling must be *glurked* while learning to feed itself. It
₁

must be protected while learning to fly. An in some species, fledglings must even

be *mexed* by their parents during their first autumn migration.
₂

In most cases, a young bird *tidly* returns once it leaves the nest. But there are
₃

some *padons*. The youth of certain kinds of woodpeckers, wrens and swallows
₄

fly back to the nest to sleep. Similarly, some eagles and large-hawks *refirk* home
₅

for weeks to feed until they learn how to catch their own *pum*.
₆

When it comes to *snerdling*, however, few fledglings need any lessons. Fifty
₇

years ago, a German scientist named J. Grohmann raised some young pigeons in

narrow tubes that prevented them from moving their *lurds*. At the same time he
₈

allowed another group of pigeons of the same age to be raised by their *medlons*
₉

in a nest in the normal way, exercising their wings vigorously. When the two

groups of pigeons were mature enough, Grohamm took them out into the open

and *possed* them into the air. Surprisingly, the pigeons raised in the *urmlews*
₁₀   ₁₁

flew away as strongly as the ones that had been unrestrained in the nest.

Grohamm thus proved that the instinctive *grumpity* to fly develops in young
₁₂

birds with or without the opportunity to practice.

Key: (1) fed   (2) accompanied   (3) rarely   (4) exceptions   (5) return   (6) prey   (7)
          flying   (8) wings   (9) parents   (10) tossed   (11) tubes   (12) ability

APPENDIX II
THE MODEL SUMMARY

Young birds go through a transition before they reach their maturity: they need to be fed before they know how to feed themselves: they must be protected while learning how to fly and they even need to be accompanied during their first autumn migration. But a German scientist's study proves that flying and the ability to fly is instinctive and needs no practice.

REFERENCES

Coady, J. (1979). A psycholinguistic model of the ESL reader. In R. Mackay, B. Barkman, & R. R. Jordan (Eds.), *Reading in a second language* (pp. 5–12). Rowley, MA: Newbury House.

Field, M. L. (1985). A psycholinguistic model of the Chinese ESL reader. In P. Larson, E. L. Judd, & D. S. Messerchmitt (Eds.), *On TESOL '84* (pp. 171–182). Washington, DC: TESOL.

Goodman, K. S. (1968). The psycholinguistic nature of the reading process. In K. Goodman (Ed.), *The psycholinguistic nature of the reading process* (pp. 13–26). Detroit: Wayne State University Press.

Haynes, M. (1984). Patterns and perils of guessing in second language reading. In J. Handscombe, R. A. Orem, & B. P. Taylor (Eds.), *On TESOL '83* (pp. 163–176). Washington, DC: TESOL.

Homburg, T. J., & Spaan, M. C. (1982). ESL reading proficiency assessment: testing strategies. In M. Hines & W. Rutherford (Eds.), *On TESOL '81* (pp 25–33). Washington, DC: TESOL.

Hudson, T. (1982). The effects of induced schemata on the 'short-circuit' in L2 reading: Non-decoding factors in L2 reading performance. *Language Learning, 32* (1), 1–31.

Kruse, A. F. (1979). Vocabulary in context. *English Language Teaching Journal, 33* (3), 207–213.

Laufer, B. (1981). A problem in vocabulary learning—Synphones. *ELT Journal, 35*(3), 294–300.

Loew, H. Z. (1984). Developing strategic reading skills. *Foreign Language Annals, 17*(4), 301–303.

Phillips, J. K. (1984). Practical implications of recent research in reading. *Foreign Language Annals, 17*(4), 285–296.

Sprenger, A. S.V.D. (1975). The reading myth. *Fu Jen Studies, 8*, 77–92.

Walker, L. J. A. (1981). *Word-identification strategies of Spanish-speaking college students in reading English as a foreign language.* Unpublished doctoral dissertation, The University of Texas at Austin.

Yorio, C. A. (1971). Some sources of reading problems for foreign language learners. *Language Learning, 21*(1), 107–115.

Editorial Comments

This chapter addresses the question of whether there are universal reading strategies that develop naturally in second-language learners, regardless of culture-bound practices. It is well known that traditional Chinese education promotes intensive word-by-word reading. Yet when Chern had a group of advanced Chinese learners of English try to interpret unknown English words, she found that they did substantial contextual guessing, similar to that of other ESL learners. Hence, this exploratory study suggests that there are indeed universal reading strategies that develop naturally, that is, without specific instruction.

This chapter takes one step further the distinction between local and global context discussed in Chapter 3 by specifying more exactly the text characteristics surrounding a nonsense word to be guessed. Using Chinese readers studying in the U.S., Chern finds that better readers appear more able to use forward context, that is, context following an unfamiliar word. Thus, Chern reports, as do Huckin and Jin (1987), that it is the use of global context clues which most readily differentiates good from poor readers.

Nevertheless, Chern reports that it was performance on backward cues (those preceding the word to be guessed) which correlated more highly with TOEFL reading proficiency. This is a sensible finding, indicating that, when readers are better at constructing meaning during reading in general, they are also better able to use clues to meaning which precede an unknown word. It thus elaborates on Walker's (1983) proposal that foreign language reading ability and the ability to guess word meanings from context are related, though there is also some research challenging this view (e.g., Bensoussan & Laufer, 1984; Palmberg, 1987).

The approach used by Chern, based on Homburg & Spaan (1982), was to set up four different categories of context cues: backward cues, forward cues, parallelism (all of which extended across more than one sentence), and sentence-bound cues. When such contextual categories are unconfounded with other variables, they can provide important information about the relative helpfulness of various contexts as well as about individual differences among readers in context use and general reading proficiency. Chern's study is thus a model research approach for others to build on.

Nevertheless, we must add a note of caution. Just as in the previous chapter (where language background was used as a variable), the way a researcher defines a factor does not mean that the true cause of difference has been pinpointed, particularly if there are potentially confounding variables present. In this case, one confounding variable is that of word-form. Sometimes Chern's nonsense words were graphophonemically or morphemically similar to the original words they had replaced: *possed* for *tossed, refirk* for *return*, and *grumpity* for *ability*. It is unclear whether readers who successfully replaced a nonsense word with its original were cued by the context independently of the word-form. In fact, some of Chern's readers reported retrospectively that they had used word-form cues to help them guess. This confounding of word-form and context makes the results of the study less clear-cut but turns it into a useful object lesson for researchers planning to use nonsense words.

In addition to contextual and word-level clues, Chern's subjects reported using topic knowledge to guess the meanings of words. This is consistent with research reported elsewhere (Adams, 1982; Bernhardt, 1986; Parry, 1987) and complements Stein's argument (Chapter 10) about the importance of cultural beliefs.

In relation to Chern's use of retrospective self-reports from her subjects about the strategies they thought they used, we must point out that—though certainly a useful investigative tool—such retrospection is not entirely reliable (see, for example, Barnett, 1989, and the thorough examination of self-report reliability in Ericsson & Simon 1984). Thus, further investigation using a variety of methods is needed to substantiate these claims.

In terms of pedagogy, we feel that Chern's results cannot easily be translated into instruction. Training studies would be necessary to find out what instructional implications can be drawn from the group differences between good and less good readers in this study. Chern's data cannot distinguish whether the use of forward global context by more successful readers is made possible by those readers' greater fluency with the language (or writing system: see Haynes & Carr, 1990), by strategic differences which might easily be taught (see Huckin & Jin, 1987), or by cognitive style differences less amenable to instruction, such as impulsivity vs. reflectivity in reading (e.g. Erickson, Stahl, & Rinehart, 1985).

Similarly, the correlation between successful use of backward cues and reading proficiency does not indicate whether it is generally good reading which facilitates the use of context, or whether, conversely, it is accurate inference from context which leads to overall better reading. Correlation does not prove causation. Thus we feel that the usefulness of this study for language teachers lies, not in its results, which cannot be directly applied to pedagogy, but in its methodology—exploring how readers comprehend nonsense words and categories of context.

REFERENCES

Adams, S. J. (1982). Scripts and the recognition of unfamiliar vocabulary: Enhancing second language reading skills. *Modern Language Journal, 66*(2), 155–59.

Barnett, M. A. 1989). *More than meets the eye: Foreign language reading.* Englewood Cliffs, NJ: Prentice-Hall Regents.

Bensoussan, M., & Laufer, B. (1984). Lexical guessing in context in EFL comprehension. *Journal of Research in Reading, 7,* 15–32.

Bernhardt, E. B. (1986). A model of L2 text reconstruction: The recall of literary text by learners of German. In A. Labarca (Ed.), *Issues in L2: Theory as practice, practice as theory* (pp. 21–43). Norwood: Ablex Publishing Corp.

Ericsson, K. A., & Simon, H. A. (1984). *Protocol analysis: Verbal reports as data.* Cambridge, MA: MIT Press.

Erickson, L. G., Stahl, S. A., & Rinehart, S. D. (1985). Metacognitive abilities of above and below average readers: effects of conceptual tempo, passage level, and error type on error detection. *Journal of Reading Behavior, 17,* 235–252.

Haynes, M., & Carr, T. H. (1990). Writing system background and second language reading: A component skills analysis of English reading by native speaker-readers of Chinese. In T. H. Carr & B. A. Levy (Eds.), *Reading and its development: Component skill approaches.* Orlando, FL: Academic Press.

Homburg, T. J., & Spaan, M. C. (1982). ESL reading proficiency: Testing strategies. In M. Hines & W. Rutherford (Eds.), *On TESOL '81.* Washington, DC: TESOL.

Huckin, T., & Jin, Z.-D. (1987). Inferring word-meaning from context: a study in second-language acquisition. In F. Marshall (Ed.), *ESCOL '86* (pp. 271–280). Columbus, OH: Ohio State University Department of Linguistics.

Palmberg, R. (1987). On lexical inferencing and the young foreign language learner. *System, 16*(1), 69–76.

Parry, K. (1987). Reading in a second culture. In J. Devine, P. L. Carrell, & D. E. Eskey (Eds.), *Research in reading English as a second language* (pp. 59–70). Washington, DC: Teachers of English to Speakers of Other Languages.

Walker, L. (1983). Word identification strategies in reading a foreign language. *Foreign Language Annals, 16*(4), 293–99.

DAN

Chapter 5
False Friends and Reckless Guessers: Observing Cognate Recognition Strategies

John Holmes
Foreign Commonwealth Office
British Council

Rosinda Guerra Ramos
Catholic University
of São Paulo
São Paulo, Brazil

The aim of this chapter is to explore the ways in which learners acquire cognate recognition skills in reading comprehension. We review and then build on previous research with Brazilian students of English for Academic Purposes to examine how students acquire greater skill in recognizing cognates. By analyzing summaries of English texts prepared in the students' L1 we identify the strategies used in recognizing cognates and the ways these first hypotheses are then monitored. We attempt to identify the role of syntactic and semantic textual clues and the importance of the students' knowledge of the world. In our final considerations we also try to identify if readers deal with cognate vocabulary differently from noncognates.

THE IMPORTANCE OF COGNATE VOCABULARY

The existence of cognate vocabulary in a target language is of crucial importance for the language learner. For this reason, native speakers of Romance languages enjoy a certain advantage in learning English when compared to speakers of non-Indo-European languages, and native speakers of English find it is much easier to read a French or Spanish newspaper than one written in Turkish or Tagalog. The English-speaking readers picks up a Brazilian newspaper and reads the headline: "PRESIDENTE DIVULGA DETALHES DO NOVO CHOQUE NA ECONOMIA" and thinks "Oh my God, the president is going to divulge details of a new shock to the economy." Portuguese-speaking students of English have a similar entry into English texts. The importance of vocabulary knowledge in reading comprehension is crucial (Alderson, 1984; Nation & Coady, 1988) and this means that for even the beginner the existence of cognates in a target language makes reading comprehension more accessible. There are, of course, other dimensions of linguistic similarity which help in reading such as syntax, rhetorical features, and cultural or formal schemata (which help in this context), but the most striking similarity for many language learners is the presence of cognate vocabulary.

Although cognate vocabulary is important, there has been relatively little systematic investigation. Perhaps the reasons for this neglect stem from the context in which most English as a Second Language (ESL) and English as a Foreign Language (EFL) teaching takes place. For example, cognates are restricted to certain language groups while much ESL and EFL research and practice concern mixed groups of language learners. Also, in much ESL/EFL methodology an emphasis on oral skills tends to reduce the importance of cognate recognition which most easily takes place in written texts. It is especially in the case of the L2 reader that the lack of vocabulary assumes proportions of a major obstacle (Ramos, 1988). Another important feature of much work in ESL/EFL methodology is the fact that the teacher is often a native speaker of English and is rarely expected to share the students' knowledge of their native language. Finally, although the role of the learner's native language has waxed and waned in importance in language learning theory it has been more commonly looked upon as a source of error, interference, or negative transfer, than as an asset in the learning process.

In the case of the Brazilian English for Specific Purposes (ESP) Project, materials incorporating cognate recognition activities have been in existence since the very beginning (1978) and have been regarded as successful and characteristic features of the Project methodology (Celani, Holmes, Ramos & Scott, 1988, Chap. 5, Part 2). The existence of cognates means that a Brazilian student of English can already recognize the majority of words of Latin origin in a reading text, an asset which is especially valuable in academic texts rather than journalism or "simplified" EFL texts, where fewer words of Latin origin are found.

We have investigated cognate recognition (CR) with the specific objective of contributing to improvements in classroom practice. Our work takes Brazilian students as subjects but we believe that our results and conclusions can be applicable for any students with a Romance L1. We will also point out how the investigation of CR throws a light on vocabulary-learning strategies in a more generally applicable way, since we are in essence focusing on the phenomenon of recognition and "misrecognition" (Haynes, 1984; Huckin & Bloch, Chap. 8, this volume) which arises when learners recognize or think they recognize a lexical item in a reading text. This occurs independently of the existence of cognates in the target language.

This chapter begins with a short discussion of what research has revealed up to this point and then gives an account of our attempts to apply these findings in the classroom. In our case we worked with graduate and undergraduate students who are native speakers of Portuguese or Spanish. They were taking short courses (30 to 45 hours) aimed at enabling them to read in English in their specialist area of study.

IDENTIFYING COGNATES

Definitions

In previous work (Holmes, 1986) we practically gave up the struggle to identify vocabulary items which could or could not be called cognates. Now our working definition for cognates is simply: items of vocabulary in two languages which have the same roots and can be recognized as such. The two principal properties of cognates lie in their orthographic and semantic similarity in the languages compared.

In terms of orthographic similarity, native English speakers identify with little difficulty words such as *internacional* in Portuguese or Spanish, *internasyonal* in Turkish as being cognate with *international* in English, while "Coca-Cola" is cognate for many world languages. However, there is a cline of orthographic similarity so that we soon come to borderline cases such as the Portuguese words *criatividade* (creativity), *recurso* (resource) and *breve* (brief).

Another important factor is the degree of semantic overlap between the two components, an issue which historically has most concerned teachers and text-book writers (e.g., Downes, 1984). Thus, we often have a great deal of attention paid to the *false cognates* or *false friends*. As languages change, two words of the same origin may change in meaning, so that at the present day they may be orthographically recognizable, but totally different in meaning. For example, the Portuguese word *marmelada* means a quince desert (marmelo = quince). This word was absorbed into English but then changed its meaning so that now the English word *marmalade*, meaning a preserve made of bitter oranges, is a false cognate.

These instances are striking, especially for the teacher, but they are part of a more general phenomenon, when we attempt to pair any lexical items in two languages. For example, the word "dog" in English does not cover the meanings of the word *cachorro* in Portuguese, and vice versa. In Portuguese a certain type of person can be referred to as a *cachorro* which would be totally inappropriate in English. However, this is a general semantic problem that any translator or language learner has to deal with, and cognates are no exception.

Identifying Cognates

As practicing teachers, our first work on cognates was to set up criteria for text selection for English for Academic Purposes (EAP) reading-comprehension materials. From the beginning, our aim in the classroom has been to expose the student to texts which are "cognate-rich" in order to motivate the student and to offer from the start an opportunity to practice vocabulary inferencing skills. Thus, we need to be able to identify in a given text the proportion of lexical items which our learners would identify as cognates. Unfortunately, this is not a simple matter.

In real life, subjects differ as to what words can be called cognates. Nakamura's (1986) findings are typical. She gave lists of English vocabulary items to Brazilian informants and asked them to identify the items which could be classed as cognates. She found many differences between subjects with a similar level of knowledge of English. Some seemed more liberal than others in admitting a word as a cognate. In a pilot study mentioned in Holmes (1986) we gave lists of English words to subjects who were fluent in both English and Portuguese and obtained a similarly wide range of results. There were some surprises, when words such as *ramp* in English were not classified as cognates (*rampa* in Portuguese) while other items were not considered since the meanings overlapped only partially (the so-called *false cognates*). Thus we could identify in our list of vocabulary a *cline of cognate-ness* from words which all the subjects agreed were cognates, like *progress* (*progresso*), to words which few or any subjects agreed were cognates, like *myth* (*mito*), and false cognates like *actual* where in Portuguese *atual* means *at the moment*. Cognate identification seemed to be personal, with some subjects inclined to be more liberal than others in admitting a word as a cognate. The same difference between liberal and conservative guessers was evident when we asked more experienced students to identify cognates in a text rather than as isolated list items. Again there was considerable spread.

COGNATE RECOGNITION STRATEGIES

The question of cognates becomes more interesting when we move from a contrastive analysis of words in isolation to the processes which cause language learners to recognize cognate items in the L2 text and construct their understanding of the text. Thus, we turned our attention to cognate recognition strategies employed by students in reading comprehension.

In Brazilian ESP a number of disparate assumptions have been made which have governed the classroom use of cognate recognition. These assumptions have arisen mainly as a result of collective experience over several years, but also due to the influence of language-learning theories and views of the reading process. This will be our starting point in investigating cognate recognition strategies.

The main explicitly taught technique could be called *skimming for cognates* and is usually employed from the very beginning of an EAP comprehension course in Brazil. The instructions in the materials are typically as follows:

Skim quickly through the text. Note the titles, subtitle, diagrams, illustrations and typographical clues. Put into capital letter any words which you think you recognize and give your opinion as to the general topic of the text.

Our aims in using this technique are as follows:

1. *Motivating.* CR can be used with beginning students as a means of motivating by showing students they can handle authentic texts.
2. *Building schemata.* There is a certain *threshold effect:* texts with a higher percentage of cognates create a context that enables more marginal cognates to be recognized. In other words, the same lexical item may not be recognized in one text while in another it is clearly and correctly identified.
3. *Training strategies.* As students develop experience they will become better guessers, not just of cognate vocabulary but of any unknown vocabulary items.
4. *Increasing grammatical sensitivity.* In the time available it is not possible to give full grammar training, but as students acquire skills for dealing with the meaning of texts they will acquire the necessary familiarity with important structural features of the target language.

Theoretical Justification

In systematizing our classroom practice we, as Brazilian ESP teachers, found little difficulty in developing a theoretical justification for working with CR strategies. We regarded lexical inference as a crucial part of the L2 reading process, and it seemed as if practice in working with cognates would be generally transferable to lexical inference of noncognates. In the skimming-for-cognates technique the reader builds up a content schema and then returns to the text where the schema now helps in the identification of further cognates. The skills involved, which range from identifying orthographic features to then checking this identification with the higher-level textual features, fit in well with interactive models of the reading process as they were emerging in the 1980s (e.g., Rumelhart, 1977; Eskey, 1986; Carrell, Devine & Eskey, 1988). Such models of interaction between data-gathering and interpretive processes were of great help to us in encouraging our investigation into what had previously been merely a successful classroom technique.

RESEARCH IN COGNATE IDENTIFICATION

After a good deal of collective experience in working with cognate recognition we thus attempted to investigate more closely the processes used by our students. Much of this is reported in Holmes (1986) and Ramos (1988). The two studies had several features in common. Working with *false beginner* students of EAP reading they attempted to analyze by means of oral summaries the product of the subjects' identification of cognates, in order to answer the following questions:

Do *false beginners* naturally look for cognates when they begin to deal with an English text, or must the strategy be explicitly taught, and justified by the teacher?

Is it easier for students to recognize cognates when dealing with texts that have a familiar subject matter, where students can construct content schemata with greater ease?

When students recognize cognates are they successful or is misrecognition common? Is this misrecognition a barrier to comprehension?

Our predictions were as follows:

1. Students would approach cognates initially with suspicion due to previous language learning experience and 'folk-linguistic' ideas about foreign language. Thus, CR would not be applied spontaneously.
2. Texts with familiar subject matter would provide content schemata to help with recognition of a wider range of cognates rather than texts with unfamiliar topics.
3. Misrecognition would occur initially, but the subjects would tend to overcome these problems when they were asked to give an overview of what they had understood of the text. In other words, students may misrecognize a cognate in isolation but when asked to give the general idea of a text or paragraph they would note inconsistencies and revise their hypotheses accordingly.

In both cases the research was carried out with the students beginning an ESP course. Holmes worked with undergraduate students of Portuguese while

Ramos' students were graduate students of educational psychology. Both groups, however, were practically beginners in English with only a vague knowledge of a few words from school experience. Thus, they brought very little previous knowledge of English to the research task.

Data was gathered by think-aloud protocols as students read silently through an English text and orally summarized their understanding of it in Portuguese. At the same time they spontaneously commented on the task.

The main insights were obtained by matching the wording of the subjects' summaries with the original text. In this way we could identify cognates and other vocabulary items which were recognized or misrecognized in the original text and were transferred directly to the summary. Some examples of this technique are given in the description of the most recent research (Figure 5.1 and 5.2, pages 24 and 25).

In order to clarify researchers' doubts, the subjects were at times asked specific questions on the meaning of words. As well as the recordings, students' comments and the notes or underlinings in the original text supplied additional data.

Conclusions

Cognate recognition is a "natural" strategy. Both investigations found that at this stage in learning, English students spontaneously sought out the cognate vocabulary in the text. Although it may be useful for the teacher to practice CR and clarify what is meant by a cognate, in the main the students bring this strategy to their first contact with English.

Previous knowledge was important. Informants were very dependent on their previous knowledge of the topic to predict the text content and the author's purpose. They also used previous knowledge to interpret cognates.

A lack of knowledge of grammar seemed to result in frequent misrecognition of cognates. Nouns were recognized as verbs, adjectives as nouns, and so on. The adjective *corrupt* became *corruption* in the summary; the phrase *the President governed* became *the President's government*, and so on. Although this did not seem to worry the informants, as teachers we were somewhat upset at what the technique could lead to. It was unclear how much this grammatical misrecognition prejudiced overall comprehension. Other difficulties created by a lack of grammatical knowledge appeared in Ramos (1988), where the informants' principal problem was in relating the components of the sentence to each other, since processing took place principally at sentence level.

One of the most striking and unexpected phenomena that was noted was the lack of a check-up or monitoring of initial guesses when summarizing. This type of behavior we called *reckless guessing*. In Holmes (1988) the informants picked out the cognates and already-familiar vocabulary from the text and wove these isolated words into a general idea of what each paragraph was about. They then started on the next paragraph, and often made no connection between the different sections of the text so that, at times, the summary of one paragraph contradicted that of the next. The 'summary' in fact was a string of isolated microsummaries which was constructed a paragraph at a time. In Ramos (1988) this type of summarizing also took place and at times students simply suppressed difficult paragraphs.

We found then, that when recklessly guessing, informants were quite happy to supply their previous knowledge of the subject to provide extra information in their summaries, often with little connection to the real content of the original text. The text spoke with the voice of the reader rather than that of the author. We should add the caveat here that we were not sure if this reckless guessing was an inherent feature of the students' understanding or was an artifact of the task we have given them. It could have been that the informants were subject to a *cognitive overload* and simply had to do too many things at once.

In reporting these results we attempted to draw pedagogical conclusions for classroom work with students.

It seemed important to encourage students to monitor their guesses and to review what they had understood in the text up to a given moment, to check that it made sense and that the text interpretation was structured coherently.

Meanwhile, by choosing texts on familiar topics we would give students the opportunity to match their initial cognate recognition with the wider context of the text, but students must also be encouraged to look for the author's purpose in writing the text and be alert for different points of view.

Finally, we as teachers should not regard CR as a magic wand which could be used from the very beginning without effort on the students' part. In particular, they must be aware of the importance of grammatical knowledge of English in order to identify cognates more accurately.

COGNATE RECOGNITION IN GROUP SUMMARY PREPARATION

Strategies of More Experienced Learners

These preliminary investigations gave us important insights into what had previously been obscure and helped us to adopt a more cautious attitude towards encouraging students to look for cognates, without falling into the opposite camp of warning students about *false friends* and emphasizing grammatical minutiae. However, there were more questions to answer:

1. How do students use cognate recognition once they have been taught to monitor their initial guesses and when their grammatical knowledge is greater? Do they really become more cautious and more successful guessers?

2. In our situation a course in reading English for academic purposes has a duration of approximately 30 to 45 hours. Is this long enough for students to acquire a background knowledge of grammar sufficient to monitor cognate recognition?

The Task: Directed Summaries

Our next step was to develop a different task type with which we could investigate students' cognate recognition in a context where they were encouraged to monitor and reflect on their hypotheses. The main problem with oral summary protocols was the lack of time for informants to reflect on the task and check back over what they had said. It was possible for the researchers to ask students about individual guesses and verify if they were monitoring or not, but in general, the task of summarizing aloud was a demanding one, and probably detracted from the monitoring of comprehension. In carrying out these tasks with beginning students of English we suspected that we were seeing an extreme form of the cognate recognition strategy. It is possible that students were concentrating more on providing protocol data and less on cognate recognition processes. This is a recognized pitfall of such protocol techniques as Cavalcanti (1984) has pointed out. Cohen (1987), in pointing out the important features that can be revealed by protocols, also voices the misgiving that some of the more deep-level processes may pass undetected in some verbal protocol data.

Accordingly, we opted for a different type of task: one which was more closely connected with classroom practice, and with the target situation in which students would eventually be working. The task chosen was the preparation of a written summary in the L1 of a text in English. This already was part of normal classroom procedures at various stages of the course so that in the experimental situation the students were carrying out a perfectly familiar activity. The type of task chosen has been given the name of a "directed summary" (Holmes, 1988). In this type of comprehension activity the students were asked to distinguish between main and less important ideas in the text and also to give a personal opinion as to the section of the text which was of most interest to them. They are also asked to note down any difficulties encountered and to evaluate their performance on the task. The instructions, translated into English, are given in Appendix A. Sarig (1987) has also investigated a similar summarizing task which she refers to as the "study-summary."

This type of activity is introduced early in the course, using short and relatively easy texts, and increasing the complexity of the text and the freedom of the student in choosing a text. In the classroom the students are encouraged to work together in groups and ask for help from the teacher. They are also allowed to use the dictionary whenever possible. Our explicit intention was to give every possible opportunity for students to acquire practice in identifying cognate items and checking on the initial inferences by discussion with peers. In preparing the written L1 summaries, the context would emerge as a check on CR strategies. Thus, we did not expect that students would write, in their summaries, the same type of incoherent and inconsistent ideas as had emerged from oral summaries, and we anticipated much less evidence of *reckless guessing*.

A final reason for choosing this task was its relevance to classroom practice. We are not extrapolating from a carefully controlled experimental situation but we were observing a procedure in the classroom with our own students.

Expected Outcomes

Our predictions relating to the processes observed in cognate recognition were as follows:

1. Students would recognize and misrecognize *raw* cognates as before, on the first reading of the text.
2. Students would check their first hypotheses in group discussion during the preparation of the written summary.
3. Hypotheses would also be checked by examining grammatical, textual and semantic contextual clues.
4. The finished product would contain few or no examples of cognate mis-recognition or of reckless guessing.

Written summaries are rich sources of data on students' comprehension although students encounter problems which go beyond the mere identification of vocabulary, such as perception of text structure, rhetorical functions, and author's purpose. In our study we were focusing on the effect of CR and we looked for the following specific features which would give us an insight into the processes involved in identifying cognates and monitoring cognate recognition.

1. *Correctly recognized cognates.* These were cognates mentioned in the summary which could be matched with the original text. This gave us a check on the occasions when students correctly identified cognates. This is useful since, although errors are easy to identify, it is often all too difficult to see what is going on when students are successful.
2. *Textual incoherencies.* This is information in the summary which did not make sense, either in the context of previous sections of the students' summaries or with the students' knowledge of the world. This would give us a chance to identify what caused the comprehension problem. As mentioned before, this was a striking feature of oral summaries and stemmed from the students' *reckless guessing* when they identified a familiar word and ignored the wider context.
3. *Syntactic switching.* Another aspect of *reckless guessing* emerges when students identify cognates but do not consider the syntactic context. There

were several ways in which this could be identified. Nouns appeared as adjectives, verbs as nouns, phrases expanded into sentences and sentences squashed into noun phrases or extended into paragraphs.

4. *Stylistic aberrations.* There were sections in the summaries that made sense but read strangely either because of syntax or choice of vocabulary. In these sections the students try to reconcile their understanding of the text with their translations of single phrases or sentences. In this situation we can observe when the recognition of a vocabulary item is difficult to fit into the reading of the text. This is a problem well-known in students' translation but it occurs frequently in summaries as well.

PROCEDURE

Informants

The study took place with a group of 15 postgraduate students of educational psychology, studying for an M.A. degree at the Catholic University of São Paulo, Brazil. The students came to the course with almost no knowledge of English, but needed to read original articles from periodicals in their specialist area of study. The study was carried out towards the end of the course which lasts one semester, in fifteen two-hour classes.

Data Collection

The data came from two sources: observation of the activity and analysis of the summaries. As the students went about the task the teacher circulated around the groups and noted in a notebook the procedures adopted in carrying out the task. Items observed were the attitudes of students to the task, the problems encountered (words looked up, questions to the teacher, etc.) and any strategies that could be explicitly identified. In particular the teacher looked for evidence of monitoring, both of initial guesses when cognates were identified and later when the main ideas of the text were being checked to see if they fitted together or made sense. All possible steps were taken to ensure that the activity was as typical of a normal lesson as possible, although the students were told that the data was to be used as part of a research project.

We are aware that there are many gaps in this data-gathering instrument and that the observer could have failed to notice many interesting features of the groups' problem-solving procedures, but alternatives were not promising. For example, it was proposed to give each group a tape recorder to record discussion, but without time for students to become accustomed this would have resulted in a certain inhibition. An initial attempt was made to carry out the activity with an extra observer, in addition to the usual teacher. The effect was dramatic and the class reacted as if they were being given a formal test. "Test-taking" strategies appeared, as the group members read the text out loud to one another, stopping at every unknown word to look it up in the dictionary and taking far more time than they usually did. Data from this attempt were discounted.

Observation

The students were given a text and the instructions for the summary, and asked to take their time, to work in groups if they wished, and to ask for help whenever necessary. A translation of the instructions is given in the appendix. The text chosen related to the recent municipal elections in São Paulo when the left-wing Workers' party had won a surprise victory, some ten days before the day of the experiment. The group reacted favorably to the topic of the text and indeed on the very day of the experiment were still euphoric over the victory of a candidate which all of them appeared to have supported. Thus, the students were interested in the topic and brought a great deal of previous knowledge to the task.

The observations confirmed most expectations with regard to the procedures used in previous situations, with a few differences. In particular, in the first stage, instead of forming groups as usually happened, practically all the students began by reading the text alone. This was not the way students normally began such a task, but we are inclined to believe this was because the subject matter was of such interest.

Silence settled on the classroom. At various intervals, students underlined unknown words, contrary to our own instructions during the semester, which were to underline what was known! This was their typical procedure, however. From time to time students would stop and go back when they came to difficult passages and rarely they would ask a classmate or the teacher the meaning of an unknown word as they came to it. This is important; they had at least acquired the habit of looking for overall meaning before asking for the meaning of an isolated lexical item.

After this first phase, there was a noticeable lightening of atmosphere, chairs were moved around and the class coalesced into groups of 4 or 5. This happened almost simultaneously within the class. Usually one person led the discussion, but not always the student with the best knowledge of English. As the students discussed the meaning of individual words and the text itself, the teacher listened to the discussion whenever possible. This was not as difficult as it sounds since not all groups were debating aloud at the same time. This was the opportunity to listen for initial cognate recognitions and any later monitoring of these guessers.

Although we had consistently discouraged word for word translations, these often took place when dealing with short sections of the text, especially with regard to the first part. Later on, as time grew short, the groups tended to summarize paragraph by paragraph and they seemed to become tired. Some groups only translated the first sentences of each paragraph, a tactic we had not taught the students explicitly in the course.

After going through the text, taking notes and scribbling translations over words within the text, the student settled down to write individual summaries. These varied in length. Some were 200 words long (with comments and self-evaluations) covering two sides of paper, other were shorter. In general, the quantity of work handed in was within the teacher's expectations.

The students as a whole said they had enjoyed the task and found the text interesting as an example of how Brazilian topics were treated by foreign journalists. A few students said that they learned nothing new from the text, and that they already knew the ideas presented by the writer.

The Product

The summaries were our raw material for identifying CR strategies and in our previous experience they had afforded rich possibilities for analysis. In this particular instance we were unfortunate as many of them were extremely general and vague, confining themselves to general details at several removes from the original text, unlike the oral summaries. In this case it was difficult to match cognates in the L2 text with the equivalents in the students' L1 summaries. This could be due to two factors: the students had a rich background knowledge of the topic and were supplementing the ideas in the text, or they understood that written summaries should always be of this degree of generality.

Comparison with different summaries written previously in the course showed that they had not been quite so general. Thus, we suspect the first alternative. It seems that in this case their good background knowledge of the topic enabled them to supply any gaps in their understanding of the text with their previous knowledge. Another interesting point emerged in the comments in Part III where students had to give personal reactions. Again, many of the informants referred to their extensive previous knowledge of the subject as motivating them but also not supplying any new ideas. However, in Section IV when students made a self-evaluation it is interesting to note that the major problem was identified as "vocabulary," following the pattern already established during the course.

RESULTS

The Summaries

Figure 5.1 comprises the first two paragraphs of the approximately 600-word article.

In the case of this sample, the first two paragraphs were more closely summarized than subsequent ones, and we are able to follow the way in which the ideas

Figure 5.1.   Original Text

Sections containing possible cognates (but see the warning at the beginning of this article) are in capital letters, but prepositions or articles occurring in these sections should not be considered.

Title: "Brazil's Elections: The People Fire a Warning Shot," taken from *The Economist,* November 19, 1988.

Three years of CIVILIAN RULE have left BRAZILIANS thoroughly DISENCHANTED. The MUNICIPAL ELECTIONS of NOVEMBER 15 OFFERED THEM A CHANCE to send a MESSAGE OF PROTEST TO PRESIDENT JOSE SARNEY AND THE MAJORITY BRA-ZILIAN DEMOCRATIC MOVEMENT PARTY (PMDB). But the country's 70m-odd voters went much further, as if warming up for next NOVEMBER'S PRESIDENTIAL ELECTION, which will be the first by DIRECT VOTE since 1960. Their swing to the left was more than a warning. It suggested a trend that does not AUGUR well for BRAZILIAN DEMOCRACY.
The PMDB took a drubbing, blamed for many misdeeds. INFLATION is close to 900% this year. Living standards are crumbling. Mr. Sarney became PRESIDENT BY ACCIDENT of a better man's death, and his only policy seems to be to keep the job for as long as he can. The PARTY HAS NO PARTICULAR IDEOLOGY. It led the OPPOSITION TO MILITARY RULE between 1964 and 1985 and on that record swept the MID-TERM ELECTION two years ago. This time it held on to very little outside the NORTH-EASTERN CITIES that have long been CONSERVATIVE strongholds. Short of an ECONOMIC MIRACLE, the party's likely PRESIDENTIAL CANDIDATE, Mr. Ulysses Guimaràes, will be an also-ran next year.

Figure 5.2.   Summary

An example from a typical student summary is given here. We provide a back transla-tion into English of one of the summaries originally written in Portuguese, quoting only the part referring to the first two paragraphs. The translation is given word-for-word so that cognate equivalents can be identified when they occur. These cognates are given in capitals, excluding those in the first paragraph which is a general overview of the text.

"The text makes a Brazilian political analysis emphasizing the municipal electoral process which happened on November 15 this year, discussing the causes and conse-quences.
The author quotes the dissatisfaction of the Brazilian people after three years of CIVILIAN GOVERNMENT, adding that the MUNICIPAL ELECTION which occurred on November 15 served as form of PROTEST against president Jose Sarney and THE MAJORITY POLITICAL PARTY the PMDB. For the writer this tendency of the Brazilian people is an AUGURY FOR DEMOCRACY.
The PMDB took a fall. INFLATION has reached 900% this year. The party doesn't have its own IDEOLOGY. For the writer, president Sarney is struggling to stay longer in power. . . ."

are transferred from the original text. Notice that the order of ideas in the summary is different from the original and that the student ignores the negative in the last sentence of paragraph 1 and comes to the conclusion that the elections augur well for democracy, exactly the opposite of the writer. We could not call this a textual incoherence, however, since it could fit in with the reader's knowledge of the world, and it certainly fits in with the rest of the summary, but this kind of misinterpretation is not rare. We could call this ignoring of the *not* an example of *reckless guessing*, where attention given to the cognates seems to lead to neglect of other contextual clues.

With regard to the student summaries in general, it is worth noting two points. In all summaries, two important words were mentioned: the *disenchantment* of Brazilians (*desencanto* in Portuguese) and the fact that the election results were a warning to the government. *Warning* is not a cognate, but in the summaries the students seemed to get the general idea without recourse to a dictionary. We would have liked to have interviewed the students to see if the idea came from their previous knowledge or from genuine lexical inference.

The analysis of the summaries focused on the four features mentioned above: cognates appearing in the summary, textual incoherencies, syntactic switching and stylistic aberrations.

Cognates Appearing in the Summaries

The cognates were almost all recognized successfully, and few misrecognitions could be identified in a comparison of the text and summaries. The presence of monitoring was evident in some cases of misrecognition which nonetheless made perfect sense in the context. For example, *military rule* was misrecognized as *military rules*, as in *rules of the game*. This made sense in an interpretation that the military had established the rules for the indirect election of the president.

In another section of the text, there was the following sentence:

The DETAILS OF VOTING in more than 4,300 MUNICIPALITIES will not be known for some days; but PRELIMINARY RETURNS CONFIRMED the exit polls which showed the left ADVANCING in most major CITIES.

The text then names the cities. The student wrote: "Preliminary results in important centres (*polos importantes*) confirm the advance of the left." Here the student had used the word *polo* which means *centre, pole* but does fit in well with the context. We hypothesize that the student misrecognized *poll* as cognate with *polo* and altered the meaning of the sentence, but certainly produced a coherent one. In this situation we could call *poll* a false cognate.

Textual Incoherencies

By encouraging students to check their hypotheses we expected that inconsistencies and incoherencies would not appear in the text, or at least would not be common. But they did appear in a different form, although we could rarely attribute them to misrecognition of cognates. For example, in one summary we found that a student interpreted sentence 6 of paragraph 2 as follows:

"The PMDB left the opposition to military rule in 1984 (sic) and 1985. . . ." Compare this with the original: "The PMDB led the opposition to military rule between 1964 and 1985."

The student's strange sentence we attribute to a misrecognition of the non-cognate *led*. Our subject confused this with *left*, but recognized the cognates in the sentence. This would have resulted in a statement which conflicted with the student's knowledge of the world (i.e., "The PMDB left the opposition to military rule between 1964 and 1985.").

She resolved the dilemma by changing the dates rather than her recognition of the word *led*, and thus changed 1964 to 1984. The summary made sense, but at the price of altering the dates in the original text. Of course we as readers have to be able to detect misprints from time to time, but it is interesting to see a relatively inexperienced reader putting more trust in her recall of a noncognate than the numbers mentioned by the author in the text.

Another example of incoherency arose from misrecognitions in a phrase that begins paragraph 3: "There was a huge turn-out for two parties on the left." In this we encountered phrases such as: "There was a return (*volta*) to the left," "The left parties returned (*retornaram*) to power," and "There was a stampede (*corrida*) to the left," where the word *turn-out* had been translated in three different ways. The students who recognized turn-out as cognate with *retorno* in Portuguese were thus caught in a dilemma since it did not really make sense to say that "the left were returning to power" in the context of their summaries. This provided us with some interesting opportunities to identify cognate mis-recognition. We found factual incoherencies in nine of the summaries, which were attempts to deal with the word *turn-out*. The high proportion of these may be due to the fact that this appeared in the first sentence of a paragraph and students devoted special care to this item. Otherwise there were only three factual incoherencies in the rest of the summaries.

The most important conclusion to draw from the cognate usage and incoherencies in the summaries is that students seem to monitor their cognate recognition more than their noncognate recall. With the exception cited in the previous paragraphs, false cognates rarely led the students astray. What is interesting is that the only other examples of textual incoherency came from the noncognates. Comparing the evidence of the summaries with our own observation data we are inclined to believe that our students have learned to monitor their initial recognition of cognates by the end of the course.

Syntactic Switching

Another feature of the summaries which reveals reckless guessing is what we have called syntactic switching, where the reader notes only the cognates and then strings them together into a coherent whole without checking the grammatical context.

One example at the very end of the text is based on the following sentence in the original:

"His INSTINCT IS TO HESITATE AND HIS GOVERNMENT is weak."

In the summary of student 11, the three cognate nouns emerged as: "His instinct is to delay and hesitation has made his government weak."

This seems to be a clear example where the reader recognized the cognates, ignored the syntactic evidence and reconstituted a phrase in line with her knowledge of the world.

Another example of ignoring syntactic clues was in the phrase in paragraph 1 which mentions a "trend which does not augur well for the future" which appeared at times as the noun "augurio" which is more common in Portuguese. We are not sure if the student failed to identify this as a verb or whether it is simply due to the rareness of the Portuguese verb, so that students may have not known it in their L1.

Another example comes from the end of paragraph 2, where the phrase: "Short of an economic miracle" emerges as "The short economic miracle." Here again, syntactic clues were ignored and the student identified the words *short, economic*, and *miracle*, and ignored the prepositional links.

Although it is difficult to quantify this data, only three students showed evidence of syntactic switches in their summary and of these only one (student 11) showed several instances, scattered throughout the text. Curiously, this student evaluated the text as "conveying nothing new" in terms of information. In general, we did not find this phenomenon to be as common in the written summaries as in the oral summaries and we are inclined to attribute this to greater opportunities for monitoring offered by the group-prepared summary.

Stylistic Aberrations

We also identified stylistic aberrations in several summaries. For example, in several summaries students dealt with the phrase: "Their swing to the left" (Paragraph 1, sentence 4) by using phrases of the type:

"Brazil is sailing/navigating/swimming to the left."

After some puzzlement we realized that in one group the word *swing* had been recognized as the noncognate *swim* and the attempts to make sense of it in the context resulted in this stylistic aberration.

Another example was the case of the word *poll* which some identified with the word *polo* (city, or central point). It was not possible to identify misrecognition if the summary used words like *city* (cidade) but when the false cognate was used it appeared stylistically out of context and it was clear that the stylistic aberration signaled a cognate misrecognition.

In all it was difficult to quantify this subjective feature, but seven summaries featured at least one example. One student (No. 11) had five examples of stylistic aberrations.

CONCLUSIONS

Our criteria for the success of the summaries were based on the match between the macrostructures of text and summary and the ability to distinguish more important from less important ideas. In the situation being investigated the students all produced satisfactory summaries of the original text, both in the opinion of the teacher and according to their own evaluation as reflected in the self-assessment. In addition, the students showed an ability to cope with unknown items of vocabulary. The main problems stemmed from the fact that the subject matter was well known to the class and so previous knowledge was called upon to bridge any gaps in the students' understanding of the original text. Although very few incoherencies and inaccuracies were noted, the main problem was the tendency to add extraneous information. However, as teachers we concluded that our students had reached a satisfactory level in reading comprehension of academic texts, even in the short time available in the course. In an evaluation of the course, which took place by questionnaire and discussion, the students were satisfied and indeed surprised at the progress they had made in acquiring strategies for reading in their specialist area.

In the students' own evaluation of the difficulties they had encountered in the task, the most consistent item cited was *vocabulary*. All the students mentioned this. Other items mentioned were the text structure, that some paragraphs did not seem to follow on from others (four students), and grammar (two students), reflecting earlier self-evaluation in the course. It is surprising that the perceived difficulties of the students have not altered during the course, and that vocabulary is still seen as the principal obstacle to comprehension, even at this stage when they are clearly more experienced and successful readers. Since the results of our analysis indicate that misunderstandings were rarely due to a lack of knowledge or misrecognition of vocabulary, the evaluation may be due precisely to this preoccupation with vocabulary. The students pay closer attention to lexis than to syntax and carefully monitor their initial guesses with regard to cognate or non-cognate vocabulary. They then state their difficulty as *vocabulary* when in fact this is a major concern rather than an obstacle, at this stage.

In general, several of our expectations appeared to be confirmed:

1. Students recognized *simple* cognates right from the beginning of the course. Greater experience of dealing with authentic texts did not appear to have inhibited their desire to identify cognates whenever they appeared.

2. Group discussions helped the monitoring process and the cognates were almost all successfully recognized in their context, as shown by observation data and the analysis of the summaries.

3. Students appeared to have acquired sufficient grammatical knowledge to check on the context of cognates. Relatively few examples of syntactic switching were encountered. Indeed, only one student (No. 11) showed anything like the strategies we had observed throughout oral summaries with false beginners.

4. There were relatively few examples of factual incoherencies in the summaries. Though they did occur, they were not due to the misrecognition of cognates but to the misrecall of noncognate items like *swing* and *led*.

This final findings seems to us one of the most interesting results of the experiment. We had assumed that the acquisition of cognate recognition strategies would be an important first step to the acquisition of lexical inference in general. It had seemed to us quite clear that cognates and noncognates should offer similar problems to the reader. The only difference would be the orthographic clues in the case of cognates, but then the reader would check the initial guess by examining the syntactic and semantic textual clues and arrive at a hypothesis which would then be reflected in the final summary.

This happened in the case of cognates. In observation of the group task we could see how the cognates were recognized and incorporated into the summary, with the meaning in almost all cases consistent with the original text. It really seemed from our observation and the finished products that students were monitoring their initial hypotheses quite carefully when they encountered cognates in the text.

What was surprising was the fact that when students recalled previously learned noncognate items they were unwilling to go through this procedure and they did not check their hypotheses in quite the same way. In fact, in two cases whole groups of students altered the meaning of the text in order to fit in with their misrecall of a noncognate item. Thus, the students in our survey seemed to behave in a different way with non-cognate vocabulary, and they did not transfer their recently acquired monitoring skills from cognates to noncognates. This behavior was noted by Ramos (1988), but at a relatively early stage in the learning process while there had been little opportunity to practice monitoring skills.

As for the much-feared *false cognates*, we certainly detected some misrecognition, but this only happened when the context made sense. There were no cases of factual inaccuracies caused by misrecognition of false cognates.

LIMITATIONS

The research technique adopted had the advantage of classroom research, in that we were observing processes and products that occur in the classroom, with the disadvantage that we could not control variables tightly and could not increase the precision of our data collection and observation without altering the circumstances drastically. Thus, as we found initial hypotheses confirmed—that the students could handle cognates with increased sensitivity by the use of monitoring strategies—we were unable to follow up in greater detail the unexpected findings with regard to noncognate recall.

The occurrence of monitoring, which is such an important feature of cognate recognition strategies, also was difficult to quantify or classify. It emerged clearly in certain group discussions, where students debated explicitly the meaning of a lexical item, but this was rare, and time-consuming. Monitoring took place at several stages in the reading and summarizing process and as such was a much more complex phenomenon than we had anticipated.

Also, in analyzing the students' summaries we had difficulties in quantifying the data. In subsequent research (Holmes & Ramos, in press) we have been able to train students to report their strategies and this has enabled us to identify the importance and frequency of use of the strategy of cognate recognition. However, we feel at present that any attempts at a greater quantitative rigor using the data-gathering technique outlined in this chapter would be misleading rather than illuminating. One avenue which seems to offer interesting possibilities is to carry out a more in-depth analysis of the processes occurring in the groups of students as they carry out summarizing tasks. It should be interesting, for example, to record the activities of each group on audio or videotape, after a period of training or familiarization. Also, useful data could be gathered by follow-up interviews or protocol analyses with a representative sample of students, after completing the summary task.

Still, this study has helped to throw some light on cognate recognition and comprehension, an aspect of vocabulary learning that has rarely been mentioned, either in research or in teaching materials, despite its immense importance to a large number of English students.

APPENDIX ONE:
Translation of Instructions for Summary Writing
READING TEXTS IN ENGLISH

1. GENERAL OBJECTIVE

    The aim of this evaluation is the preparation of a summary which shows your ability to read texts in English at a suitable level of comprehension and use the information in your academic work.

2. READING PROCEDURE

    First of all, skim through the whole text and determine:

    a) which are the principal divisions
    b) what is the author's purpose in writing the text
    c) for what kind of readership was the text written

d) read the text again, distinguishing the main idea and the less important ideas.

3. THE SUMMARY

Divide your summary into the following parts:

Part I–2 points

Write down the title and the bibliographical reference and indicate the intended readership of the text.

Part II–General idea: 2 points

Supporting ideas: 4 points

Make a short summary of the text pointing out the relationship between the more and less important ideas of the text.

Part III–2 points

Identify the parts of the text which were most important for you personally. Justify your choice. (You could mention a main idea in the text, a detail that caught your attention, or an item of information not mentioned in the text).

Part IV

Evaluation of your own performance.

Mention the problems that you experienced (vocabulary, grammar, the topic of the text, etc.).

Which section of the text was most difficult to understand?

What is your opinion of the text? How useful was the text for you?

Don't forget: your self-evaluation can help the teacher in grading your summary and helping you.

REFERENCES

Alderson, J. C. (1984). Reading in a foreign language: A reading problem or a language problem? In J. C. Alderson & A. H. Urquhart (Eds.), *Reading in a foreign language* (pp. 1–27). New York: Longman.

Carrell, P., Devine, J., & Eskey, D. (Eds.). (1988). *Interactive approaches to second language reading.* Cambridge, UK: Cambridge University Press.

Cavalcanti, M. (1984). Investigating FL reading performance through verbal protocols. *The ESPecialist, 10,* 9–31.

Celani, M. A. A., Holmes, J. L., Ramos, R. de C. G., & Scott, M. R. (Eds.). (1988). *The Brazilian ESP project: An evaluation.* São Paulo, Brazil: EDUC.

Cohen, A. (1987). Recent uses of Mentalistic Data in Reading Strategy Research. *DELTA, 3*(1), 57–84.

Downes, L. S. (1984). *Palavras Amigas-da-Onca: A Vocabulary of False Friends in English and Portuguese.* Rio de Janeiro: Ao Livro Tecnico.

Eskey, D. E. (1986). Theoretical foundations. In F. Dubin, D. E. Eskey, & W. Grabe (Eds.), *Teaching English for academic purposes* (Chap. 1). Reading, MA: Addison-Wesley.

Haynes, M. (1984). Patterns and perils of guessing in a foreign language. In J. Handscombe (Ed.), *On TESOL '83* (pp. 163–176). Washington, DC: TESOL.

Holmes, J. (1986). Snarks, quarks and cognates: An elusive fundamental particle in reading comprehension. *The ESPecialist, 15,* 13–40.

Holmes, J. (1988). Nine products in search of a process: The use of summaries in EAP. *The ESPecialist, 5,* XX–XX.

Holmes, J. L . & Ramos, R. de C. G. (in press). Learners talking about learning: Establishing a framework for discussing and changing learning processes. In C. James & D. Garret (Eds.), *Language awareness in the classroom.* London: Longman.

Nakamura, L. K. (1986). Students identification of English/Portuguese cognates. *The ESPecialist, 13,* 19–25.

Nation, P. & Coady, J. (1988). Vocabulary and reading. In R. Carter & M. McCarthy (Eds.), *Vocabulary and language teaching* (pp. 97–110). London: Longman.

Ramos, R. de C. G. (1988). *Estratégias usadas por falsos principiantes na leitura de textos acadêmicos em Inglês* [Strategies used by false beginners in academic texts in English]. Unpublished Master's thesis, Pontificia Universidade Catolica de São Paulo, Brazil.

Rumelhart, D. E. (1977). Toward an interactive model of reading. In S. Dornic (Ed.), *Attention and performance* (Vol. 6 pp. 573–603). New York: Academic.

Sarig, G. (1987). *Composing a Study Summary: a Reading-Writing Encounter,* Mimeo. The Open University of Israel.

Editorial Comments

The series of studies summarized in this chapter explores the complexities of cognate recognition for Portuguese literates reading in English. The authors find individual differences among learners and among words. Instead of defining a dichotomy between cognates and noncognates, the authors trace what they term "a cline of 'cognateness' " in which some words are clearly familiar to readers, while others are not easily recognized as related to items in the L1. In addition, the authors show us cases of misrecognition (e.g., "led" is misrecognized as "left") which involve similar-looking words in L2, without reference to L1 cognates, and which suggest that cognate recognition is a special case of the more general process of word identification in reading. Thus, as these readers apply their prior knowledge of the Portuguese lexicon to the reading of English, the problem of word-form recognition resurfaces here.

The authors also demonstrate the grammatical sloppiness of cognate recognition with language learners who have less experience. As in Haynes (1984, Chap. 3), readers' natural attention to word-form seems to override attention to other information in the text, especially syntactic information, which, in contrast with L1 learners, remains relatively fragile for L2 readers. Their last study, however, suggests that such difficulties can be dealt with pedagogically through group negotiation of summaries. By discussing various interpretations, learners seem to better monitor their cognate recognition and other reading inferences. Thus, in some cases they can revise incorrect construction of meaning.

The authors also demonstrate that plentiful background knowledge about the content addressed in the text is not always a good thing. In particular, when background knowledge contradicts textual information, it can actually interfere with close construction of meaning from the language on the page. In general, Holmes and Ramos found cognate recognition to be quite sensitive to the reader's content schemata (topic knowledge—see also Bensoussan, 1986; Carrell, 1988; and Haynes & Baker, Chap. 7, this volume).

We feel this chapter models several aspects of good linguistic research. First, the authors' ongoing research agenda has allowed them to explore the topic of cognate recognition in greater depth than they could in a single study. Also, to support their conclusions they have drawn on several sources of evidence, including analyses of the written product (students' L1 summaries of an English text) with observation of classroom process (the interaction of students in groups while discussing how to construct written summaries). Furthermore, Holmes and Ramos have used classroom-centered research, offering teachers not only a research tool but also a pedagogical technique for enhancing individual inferencing with group negotiation of text interpretation.

One difficulty with classroom-centered research is also addressed here. The authors discuss the negative effects of bringing recording equipment or outside researchers into the classroom, yet their study also demonstrates the limitations of a single teacher-observer conducting researcher in his or her own classroom. (Few details about the specific effects of group discussion on reader interpretation could be gathered because a single observer could not be present in all groups, tracing students' thinking at each step of the discussion.) Clearly, the dynamics and the effects of group interaction, though essential for our understanding of collaborative learning, do not lend themselves readily to observation.

REFERENCES

Bensoussan, M. (1986). Beyond vocabulary: Pragmatic factors in reading comprehension—culture, convention, coherence and cohesion. *Foreign Language Annals, 19*, 399–407.

Carrell, P. L. (1988). Some causes of text-boundedness and schema interference in ESL reading. In P. L. Carrell, J. Devine, & D. Eskey (Eds.), *Interactive approaches to second language reading* (pp. 101–113). Cambridge: Cambridge University Press.

Chapter 6
Too Many Words: Learning the Vocabulary of an Academic Subject*

Kate Parry
Hunter College
City University of New York
New York, NY

This chapter reports a longitudinal case study of a Japanese university student's acquisition of vocabulary in English. The student was asked to record all the new words encountered in the reading assigned for an anthropology course at an American university, and to record also her guesses as to what the words meant. The resulting lists show that she was remarkably successful in her guesses, much more so than studies of first language vocabulary acquisition would lead us to expect. The success is attributed, first, to the student's experience and knowledge as an adult—as opposed to the lack of experience that characterizes children—and, second, to the breadth of the context in which the vocabulary was encountered, it being part of an academic course that continued over a full semester. The lists also, however, show significant problems with syntax and morphology, suggesting that this student, at least, needs to adopt a more analytical approach to vocabulary if she is to use it productively as well as receptively. In addition, the study provides evidence that even though words may be understood quite well in context they cannot be said to have

* I should like to express my thanks to Yuko, without whom this study would have been impossible; to her anthropology teacher, Karen Frojen, for allowing me to survey her class and giving me information on the course requirements; and to John Ingulsrud and Yasuko Watts, both of whom helped me to interpret Yuko's glosses.

been learned in the sense that they can be individually defined. The process of ascribing a precise set of semantic features to a particular word is necessarily a gradual one and will usually require several encounters in informative contexts. It is suggested, therefore, that teachers of English as a second language should provide as rich contextual support as possible for the vocabulary they teach, as well as giving some explicit instruction in syntactic and morphological analysis.

Anyone who has seen *Amadeus* will remember the Emperor Franz Josef's complaint about Mozart's music: "Too many notes." Students of English as a second language might well say something similar about English, especially when they go beyond the graded material of ESL classes to the linguistically uncontrolled texts of content courses. There are too many words. Consider, for example, the findings of Kučera and Francis (1967) in their count of a million running words of American English. In the whole corpus there were over 50,000 different words (word types, as the authors call them, in opposition to word tokens) of which more than 84% occurred no more than 10 times—and this 50,000 represents only a small proportion of the total lexicon (Hofland & Johansson, 1982, p. 39). Thus, once students have learned a basic vocabulary, they have an increasingly difficult task of expanding it to include those specialized, exact, or evocative terms that are the mark of the fully proficient language user.

These words—or at least most of the them—are not taught in their language classes. Vocabulary teaching takes a good deal of time, and it is simply not economic to spend precious minutes on items whose chances of reoccurrence are only 10 in a million. Consequently, the tradition in ESL teaching has been to consciously teach only the two thousand or so most frequent items (Thorndike, 1921; West, 1964; Bright & McGregor, 1970; van Ek & Alexander, 1975; Hindmarsh, 1980; Allen, 1983; Coady et al., Chapter 11, this volume); as for the less frequent ones, they are glossed in ESL textbooks when they crop up, but the purpose here is to facilitate comprehension of the text as a whole rather than to teach individual word meanings. There is no attempt—for how could there be?—to present new lexical items in a systematically representative way. So what it comes down to is that students have to expand their vocabularies on their own, learning the meanings of new words from the contexts in which they come across them, with, perhaps, the aid of a dictionary.

How successful are they likely to be? Not very, according to recent psycholinguistic research. Jenkins and Dixon (1983) report an experimental study of the acquisition of word meanings from context on the part of 5th graders: they found that learning did indeed take place, but "this learning does not come easily" and "the amount learned is not imposing" (p. 257), even though the students were reading in their first language (see also Jenkins, Stein & Wysocki, 1984). Van Daalen Kapteijns and Elshout-Mohr (1981), in a different kind of experiment, also found that adults had difficulty inferring the meaning of neologisms in their first language; the inferences they made were often incorrect. Again, more general work on the problems of Nigerian students reading in English (which is their third language) showed that the students had great difficulty in inferring the meanings of unfamiliar words, although these represented less than 1% of the whole text, and that, even when a word was familiar, students could misinterpret it, because they were unduly influenced either by the context in which they had originally learnt it or by relationships suggested by the lexicon of their second language, Hausa (Parry 1986, 1987a).[1] All these studies, then, raise serious questions about the challenge facing ESL students in the United States: What do such students do about the new vocabulary that they must come across as they study for content courses? What difficulties does it present for them? And is there any way in which these difficulties can be reduced? We cannot tell until we know a bit more than we do at present about what happens.

This chapter reports a longitudinal case study that was designed to address such questions, one of a series conducted at Hunter College of the City University of New York between 1986 and 1988. Selected ESL students who were enrolled in an Introductory Anthropology course were asked to record every new or difficult word that they came across in their anthropology textbooks and also to gloss, in their first language if they wished, what they guessed its meaning to be. They might then, but it was again optional, look the word up in a dictionary and record the definition they found there. From the lists produced by each student, the glosses were extracted and passed on to an interpreter who was proficient in both the student's language and English; this interpreter translated them back into English and then discussed with the researcher the degree to which each gloss represented the original. The results of the first such study are reported in Parry (1987b); this chapter reports the results of the second, which was conducted with a Japanese student called, for the purposes of discussion, Yuko.

At the beginning of this study in September 1987, Yuko had been in the United States for less than a year, and, since she was living with her family, she still spoke Japanese for much of the time. On her admission to Hunter she had been placed in the lowest level of the college's sequence of three ESL writing courses, and in the upper of its two developmental courses in reading. As for vocabulary knowledge, she scored 23 out of 40, or 57.5%, on the relevant section of the Michigan Test of English Language Proficiency. Thus she could expect to have language difficulties in her work for anthropology, a fact of which she was well aware and which made her more than willing to participate in this project.

In the course of the semester Yuko read some 93 pages of anthropology text,[2] representing a total of about 48,000 words. She recorded 168 of these, and made guesses at the meaning of 148 of them. Table 6.1 gives a classification of those guesses in terms of their relationship to the original items.

There are several striking points about these figures. First is the relatively small number of words glossed. This does not mean, of course, that Yuko really

Table 6.1. Overall Results

Estimated number of words read	48,000
Number of words recorded (c. 0.35% of words read)	168
Number of words glossed (89% of words recorded)	148
Correct glosses (33% of words recorded)	55
Incorrect glosses (20% of words recorded)	33
Partially correct glosses (36% of words recorded)	60

knew all the other words that she read—indeed, there is clear evidence that she did not, for sometimes a particular word is passed by, as if she knows it, and then it is recorded and glossed when it appears on a subsequent page; but it does indicate that she was able to read the rest without feeling that the unfamiliarity of many words was an impediment to comprehension. Much vocabulary acquisition is probably, therefore, unconscious; a new word is often not noticed because it appears in a text of which the general sense is understood. Some association, however, may be established for the word, an association which may well be reinforced at the next encounter and may perhaps be expressed in a gloss. To use a metaphor suggested by Aitchison (1987), a new "tunnel" may be opened in the network that connects auditory representation with semantic representation and general knowledge; the tunnel is neither "well worked" nor "well lit" at this stage, but it may become increasingly so with each subsequent encounter, and it also may be taken deeper so that the association becomes more detailed and precise (pp. 194–196).

A second point to note about the figures above is that Yuko, like the Rumanian student in the previous study (Parry, 1987b), is able to make a guess at the meaning of a very large proportion of those words that she records. It suggests that a second-language reader, even one of such limited proficiency as Yuko, puts an enormous amount of meaning into the text read, more than a child reading such texts in the first language is able to do. For Yuko, as an adult, has a far richer store of background knowledge, so that she is able to consider a wider range of potential meanings for the word in question, and has a much stronger sense of what might be plausible. This means that we cannot assume that people will learn vocabulary in the same way in their second language as in their first.

A third, and still more striking, point is the high degree of success that Yuko has in her guesses. Of 148 glosses more than a third were judged by the interpreters to be good translations, and less than a quarter were considered definitely wrong. As for the remaining two-fifths, they all were found to be in the right general area of meaning, although the glosses were not considered good Japanese representations of the originals. It seems that not only is an ESL reader able to bring a great deal of meaning to an English text, but for a remarkably high proportion of the time it is the right meaning. But in order to see just how right or wrong the meaning is, it is necessary to look at each of these categories in greater detail.

A gloss is most obviously correct when the interpreter, in translating it back into English, uses the same lexical item as the original. This occurred with the words *sap, emission, norm, carbohydrate, census, penitent,* and *shirk,* and in six other cases the interpreter used a different form of the same item, as when *altruism* was translated back as "to be altruistic." In 22 other cases the process of back-translation produced a synonym of the original, like "excrement" for *feces,* or "specialized knowledge" for *expertise.* The remaining "good translations" were ones where there is no exact equivalency between the two languages, the most frequent type being instances of imagery. For the English word *breakthrough,* for instance, Yuko produced a totally different image, "the mouth of the thread," but that was translated back by my interpreter as "clue to discovery," which means much the same thing as *breakthrough.* There were eight examples of such variation in imagery. Then there were five cases where Yuko had written a circumlocution that defines the word adequately, though it is not an exact equivalent, an example is "a person that researches genes biologically" for *geneticist.* There were three cases where the gloss was a superordinate, like "artificial things" for *artifacts,* which, in the absence of an exact equivalent in Japanese, my interpreter said was the best translation possible, and there were two instances of the correct meaning being given but in a different word-form class from the original. Finally, in the "good translation" category, there was one marvellously illustrative example of the impossibility of translating certain cultural concepts: Yuko gave "a male-only group" for *fraternity,* which, given that fraternities exist only in the United States, was, my interpreter said, as good a rendering as possible.[3]

The criterion for "wrong" is that, when the words are decontextualized, there seems to be no relationship between each original item and its gloss. This, as can be seen, is the case with all those listed in Table 6.2.

Of these 33 glosses, there are 4 that seem to make no sense at all. It is hard, for example, to imagine what Yuko was thinking when she guessed *patrilineal* to mean "leaning toward one position," having come across it in the sentence "Kinship is patrilineal, and a typical village consists of two lineages that have intermarried" (Plog & Bates, 1980, p. 125); and her guesses for *arbitrary, stymie,* and *etic* are similarly inexplicable. In the other 29 cases, however, the gloss does make sense in the context; the problem is that that sense is the wrong one. Sometimes this happens because Yuko is misled by the other words in the immediate environment. Her guess for *sedentary,* for example, as "to use vehicles" is reasonable enough in this passage:

The most obvious change that Kemp observed on Baffin Island is that the people have become *sedentary.* The snowmobiles and boats enable hunters to travel to their hunting grounds in a relatively short time. Thus it is not necessary for the whole village to pack up and move, as in the past. (Plog & Bates, 1980, p. 102)

Table 6.2. Incorrect Glosses

Original Word	Back Translation
refinement	idea, intuition; thinking
arbitrary	other decision, has decided
postulate	to mean
firsthand	basic, fundamental. primary
elucidation	results
sleds	furrow, track
stymie	perhaps, in general
stampede	gather (household objects)
sedentary	to use vehicles
patrilineal	leaning toward one position
intriguing	prosperous
lineage	assets
sire	to be separated
vernacular	standard, construction
etic	the goal is clear
bifurcation	discriminate
genealogy	typology
legitimize	give birth to, raise
prerequisite	stop, withdraw
embellishment	ceremony, festival, special occasion
predominantly	authoritarian
assertion	ability to choose, decision
rift	relation
facilitate	stop, withdraw
acquisition	quality, quantity
circumvent	devise, manage, contrive; manage carefully
besiege	pliable; receive
reverberation	natural resource, support
arbitrary	shape, pattern
terrace	equip, fix, consolidate; tame, break in
aggrandizement	sacrifice
astute	close, intimate; long
intrinsically	natural; normal

Although a clue to the correct meaning is given in the last sentence of the quotation, it is not surprising that Yuko is more attracted by the suggestion given in the sentence that immediately follows the word. In other instances the effect of the immediate context is not so obvious; the wrong—but entirely reasonable—interpretation seems to be derived from her general knowledge. That is probably how she guessed that *refinement* must mean "idea," having come across it in the following sentence:

> When a bird emits its danger call, that is the only call it can produce in that situation, and the bird cannot add any *refinement* to the call to indicate, for example, the source of the danger. (Plog & Bates, 1980, p. 16)

"Idea" is a good guess, but that is not what it means. Sometimes such guesses could lead to radical misinterpretation of the text. Consider, for example, *facilitate* in this sentence:

> During the colonial era, British officials attempted to organize and politically consolidate the Tiv of northern Nigeria in order to *facilitate* colonial administration. (Plog & Bates, 1980, p. 329)

Yuko glossed it as "stop" or "withdraw"; perhaps she was employing her knowledge of Britain's withdrawal from empire, which parallels Japan's, and the setting up of independent states. The results are disastrous as far as interpretation of this sentence is concerned.

It was far more common, however, for Yuko to get her glosses at least partly right; she did so for 36% of the words she listed. This means that even when the words and their glosses are decontextualized, there is a clear semantic relationship between them; although, since there is a much closer Japanese equivalent in each case, they cannot be said to be good translations. Such glosses are perhaps the most interesting, not only because they are the largest group (as they were in the previous study, Parry, 1987b), but also because they may tell us more than do either the right or the wrong glosses about how semantic representations come to be put upon lexical items, or, to revert to Aitchinson's metaphor, how the tunnels in the mental lexicon come to be built. What follows, therefore, is an attempt to define more precisely the relationship between each original item and the back-translation of its gloss; the resulting classification of these relationships is not watertight (for semantic categories are notoriously permeable), but it may prove to be provocative and therefore valuable.

First, there are relationships which are quite readily characterized in the terms used by such semanticists as Lyons (1977): superordination, hyponymy, and part-of relationships. There are a number of examples of superordination, where Yuko glosses a word by naming, not the equivalent in Japanese, but the superordinate category to which it belongs. The relationship might be indicated in a diagram, as in Figure 6.1.

Figure 6.1.   Superordination

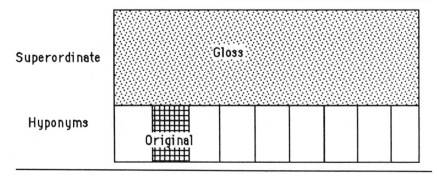

Here is a list of those cases (Table 6.3):

Table 6.3. Glosses Representing Superordinate Categories

Original Word	Back-Translation of Gloss
flogging	hit
forage	gather
husbandry	agricultural
substantivist	modernism person
staple	necessary articles
glean	gather
vagary	change
tenure	control, have
vengeance	punishment

Hyponymy is illustrated in Figure 6.2:

Figure 6.2. Hyponymy

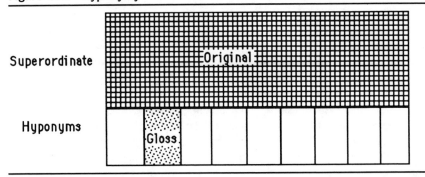

It occurs much less frequently, and this study produced only one example (see Table 6.4):

Table 6.4. Gloss Representing a Hyponym of the Original

Original Word	Back-Translation of Gloss
vegetation	a cluster of plants

Part-of relationships are illustrated in Figures 6.3 and 6.4:

Figure 6.3. Part-of relationship

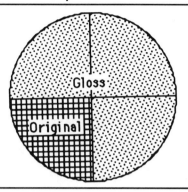

Figure 6.4. Part-of relationship

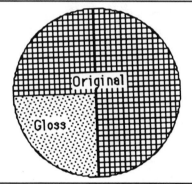

This kind of relationship is also rare; Yuko's gloss in one case names the whole of which the original is a part, and in another it names a part of which the original is the whole (see Table 6.5):

Table 6.5. Glosses That Have a Part-of Relationship with the Original

Part-whole

Original word	Back translation
nutrient	fertilizer

Whole-part

Original word	Back translation
platform	board

It is slightly more common for Yuko to name in her gloss another member of the same class as the original. This is illustrated in Figure 6.5:

Figure 6.5. Members of the same superordinate category

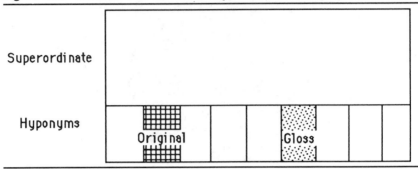

The instances are in the following list (Table 6.6):

Table 6.6. Glosses Representing Different Members of the Same Superordinate Category as the Original

Original Word	Back Translation
harpoon	javelin
vex	to frighten
avunculocal	the family of my paternal grandfather
artisan	artist
silt	sand
reservoir	well

By far the largest group, however, cannot be described in such terms but rather in terms of componential analysis (cf. Nida, 1964, pp. 90–93). In these cases the gloss overlaps with the original word in meaning, sharing with it some semantic components but differing from it in others. There are three possible variations of this relationship, as shown in Figures 6.6–6.8.

To classify glosses in terms of these variations it is necessary to identify the components in question. This is done in the lists given in Tables 6.7–6.9.

Generally speaking, when meaning is added or subtracted in this way, it has little adverse effect on the interpretation of the text; in other words, Yuko does seem to have got the defining feature for the word in that particular context. She glosses *lurid*, for example, as ''frightening'' or ''repellent,'' thus both adding

Figure 6.6.   Gloss subtracts meaning

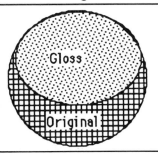

Figure 6.7.   Gloss adds meaning

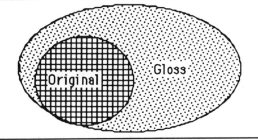

Figure 6.8.   Gloss both adds and subtracts meaning

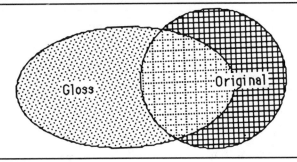

and subtracting components; but her interpretation is quite adequate for the word as it appears in this passage:

> Ignorant of Christianity and bent on strange and exotic practices, these societies were usually portrayed in the most *lurid* terms. Cannibalism in particular caught the imagination of the European observers. (Plog & Bates, 1980, p. 3)

Table 6.7.   Glosses that Subtract from the Meaning of the Original

Original Word	Back Translation	Common Component(s)	Different Component(s)
vitally	in an important way, in a valuable way	[important] [in a way]	– [to life]
predominantly	dominating	[dominance]	– [in a way]
demise	failure	[cessation]	– [death]
pool (verb)	present (verb)	[give]	– [with others]
demographer	population count, statistic	[population] [numbers] [documentation]	– [person knowledgeable in]
encampment	lodge; lodging	[dwelling place] [temporary]	– [out of doors]
infrastructure	structure, organization	[organization]	– [backing for other activity]
ecosystem	ecological connection	[ecology]	– [system]
fallow	not cultivated	[lack of cultivation]	– [restorative purpose]
criterion	importance, foundation	[basis]	– [for judgement]
vis-a-vis	to be involved, to relate	[relationship]	– [towards]
stipulate	point out	[state]	– [require]

Table 6.8.   Glosses that Add to the Meaning of the Original

Original Word	Back Translation	Common Component(s)	Different Component(s)
egalitarian	a person who is egalitarian	[belief] [equality]	+ [person]
segment	example	[part of whole]	+ [purpose] + [illustration]
indigenous	the natural resources of the locality	[of the locality]	+ [natural] + [resources]
depletion	misuse, waste	[reduction]	+ [irresponsibility]
proportionate	balance	[ratio]	+ [equality]
vie	conquer	[competition]	+ [battle] + [win]
devolve	responsibility	[pass down]	+ [responsibility]
locus	society, status, origin	[position]	+ [social] + [starting point]
estrange	separated, divorce	[relationship] [failed]	+ [marriage] + [legal]
depleted	to be used	[reduction]	+ [use]
hereditary	a fortune, legacy, inherit	[inheritance]	+ [property]
corollary	result	[link]	+ [causation]

Table 6.9. Glosses that Both Add To and Subtract From the Meaning of the Original

Original Word	Back Translation	Common Component(s)	Different Component(s)
lurid	frightening, repellent	[unpleasant]	+[frightening] −[sensational]
predator	looter, raider	[hostile]	+[human] +[theft] −[animal]
cognitive	already knows, known	[knowing]	+[state] −[purpose]
converge	is being influenced	[similarity]	+[effect] −[independence]
disruptive	chaotic, crazy	[confusion]	+[state] −[causative]
nurturance	raise (of education)	[care]	+[education] −[food-giving]
informants	a person who gathers information	[person] [information]	+[gathers] −[gives]
preposterous	low, vulgar, not good	[unacceptable]	+[low social rank]
stratification	policy, status	[social rank]	+[position] −[process]
herding	raise (of animals in a barn)	[care of animals]	+[barn] −[open range]
terminology	quotation, citation	[language]	+[quotation of text] −[individual words]
exogamous	intermarriage	[marriage]	+[between groups]
realm	within the limits of	[area]	+[limit] −[kingdom]
sever	let go	[terminate]	+[release] −[cut]
incense	to be afraid	[emotion]	+[fear] −[anger] −[causative]
predator	enemy, foreign enemy	[hostile]	+[person] −[animal]
dissemination	exchange	[passing from one person to another]	+[reciprocity] −[direction from center]
exacerbate	deteriorate, grow worse	[change] [worse]	+[inchoative] −[causative]

The sense of the whole is obviously understood. The same can be said of *terminology* in this passage, a word which Yuko glossed as "quotation," thus again adding and subtracting meaning:

Without using the *terminology* of Frank's thesis, Neichtmann describes the development of poverty and under-development among the Miskito Indians. (Cole, 1982, p. 216)

There is a more serious problem, however, when the difference is in a more general feature, one that determines the syntagmatic relations into which the item may enter rather than its paradigmatic, or associative, relations with other items in the lexicon (Saussure, 1966, pp. 123–124). Yuko interprets *exacerbate*, for example, as "deteriorate," having encountered it in this context:

> Intensification *exacerbated* the problems it was designed to solve. Farmers found they were working longer hours for diminishing returns. (Plog & Bates, 1980, p. 165)

In the paradigmatic dimension the guess is a good one, for both *exacerbate* and the Japanese word expressed here as "deteriorate" contain the defining feature [worsen]; but in the syntagmatic dimension it is wrong, for while *exacerbate* is transitive, "deteriorate" is what is technically known as an *inchoative* verb, or one that expresses a change in its subject (Dillon, 1977, p. 35). Yuko, it seems, has interpreted *the problems* as the subject of this verb, and so, though she has understood the general sense of the text, she has misinterpreted the syntax. This does not matter much here, but it could well cause misunderstanding in other instances, and such an interpretation of the verb is, of course, likely to lead to mistakes in her own writing.

There is also a problem when Yuko fails to interpret the morphological structure of the words she encounters. Her glosses for *disruptive* ("chaotic, crazy") and *cognitive* ("already knows, known"), for instance, show that, although she is in the right area of meaning, she does not appreciate how the adjective relates to the noun it qualifies. That relationship is expressed by the suffix *-ive*, which, in each case, signals an underlying proposition: *disruptive* in the context qualifies *behavior*, so that the underlying proposition is "behavior causes disruption"; *cognitive* qualifies *structures*, thus signaling the proposition "structures cause (or enable) cognition." Similarly she interprets *informant*, as "someone who collects information," whereas the underlying proposition, signalled by the suffix *-ant*, is quite the opposite: "someone *gives* information." This is quite a serious mistake, for it radically alters the referential meaning in the sentence, "Informants often do not remember relevant details accurately" (Plog & Bates, 1980, p. 47). Yuko is evidently not yet sensitive to such morphological clues, not surprisingly, for it is difficult to define precisely how they work.

In addition to showing something of both the potential and the limitations for ESL learners of guessing word meanings from context, this study also shows a little of the incremental process by which precise representations of word meaning are presumably built up; for it will be noticed that several items appear more than once. One of these is *predator*, which appears on the list she made on September 9, and then on the one dated December 7; she had obviously had plenty of time to forget the word. Her first guess for it is "looter, raider"— definitely a person, and one who robs, so she has added at least two semantic components, as well as losing the original's primary sense of a nonhuman animal. Then a correct dictionary definition is given: "carnivorous animal, predatory person." Her second guess again drops the component of [animal] and adds that of [person]; but the notion of robbery is now lost, for the gloss translations back as "enemy, foreign enemy." Can we interpret this as a first step towards the correct representation of the word? The changes in the guesses are not always positive, however, for, in the case of *artisan*, Yuko guessed the meaning correctly on the first occasion, when the gloss translated back as "craftsman"; but on the second she added a component which made it slightly wrong, her gloss being translated as "artist."

The fact that Yuko looked a word up in the dictionary could itself sometimes lead her to a wrong guess the second time the word appeared. On September 14, for example, she noted *predominantly* and glossed it as "dominating," a correct gloss, except that it lacks one of those morphologically marked components that determine the possible syntagmatic relations into which the item may enter; but in the context "The *predominantly* speculative nature of early evolutionary theories," this deficiency does not much matter. Then she looked the word up in the dictionary and wrote down "having superiority in power, influence, or control," still missing the morphological marker. Not long afterwards, on September 29, the word came up in a passage about marriage practices among the Eskimo:

> Beyond these *predominantly* economically oriented activities and sexual intercourse, there was little involved in the relationship, at least ideally. (Cole, 1982, p. 120)

Yuko's gloss is translated as "authoritarian," suggesting that her guess was inspired by some, probably unconscious, recollection of the definition found 3 weeks previously. There is no way of knowing her exact interpretation of the word in the sentence, but it seems clear that she missed the significance of the suffix once again, and this, together with the broader context, may have led her to think that the word referred to the authority of the husband over the wife, in which case she missed the point entirely.

A final instance is the word *arbitrary* and its derivatives, which appeared three times, in these three contexts:

> What distinguishes symbols from signs is that a symbol is *arbitrary*. It stands for a thing only because the people who use the symbol agree that it does. (Plog & Bates, 1980, p. 16)

> This does not mean a haphazard selection, such as going into a room and *arbitrarily* interviewing ten people. (Plog & Bates, 1980, p. 51)

> This flexibility is made possible by the *arbitrariness* of human language. Unlike animal calls, the sounds of a language have no fixed meaning. (Plog & Bates, 1980, p. 196.)

Yuko seems to have had difficulty with this item: Her first guess for it is "other decision; has decided," which is one of those glosses which apparently make no sense at all; the second time no gloss is even attempted; and the one for the third time is "shape, pattern" which does make sense, but not the right one. Here there is no apparent building up towards the right meaning. Maybe, however, that is again because Yuko was misled by her dictionary, for the dictionary definition she records on the first two occasions is little better than her guesses: "not absolute, having only relative application." The third time she records the dictionary definition, she is, interestingly enough, nearer the mark: "founded on or subject to personal whims, prejudices; not absolute." Perhaps, after all, there is a progression, and her growing sense of the word's meaning has helped her to interpret the dictionary definition more accurately.

Overall, however, Yuko seems to be doing rather well—much better than might have been expected. Her success, however, does not allow ESL teachers to abdicate responsibility for vocabulary: They should at the least know what is happening and help the process along if they can. So the question now is what these observations show about vocabulary acquisition in general, and whether they offer any suggestions for ESL classes. For, while Yuko is only one individual, and individuals can vary greatly, this study has provided some important information.

First, Yuko has demonstrated conclusively that she can and does derive representations of meaning from context, and in this she confirms the findings of a previous study with a more advanced Rumanian student (Parry, 1987b), as well as those of Saragi, Nation, and Meister (1978) in their study of readers learning the *nadsat* vocabulary in *A Clockwork Orange*. Note, however, that the context in all these cases is a very broad one: Yuko, for instance, could draw on information that went far beyond the individual sentence or paragraph, for she was reading two books on the subject and listening to lectures on it every week. That explains why her guesses are so much more successful than the experimental studies cited at the beginning of this article would lead us to expect; for these studies were based on only short passages. The observation suggests a moral for language teaching: To facilitate vocabulary growth, instructors should try to replicate this richness of context by constructing their own courses on thematic rather than grammatical or rhetorical lines, and by using as reading materials whole books, or else selections that are grouped according to their unity of content.

Second, Yuko has shown that, while a guess from context is usually in the right general area of meaning, it is also, more often than not, different in some respect from the generally accepted interpretation of the item in question. Often this does not matter as far as general comprehension is concerned; but it can lead to serious misunderstanding if the different components have to do with the syntagmatic relations into which the item may enter (as with *predominantly*), or with the relations that obtain between the components within the item (as in the case of *informant*). For students like Yuko, therefore, it seems important to teach something of English morphology, so that they can recognize both signals of syntactic function, like the *-ly* suffix, and those of an underlying proposition, like *-ant*. Yuko would also probably profit from some lessons in understanding the sentence patterns in which new items appear; for it is native speakers' knowledge of the constraints of English sentence structure that make it impossible for them to interpret the blank in "Intensification _____ed the problems" as an inchoative verb.

Third, the fact that a word is encountered and its meaning is guessed does not mean that it will be immediately learned—even when the student is asked, as in this case, to write the word and its guessed meaning down. Vocabulary learning is clearly a gradual business; but this does not matter as much as it would seem, because so much can be derived from context, if the context is sufficiently broad. This explains why Yuko could do so well in her guesses and still do badly on vocabulary and reading tests: at the end of term she was given a second form of the Michigan Test, in which she did little better than previously, getting 23 out of 40; nor did she pass the exit exam for her reading course, which like most reading tests consists of a series of short passages with three or four tasks on each. Such a low score suggests that both these kinds of test may, in cases like Yuko's, seriously underestimate the students' linguistic ability.

Yuko has, therefore, provided some helpful insights into how a vocabulary in a second language can be extended by general reading. Moreover, these insights are not entirely idiosyncratic, for the analysis of Yuko's glosses reproduced the pattern found in the previous study, and the findings of two subsequent studies have proved in many ways similar (Parry, 1991). Nevertheless, a great deal of work remains to be done. We need to know more about the process by which Yuko and others arrive at their guesses (see Huckin & Bloch, Chapter 8, this volume), on how the words guessed at are stored in memory, and on the differences both of background knowledge and of strategy that must exist between individuals. The case study method described here has proved productive, but many more cases must be examined—in even more detail than is this one here—before teachers can give informed advice to their students on how to deal with the multitudinous words of English.

REFERENCES

Aitchison, J. (1987). *Words in the mind: An introduction to the mental lexicon.* Oxford: Basil Blackwell.

Allen, V. F. (1983). *Techniques in teaching vocabulary.* New York: Oxford University Press.

Bright, J. A., & McGregor, G. P. (1970). *Teaching English as a second language: Theory and techniques for the secondary stage.* London: Longman.

Cole, J. B. (Ed.). (1982). *Anthropology for the eighties: Introductory readings*. New York: The Free Press.

Dillon, G. L. (1977). *Introduction to contemporary linguistic semantics*. Englewood Cliffs, NJ: Prentice-Hall.

Hindmarsh, R. (1980). *The Cambridge English lexicon*. Cambridge, UK: Cambridge University Press.

Hofland, K., & Johansson, S. (1982). *Word frequencies in British and American English*. Harlow, UK: Longman.

Jenkins, J. R., & Dixon, R. (1983). Vocabulary learning. *Contemporary Educational Psychology, 8,* 237–260.

Jenkins, J. R., Stein, M. L., & Wysocki, K. (1984). Learning vocabulary through reading. *American Educational Research Journal, 21,* 767–788.

Kučera, H., & Francis, W. N. (1967). *Computational analysis of present-day American English*. Providence, RI: Brown University Press.

Lyons, J. (1977). *Semantics*. Cambridge, UK: Cambridge University Press.

Nida, E. (1964). *Toward a science of translating*. Leiden: E. J. Brill.

Parry, K. J. (1986). *Readers in context: A Study of Northern Nigerian students and School Certificate texts*. Unpublished Doctoral dissertation, Teachers College, Columbia University.

Parry, K. J. (1987a). Reading in a second culture. In P. Carrell, J. Devine, & D. Eskey (Eds.), *Research in reading in English as a secónd language*. Washington, DC: TESOL.

Parry, K. J. (1987b). Learning vocabulary through an academic subject: A case study. In S. Dicker & L. Fox (Eds.), *Improving the odds: Helping ESL students succeed: Selected papers from the 1987 CUNY ESL Council Conference*. New York: Instructional Resource Center, Office of Academic Affairs, the City University of New York.

Parry, K. J. (1991). Building a vocabulary through academic reading. *TESOL Quarterly, 25* (4), 629–653.

Plog, F., & Bates, D. G. (1980). *Cultural anthropology*. New York: Alfred Knopf.

Saragi, P., Nation, I. S. P., & Meister, G. F. (1978). Vocabulary learning and reading. *System, 6*(2), 72–78.

Saussure, F. (1966). *Course in general linguistics*. New York: McGraw Hill.

Thorndike, E. L. (1921). *The teacher's word book*. New York: Teachers College, Columbia University.

van Daalen-Kapteijns, N., & Elshout-Mohr, M. (1981). The acquisition of word meaning as a cognitive learning process. *Journal of Verbal Learning and Verbal Behavior, 20,* 386–399.

van Ek, J., & Alexander, L. (1975). *Threshold level English*. Oxford, UK: Pergamon Press.

West, M. P. (1964). *A general service list of English words*. London: Longman.

ENDNOTES

1. These students, as is common in Nigeria, all spoke at least three languages: their mother tongue, such as Higgi or Chamba; Hausa, which is a *lingua franca*; and

English. I am able to comment only on the influence of Hausa, rather than that of their first languages, because the latter are too numerous, and I do not know them.

2. The texts used were *Cultural Anthropology*, by Fred Plog and Daniel G. Bates (1980), and *Anthropology for the Eighties*, edited by Johnetta B. Cole (1982).

3. The context was: ''All men are likewise of one category, but when combined with other criteria, they can form business*men*'s clubs, social organizations like *fraternities*, and hate groups such as the Ku Klux Klan'' (Cole, 1982, p. 102).

Editorial Comments

This longitudinal case study of a fairly weak L2 reader literate in a noncognate language focuses on the accuracy of her glosses for words which she judged to be new or difficult in the required textbook for her anthropology course. She provided glosses for 90% of the words she selected. About a third of these glosses were adequate, while incorrect interpretations were given for about a fifth of them. The remaining words, a little over a third of those recorded as new, had glosses with appropriate components of meaning, but the glosses were either too general, too specific, or lacked critical features of the English word's meaning in that context. Parry interprets these findings as generally favorable toward learning vocabulary from reading, since vocabulary learning should be seen as a long-term process in which the reader moves through multiple encounters with a word toward more precise grasp of the concept that word represents.

Parry's research is particularly important, because it is a longitudinal case study, a type of study needed to supplement what we can learn from group studies in this area of language research. This type of analysis is not common because it is so time consuming and painstaking for both researchers and participants. Working with qualitative data (glosses which were translated, back-translated, and then evaluated in terms of the original word's meaning) also presents difficulties with rater reliability (or translator reliability) and subjectivity. But such research is especially worthwhile for the insights it gives us into vocabulary acquisition—insights such as the surprising accuracy of the reader's glosses, the systematicity of her deviations from original word meaning, and the incremental nature of her vocabulary learning.

Parry arrives at some conclusions that have important implications for pedagogy. First, learners can make successful guesses at the meanings of unknown words when they encounter them in a rich and meaningful context, and especially when they have good background knowledge of the material being studied (as long as this background knowledge does not conflict with information in the text—see Holmes & Ramos, Chapter 5, and Haynes & Baker, Chapter 7, this volume). Reading in the context of class instruction is in many ways an ideal case for vocabulary acquisition. If the student has already been exposed to some of the content through class lectures, there should be a significant amount of cognitive processing time/space left available for interpreting new words in context. This would suggest that we should give learners longer texts which treat material they are already familiar with, even if there are large numbers of unknown words.

However, this approach may help content learning more than word learning, according to Stahl et al. (1989). In a series of carefully controlled group studies with one social studies text, these researchers failed to find interaction between content instruction and difficulty of vocabulary in the text. They suggest that instruction helps readers' "macroprocessing" (developing a summary of the text) but does not aid their "microprocessing" (developing a detailed construction of the ideas in the order they appear in the text—see Kintsch & van Dijk, 1978, who introduced these terms). Thus Stahl et al. propose that gaining richer background knowledge only enables students to get a better general idea of the text, not to learn specific word meanings. A related finding from another group study is Omanson's (1985) conclusion that, rather than substituting appropriate synonyms or concepts for unknown words, readers tend to leave a conceptual blank for them. This might explain why it would be difficult for prior knowledge to have a positive effect when new words are encountered. In any case, Parry's work demonstrates clearly that group studies need to be complemented by case study approaches in order to sort through such conflicting conclusions. Both approaches are needed to address key questions, such as when and how comprehension of content and learning of new vocabulary *do* interact, across texts and context, longitudinally.

Parry concludes that, although "vocabulary learning is clearly a gradual business," this is not such a crucial handicap if students can, in fact, take advantage of the rich and extensive contexts of an academic course, encountering words a number of times within a single discipline (see also Brown, Chapter 13, this volume, for unusual evidence in support of multiple encounters for word learning). Thus, vocabulary learning from reading should be seen as a long-term process in which the reader moves through multiple encounters with a word toward more precise grasp of the concept that word represents.

Another pedagogical implication of Parry's work involved the near-misses of her guesser. Parry reports that, although guesses are usually close to the meaning intended, they are often not appropriate in their syntactic interpretation. This can lead to problems when the same word is encountered in other contexts. Accordingly, Parry suggests that we teach English morphology directly.

Parry's learner, like Werner and Kaplan's (1952) young L1 guessers, also seemed sometimes to focus on features of meaning more closely tied to the sentence as a whole than to the lexical item's unique contribution to the meaning of the sentence. In other words, Parry's reader missed the meaning of words in ways which showed the focus of attention was on the ongoing meaning of the text. This is not a wholly unfavorable tendency, but it, too is likely to cause problems when readers encounter the same word later in a different context. It appears that, for both L1 and L2 readers, there may be a developmental universal, that readers have difficulty isolating a concept from the ongoing message.

One of the most valuable contributions of Parry's work, we feel, is the systematic examination of the similarities and differences between intended meaning of the author and inferred meaning of the reader. Parry's Venn diagrams and specific examples of convergent and divergent word meanings provide a fascinating introduction to lexical semantics, a relatively neglected area of linguistics. Her work also demonstrates the paradoxical situation in which we find ourselves today. On the one hand, models of human word knowledge which are built from individual features appear to be wrong, because human conceptual categories are more indefinite and flexible than feature models would allow (Smith & Medin, 1981). On the other hand, Parry shows us that, as researchers, we can learn a great deal about vocabulary acquisition by adopting a feature model of word meaning as a reference point, a heuristic for analyzing the degrees to which a word's meaning is understood.

REFERENCES

Kintsch, W., & van Dijk, T. A. (1978). Toward a model of text comprehension and production. *Psychological Review, 85*, 363–394.

Omanson, R. C. (1985). Knowing words and understanding texts. In T. H. Carr (Ed.), *The development of reading skills* (New directions for child development, No. 27, 35–54), San Francisco: Jossey-Bass.

Smith, E., & Medin, D. (1981). *Categories and concepts.* Cambridge, MA: Harvard University Press.

Stahl, S. A., Jacobson, M. G., Davis, C. E., & Davis, R. (1989). Prior knowledge and difficult vocabulary in the comprehension of unfamiliar text. *Reading Research Quarterly 24* (1), 27–43.

Werner, H., & Kaplan, B. (1952). The acquisition of word meanings: a developmental study. *Monographs for the Society for Research in Child Development 15*. Evanston, IL: Child Development Publications.

Chapter 7
American and Chinese Readers Learning from Lexical Familiarization in English Text

Margot Haynes
English Division
Delta College
University Center, MI

Ila Baker

This study explores the reasons that college students in Taiwan are less successful than their American counterparts in learning new word meanings from reading an English text, whether picking up meanings incidentally or attending to the task of word learning. Focusing on lexical familiarizations—relatively overt clues to word meaning often provided by writers of textbooks or technical texts—the authors argue that linguistic factors rather than reading strategies provide the most convincing explanation of the differences between these L1 and L2 readers. The evidence includes: (a) performance of the groups on grammar, vocabulary, and L1 reading tests; (b) observation of strategic scanning and illustration use; and (c) differences in comprehension of stipulations, the specific meanings given to certain words in this text about skin wounds. From this study of reading process and product, the authors conclude that the most significant handicap for these L2 readers is not inflexible reading strategies but insufficient vocabulary knowledge in English.

INTRODUCTION

When a word-form and its new concept are introduced and explained in a text, a reader's comprehension of that new word is an important indicator of that reader's general ability to learn from reading. Thus, when a text gives information about a new concept, word-learning becomes a microcosm of reading comprehension.

For this reason, a careful look at the product and process of word-learning may provide some answers to basic questions about learners' comprehension difficulties in L2 (second language) reading: To what extent are problems due to readers' strategic inflexibility (Coady, 1979; Hosenfeld, 1984; Block, 1986), their lack of reading strategies in both L1 and L2? To what extent is limited linguistic proficiency in English to blame (Yorio, 1971; Clarke, 1979)? Would better knowledge of the grammar or vocabulary of the language enable them to comprehend, regardless of reading strategies? Most studies have not provided enough information to address these questions fairly, since they lacked background information about participants' native language reading skill and L2 linguistic proficiency (Alderson, 1984). The research project reported here explores the similarities and differences between Chinese and Americans who are learning new words from reading, in order to project a clearer picture of the components of L2 comprehension success.

In this chapter we have three goals: (a) to compare the word-learning success of L2 college readers with that of comparable American readers; (b) to compare the effects of strategic and linguistic skill on learning new vocabulary from reading; and (c) to better understand the process of concept learning from reading by looking closely at an important type of guessing-from-context task, learning from lexical familiarization in written text.

According to Bramki and Williams (1984), *lexical familiarization* is "a contextual aid, intentionally and explicitly provided by the author" in order to familiarize a specific readership with words appearing for the first time in the text (p. 170). Sometimes lexical familiarization appears as a direct definition in the text, but it can take other linguistic form through a synonym or example as well as nonlinguistic form in illustrations or diagrams. Bramki and Williams consider lexical familiarization to be a unique type of contextual clue in that the author has intentionally provided it to assist readers in dealing with new terminology.

There are many good reasons for studying how readers learn from lexical familiarization. First, if students can comprehend lexical familiarizations in scientific or technical text, they will be better prepared to gain new knowledge from reading in educational and professional contexts. Also, since lexical familiarization is deliberately supplied by an author aware of the limited knowledge of the intended readership, it should be among the more obvious types of context clues. Thus a study of how readers handle lexical familiarization provides a strong test of readers' ability to use context in learning vocabulary through reading. In addition, as mentioned at the outset, lexical familiarization presents an opportunity to study comprehension processes and outcomes in a relatively well-defined, specific domain, that of word learning from reading.

SELECTION OF TEXT, WORDS, AND FAMILIARIZATIONS

The first step was to find an appropriate text for both American and Chinese readers, one which had enough examples of lexical familiarization yet was still understandable to readers with no prior expertise in the content area. In fact, given what we have learned from schema-theoretic studies of reading about the potential impact of differential background knowledge (Anderson & Pearson, 1984; Carrell, 1983), the ideal was a text with universally accessible topic and organization. Originally the goal was to find such a text with a number of examples of linguistic familiarization of new concepts. However, academic texts with a high proportion of lexical familiarizations tended to use illustrations as well as linguistic devices. It was finally decided, on grounds of ecological validity, to choose a text which included both linguistic and nonlinguistic lexical familiarizations.

The choice which best satisfied criteria of universality as well as of richness in lexical familiarizations was one about the treatment of skin wounds. It is the beginning of the second chapter of *Childhood Injury*, by J. Shiller, M.D. (1977).[1] This book was written for a lay audience, in particular parents, to help them decide when an injured child needs special medical care. Though the content is technical, with frequent reference to medical terminology, the author takes care to familiarize his readership with new terms or restricted meanings for familiar terms (the first two pages of the text are shown in Figure 7.1).

A total of 15 words from this text were included in the study, but only six of these will be discussed in detail here: *cuts, lacerations, Langer's lines, approximation, suturing,* and *bandaging.*

The words *cuts* and *lacerations* are both defined as types of skin wounds; however, their definitions include a narrower meaning than in common usage. In this case *cuts* mean "smooth, clean slices," in contrast with *lacerations,* which are "jagged, rough tears." This narrowing of meaning has been classified by Bramki and Williams (1984) as a special type of lexical familiarization, called *stipulation.* For Bramki and Williams, a stipulation is defined by the fact that the author explicitly "restricts the use of a term to a particular subject-field" (p. 178). Here is one example of a stipulation:

Figure 7.1.

2

Cuts and Lacerations— Do They Need Stitches?

Cuts, meaning smooth, clean slices through skin, and lacerations, which are jagged, rough tears of the skin, occur in a variety of sizes, shapes and locations. They usually heal, with or without help and with more or less scarring, if a reasonable amount of care and cleanliness is provided.

However, they will heal more quickly and with less scarring if the edges of the wound are brought together. How best to do this is the problem and an understanding of the properties of skin and how wound healing occurs will be helpful in solving it.

PROPERTIES OF SKIN THAT INFLUENCE HEALING

Mobility and Elasticity

Skin is both *mobile* and *elastic*. The mobility of skin is best demonstrated where it covers a joint. Consider the skin of your wrist. As the wrist is cocked up and down, the skin moves considerably to accommodate the swing of the hand.

Look at your wrist closely. It has furrows or ridges which run transversely across the wrist. These are called

CUTS AND LACERATIONS—NEED STITCHES?   43

Langer's lines. (Fig. 2-1) Because of the mobility of the skin, when it is cut in the *same* direction as these lines, the wound edges are easy to pull together and less scarring is apt to occur.

On the other hand, when skin is cut perpendicular to Langer's lines, the *elasticity* of skin becomes more obvious because the wound edges *retract* and even the most finely incised line becomes a gaping wound. As you will see below, the direction of a skin cut as it relates to Langer's

Figure 2-1.

In the Penguin Dictionary of Economics (1972), for example, the term land is stipulated in the following way: 'Land' in Economics is taken to mean not simply that part of the earth's surface not covered by water, but also the 'free gifts of nature' such as minerals, soil, fertility, etc. (Bramki & Williams, 1984, p. 178)

In this study, we extended the meaning of stipulation to include components of word-meaning which were particularly salient in the context of this particular subject-matter and text, even if the author did not directly state a contrast with the common meaning. For example, here *cuts* are not any kind of wound to the skin, but only those wounds which break the skin in a straight line, while the stipulation for *lacerations* is that they are uneven wounds.[2]

The term *Langer's lines* is given explicit definition in the text. In addition, we decided that this term should be characterized by a stipulated meaning, so that we could capture experimentally the distinction between comprehending the illustration (see Figure 7.1) and comprehending the text. Pilot testing with both native and nonnative readers had indicated that readers tended to interpret the picture as showing muscle lines beneath the skin. However, in the context of the topic, how to deal with skin wounds, and of the familiarization devices "Look at your wrist closely" and "furrows or ridges which run transversely across the wrist," *Langer's lines* must be pictured on the surface of the skin. It was apparent that, for some readers, overreliance on the picture was leading to misinterpretations. Therefore we decided to treat the concept that the lines were on the surface of the skin as a stipulated meaning so we could distinguish between readers who overrelied on the illustration and those who successfully integrated text with illustration.

For the words *approximation, suturing*, and *bandaging*, the stipulation was determined by the fact that, in this particular text, the emphasis is on the purpose of these techniques: to hold the edges of a wound together (see Figure 7.2). This stipulation is closely connected to the theme of the text as a whole, the relation between characteristics of the skin and methods of treating wounds.

Comprehension of stipulated meanings requires a fine-tuning of word interpretation rather than the automatic activation and selection of already-known word meanings (Swinney, 1979; Kintsch & Mross, 1985), which, according to Rayner and Pollatsek (1989), is more characteristic of fluent reading. However, Clark and Gerrig (1983) suggest that much of L1 spoken language comprehension involves the listener in "sense creation" rather than automatic activation and selection of each word's meanings, which they call "sense selection." For the reader, as for the listener, interpretation of word-forms such as *Langer's lines* involves creation of a new meaning from the elements of lexical familiarization in the text. With already familiar word-forms such as *cuts, lacerations, approximation*, or *bandaging*, however, there may be various degrees of conflict between (a) the word meaning(s) automatically activated by the familiar form, and (b) the meaning specified by the lexical familiarization (see Duffy, Morris &

Figure 7.2.

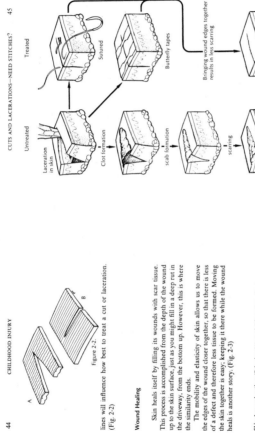

44   CHILDHOOD INJURY

Figure 2-2.

lines will influence how best to treat a cut or laceration. (Fig. 2-2)

Wound Healing

Skin heals itself by filling its wounds with scar tissue. This process is accomplished from the depth of the wound up to the skin surface, just as you might fill in a deep rut in the driveway, from the bottom up. However, this is where the similarity ends.

The mobility and elasticity of skin allows us to move the edges of the wound closer together, so that there is less of a defect and therefore less tissue to be formed. Moving the skin together is easy; keeping it there while the wound heals is another story. (Fig. 2-3)

Skin Approximation (Bringing Wound Edges Together)

The two most common methods of keeping wound edges together are suturing (stitching) and bandaging (taping). From time to time, other methods have been

CUTS AND LACERATIONS—NEED STITCHES?   45

Untreated   Treated

Laceration in skin

Sutured

Clot formation

Butterfly tapes

scab formation

Bringing wound edges together results in less scarring

scarring

Figure 2-3.

Rayner, 1988). Thus, by including the dimension of stipulation in this study we can begin to look at how successfully readers operate when the context calls for more conscious "sense creation" instead of or alongside their more typical process of automatic "sense activation" (see Rayner & Pollatsek, 1989, pp. 19–36).

PARTICIPANTS

In this study, there were two L2 learner groups and one L1 group. The L2 learners were college freshmen and seniors in Taiwan, the Republic of China (25 freshmen and 29 seniors). The freshmen had completed 6 years of secondary school English, taught largely through grammar-translation. Having passed a highly competitive exam which placed them in a prestigious university, they were among the top 10% of graduating high schoolers. The seniors were similar in background, except that they had had considerably more experience with reading English for information. They had all finished a year of college English, taught for the most part by native speakers of English, and had all completed 3 years of coursework requiring mostly English textbooks.

These Taiwan college students represent the intellectual capital of the country. Many of them will come to the U.S. for further study, entering programs in which they must keep up with American graduate students. It makes sense to compare their learning from lexical familiarization with that of American students like those with whom they may study upon graduation. Thus the third group in this study included nine American undergraduates from a large midwestern university.

PROCEDURE

This study included three meetings with each subject. During the first meeting, students were given group-administered vocabulary, grammar, and L1 reading tests. During the second meeting, an individual session, various measures of reading speed and comprehension were taken.[3] The third session is the one of concern here (see Table 7.1).

Before focusing on word guessing, the individual student was asked to read the passage, then write a free recall in order to construct a global sense of the passage. After this, the student reread the passage, underlining any words which had caused comprehension problems on the previous reading. This yielded a set of words for which the reader had conscious awareness of difficulty. Then the student was given a list of the 15 words in the experiment and asked to provide a category and definition for each one, without referring back to the text. At the end of the list any other words marked by the students were also included for definition. The categories and definitions written for the 15 lexically familiarized words provided the first measure of word learning from reading.

The student was then guided through a focused rereading of the text. After rereading a paragraph silently, the individual was asked to point out words which were still confusing and was questioned about each of those words (see Table 7.1). This rereading interview was designed to focus the student's attention on learning as much as possible from the text about the words which were problematic. Following this, a few integrative questions were asked; then the student was invited to revise the original categories and definitions he or she had written, without referring back to the text.

The key task difference concerns the two definition writings. The first definition writing measured *incidental learning from context*, since readers were not forewarned that they would be expected to define words from the text. In contrast, the second definition writing constitutes a measure of *attended learning from context*, since readers had been encouraged to maximize their word learning by rereading and by seeking further clues in the text, knowing that they would be asked at the end of the interview to improve upon their original definitions.

SCORING

For each of the 15 words, one point was awarded for category and one for definition. But in the case of the six stipulation-restricted words—*cuts, lacerations, Langer's lines, approximation, suturing, bandaging*—raters awarded a total of three possible points: one point for a meaning in the correct category area (e.g., a kind of wound or a kind of healing), one point for an acceptable

Table 7.1.   Procedures of the Reading and Guessing Interview

1. *Read* the passage
2. *Write* free recall of the passage
3. *Reread* the passage to underline any confusing words
4. *Write* definitions—(without passage available)—
   INCIDENTAL LEARNING FROM CONTEXT
5. *Reread* passage paragraph by paragraph, stopping to *answer* questions on confusing words (Questions asked students to reevaluate their written definitions in terms of the text, look for other clues in the text, weigh the importance of the word in the passage, and consider how they would deal with the word if they were reading in their room, with other resources available)
6. *Answer* post-reading questions (Questions designed to help the reader integrate what had been learned from the text and how the 15 words related to one another)
7. *Revise* definitions—(without passage available)—
   ATTENDED LEARNING FROM CONTEXT

definition for the meaning of the word (e.g., *cuts* is a skin wound, *bandaging* is a method of treating a skin wound), and one point for the stipulation (e.g., *bandaging* is to hold the skin together while healing, that is, not to keep a wound sterile or protect it from injury from other impacts, as it might mean in other contexts). This scoring method yielded two points for nine words and three points for the six stipulated words, so the maximum possible word-learning score was 36 points. Because in some cases the students' written definitions were ambiguous, it was decided to include gradations of half a point for definitions which either echoed the wording in the text exactly (thus possibly representing rote memorization rather than comprehension) and definitions which seemed to be on the right track but were not unequivocally correct (see the latter part of this chapter for examples).

Each written definition was scored by at least two raters. The average of the two ratings was used as the score for each individual word. Interrater reliability was measured in two ways. First, the number of exact agreements on each word definition was used as the numerator, total possible items for the respondent as the denominator, to determine reliability for rating of each student's definitions. By the second method, number of agreements within half a point were taken as the numerator. Average reliability for the American students, using exact agreement, was .68; using half-point range agreement, .91. For the Chinese readers, interrater agreement was calculated for 20% of the responses. Exact agreement was .81; half-point range agreement was .91. When discrepancies of more than half a point were found on individual word definitions, they were discussed by the two raters and in most cases resolved. With the few cases in which agreement could not be reached, the third rater was asked to consider the category and definition, and her rating was averaged into the final rating for that specific definition.

GENERAL RESULTS

The first question of interest was the difference between American and Chinese readers. Results showed that the American readers were significantly more successful than the Chinese readers in both incidental and attended word learning. In fact, even after the Chinese readers reread the text to derive more information about target words, their group mean was still far below the level that American readers had achieved even before they had reread the passage with word learning as their focus. Thus the mean of the Americans' incidental learning was higher than the mean of the Chinese readers' attended learning from context (see Table 7.2).

One might argue that the difference between Americans and Chinese was to be expected, since the American group probably knew some of the 15 key words to begin with. In anticipation of this problem, the first author had arranged for

Table 7.2. Word-comprehension From Reading (Raw Scores) Out of a Maximum of 36 Points

	Incidental Word-learning	Attended Word-learning
Taiwan college freshmen		
Mean	6.9	12.5
Standard deviation	4.4	5.0
Taiwan college seniors		
Mean	13.6	19.7
Standard deviation	7.1	6.2
American college students		
Mean	26.5	29.3
Standard deviation	3.1	2.0

students at the initial testing session to take a vocabulary pretest that included words from this text. The target words were mixed in with 40 items on a multiple choice vocabulary proficiency test so readers would not be alerted to remember these words. In addition, since the format for the multiple choice test was a sentence with a blank, followed by four options, readers' attention was not focused in particular on the form of the correct response as it would have been if the correct response had been in the sentence with synonym options listed below. Also, an effort was made to control for guessing, since it was necessary to estimate as accurately as possible whether the individual word was known or not. The response format for the vocabulary test included confidence ratings on a 5-point scale. Thus it was possible to distinguish words which had been guessed correctly by chance (below average confidence) from words for which a student showed strong confidence (average or above-average confidence). Using this information, we could correct guessing scores so they more accurately reflected the actual amount of learning which had taken place.

The results of this vocabulary pretest showed that the American readers did indeed know with confidence a substantial proportion of the 15 key words to be tested. They demonstrated knowledge of a mean of seven words, while the Chinese students had a mean of between one and two words. Table 7.3 shows the individual guessing scores corrected according to prior vocabulary knowledge. Any words for which a student showed a confident correct answer on the pretest were eliminated from the analysis for that individual student. (To maintain comparability, scores on definitions were converted to percentages of the total possible score on words remaining that a student did not know.) The outcome was surprisingly similar to the raw score results. Comparing performance on only those items for which no previous knowledge had been shown, we found that Americans still outperformed the Taiwan seniors, and the seniors still learned significantly more words from context than the freshman group.

Table 7.3. Word-learning From Reading (Scores are Corrected According to Prior Word Knowledge) in Percentage of Unknown Words Learned

	Incidental Word-learning	Attended Word-learning
Taiwan college freshmen		
Mean	18.3%	34.2%
Standard deviation	10.2	14.4
Taiwan college seniors		
Mean	33.7%	51.3%
Standard deviation	19.0	17.0
American college students		
Mean	59.2%	69.7%
Standard deviation	12.7	10.4

DISCUSSION AND FURTHER ANALYSIS: WHAT MIGHT EXPLAIN THESE DIFFERENCES?

Which of the two competing explanations—reading strategies or language proficiency—better accounts for these differences in word learning from reading? We approach this question from three directions: First we review some reading strategies used as students first read through the "Cuts and Lacerations" passage; second, we consider converging information from first language reading and second language proficiency test scores; finally, in the last section of this chapter, we analyze both quantitatively and qualitatively the understanding of stipulations which was demonstrated in readers' written definitions.

While students first read through the "Cuts and Lacerations" text, their more obvious eye movements had been observed. Overt indicators of two reading strategies were recorded: (a) students' gaze times at illustrations during reading (see Mohammed & Swales, 1984, the inspiration for this observational approach), and, (b) their backward scanning across segments of text. Both illustration use and backward scanning can be taken as indications that readers searched for additional information when they became aware of not understanding the immediate text. In other words, we consider both illustration use and scanning to be strategic responses of readers who are closely "monitoring" their comprehension (Baker & Brown, 1984).

Most Chinese and American readers looked down at the illustration of Langer's lines when the new term was encountered in the text (see the illustration in Figure 2-1 of Figure 7.1 of this chapter). This showed that students in both groups sought additional clarification of the new term. However, among the American readers, there were very few other examples of illustration use or scanning. We compared the proportion of readers in each group who studied the flowchart (see Figure 7.2) demonstrating the scarring process and the techniques of suturing and bandaging. Even though quite a few readers ignored it or only glanced at it quickly as they turned the page, a significantly higher percentage of the Chinese readers looked at it carefully, most often from between 10 to 40 seconds. There were also proportionally more Chinese than American readers who scanned from one location in the text back to another. This more frequent use of illustrations and backward scanning suggests that Chinese readers *were* aware of their need for more information and took active steps to seek it during their reading.

This preliminary evidence, that Chinese readers showed more strategic behavior than the Americans, suggests it might not be limited strategies but limited language proficiency that explains the Chinese students' relative lack of success in comprehending new words. From language proficiency pretests of the participants, we can provide some converging evidence on this point.

Table 7.4 shows a comparison of performance on various proficiency pretests. On vocabulary and grammar tests, the American group performed near ceiling, while the Chinese groups got only a little more than half the items correct. In contrast, on a first language reading test (given in English to the Americans and in Chinese to the Taiwan students), there were no significant differences between the groups. Thus, when they are reading in their own language, this group of Chinese readers appears generally comparable to the American group in reading comprehension, sharply contrasting with their performance in guessing while reading in English. When we looked at correlations between Chinese students' definition scores and these three measures, we found that English vocabulary scores correlated much more highly ($r = .62$) with definition outcomes than did L1 reading or English grammar ($r = .31$, and $r = .38$, respectively; for all three correlations, $p < .05$).

Table 7.4. English Vocabulary and Grammar Tests and Native Language Reading Tests (in Percentages)

	English Vocabulary	English Grammar	Native Lg. Reading
Taiwan freshmen			
Mean	55.6%	65.1%	79.4%
Standard deviation	10.8	12.1	7.3
Taiwan seniors			
Mean	61.9%	64.2%	82.1%
Standard deviation	13.9	12.7	7.9
American students			
Mean	97.8%	94.2%	81.9%
Standard deviation	2.4	3.8	9.1

There is further evidence that prior vocabulary knowledge may be the central roadblock to comprehension experienced by these Chinese readers. The difference between freshmen and senior groups in grammar proficiency was not significant, while the difference in their vocabulary knowledge was marginally significant. Recall that in word learning from context the seniors also performed better than the freshmen on both incidental and attended word learning. The pattern of proficiency differences shown here suggests that grammatical competence may have less impact on learning new words from reading than does prior vocabulary knowledge.

This finding—that word learning from reading is especially sensitive to prior vocabulary knowledge—is consistent with other research showing that vocabulary knowledge has a strong impact on reading comprehension, both in L1 (McKeown & Curtis, 1987) and in L2 (Saville-Troike, 1984).

INTERIM SUMMARY

Though certainly not conclusive, this analysis of group differences between American and Chinese readers, on the one hand, and between freshmen and senior Chinese readers, on the other, suggests that what second language readers need in order to gain new word and conceptual knowledge from reading is not only better reading strategies, but greater language proficiency, specifically broader vocabulary knowledge. But to understand why this is so we need to look more closely at readers' definition performance.

QUANTITATIVE AND QUALITATIVE ANALYSIS OF STIPULATIONS IN DEFINITION RESPONSES

Before comparing American and Chinese readers' definitions, it is important to convey a sense of the data and how we turned qualitative responses into quantitative scores for group comparisons. In evaluating subjects' written definitions, raters gave an extra ''stipulation'' point if the student demonstrated knowledge of the word's stipulation. Here are some examples of definitions receiving a stipulation point. The response for *cuts*, ''smooth hurted lines caused by knives,'' earned a stipulation point because the subject conveyed the crucial notion that cuts are smooth-edged wounds. That *lacerations* are jagged wounds is mentioned by another subject's definition: ''Lacerations are a kind of wound. It's caused by jagged and tore on the body. And it's always harder to heal than cuts.'' The response that *Langer's lines* ''cover on the skin all over the body'' demonstrates recognition that Langer's lines are on the surface of the skin. Another definition shows that the student has clearly understood the author-intended meaning for approximation, to bring wound edges together: ''Approximation is a kind of movement of skin''; ''the approximation means the closing of the skin beside the wound.'' Both of the following definitions include the stipulation that *suturing* and *bandaging* are methods for closing a wound:

Suturing is a processing method of wounds which use sewing needle tissue line to get the cuts closed.
Bandaging uses some tapes to bring tight the hurted part.

A comparison of the percentage of students in American and Chinese groups that earned stipulation points for each of the six words is shown in Table 7.5 (the percentages include all responses, with no corrections made for prior knowledge on the vocabulary test, since stipulations could be considered to be passage-specific, representing new knowledge acquired from this specific reading). The Chinese earned an average of 37% of the total possible stipulation points compared with the Americans, who averaged 61%.[4]

A comparison of the individual words tested shows that the Chinese had significantly more difficulty than the native speakers with *cuts, lacerations*, and *Langer's lines*. The poorer performance of the Chinese on *cuts* and *lacerations* was due in large part to their unfamiliarity with the defining words *slices, jagged*, and *tears*. This lack of vocabulary knowledge became obvious in the interviews, when the subjects discussed difficult words in the text, paragraph by paragraph. Many of the Chinese readers indicated that they did not know the meaning of these defining terms. This fact, combined with the high correlation between vocabulary knowledge and word-learning performance ($r = .62$, as discussed above), confirms that vocabulary knowledge forms the foundation of word-learning from lexical familiarization.

The Chinese also got significantly fewer of the possible stipulation points given for *Langer's lines* than the Americans. Recall that the stipulation for *Langer's lines* required subjects to integrate the text definition (''furrows or ridges which run transversely across the wrist'') with an illustration and an

Table 7.5. Percentage of Chinese and USA Subjects Given Stipulation Points

	Chinese	USA	Difference
Cuts	31%	67%	−36%*
Lacerations	25	78	−53*
Langer's Lines	51	89	−38*
Approximation	16	11	5
Suturing	67	89	−22
Bandaging	29	33	−4
$\overline{X}$	37	61	−24

*$p < .05$ level

example, "Look at your wrist closely." The Chinese showed some difficulty integrating the text cues with the illustration, as seen in definitions which restricted the lines to the wrist rather than extending to the whole body. In addition, many Chinese did not know the text definition words *furrows, ridges*, and *transversely*. The role of vocabulary in building knowledge through reading is again obvious.

Both groups found *suturing* to be the easiest. This is not surprising, since the text gives *suturing* extensive lexical familiarization (see Figure 7.2). There is a parenthetical definition immediately after the word "(stitching)" and a clearly labeled illustration in Figure 7.2, complete with needle and thread. Finally, to support comprehension of this word, there is a paragraph-long description of the process of suturing on the final page of the text:

> Suturing requires professional care. It is necessary to sterilize the wound, use sterile needles, thread and instruments, and know what one is doing. This type of closure provides the best cosmetic result, with the least amount of scarring and the shortest healing time. But all wounds do not need to be sutured. As a matter of fact, I believe that some wounds should not be stitched. (Shiller, 1977, p. 46)

Given such multiple sources of lexical familiarization, it is not surprising that a high percentage of readers in both groups comprehended the stipulation that suturing was for holding the skin together.

Both groups found *approximation* the most difficult. In part this is related to the word-form's more common meaning in mathematics, which many readers seemed to rely on for their written definitions. But we believe an even greater source of difficulty to be the fact that the new concept is introduced in parenthetical material in a heading:

Skin Approximation (Bringing Wound Edges Together)

A lesson for textbook publishers in this example is that, apparently, readers do not pay much attention to the headings in the normal course of reading a text. Therefore, important new concepts should not be introduced in headings.

Another word equally difficult for both the Chinese and the American readers was *bandaging*. Most of the students in both groups defined *bandaging* as "to cover a wound" and therefore failed to understand the stipulation explicitly stated in introducing *suturing* and *bandaging* ("The two most common methods of keeping wound edges together") and implied by the parenthetical synonym ("taping") and the illustration of butterfly tapes (see Figure 7.2). We suspect that for *bandaging* an important source of difficulty for both groups was the prior knowledge readers brought to the text. Responses to *bandaging* that emphasized "covering the wound" indicate that readers' experiential knowledge—that is, readers' wound treatment schema—caused readers to overlook the stipulation in this text. Thus, it appears that prior knowledge evoked by either familiar word-forms or familiar schemata may result in misconceptions about word meaning in a text (see Roth, 1986, concerning the difficulties American science students have in biology when they must replace common definitions of a given word-form with a stipulated one). More research is needed with lexical familiarization to determine to what extent first- and second-language readers may differ in the strength of their preconceptions about word meaning and their ability to override them through close reading of the text and "sense creation" (Clark & Gerrig, 1983) of their own.

This tendency to miss the stipulation for familiar words was common among the Americans. Notice (Table 7.5) that the three most difficult words for the native speakers were *cuts, approximation*, and *bandaging*, all of which have other more common meanings and associations. Although the subjects had been instructed to define the words as they were used in the text, we found that many of the Americans' definitions reflected a word's more common or dominant meaning. Our data show that it was the common meaning, rather than the restricted one, that persisted in memory. We speculate that, when the Americans encountered a familiar word-form like *cuts*, their prior knowledge about the word was activated automatically, causing them not to attend closely to the lexical familiarization that accompanied the word.

Interim Summary

There appear to be contrasting sources of difficulty for the American and Chinese readers. The Chinese seemed to have been handicapped in their ability to use lexical familiarization by their overall weaker English vocabulary knowledge. This was not the case for the Americans. We observed during the rereading interviews that the Americans understood the cue words in the lexical familiarizations; they sometimes failed to use them, however, probably because of their familiarity with the more common meanings for some of the target words.

For both groups, the illustrations were not always helpful in defining the words. Many Chinese seemed to have difficulty integrating text definitions and illustrations, especially when they did not know the meaning of the defining words. The Americans tended to rely more on the text—and then more selectively—generally not paying much attention to the illustrations for words they thought they already knew (see Winn, 1987, for similar findings on illustration use by good and poor readers).

Some Defining Strategies of Chinese and Americans

When the subjects had not understood the author-intended cues defining a technical term in the text, they tended to fill the gap in their lexical knowledge by using a combination of *text-based responses* and *reliance on prior knowledge* in order to define the term. But there were similarities and differences in the way the Chinese and Americans employed these strategies.

One example of a text-based strategy that both Chinese and American readers employed was to rely on the illustrations without integrating them with the text definition. For example, a Chinese student gave the following definition for *Langer's lines*, misinterpreting the illustration to be about muscles rather than skin lines: "Langer's lines are a kind of muscle tracks. Langer's lines mean the directions the muscles grows." Several of the American subjects also employed this strategy, defining *Langer's lines* as "muscle lines."

Here, the difficulty of integrating multiple cues made the Americans' responses more closely resemble the Chinese responses. It was crucial for readers to integrate the text cues in order to grasp the implied stipulation that *Langer's lines* are on the surface of the skin. Each text cue, like a piece in a jigsaw puzzle, gives specific information about how to construct the whole picture (Werner & Kaplan, 1952; van Daalen-Kapteijns & Elshout-Mohr, 1981), in this case, the meaning of *Langer's lines*. The cue "Look at your wrist" tells readers that *Langer's lines* occur on the wrist. If readers fail to integrate the illustration, which shows lines all over the body, they construct definitions of *Langer's lines* that are too restrictive, as did the Americans and the Chinese who said *Langer's lines* were skin lines on the wrist. Conversely, overreliance on the illustration without integrating the notion that *Langer's lines* are skin lines led some Chinese and Americans to wrongly define *Langer's lines* as muscle lines.

Another text-based strategy Chinese subjects employed in their definitions was to echo words from the text even if they did not know their meanings. In this definition, "Langer's lines are a kind of body tissue. Furrows and ridges combine the Langer's lines," the student correctly defined *Langer's lines* as composed of furrows and ridges, but when this subject had been asked to define *furrows* and *ridges*, the response was "Langer's lines." None of the Americans gave this type of circular definition.

In addition to text-based strategies, both the Chinese and the Americans relied on their prior knowledge of words and on their injury schemata in defining terms. Subjects used their schema of the treatment of wounds to define bandaging. Some seemed to mistake the lexical familiarization synonym "(taping)" to mean something like "Band-Aid," as in this definition: "Bandaging is a kind of packing. If you get injured you must bandage place where the hurt is. 'OK-band' is used for bandaging." ("OK-band" is the Taiwan equivalent to our Band-Aid.) In a slightly different twist of interpretation, another student interpreted "(taping)" to mean adhesive tape to hold the bandage in place: "Bandaging is a kind of treatment method. Use cloth and tape to cover the wound."

Despite the fact that both Chinese and Americans called on their background knowledge in defining individual words, they seemed to differ in the way they used prior knowledge of word meanings. Some of the Chinese readers recalled meanings learned in other contexts (as in Parry, 1987; see also Lipson, 1982).

This was quite clear in the definitions the Chinese wrote for cuts. Here the student defined the verb *cut* and did not even try to frame the definition within the context of the reading: "Cuts are a kind of divide to some part or shape. We can divide fruit or paper by cutting it is always to use in the kitchen." Another subject defined *cuts* as instruments for cutting: "Cuts are a kind of instruments. For examples knife." This seems to be an attempt to adapt a known verb meaning to define a noun. It is only after the word-focused rereading interview that this subject adopted a more suitable interpretation: "Cuts are a kind of wound. Cuts mean that cut the skin by knife." In contrast to the difficulties of the Chinese readers, none of the American subjects said *cuts* were anything other than wounds. The Chinese, having had fewer encounters with the various meanings and contexts in which *cuts* may be used, had more difficulty writing definitions appropriate to the semantic context of the passage than did the Americans, who were quite familiar with the nominal "wound" sense of the word *cuts*.

In general, then, the Chinese had less prior word knowledge in English than the Americans. When the Chinese did not know the defining words, they tended to write definitions that parroted the text or that showed heavy reliance on the illustrations. Chinese readers who had minimal linguistic experience with the words they were defining, as in the case of *cuts*, tended to write definitions for words that did not fit the meaning of the text. The Americans, in contrast, could usually rely on their extensive linguistic experience. They knew most of the defining words and target words and thus wrote definitions that fit the meaning of the passage. But the Americans tended to overrely on this prior knowledge when defining some of the target words in that they failed to pay close attention to some text definitions. In the case of *Langer's lines*, however, where both the word-form and the concept were new, U.S. subjects paid more attention to the lexical familiarizations. Nevertheless, with this completely new word, they were not always successful at integrating multiple cues, a process which requires complex inferencing as well as linguistic knowledge (Werner & Kaplan, 1952; van Daalen-Kapteijns & Elshout-Mohr, 1981).

CONCLUSIONS

When we combine this analysis of stipulations and defining strategies with the large differences seen between Chinese and American readers' comprehension in the first section of this report, we begin to distinguish a pattern in which prior knowledge plays a dominant role. But we must distinguish between prior experiential knowledge and prior linguistic knowledge.

Experiential knowledge can interfere with the learning of new word meaning when readers overemphasize illustrations (Langer's lines) or situations (bandaging) which connect with their knowledge of the world. Misconceptions resulting from experiential knowledge were observed in both Chinese and American readers. In addition, this experiential knowledge could apparently combine with vocabulary knowledge to prevent comprehension of stipulated meanings within a particular text (cuts, bandaging). American and Chinese readers' comprehension tended to remain incomplete when prior vocabulary and experiential knowledge was not modified by close reading of the text. Familiar word-forms seemed to lead readers to rely on automatic "sense selection" rather than engaging in more deliberate and effortful "sense creation" (see Clark & Gerrig, 1983, and Kintsch & Mross, (1985), for discussions of such lexical inferencing processes). Furthermore, when readers were forced to engage in "sense creation," as with the new form and concept *Langer's lines*, both American and Chinese readers found it difficult to integrate various cues in the text, tending to focus on one dimension of meaning to the exclusion of others.

In spite of these shared difficulties, the American group's comprehension was still much more complete than that of the Chinese. For the Americans prior vocabulary knowledge served mainly to facilitate comprehension of new concepts, whereas for the Chinese limited vocabulary knowledge restricted comprehension of lexical familiarizations. There were just too many new words in the lexical familiarizations. When we combine this observation with the converging view of word comprehension presented in the first part of this chapter, it is clear that vocabulary knowledge constitutes the central difficulty for this group of L2 readers: Even though the Chinese subjects read closely, with considerable strategic flexibility, they could not compensate very well for their limited vocabulary.

REFERENCES

Alderson, J. C. (1984). Reading in a foreign language: A reading problem or a language problem? In J. C. Alderson & A. H. Urquhart (Eds.), *Reading in a foreign language* (pp. 1–27). New York: Longman.

Anderson, R. C., & Pearson, P. D. (1984). A schema-theoretic view of basic processes in reading. In P. D. Pearson (Ed.), *Handbook of reading research* (pp. 255–291) New York: Longman.

Baker, L., & Brown, A. L. (1984). Metacognitive skills and reading. In P. D. Pearson (Ed.), *Handbook of reading research* (pp. 255–291). New York: Longman.

Block, E. (1986). The comprehension strategies of second language readers. *TESOL Quarterly, 20*(3), 463–494.

Bramki, D., & Williams, R. (1984). Lexical familiarization in economics text and its pedagogic implications in reading comprehension. *Reading in a Foreign Language, 2*, 169–181.

Carrell, P. L. (1983). Background knowledge in second language comprehension. *Language Learning and Communication, 2*, 5–34.

Clark, H. H., & Gerrig, R. J. (1983). Understanding old words with new meanings. *Journal of Verbal Learning and Verbal Behavior, 29*, 591–608.

Clarke, M. (1979). Reading in Spanish and English: Evidence from adult ESL students. *Language Learning, 9,* 11–150.

Coady, J. A. (1979). A psycholinguistic model of the ESL reader. In R. Mackay, B. Barkman, & R. R. Jordan (Eds.), *Reading in a second language* (pp. 5–12). Rowley, MA: Newbury House.

Duffy, S. A., Morris, R. K., & Rayner, K. (1988). Lexical ambiguity and fixation times in reading. *Journal of Memory and Language, 7,* 49–446.

Haynes, M. (1989). *Individual differences in Chinese readers of English: Orthography and reading.* Unpublished doctoral dissertation, Michigan State University.

Haynes, M., & Carr, T. H. (1990). Writing system background and second language reading: a component skills analysis of English reading by native speaker-readers of Chinese. In T. H. Carr & B. A. Levy (Eds.), *Reading and its development: component skills approaches* (pp. 375–421). New York: Academic Press.

Hosenfeld, C. (1984). Case studies of ninth grade readers. In J. C. Alderson & A. H. Urquhart (Eds.), *Reading in a foreign language* (pp. 231–249). New York: Longman.

Kintsch, W., & Mross, E. F. (1985). Context effects in word identification. *Journal of Memory and Language 4,* 336–349.

Lipson, M. Y. (1982). Learning new information from text: the role of prior knowledge and reading ability. *Journal of Reading Behavior, 14*(3), 43–61.

McKeown, M. C., & Curtis, M. E. (1987). *The nature of vocabulary acquisiton.* Hillsdale, NJ: Erlbaum.

Mohammed, M., & Swales, J. (1984) Factors affecting the successful reading of technical instructions. *Reading in a foreign language, 2*(2), 206–217.

Parry, K. (1987). Reading in a second culture. In J. Devine, P. L. Carrell, & D. E. Eskey (Eds.), *Research in reading in English as a second language* (pp. 59–72). Washington, DC: TESOL.

Rayner, K., & Pollatsek, A. (1989). *The psychology of reading.* Englewood Cliffs, NJ: Prentice-Hall.

Roth, K. J. (1986). *Conceptual-change learning and student processing of science texts* (Research Series #167). East Lansing, MI: M.S.U., Institute for Research on Teaching.

Saville-Troike, M. (1984). What really matters in second language learning for academic achievement? *TESOL Quarterly 18,* 199–220.

Shiller, J. G. (1977). *Childhood injury.* New York: Stein and Day.

Swinney, D. A. (1979). Lexical access during sentence comprehension: (Re)consideration of context effects. *Journal of Verbal Learning and Verbal Behavior, 18,* 645–659.

van Daalen-Kapteijns, M. M., & Elshout-Mohr, M. (1981). The acquisition of word meanings as a cognitive learning process. *Journal of Verbal Learning and Verbal Behavior, 20,* 386–399.

Werner, H., & Kaplan, E. (1952). The acquisition of word meaning: A developmental study. *Monographs of the Society for Research in Child Development, 15,* 3–10.

Winn, B. (1987). Using charts, graphs, and diagrams in educational materials. In D. M. Willows & H. A. Houghton (Eds.), *The psychology of illustration: Basic research* (Vol. 1). New York: Springer-Verlag.

Yorio, Carlos A. (1971). Some sources of reading problems for foreign language learners. *Language Learning, 1*(1), 107–115.

ENDNOTES

1. Copyright ©1977 by Jack G. Shiller. From the book *Childhood Injury* (pp. 42–46), originally published by Stein & Day, reprinted with permission of Scarborough House Publishers.
2. The initial features of each definition and stipulation were discussed and agreed upon by the first author and Dr. Thomas Carr. During the training sessions before rating, these criteria were again discussed and slightly adjusted by the three raters, Margot Haynes, Ila Baker, and Elise Lue. Thus the criteria for all of the stipulations are those used by the raters in scoring student definitions.
3. Details of the complete study are reported in Haynes (1989). A shorter version of the large study can be found in Haynes and Carr (1990).
4. Even though this is a fairly large difference, it just missed significance ($p < .08$), possibly because the number of subjects in the American group was so small.

Editorial Comments

The main claim of this chapter is that L2 learners have difficulty guessing word meanings in context not because of ineffective reading strategies but because of linguistic deficiencies—specifically, inadequate vocabulary knowledge. This is not a new claim: It has been made before by van Parreren and Schouten-van Parreren (1981) and by Haynes (1984, Chapter 3), among others. Haynes and Baker's major contribution, we think, is the use of multiple methods to make the claim significantly stronger. It should be noted, however, that it is not immune to challenge. Bensoussan and Laufer found in their 1984 study that the size of a learner's vocabulary had no bearing on his/her ability to guess unknown words from context.

Why is there such a difference in these results? One explanation may be that these researchers are looking at different aspects of the word-guessing process. Haynes and Baker's subjects had difficulty guessing word meanings because they didn't know other nontarget words that were supposed to serve as context clues, such as *jagged, slices,* and *tears*. Bensoussan and Laufer's subjects, by contrast, often had difficulty because they misidentified the target words in the first place and didn't even try to use the context clues. It is worth noting as well the possible role of methodology in inducing these differences. Haynes and Baker had students first read a text for global meaning, then try to guess the meanings of specific words. Bensoussan and Laufer worked in the opposite direction, asking students to first define words from a list and only later letting them see these words embedded in a text. Furthermore, even something as simple as scoring methods might explain the difference. Bensoussan and Laufer used raw scores and number of words learned, while Haynes and Baker used percentages of words learned out of the total number of words remaining for each person to learn (after subtracting out words shown to be already known on the vocabulary pretest). These different methods might in particular affect scores for those with larger vocabulary knowledge, since in Bensoussan and Laufer's study they would have a small number of possible words left to learn, while in Haynes and Baker's study they would have the same percentage of information to learn as did those who knew less to begin with. Perhaps this is why the former study found that size of vocabulary had no effect on new learning, while here Haynes and Baker found a strong correlation between vocabulary knowledge and learning of new words.

Haynes and Baker's chapter underscores an important cognitive distinction that runs throughout much of the literature on reading and vocabulary learning, namely, the distinction between attended and automatic processing. Attended processing includes conscious use of reading strategies and metacognitive monitoring techniques, requiring space in working memory; automatic processing includes rapid graphemic identification, lexical access, and syntactic analysis when these take place without requiring working memory resources (see Brown, 1985, for detailed discussion of the psychological distinction). The former requires more effort but provides adaptability; the latter is not as flexible but provides speed and leaves cognitive space free for higher level processes. For optimal use of one's cognitive capacities, there needs to be an appropriate balance between attended and automatic processing.

By focusing on lexical familiarizations, Haynes and Baker give us a unique and naturalistic look at how some L1 and L2 learners try to manage this tradeoff. These learners are exposed to familiar word forms (*cuts, bandaging*) that appear to require only sense selection (a form of automatic access to meaning for familiar word forms), yet the context makes it clear—or *should* make it clear!—that these word forms are being used in an unusual way requiring "sense creation" (a form of attended processing). Under these circumstances, it is interesting to note that although vocabulary knowledge generally helped Haynes and Baker's subjects to guess other unfamiliar words, it sometimes had the undesirable effect of causing them to overlook unusual, context-specific meanings of familiar words. This behavior, shown by both L1 and L2 readers, is similar to that observed by Laufer (1981), Holmes and Ramos in chapter 5, Huckin and Bloch in chapter 8, and others. It leads to a pedagogical suggestion that teachers encourage students to monitor not only their guesses about new word forms but their assumptions about meanings for familiar forms in particular contexts.

There are a few methodological difficulties with this study that should be mentioned. First, the authors appear to apply the term "stipulation" more loosely than it was originally intended, and thus skew the scoring system for vocabulary learning. For example, though "holding skin edges together" may be a stipulated part of the meaning of "bandage" in this text about healing skin wounds, the same purpose feature would seem essential to the meaning of "suturing" *wherever* it might appear and thus perhaps should not have counted an extra stipulation point. Furthermore, the whole scoring system raises many questions, such as whether equal points should have been awarded for category, definition, and stipulation. Such questions, along with questions of rater reliability, necessarily arise when one attempts to fit qualitative data into a quantitative mold. It is our conviction that more may be learned by looking closely at the qualitative data (as do many of the researchers in this volume) and raising these openly than by possibly influencing subjects in uncontrolled ways by testing with multiple choice questions that conceal, but do not resolve, issues of reliability and validity.

Finally, Haynes and Baker's design and methodology should be applauded, we think, for its thoroughness and ecological validity. Their use of both L1 and L2 readers provides the kind of baseline comparison too little represented in L2 research. Their contrast between incidental and attended guessing allows us to see comprehension as a dynamic process in which individual learners show varying amounts of learning potential as they allocate attention according to different purposes during reading. The authors' use of both quantitative and qualitative measures, including observation of the subjects' scanning behavior, strengthens their findings. And their choice of a text that neutralizes cross-cultural differences in topic knowledge and contains both visual and linguistic information gives the study a naturalness and validity that future researchers might well want to emulate.

REFERENCES

Bensoussan, M., & Laufer, B. (1984). Lexical guessing in context in EFL comprehension. *Journal of Research in Reading, 7,* 15–32.

Brown, T. (1985). Defining the role of automaticity in skill acquisition: Interactions between working memory and practice in task performance. Unpublished doctoral dissertation, Michigan State University.

Laufer, B. (1981) A problem in vocabulary learning—synophones. *ELT Journal, 33*(3), 294–300.

van Parreren, C.F., & Schouten-Van Parreren, M.C. (1981). Contextual guessing: A trainable reader strategy. *System, 9*(3), 235–241.

Chapter 8
Strategies for Inferring Word-Meanings in Context: A Cognitive Model

Thomas Huckin
University Writing Program
and Department of English
University of Utah
Salt Lake City, UT

Joel Bloch
Department of English
Carnegie-Mellon University
Pittsburgh, PA

This chapter describes an exploratory study that used think-aloud protocols to track the problem-solving strategies of three intermediate-pro-
ficiency NNS graduate students encountering unfamiliar words in their
course readings. In general, these students relied mainly on context clues
for guessing (especially local clues) and were usually successful when they
did so. The most common cause of unsuccessful guessing was when students thought they knew a word but didn't—and therefore didn't really
make a "guess." The chapter concludes by proposing a dynamic model of
hypothesis generation and testing that incorporates both parallel and serial
processing.

INTRODUCTION

Of the four general skills that need to be mastered to become proficient in a
second language—speaking, listening, reading, and writing—reading is certainly

the most crucial to a student entering into a second-language academic environment. Reading is the primary means by which academic knowledge is transmitted, and it is also a useful secondary source for information that might be missed in a class discussion or lecture. For many foreign students whose command of spoken English is quite tenuous, reading is the skill they most often depend on to help get them through a program of study.

Research has shown that second-language readers rely heavily on vocabulary knowledge, and that a lack of vocabulary knowledge is the largest obstacle for second-language readers to overcome (Ulijn, 1981; Alderson, 1984). Probably the most common way for adult second-language learners to acquire new words in an academic setting, as a glance at the margins of a typical L2 reader's book will show, is to look them up in a bilingual dictionary. Many second-language learners depend heavily on such dictionaries. But dictionaries, especially the small pocket-size ones favored by L2 readers, often do not contain sufficient accurate information to serve the L2 reader's needs. Consequently, second-language learners who wish to maximize their reading comprehension and vocabulary building must also learn strategies for guessing word-meanings in context.

Though there has been some scattered research on the strategies that second-language learners use when trying to guess word-meanings in context (e.g., Hosenfeld, 1977; Van Parreren & Schouten-van Parreren, 1981; Bensoussan & Laufer, 1984; Huckin & Jin, 1987), none of this research has attempted to model the process in a comprehensive way. The purpose of the present investigation was to trace the behaviors exhibited by one group of L2 students trying to guess unfamiliar words in their course readings and, on the basis of this data, to construct a tentative working model of these behaviors. We cannot claim generality for our model, but we do feel that it can serve as a starting point for further studies, the result of which could be a more generalized theory of second-language word-guessing strategies.

EVOLVING PERSPECTIVES

In the 1960s, the development of psycholinguistic models of reading, such as Goodman (1976) and Smith (1971), shifted the emphasis in teaching vocabulary from learning words in isolation to learning words in context. Smith argued that, instead of looking words up in a dictionary, the best way to identify an unfamiliar word in a text is to draw inferences from the rest of the text. Interest in the use of context as a means of aiding vocabulary learning was given a strong boost by the development of the psychological concepts of *priming* and *spreading activation*, which showed that the recognition and understanding of a given word can be affected by the words which have preceded it (Collins & Loftus, 1975). This emphasis on guessing from context has had a salutary effect on second-language teaching insofar as it has sensitized both teachers and learners to the fact of context-dependence in the interpretation and use of words. But it has also seriously underplayed the problems learners might have in using this context, as well as more fundamental problems they might have in simple bottom-up processing (e.g., graphemic identification). In the past 10 years, the development of interactive models of reading has renewed interest in researching lower order reading skills. Interactive models propose that language processing is organized into levels ranging from graphic recognition to high-level schemata representing world knowledge (Rumelhart, 1977). Activation flows in both directions between these levels (see Rumelhart, McClelland, & the PDP Research Group, 1986), so that bottom-up processing is influenced by top-level schemata, and vice versa. This model of activation was used by Stanovich (1980) to develop what he called an *interactive-compensatory* model of reading, in which processing at one level can compensate for deficiencies at another level. According to this theory, a reader who lacks fast automatic word recognition skills would try to compensate by using more controlled activation of processes at higher levels, for example, contextual information and top-level schemata. Stanovich notes that increased dependency on higher-level processing does not necessarily mean more effective use of it; deficiencies in automatic word recognition may seriously hamper the reader's use of higher-level processing. Indeed, Eskey argues that, for second language readers, lower level decoding skills are essential to rapid comprehension (Eskey 1988; Eskey & Grabe 1988).

Research Questions

Whether or not interactive models are consistent with successful word-guessing is an empirical question. By observing the performance of second-language readers confronting unknown vocabulary, we hoped to provide a tentative answer to this question and also see whether some word-guessing strategies work better than others. Specifically, we were interested in these questions:

1. What strategies do second-language learners use when they encounter unknown vocabulary in context?
2. How does context function to aid second-language learners in dealing with unknown words?
3. In what ways do second-language learners fail to take full advantage of context clues; that is, how might teachers help these learners to make better guesses when vocabulary knowledge is not sufficient?

RESEARCH DESIGN

Given the complexity of an interactive conception of reading and the difficulty of controlling all the variables involved, we decided to explore the questions listed above via case studies rather than controlled experiments. A further consideration in our choice of approach was that previous research has shown that gains in vocabulary learning from context tend to be gradual (Nagy, Herman, & Anderson, 1985) and are therefore often difficult to measure empirically in a controlled experiment. To this end, a qualitative study using think-aloud protocols was designed to examine the research questions. We felt that a translation task would be a useful means of achieving this goal, since it allowed the participants to work in both their native and target languages while focusing on the problem of understanding unknown words.

Subjects

Three students currently enrolled in the second semester of the Masters Degree program in International Business at Point Park College in Pittsburgh were asked to participate in the study for a small payment. All three were natives of China and had come to the United States within the last 3 years. Though no test of prior knowledge was given to the subjects, interviews showed that none had extensive knowledge of business or international economics before entering the program. Their instructor evaluated them as having sufficient knowledge in the course to understand the texts described below. The Michigan Test of Language Ability was administered to each of the students to obtain a measure of their proficiency in English. Their scores, ranging from 69 to 82, indicated that they were at an intermediate level of English proficiency. None reported having had systematic training in how to use context clues to infer the meaning of unknown words.

Texts

Since this study was designed to examine how students use vocabulary-learning strategies in an academic situation, materials for the experiment were chosen from the students' current assigned readings. A 450-word passage from a textbook (see Table 8.1) and a 260-word passage from a journal article were selected. Although readability formulas are not entirely accurate or reliable in depicting the actual difficulty of a text for any particular reader (Seltzer, 1983; Duffy, 1985), we decided to run these texts through the computer program *Writer's Workbench* to get a rough approximation of the linguistic differences between them. According to three standard readability formulas included in this program (Kincaid, Flesch, Coleman-Liau), the longer passage was written at the 11th grade level and the shorter one at the 17th.

Identification and Testing of Target Vocabulary

Target words were selected by the two investigators (who are experienced ESL instructors) as the words that these students would be least likely to know. This resulted in a list of 17 words for the first text and 10 words for the second. While a few of the words on the list, such as *tariffs*, could be considered technical terms with specialized meanings, the majority of the words were nontechnical. One study (Cohen et al., 1988) found that their informants had greater difficulty with

**Table 8.1. The "Tariff" Text with Sentences Numbered
and Target Words Underlined (from Lindert, 1986)**

The Basic Analysis of a Tariff

A majority of economists has consistently favored letting nations trade freely with few tariffs or other barriers to trade [1]. Indeed, economists have tended to be even more critical of trade *barriers* than have other groups in society, even though economists have taken great care to list the *exceptional* cases in which they feel trade *barriers* can be justified [2]. Such consistent agreement is rare within the economics profession [3].

The *presumption* in favor of free trade is based primarily on a body of economic analysis demonstrating that there are usually net gains from freer trade both for nations and for the world [4]. We caught an initial *glimpse* of this analysis in Chapter 3 above, which showed that free trade brings greater *well-being* than no trade [5]. The main task of this chapter and the following chapters of Part Two is to compare free-trade policies with a much wider range of trade barriers, barriers that do not necessarily shut out all international trade [6]. It is mainly on this more detailed analysis of trade policies that economists have based their view that free trade is generally preferable to partial restrictions on trade, with a list of *exceptions* [7]. Once this analysis is understood, it is easier to understand what divides the majority of economists from groups calling for restrictions on trade [8].

A PREVIEW OF CONCLUSIONS

The economic analysis of what is lost or gained by putting up barriers to international trade starts with a close look at the effects of the *classic* kind of trade barrier, a tariff on an imported good [9]. This chapter and the next *spell out* who is likely to gain and who is likely to lose from a tariff, and the conditions under which nation or the world could end up better off from a tariff [10]. Later chapters take up other kinds of barriers to trade [11].

Our *exploration* of the *pros and cons* of a tariff will be detailed enough to *warrant* listing its main conclusions here at the *outset* [12]. This chapter and the next will find that:

1. A tariff almost always lowers world *well-being* [13].
2. A tariff usually lowers the *well-being* of each nation, including the nation imposing the tariff [14] .
3. As a general rule, whatever a tariff can do for the nation, something else can do better [15].
4. There are exceptions to the case for free trade [16]:
    a. The "national *optimal*" tariff: When a nation can *affect* the prices at which it trades with foreigners, it can gain from its own tariff [17].
    b. "Second-best" arguments for a tariff: When other *incurable distortions* exist in the economy, imposing a tariff may be better than doing nothing [18].
    c. In a narrow range of cases with *distortions* specific to international trade itself, a tariff can be better than any other policy, and not just better than doing nothing [19].
5. A tariff absolutely helps groups tied to the production of import substitutes, even when the tariff is bad for the nation as a whole [20].

greater difficulty with nontechnical words than technical words. In this study, it was expected that, from the class lectures and previous reading, the participants would have enough content knowledge to understand most of the technical vocabulary.

The subjects were then tested on these target words, both before the actual reading of each text and after. In addition to target words, other words were added as distractors to minimize any priming effect, that is, to avoid having the full set of test words itself suggest definitions for individual test words. The vocabulary words were randomized twice to be used in two lists, one for the pretest and one for the posttest. The pre- and posttests were designed to show differences in vocabulary knowledge before and after the words were seen in context. They also allowed the researchers to identify words unknown to a specific reader and then focus on the strategies the participants used for those words during contextual guessing

For the pre- and posttests, the researchers used an interview and probe strategy modified from one developed by Nagy et al. (1985). The participants were asked the meaning of each word. If they did not know the word, they were asked to make a guess; if their guess was partly or possibly correct, the participants were asked to think of another possible meaning. After this probe was completed, the participants were asked to translate that word into Chinese. This translation task was added to safeguard against the possibility that a subject might not know the English definition even though he or she actually knew the meaning. This process gave the researchers a record of what the subjects thought a word actually meant in both Chinese and English. This information could then be compared to what they said in their protocols and written translations to see if there was any change in what they thought the word meant.

To try to determine the amount of contextual support there is for each target word, a cloze test was developed by blanking out all the target words in the two texts. The passages were then given to 12 native speakers who were asked to fill in the blanks.

Protocol Analysis

We elected to use protocol analysis (Ericsson & Simon, 1984) as the investigative tool most likely to yield the rich body of data one needs in an exploratory study. Previous research has shown that the ''think-aloud'' procedure could be effectively used with second-language learners (Hosenfeld, 1977; Van Parreren & Schouten-van Parreren, 1981; Raimes, 1985; Huckin, 1986). The subjects were asked to translate the texts into Chinese while ''thinking aloud'' either in Chinese or English. All of their verbalizations were recorded on audio tape and later transcribed by a bilingual Chinese-American and analyzed by the two authors.

The subjects were tested individually as follows:

1. Each subject was given the pretest with probes from the researcher.
2. Each subject wrote a translation of the passage while "thinking aloud."
3. Each subject was given the posttest with probes from the researcher.

The participants were given a short training session before the first translation task to gain familiarity with the thinking-aloud procedure. During the actual task, each subject was asked to think aloud while translating, but not to reflect on what he or she was doing (we wanted to tap the subjects' stream-of-consciousness, not have the subjects tell us what they thought we wanted to hear). An experimenter was present to urge the participant to continue talking if he or she lapsed into silence; however, he did not answer questions the participant might have about the text. The protocols were transcribed, checked for accuracy against the tapes, and then divided into units corresponding to what were perceived as the individual subgoals of each participant. As Ericsson and Simon (1984) have argued, verbal protocols capture only a fraction of a subject's thoughts, but they usually provide enough information to trace the thinking process and build a rough model of it.

The participants were asked to make their translations as meaningful as possible but not concern themselves with grammatical correctness. All of the Chinese spoken in the protocols was translated by a native Chinese speaker into English. The translator was instructed to make the translation adhere as closely as possible to the meaning of the Chinese lexical items.

FINDINGS

With 27 target words on the two pretests and three subjects participating, there were 81 cases (3 × 27) where subjects could indicate prior knowledge of a word. Of this number, the subjects gave reasonable definitions (as judged by the two authors) of 37. This meant that, during the actual reading of the two passages, there were 44 cases where subjects had to guess at the meaning of a target word.

We used both the tape-recorded protocol and its written transcription to analyze each of these 44 cases. It should be emphasized that, although think-aloud protocols provide more information about cognitive processes than any other single technique, they are able to capture only traces of the cognition that actually takes place. Instead of making definitive claims about the subject's cognitive behavior, the investigator can only make educated guesses and must use his or her interpretive skills to create a coherent picture. That is what we have done here. The overall results are given in Table 8.2, and the discussion that follows should be understood in this light. Although our interpretations are all based on data from the protocol record, they represent only our "best guess" of how our subjects proceeded through the task. Each sentence in the step-by-step descriptions given below should be read as if it contained the word *apparently*. We have omitted this qualifier simply to avoid heavy repetition.

As Table 8.2 shows, subjects made 25 successful guesses out of 44 opportunities. In so doing, they relied mainly on context clues (23 of the 25). Subjects were unsuccessful in 19 of the 44 guessing opportunities, and these failures can be attributed largely to the subjects' failure to use context clues. In nine of these cases, they apparently mistook the word for another that resembles it (e.g., *pillars* for *appliers*). We call these cases instances of *mistaken ID* (Holmes & Ramos, Chapter 5, this volume, call them *mismatches*; Laufer, 1988, calls them *synforms*). In seven other cases (the "pothole" cases), the subjects detoured around the word without even making a guess. In one case, the subject relied on incomplete knowledge of the word. In another, the subject tried unsuccessfully to use morphological analysis. In only one case did the subject rely mainly on context and fail to guess the word.

In general, all three subjects seemed to follow the same pattern for each word they encountered. First, they would simply access their store of vocabulary knowledge. If they thought they recognized the word and knew its meaning, they would stick to that meaning and try to incorporate it in a coherent way into their mental representation of the text, without checking any context clues. This worked well for the many words they really knew—approximately 95% of the 710 words in the two texts. It failed badly, however, for those relatively few words they only *thought* they knew (i.e., the "mistaken ID" cases). If they did not recognize the word as a whole, they would often try morphological analysis to make guesses, concentrating on the word stem. In most cases, however, they would check these guesses against various context clues, which then became the primary determinants of the subject's guess. This was usually successful in generating correct or near-correct guesses.

Finally, if they did not recognize either the word or its stem, they would look for a variety of context clues. This tactic was usually successful. The clues involved were of three general types:

Table 8.2.   Totals for All Target Words, with Main Guessing Strategies Used. (3 Subjects, 2 Texts, 81 Target Words)

Target words already known   37
Guesses   (44)
Successful   (25)
Used context*   23
Latent word knowledge   1
Morphological analysis   1
Unsuccessful   (19)
Mistaken ID   9
Potholes   7
Incomplete knowledge   1
Morphological analysis   1
Used context   1

*Includes "late bloomer" case

- local linguistic constituents (e.g., syntactic or semantic collocations),
- global text representations (including text schemas and "permanent memory," that is, the translation up to that point), and
- world knowledge.

Although they would often appear to use two or more of these different clues in combination, the overwhelmingly most popular and most effective type of clue appeared to be some local linguistic constituent—especially a collocating clue-word that tipped off the meaning of the target word. Of the 23 cases of successful contextual guesswork, 16 were governed by some clue-word. These clue-words were distinctly *local*: all but one of the 16 occur in the same sentence as the target word.

On seven occasions, after not finding sufficient contextual evidence to support a hypothesis or not being able to generate a hypothesis in the first place, the subjects apparently decided that they could get by, or "make do," without it. These are the "pothole" cases. We suspect, on the basis of two other cases (discussed below), that the subject put these words into some sort of interim memory store before going on to the next word.

Successful Guessing

In generating successful guesses, our subjects relied mainly on clue-words. However, they used other context clues as well, and showed a variety of strategies in their guesswork, even within subjects. Using Text 1, the following sections describe and illustrate these strategies.

The Clue-Word Strategy. In 16 of the 25 cases where they successfully guessed a word's meaning, our three subjects used some other word or words in the immediate context to provide clues to the meaning of the target word. In all but one case, this clue-word was located in the same sentence; usually it was the nearest content word. Table 8.3 summarizes these findings:

For example, one subject (Xia) did not know the word *distortions*. On the pretest, he offered no definition for it at all, either in English or in Chinese. Then he encountered it in the reading (sentence 18). Here is the transcript of his protocol (italics indicate words that the subject spoke in Chinese but that we have

Table 8.3. Location of Clue-Words Relative to Target Words

Distance from Target Word	Number of cases
1 content word away	12
2 content words away	1
3 content words away	1
5 content words away	1
27 content words away	1

translated here for the reader's convenience; Roman type and parentheses indicate words the subject spoke in English):

> . . . *When other incurable* (distortion) *whatever, when other, when other incurable problems, it's incurable then it must be problem exist in the economics, setting up tariffs is better than doing nothing, something is better than nothing.*

His written Chinese translation (actually, our back-translation) reads as follows:

> *When other incurable problems exist in the economy, setting up tariffs may be better than doing nothing.*

As reconstructed from the protocol record, Xia begins by fixating on the target word (*distortions*), with the goal being to translate it. He then tries to generate a hypothesis about its meaning. It is not part of his vocabulary knowledge, so he considers other forms of knowledge he has (syntactic, morphological, text schematic, collocational, etc.). He knows the word *incurable* (he defined it correctly on the pretest and also in his protocol) and he apparently knows English syntax well enough to see it as a modifier of *distortions*. He then accesses his world knowledge and infers, in effect, that if it is incurable, it "must be a problem."

A "late bloomer" case. A more unusual example of the clue-word strategy can be found in another subject's (Ran) attempts to guess the meaning of *barriers* (sentences 1 and 2). On the pretest, he correctly translated it as *obstacles*. Yet, when he encountered it in the text a few minutes later, he did not seem to recognize it. Here is the transcript of his thinking aloud as he dealt with the text phrase, "with few tariffs or other barriers to trade":

> *with very free, free, . . . free . . . , free, low, low, few, few, with very few* (tariffs) *very few tariffs, tariffs, tariffs . . . , tariffs, or other. tariffs, or other . . . , other, other, what, few tariffs or other, other . . . , tariffs . . . , (Indeed) really, indeed, indeed . . .*

He fixates on *barriers* but does not seem to be able to generate a guess as to what the word means. In his written translation (done almost concurrently with his thinking aloud), he translates it as "types of duties":

> *with little tariffs or other types of duties between countries.*

Apparently, the modifier *other* serves as a clue-word here, telling him that *barriers* is a superordinate of tariffs. If so, this might help to explain why he does not translate *barriers* as 'obstacles,' as he had on the pretest. Perhaps he does not think of tariffs as obstacles, and therefore assumes that *barriers* must have some other meaning in this context. But since we do not have any protocol data to support this interpretation, it is merely speculative. This is the only case in our entire study where the subject correctly translated a word on the pretest and then failed to even articulate this meaning during the translation process.

He then goes on to sentence 2, where he encounters the word two more times. Here he avoids the word entirely, going around it the way one drives around a pothole in a street (hence, our use of the term *pothole* as a descriptor). The text sentence reads:

> Indeed, economists have tended to be even more critical of trade barriers than have other groups in society, even though economists have taken great care to list the exceptional cases in which they feel trade barriers can be justified.

Ran translates it in writing as follows:

> *Indeed, economists want to have a more critical point of view than in other social sectors.*

In general, one might imagine either of two reasons for potholing on a word, that is, for not even trying to guess it. First, the subject might feel that the word is not essential to the meaning of the sentence and therefore not worth expending a lot of time and energy on.[1] Or, second, the subject might simply have no idea what it means. In the case at hand, the first reason seems unlikely. *Barriers* plays a major role in the text sentence, and by detouring around it the subject has produced a translation that differs greatly from the text sentence. Given his behavior on other parts of the task, it is implausible that he would not have been aware of this difference. On the other hand, the second explanation does not hold up well either, for it seems very unlikely that the subject had no idea what the word meant. After all, he had translated it correctly on the pretest and had come up with a near-synonym for it in the first sentence. So we are quite puzzled why he failed to even attempt a guess in this particular case.

In any event, the subject continued reading and translating. In view of his potholing behavior in sentence 2, one would suppose that he had given up on *barriers*, discharging it, in effect, from working memory. And yet there is clear evidence that he had merely put it into some kind of interim memory buffer. When he got to sentence 6, he encountered the word *barriers* again:

> The main task of this chapter and the following chapters of Part Two is to compare free-trade policies with a much wider range of trade barriers, barriers that do not necessarily shut out all international trade.

Here is how he dealt with it:

> *to compare free-trade policies with* (much wider range of trade barriers) *free-trade policies with wider, wider . . . , wider . . . ,* (much wider) *much wider . . .* (trade barriers and barriers) *much wider range of tariffs . . . range,* (barriers that do not

necessarily shut out all international trade) *wider tariffs . . . or . . . or* (barriers that do not necessarily shut out, barriers that do not necessarily shut out all international trade) *and, and the, and those . . . , those . . . , cannot, cannot prevent, preve-, prevent,* (god!) *preve-, preve- . . . , cannot prevent . . . , cannot prevent . . .* (international trade) *cannot prevent . . . international trade, international trade . . . the tariffs that cannot prevent, prevent international trade, tariffs that cannot prevent . . . international trade, what does this mean? tariffs cannot prevent international trade.*

Suddenly he seems to equate *barriers* with *tariffs.* The only previous mention of tariffs in the text occurs in sentence 1, where it is closely linked, both physically and semantically, with barriers. Thus it appears that Ran must have created an association between these two words and put them together into a memory buffer. His written translation of sentence 6 shows that he indeed now sees *barriers* as meaning 'tariffs':

> The main task of this chapter and the chapters in part two is to compare the free trade policies with tariffs in more extensive areas or the tariffs that cannot prevent international trade.

Thereafter, for the rest of the text, he consistently translates *barriers* as 'tariffs' (it appears three more times). And on the posttest, he translates it the same way.

This is a case, therefore, where the subject's sensitivity to context actually overrode independent word knowledge. In a sense, understanding *barriers* to mean 'tariffs' worked quite well in this context. But if he retains this meaning in lieu of the more general meaning of 'obstacles,' then his performance in other contexts, where *barriers* does not mean 'obstacles,' may suffer. In that case, it could be said that contextual guessing helped his reading but did not help his vocabulary building.

A variety of strategies. Another word that Ran did not know was *presumption.* On the pretest he defined it as 'guess.' When he encountered it in the text (sentence 4), he continued reading the rest of the sentence. Then, he went back to it, fixated on it, and tried a variety of hypotheses. Here is the relevant protocol segment:

> (Such consistent agreement is rare within the economics profession.) *such,* (such consistent) *such . . . , such consistent, consistent* (agreement) *consistent . . . ,* (agreement) *consistent . . . ,* (agreement) *consistent, consistent* (agreement . . . , aiya, I see, agreement) *. . . agree, not "agree" . . . agree, consistent agree, consistent* (agree) *agree,* (agreement) *agree about a event* (agreement) *approve, agree . . . , agree, consistent agree . . . , economics, in economics . . . , in economics circle, in economics circle . . . , in economics circle . . . , it's rare in economics circle . . . ,* (The presumption in favor of trade . . . , presumption in favor of trade is

based primarily on a body of economic analysis . . . , presumption) *such approval,* (presumption, presumption . . . , presumption) *is* (predict, prediction, in favor) *such predi-, predict, such prediction . . . , such . . . , such . . . , about free trade . . . , free trade . . . , such . . . free trade . . . expectation,* (favor of) *free trade. . . . ,* (favor) *appreciation . . . , appre-, appre- . . . appre, admire . . . , appreciation, -tion . . . , appreciation* (presumption, oh, my god, presumption) *is it* (prediction?) *. . . the appreciation of free trade, point of view, point of view . . . , the point of view* (is based primarily) on . . .

His written Chinese translation reads as follows:

This view of free trade is based on the analysis of the nature of . . .

Based on Ran's protocol, our interpretation of his attempts to guess the meaning of *presumption* is as follows: First, he tries to see it as an anaphoric reference to the preceding sentence. That sentence is still active in his working memory (note the recurring phrase *such approval*), and he probably knows that, in formal written English, a common way of creating intersentential cohesion is by beginning a sentence with a definite noun phrase that refers anaphorically to all or part of the preceding sentence.

Thus his first guess is that *presumption* means 'approval.' He quickly rejects this guess, for reasons that are not made clear in the protocol. Perhaps he recognizes that ''approval in favor of'' would be redundant.

He then tries 'prediction.' The fact that he makes this guess in English rather than Chinese is a tipoff, we feel, to the underlying source of the guess: *prediction* and *presumption* are somewhat similar in word-shape, differing only in their internal syllable. Thus it is plausible to suspect that he uses word-level morphology to generate this particular guess. Notice that this is strictly a *local* guess: there is no suggestion of any ''predicting'' in the text up to this point, and no reason that we can see for him to have it in his mental text representation. Perhaps this is why he rather quickly abandons this guess. When he tries it out in context, it doesn't work.

Next he tries 'expectation,' which is a near-synonym of 'prediction' but which has more of a positive connotation. This guess, we believe, reflects the subject's attempt to capture the meaning of the phrase *presumption in favor* of; note his protocol comment ''prediction, in favor.'' But he quickly rejects 'expectation,' preferring the even more positive 'appreciation'; note how he continues to key on the text word *favor* in his protocol comments. At one point, he even tries the very positive term 'admire.'

Finally, though, he seems to recognize that a positive term like 'appreciation' or 'admire' does not go well with *in favor of*. Perhaps he realizes that a phrase like ''appreciation in favor of'' would be redundant. He briefly returns to 'prediction,' then tries ''point of view,'' without giving any clues as to why.

Perhaps it is the connotative neutrality that appeals to him: ''point of view'' has neither a positive nor negative nuance and thus might be a safer guess for someone who does not know what *presumption* means. At the same time, it fills the role of a reiterative superordinate (Halliday & Hasan, 1977), providing a lexical transition from the first paragraph to the second. 'View' is the word he settles on for his translation.

This is a good example of a subject trying multiple, varied guesses, all of them using context. His guesswork also benefits from morphological analysis (presumption = prediction) and from the exploring of a semantic field: prediction > expectation > appreciation > admir(ation) > point of view > view. Although 'view' is not a fully successful translation for *presumption*, it is close enough in this context, we feel, to count as an instance of successful guesswork.

Unsuccessful Guessing

As Table 8.2 shows, our subjects failed to make correct guesses on 20 of the 44 guessing opportunities they had. In 17 of these 20 cases they did not use context clues, relying instead on vocabulary knowledge, which turned out to be deficient. The most common cause of unsuccessful guessing was simple misidentification of the word. Sometimes our subjects would try to use this ''mistaken ID'' in their translation; sometimes they would sense that something was seriously wrong with their interpretation and would detour around the word (the ''pot-hole'' cases). This section discusses both of these types of errors and a third category, that of incomplete knowledge.

Mistaken ID.   There were nine cases where the subject misidentified a word and forced this misinterpretation into his translation. In most of these cases, there were context clues available which were inconsistent with the mistaken interpretation and which could have alerted the subject to the error, but the subject apparently either failed to notice these clues or failed to take them seriously. This may be due partly to the nature of the clues themselves: in eight of these nine cases, our cloze tests with native speakers indicated that the context clues were not at all obvious. But it is also related, we feel, to a phenomenon reported in Haynes (1984) and Bensoussan and Laufer (1984), namely, that word-shape familiarity will tend to override contextual factors.

A good example of mistaken ID can be found in Xia's attempts to guess the meaning of *optimal* in sentence 17. On the pretest he showed no familiarity with the word, not even venturing a guess. When he encountered it in the text, he apparently mistook it for *optional*. Here is the relevant protocol segment:

Four . . . , there are exceptions in free trade, (A, tariffs, the national optimal) *nation . . . A, a nation can choose tariffs, a nation can choose tariffs, what does that mean? When a nation can influence the prices that it trade with other nations, it may gain from the tariffs* (right, that's right)

He reads the entire text phrase, "The 'national optimal' tariff", and quickly generates 'can choose' for 'optional'. He apparently senses that this interpretation does not quite fit the context ("what does that mean?"), but he uses it anyway. His written translation reads, "National selective tariffs," with 'selective' clearly being a rendition of 'can choose.'

There are few context clues to draw on in this case, either positive clues supporting an "optimal" interpretation or negative clues denying an "optional" one. And those few clues are hardly clear and unambiguous. One could point to the fact that, in talking about how tariffs affect the well-being of a nation, the entire paragraph focuses on their *degree* of effectiveness. The word *better* is particularly prominent, appearing four times, all as part of the main clause predicate. But these clues appear in adjoining sentences, not in the sentence in which the target word itself appears. When we had 12 native speakers (graduate students and undergraduates) complete a cloze test with *optimal* blanked out, they made wild guesses like 'trade' (2), 'income,' 'brand,' 'price,' 'profit,' 'variable,' 'good,' and 'debt'; three of them left it blank. Thus we have independent evidence that the context clues in this case are not obvious.

Potholes. The other major category of unsuccessful guesses consisted of "pothole" cases, that is, cases where the subject simply avoided the word in his written translation. We have already illustrated this kind of avoidance in Ran's response to *barriers*. After first encountering the word and then seeming to hang on to it in some temporary memory store for several sentences, he eventually succeeded in figuring out its meaning; and so what started out as a pothole case became instead a "late bloomer" case of successful guessing from context. But in the other seven pothole cases in our corpus, involving four words, this was not so; the subject avoided the word indefinitely.[2] And in these cases, it is not because of any lack of context clues. Our cloze tests with native speakers indicated that all four of these words had strong contextual support. Thus, in these cases, it seems that the subject misidentified the word, recognized from context clues that it did not fit the context, but then could not think of a good alternative. In other words, there was probably a clash between the subject's supposed knowledge of a word and his text representation as derived from context clues. Not knowing how to resolve this contradiction, he or she apparently opted to evade it.

A good example of potholding can be found in Xia's response to the text word *warrant* (sentence 12). On the pretest, Xia translated *warrant* as 'guarantee.' Like our other two subjects, he apparently confused it with *warranty*, a word probably known to many Chinese students in the United States through their exposure to consumer product documentation. The text sentence reads as follows:

> Our exploration of the pros and cons of a tariff will be detailed enough to warrant listing its main conclusions here at the outset.

and Xia's protocol reads like this:

Our exploration about the good and bad points of tariffs (exploration) *exploration is better . . . exploration will . . . be in great details detail* (detail enough) *will be detailed enough to . . . sure* (sure, sure) *sure to list out . . . the main conclusion, be sure to list here the main, what? confused, will be detailed enough to sure, list out at the beginning the main conclusion—This sentence doesn't feel right—then why, why at the beginning list out the main conclusions, will be detailed enough, . . . Actually it's like this, our exploration about the good and bad points of the tariffs will be in great detail, . . . then will guarantee, list out at the beginning . . . not right, we, didn't get the right style, will be described here in great detail at the beginning, use "explore," not "explain." Our exploration of the pros and cons of tariffs will be detailed enough . . .* (to warrant, to warrant, to warrant) *enough to do what? Indeed, this chapter and the next . . .*

He apparently begins his guesswork on *warrant* by accessing his vocabulary knowledge. Immediately upon encountering the word, he translates it as 'sure.' This is not the word he used on the pretest, but it is fairly closely related: A warranty or a guarantee is an 'assurance' of something. However, when he checks it against the rest of the sentence, he notices that it doesn't fit: "This sentence doesn't feel right." At this point, one would think he might abandon the warranty/guarantee/sure hypothesis and try another, but he doesn't. Instead, he tries "guarantee." When that doesn't work, he simply evades the problem by rephrasing the sentence. His written translation comes out like this:

Our exploration of the advantage and disadvantage of tariffs will be introduced in great detail, so that the major conclusions are listed at the beginning.

Most of our native speakers who took the cloze test produced good guesses on this item: 'merit, start, justify (5), encourage, warrant.' (Two others left it blank.) Thus there appears to be substantial contextual support for this word. Anyone familiar with the text-schema for academic textbook discussions (as our three subjects were) should be able to recognize that pro-and-con explorations typically lead to, or warrant, certain conclusions. Thus it should have been relatively easy for our subjects to guess the word's meaning, even if (as in the case of one subject), a key word like *exploration* is not fully known.[3] Yet there is no evidence from Xia's thinking aloud or from his translation that he used any of this contextual support in his guesswork. Rather, he clings to two types of commitments: (a) the warrant–warranty misidentification, and (b) the definition of warranty as "guarantee, assurance." In the case at hand, it is the first type of commitment that apparently causes the problem: Were it not for that word-form misidentification, the second commitment would presumably not come into play. But this does not reduce the overall force of the point we wish to make here, namely, that context clues seem to have little effect when the learner has word-level commitments in his mind. For we have evidence from other cases (see also Huckin & Jin, 1987) that, where polysemy is involved, learners who know only one meaning of a word will try to stick to that meaning even in the face of negative context clues.

Incomplete Knowledge. On two occasions, our subjects relied on partial knowledge of a word and were unable, despite serious attempts to use context clues, to guess the full meaning of the word in that context. Here is an example: On the pretest Xia defined the word *liquidity* as "not solid" (Chinese: *ye ti*). When he encountered it in the reading text ("Balance of payments deficits and problems of national liquidity depend to some degree on enterprises"), he first tried using the "not solid" definition ("fluidity"). But then he quickly recognized that "fluidity" did not fit the context. Going back two sentences, he noticed the word *instability* and decided to key on that. His protocol for this section reads as follows:

> *The balance of payments and . . . and* (liquidating, national liquidating . . .) *fluidity, national fluidity,* (national liquidating) *problem, not, national, national, fluidity, fluidity, nation, national impossibility, national fluidity, the instability . . . yes, instability . . . [PAUSE] . . . it's impossible to translate this second part . . .* (problems of . . . liquidating) *depend on enterprise. That means the instability problem of the nation depends on enterprise, to a certain extent . . . the instability problem of a nation . . . depend . . . on enterprises. Enterprises are facing . . .*

And he translates the text using *instability* for *liquidity*:

> *To a certain extent, the balance of payments and the instability problem of a country depend on enterprises.*

Apparently he is not confident of this translation: on the posttest, he reverts to his original definition of *liquidity* as 'not solid.' This and another case like it represent two of the three cases where a subject used context clues but failed to guess the meaning of the word. (See Haynes & Baker, Chapter 7, this volume, for other illustrations of the problems caused by polysemy.)

A Cognitive Model

Figure 8.1 is a tentative working model of the behavior just described. This cognitive model incorporates both *serial* and *parallel processing*. The metalinguistic control steps (e.g., "Try to generate hypothesis," "Test hypothesis?", "Make do?" "Need more context?" and "Generate more context") are done in serial order and appear to be governed by conscious decision making. There is clearly a natural ordering to at least some of these steps (e.g., a hypothesis must

Task Representation

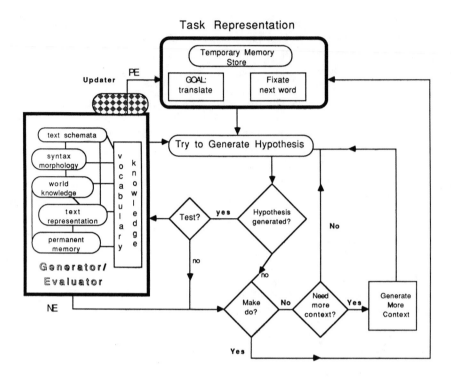

PE= positive evaluation
NE= negative evaluation

be generated before it can be tested), and one can fairly easily follow, in the protocol, a subject's path through these steps. But this path, though made up of a sequence of steps, is not always straightforward. Our subjects displayed false starts, tried multiple hypotheses, ran into dead ends, and generally showed behaviors that one might expect of readers with limited vocabularies. For example, sometimes they would generate several quick hypotheses in a row, without testing them. This would usually result in a negative answer to the question "Make do?" and cause them to read ahead beyond the target word ("Generate more context"). On the other hand, sometimes they would generate an unsuccessful hypothesis (negative evaluation, or "NE") but use it anyway—an example of making do. On two occasions a subject failed to generate a hypothesis, went on past it, and then much later suddenly came up with an appropriate guess. We take this as evidence of some kind of temporary memory store intermediate between the two traditional types of memory (working and long-term) often discussed in the cognitive psychology literature.

The modules in the Generator/Evaluator—which represent only some of those that may have to be included in a more refined model—are linked together in a network. The module labeled "Vocabulary Knowledge" refers to the subject's knowledge of words, including such aspects as register, frequency, syntactic behavior, pronunciation, orthographemic form, derivational relatives, different meanings, and collocations (Richards, 1976). It is, of course, the single most important module for word-guessing in context. The "Text Schemata" module contains the subject's mental representations of prototypical discourse patterns. The "Syntax and Morphology" module contains the subject's general knowledge of sentence-formation and word-formation rules, apart from specific syntactic and morphological knowledge associated with any particular word (which we are treating as part of Vocabulary Knowledge). "World Knowledge" refers to all the facts, beliefs, and other concepts that comprise the subject's nonlinguistic knowledge of the world. The "Text Representation" is the subject's evolving conception of the meaning of the text-at-hand. "Permanent Memory" refers to the subject's written translation of the text up to that point.

In contrast to the linear nature of the metalinguistic control steps, the cognitive processing that takes place within and among the various modules in the Generator/Evaluator is much more rapid and complex, and much less readily analyzable. Indeed, our depiction of this part of the model is based largely on inferences that we have made using relatively fragmentary data. The different modules in the Generator/Evaluator, as we hypothesize them to be, are interconnected in such a way as to operate in parallel. For example, vocabulary knowledge is related to world knowledge inasmuch as words have ranges of possible referents in the world; conversely, world knowledge is partially codified, so to speak, in vocabulary. Vocabulary knowledge also includes knowing a word's part of speech (syntax), its morphological composition, and its collocability in various text schemata. It also involves knowing how to adjust the word's conventional sense to actual text representations. Conversely, one's knowledge of syntax, morphology, text schemas, etc. can alter one's vocabulary knowledge, especially in the context of particular texts. Seeing a word used in a certain way in a certain text can cause a reader to revise his or her mental representation of that word, not just to make it fit the reader's global sense of the text up to that point (the "text representation") and the written translation ("permanent memory"), but also perhaps more generally and more permanently. For this reason, we see the contents of these different modules as being not fixed but *dynamic*: Whenever a hypothesis receives a positive evaluation (PE), it is used to update the subject's mental text representation, vocabulary knowledge, world knowledge, and other components of the Generator/Evaluator (hence our inclusion of an "Updater" in the model). The way in which subjects access these different components also varies, even for a single subject working on a single word: When our subjects tried to test hypotheses, they did not appear to use the same modules in quite the same way they had used to generate those hypotheses. For example, they might key on morphology to generate a hypothesis but then rely more on world knowledge to test it, or vice-versa.

We wish to emphasize that the model just described is merely a tentative one. It is based on the cognitive processing behavior of only three students doing translation tasks on only two texts. Further studies with a variety of students, texts, and tasks are needed to see if the model has more general validity.

Summary

Vocabulary knowledge seems to be the learner's primary resource in a translation task, at least in the case of our three students. When they know the word, it works to the students' advantage. When they clearly don't know the word, it also works, because they can then direct their attention to context clues. Where this reliance on vocabulary knowledge can cause serious problems is in cases where learners think they know a word but really don't. Instead of using context to help them correct their error, they simply persist in the error.[4] And our data suggest that learners do not learn from these errors: Of the 16 cases of misidentification in our study, subjects did not show any pretest–posttest improvement on 15 of them. The one exception, interestingly, occurred in the case just discussed. Instead of translating *warrant* as 'guarantee,' as he had on the pretest, Xia left it blank on the posttest. This may not seem like much of an improvement, but if it indicates awareness of a possible misidentification, it could be the kind of incremental change that Nagy et al., and others, have claimed to be typical of vocabulary growth.

CONCLUSION

This study was motivated by three research questions pertaining to the word-guessing strategies that second-language learners use, the role of context in these strategies, and the limits of context. Since only three subjects were studied, our findings cannot be taken as "answers" to these questions, even tentative ones. But the findings are consistent and coherent enough to raise interesting hypotheses for further research. Let us conclude by summarizing these findings.

What strategies do second-language learners use when they encounter unknown vocabulary in context? In general, our learners first studied the word-form itself to see if they recognized any of its parts. If they did, they would generate a hypothesis as to what the word might mean; then they would generally use one or more context-based strategies to evaluate this hypothesis. If they did not recognize any part of the word at all, they would typically use context-based strategies to generate a guess. The most popular of these strategies was the use of some collocating clue-word in the immediate context. Clue-words seemed to serve as a link between the target word, on the one hand, and various levels of representation, including syntax, text schemata, text representation, permanent memory, and world knowledge, on the other. If they could not find any clue-words or other contextual aids, and if they could get by (i.e., generate a co-herent text representation) without using the target word, they would "detour" around it.

How does context function to aid second-language learners in dealing with unknown words? As described in the preceding paragraph, context helps the learner both to generate and to evaluate guesses. Sometimes learners can guess at the meaning of a word through morphological or other word-level clues, and use context only to evaluate their guesses. In other cases, learners may need to use context clues to generate a guess in the first place. In either event, the subjects in our study relied mainly on local context clues to help them guess unknown words. In 16 of the 23 cases where they successfully exploited the context, the principal type of clue they used was some clue-word located in the same sentence. But they sometimes used other kinds of context clues as well, either in support of a clue-word or independently. For example, the general language of the text sometimes seemed to evoke world knowledge that the learner could apply to the evolving text representation, which in turn could be applied to the target word. In the seven successful cases where our subjects did not seem to be using clue-words as such, they were apparently relying exclu-sively on these broader forms of contextual support.

In what ways do second-language learners fail to take full advantage of context clues; that is, how might teachers help these learners to make better guesses? By far the major condition associated with our subjects' failure to use context clues to guess word-meanings was when they thought they knew the word in question but didn't. As in Bensoussan and Laufer (1984) and Haynes (1984), word familiarity—either apparent or real—caused our subjects to ignore contextual factors. In most cases the word was correctly identified, and failure to use context to verify a guess was unproblematic. Indeed, one could argue that it is actually the most efficient way to proceed, since it puts less strain on working memory. But in many other cases, the word was mistakenly identified and failure to examine the context in these cases led to serious problems of comprehension. This pattern has also been noted by Van Parreren and Schouten-van Parreren (1982) and others. Teachers should alert their students to the problem and encourage them to use context clues to double-check word interpretations, *even when they think they know the word.* And they should show them how to use larger discourse-level clues to do this (as discussed in Huckin, 1986, and Huckin & Jin, 1987), not just local clues. Since these metacognitive skills are an important part of reading itself, helping students to develop such skills would benefit them not only in vocabulary building but in reading as well.

At the same time, teachers should encourage students to improve their gra-phemic identification of words. In our study, most of the unsuccessful cases of word guessing resulted from misidentification of word-forms. Our subjects were apparently lulled into thinking that they knew such words and did not have to check them against the context. But the fact is that they did not know these words. The problem can be attributed partly to the fact that our subjects were all native speakers of a language whose orthography and lexis are radically different from those of English. But students from a cognate language can have analogous problems, as is discussed by Holmes (1986). Sensitizing second-language learners to the existence of homographs, near-homographs, and other potential sources of graphemic confusion would serve the valuable purpose of encouraging such learners to use context clues to confirm their guesses.

Our study echoes Stanovich's research with first-language readers in which he found that slow readers compensate for word-recognition deficiencies by making more use of context. Our second-language learners relied heavily—and often successfully—on context clues for words they did not recognize. But we also found that this process of using the context often took considerable time. As Segalowitz (1986) notes:

> If the reduced automaticity of word recognition does result in increased dependency on contextual information, then obviously the quality of that information becomes very important. Bilinguals who have a poor grasp of paragraph structure or the sense of certain syntactic structures will have poor quality contextual information to assist word recognition. Their increased reliance on context may thus result in yet slower reading rates and in reading marked by difficulties. (p. 9)

This study is merely an exploratory one, with obvious limitations. For one, it does not tell us anything about beginning second-language learners or about advanced second-language learners. Research reported elsewhere (e.g., Huckin, 1986) suggests that beginners are *unable* to use many of the context clues discussed here, and it is possible that advanced learners may find less of a *need* to use them. Also, this study looked at learners from only one language group. Learners from other language groups, especially from cognate languages, may behave differently. Furthermore, it used subjects who had been residing in an English-speaking country for at least a year. Thus it may not be reflective of subjects learning English in their native country. And, of course, it used only three subjects. Other limitations could be cited as well. We hope that, rather than being seen simply as flaws in the research, these limitations will be seen as raising important questions for further study.

REFERENCES

Alderson, J. C. (1984). Reading in a foreign language: A reading problem or a language problem? In J. C. Alderson & A. H. Urquhart (Eds.), *Reading in a foreign language*. New York: Longman.

Bensoussan, M., & Laufer, B. (1984). Lexical guessing in context in EFL reading comprehension. *Journal of Research in Reading, 7*(1), 15–32.

Cohen, A., Glasman, H., Rosenbaum-Cohen, P., Ferrara, J., & Fine, J. (1988). Reading English for specialized purposes: Discourse analysis and the use of student informants. In P. Carrell, J. Devine, & D. Eskey (Eds.), *Interactive approaches to second langauge reading* (pp. 152–167). Cambridge, UK: Cambridge University Press.

Collins, A. M., & Loftus, E. F. (1975). A spreading-activation theory of semantic processing. *Psychological Review, 82,* 407–428.

Duffy, T. M. (1985). Readability formulas: What's the use? In T. Duffy & R. Waller (Eds.), *Designing usable texts* (pp. 113–143). New York: Academic Press.

Ericsson, L., & Simon, H. (1984). *Protocol analysis: Verbal reports as data.* Cambridge, MA: MIT Press.

Eskey, D. (1988). Holding in the bottom: An interactive approach to the language problems of second language readers. In P. Carrell, J. Devine, & D. Eskey (Eds.), *Interactive approaches to second language reading* (pp. 983–100). Cambridge, UK: Cambridge University Press.

Eskey, D., & Grabe, W. (1988). Interactive models for second language reading: Perspectives on instruction. In P. Carrell, J. Devine, & D. Eskey (Eds.), *Interactive approaches to second language reading* (pp. 223–238). Cambridge, UK: Cambridge University Press.

Goodman (1976). Reading: A psycholinguistic guessing game. In H. Singer & R. Ruddell (Eds.), *Theoretical models and processes of reading* (2nd ed., pp. 497–508). Newark, DE: International Reading Association.

Halliday, M. A. K., & Hasan, R. (1977). *Cohesion in English.* London: Longman.

Haynes, M. (1984). Patterns and perils of guessing in second language reading. In J. Handscombe, R. A. Orem, & B. P. Taylor (Eds.), *On TESOL '83* (pp. 163–176). Washington, DC: TESOL.

Holmes, J. (1986). Snarks, quarks, and cognates: An elusive fundamental particle in reading comprehension. *The ESPecialist, 15,* 13–40.

Hosenfeld, C. (1977). A preliminary investigation of the reading strategies of successful and nonsuccessful second language learners. *System, 5,* 110–123.

Huckin, T. (1986). The use of discourse patterning in foreign-language reading and vocabulary acquisition. *DELTA, 2*(1), 57–75.

Huckin, T., & Jin, Z.-D. (1987). Inferring word-meaning from context: A study in second-language acquisition. In F. Marshall (Ed.), *ESCOL '86* (pp. 271–280). Columbus, OH: Ohio State University Department of Linguistics.

Laufer, B. (1988). The concept of 'synforms' (similar lexical forms) in vocabulary acquisition. *Language and Education, 2*(2), 113–132.

Lindert, P. H. (1986). *International economics* (8th ed.). Homewood, IL: Irwin.

Nagy, W., Herman, P., & Anderson, R. (1985). Learning words from context. *Reading Research Quarterly, 20*(2), 233–53.

Raimes, A. (1985) What unskilled ESL students do as they write: A classroom study of composing. *TESOL Quarterly, 19*(2), 229–258.

Richards, J. (1976). The role of vocabulary teaching. *TESOL Quarterly, 10*(1), 77–89.

Rumelhart, D. E. (1977). Toward an interactive model of reading. In S. Dornic (Ed.), *Attention and performance VI.* Hillsdale, NJ: Erlbaum.

Rumelhart, D. E., McClelland, J. L., & the PDP Research Group (1986). *Parallel distributed processing: Explorations in the microstructures of cognition: Vol. I. Foundations. Vol. II. Psychological and biological models.* Cambridge, MA: MIT Press.

Segalowitz, N. (1986). Skilled reading in the second language. In J. Vaid (Ed.), *Language processing in bilinguals: Psycholinguistic and neuropsychological perspectives* (pp. 3–19). Hillsdale, NJ: Erlbaum.

Seltzer, J. (1983). What constitutes a 'readable' technical style? In P. V. Anderson, R. J. Brockmann, & C. R. Miller (Eds.), *New essays in technical and scientific communication: research, theory, and practice* (pp. 71–89). Farmingdale, NY: Baywood.

Smith, F. (1971). *Understanding reading*. New York: Holt, Rinehart, and Winston.

Stanovich, K. E. (1980). Toward an interactive-compensatory model of individual differences in the development of reading fluency. *Reading Research Quarterly, 16*, 32–71.

Ulijn, J. (1981). Conceptual and syntactic strategies in reading a foreign language. In E. Hopkins & R. Grotjahn (Eds.), *Studies in language teaching and language acquisition* (Vol. 9, pp. 129–166). Bochum: Brockmeyer.

Van Parreren, C. F., & Schouten-van Parreren, M. C. (1981). Contextual guessing: A trainable reader strategy. *System, 9*(3), 235–241.

ENDNOTES

1. For example, when he encountered the unfamiliar word *lexicon* (in another text), Xia apparently decided that it was not important enough to worry about. The text sentence reads like this: "Political risk has long been a familiar term in the lexicon of international business," and Xia's protocol reads as follows:

    > In what? (lexicon) *but the political risk recently still not . . . the political risk . . . in administrative system, political risk for a long time, for long time, turn it over, political risk has become a familiar word, term, another? in, in the world, has become the international business, what IS this! Pass it, useless, insignificant.*

    He then potholed on it.

2. We observed a second instance of this "late bloomer" phenomenon in another part of the study that is not included in this chapter. Reading a third text, Xia encountered the word *cataclysmic*. He avoided it at first, but then—four sentences later—suddenly came up with a successful guess ("explosive").

3. Our native speaker subjects had to work from this sentence: "Our _____ of the _____ and _____ of a tariff will be detailed enough to _____ listing its main conclusions here at the _____." Thus they actually had less context available to them than did our nonnative subjects.

4. For other discussion of this phenomenon, see Bensoussan and Laufer (1984), Laufer (1988).

Editorial Comments

These researchers combine a powerful technique for looking at cognitive processes during L2 reading (L1 translation with think-aloud) with a range of other information sources: a careful look at texts, reader error patterns, and vocabulary knowledge shown in pretests and posttests.

Using these multiple information sources, Huckin and Bloch focus closely on the relations between reading process and learning product. From this they develop a useful cognitive model of word guessing from context. In addition, they offer us an important distinction between *comprehension* while reading and *vocabulary building*, which may or may not result from this comprehension. In harmony with cognitive theories of attention and learning, they suggest that adequate comprehension does not always lead to long-term retention of word meanings (see also Mondria & Wit-de-Boer, 1989, who found for Dutch students learning French that guess-ability was inversely related to retention—the richer the context and the easier the guess, the less likely were readers to remember a word's meaning).

We applaud several aspects of Huckin and Bloch's methodology: (a) The vocabulary pretest is more than the simple checklist used by Nagy, Herman, and Anderson (1985), since it includes probes for definitions and translations; (b) the pretest–posttest design allows for a more precise estimate of vocabulary learned during the reading than does a posttest, which assumes everything to be new; (c) the use of written translation from L2 to L1 with concurrent L1 think-aloud is a powerful alternative to the more typical think-aloud procedure, for it allows more precise insight into the online comprehension, since think-aloud and written protocols can be compared (although, as with any data, the sources of a given difficulty and of its resolution are still not always apparent and thus still depend on researcher interpretation); (d) using texts actually assigned for coursework in the ESL setting, as Parry (this volume) does, enhances the ecological validity of the study; and (e) careful delineation of context through the authors' analysis of texts and their provision of the whole texts within the research report allows us to closely scrutinize their work.

We also learn a great deal from Huckin and Bloch's categorization of strategies leading to successful and unsuccessful guesses (Table 8.1). This confirms a difficulty mentioned by Haynes (1984 and this volume; Chapter 3, and Holmes & Ramos, Chapter 5, this volume), which has been given a name by Laufer (1989): that mistaken identities or "syn-form" confusions may be a major unrecognized source of miscomprehen-sion. In contrast with L1 children, this confusion among similar word-forms in memory may represent a special difficulty for L2 learners, whose unstable knowledge of L2 phonology probably creates less efficient patterns of storage and retrieval in memory. Huckin and Bloch find that about 20% of guesses for unknown words involve some type of word-form misrecognition. It also appears that word-form misidentifications easily short-circuit the guessing from context process. But the pedagogical implications of these findings remain cloudy: How can we increase the accuracy of word-form representation in learners' memory or their atten-tion to form during word identification in reading? Without going beyond the evidence we have presented here, we can only stress that teachers need in some way to work on word-form accuracy, probably approaching word-form both phonologically, graphemically, and morphemically.

Huckin and Bloch find, as have other researchers (Haynes, 1984, Chapter 3; Chern, Chapter 4, and Dubin & Olshtain, Chapter 10) that most acceptable guesses grow out of clues in the local context (immediate sentence context). The pedagogical implications of this finding remain to be worked out through training studies and classroom research. However, teachers should be aware that they can expect students to experience more success with lexical inference when there are clues in the immediate sentence. Likewise, they should know that students will need more direction from teachers in order to benefit from global contextual clues.

Finally, the authors' inclusion of parallel processing and attentional considerations in their discussion of context raises the question of whether it may be as important to directly teach some vocabulary to a satisfactory level of automatic recognition (see Coady et al., Chapter 11) as to stress strategic but attention-demanding processes of contextual inference. For developing readers, the more automatic lower level cognitive processes can become (processes such as word identification and meaning selection among alternative senses of words), the more attention or cognitive capacity the reader will have left to deal with higher level processing (Perfetti, 1985; Rayner & Pollatsek, 1989) such as inferring the meanings of new word-forms, relating sentence meaning to the global context, and so on. Which approach is more important—direct teaching of vocabulary toward automaticity, or more indirect teaching of guessing strategies which use the broader context? At this point we can only say that teachers need to be aware of the benefits and drawbacks of each approach; indeed, that is one of the major goals of this volume as a whole.

References

Laufer, B. (1989). The concept of 'synforms' (similar lexical forms) in vocabulary acquisition. *Language and Education, 2*(2), 113–132.

Mondria, J., & Wit-de-Boer, M. (1989). Worden leren door raden? De invloed van context op het raden en outhouden van woorden [To learn words through guessing? The influence of context on the guessing and retention of words]. *Levende Talen*, pp. 497–500.

Nagy, W., Herman, P., & Anderson, R. C. (1985). Learning words from context. *Reading Research Quarterly, 10*, 233–253.

Perfetti, C. A. (1985). *Reading ability.* New York: Oxford University Press.

Rayner, K., & Pollatsek, A. 1989. *The psychology of reading.* Englewood Cliffs, NJ: Prentice Hall.

III
Examination of Context

Chapter 9
Predicting Word Meanings From Contextual Clues: Evidence From L1 Readers

Fraida Dubin
University of Southern California
Los Angeles, CA

Elite Olshtain
Tel Aviv University
Ramat-Aviv, Israel

This chapter poses the question: In what instances are adult, educated L1 readers able to predict or generate word meanings to fit a particular textual context? In what instances are they not? What are some of the specific features in a text which aid or hinder the task? It is believed that, by delineating the elements in texts which make it possible or not for L1 readers to supply word meanings, we can help both teachers and materials preparers who work with L2 learners be better prepared to deal with unedited texts.

BACKGROUND

Guessing word meanings from the context as a way to deal with unfamiliar vocabulary in unedited selections has been suggested so widely by both L1 and L2 reading specialists that it is the prevailing conventional wisdom. In one such source (Gairns & Redman, 1986), the strategy of ''contextual guesswork'' is described in some detail. Among other caveats, the authors emphasize ''that students should not be asked to guess the meaning from context when the context is wholly inadequate to the task'' (p. 84). However, the question of what kind of context is adequate for guessing word meanings in context remains unanswered.

Theories about the nature of reading put a great deal of emphasis on strategies of guessing and predicting in the 1960s, 1970s, and well into the 1980s. Reading, from that point of view, was labeled a "psycholinguistic guessing game" (Goodman, 1967). The approach focused on so-called top-down, or cognition-driven, strategies such as predicting and guessing. More recently, however, a later, competing model of the reading process has developed which combines top-down strategies and bottom-up, or data-driven, strategies (Eskey, 1986), an "interactive" model of reading (Rumelhart, 1977). According to interactive theory, effective readers use both top-down and bottom-up processing, although they are not always aware of the latter: They predict overall meaning, but they also use local graphemic signals to get meaning from print.

Along with more sophisticated, complex notions of the reading process as formulated by interactive theorists, there is a growing literature on the limitations of guessing for developing vocabulary knowledge (Huckin, 1988; Parry, 1987; Dubin & Olshtain 1987a, b). When does guessing work? When doesn't it work? What are its parameters? For example, Parry (1987) has described the role which the reader's own cultural background plays in the process of guessing. Haynes' study (1984), one of the first in the L2 literature that referred to interactive reading theory, found that ESL learners could guess but still not comprehend a text. Dubin and Olshtain (1987a) found that L2 students scored well in answering overall comprehension questions after reading a passage but were not able to recognize the meaning of key terms within it; or that, at least at that stage of their interlanguage development, they were still acquiring the knowledge of specific lexical items.

One aspect of the strategy of guessing involves the knowledge which the reader brings to the text since meaning in all written material goes beyond the domain of the text itself. As pointed out by Drum and Konopak (1987),

> Although the within text cues can refine and enrich previous meanings for words, if the reader has no understanding of the topic, then learning will likely be confined to a possible recognition memory for the words. Word knowledge accrues with domain knowledge. (p 85)

In delineating the components of textual support for particular lexical items, we wanted to be able to capture the full range of knowledge which readers must possess, from "domain knowledge" to recognition of local, linguistic clues.

THE CONSTRUCT: TEXTUAL SUPPORT

The main objective of the study reported in this chapter was to further delineate the components of textual support. In an earlier paper (Dubin & Olshtain, 1987b), we noted that some words seem to be rather easy to guess while others are almost impossible. The difference, we proposed, was the degree of textual support, a construct for describing a complex set of elements which include:

1. Extratextual knowledge: the reader's general knowledge extending beyond the text.
2. Thematic knowledge: the reader's overall grasp of the content of this particular text.
3. Semantic I: information extending over larger discourse units in the text beyond the paragraph level.
4. Semantic II: information available locally at the sentence or paragraph level.
5. Syntactic: relationships within the immediate sentence or paragraph.

The five elements of textual support are presented here in a hierarchy which moves from the most global type of processing to the most local. The first two components (1 & 2) are more closely related to top-down (knowledge driven) processing at both the extratextual and textual level. The last two (4 and 5) are more directly tied to bottom-up processing (data-driven), while the middle component (3) involves substantial top-down and bottom-up processing. Furthermore, the four subtypes of textual support that are not extratextual in nature (2, 3, 4, 5) can be described under 2 and 3, which rely more heavily on features of coherence, and 4 and 5, which rely mostly on features of cohesion.

In this chapter, we propose that the degree of textual support, which is linked with a word's guessability, can range from high to low. Textual support can occur either locally or globally in a text. Global textual support requires more top-down processing skills and often extratextual knowledge. Local textual support is tied to the sentence or clause level; it calls forth primarily bottom-up processing skills.

Since this ability to guess from context—at least in the case of some words in a text—is evidenced by native speakers, it was clear from the start that they would be the subjects in any further study. Establishing native speakers' ability to guess correct word meanings provides a norm of retrievability for items deleted from a text. Second-language teachers need to know what native speakers can do with a text before making suggestions to L2 learners. However, it has not been at all clear how L1 readers go about using textual support as an aid for discovering word meanings. Moreover, the conditions which make guessing possible or not need clarification.

One facet of guessing from context is the text. But behind every page there is a writer. In fact, the hypothesis of textual support connects readers and writers through the element which mediates them, the text. Readers, of course, bring their own background knowledge and experience to the process of getting meaning from print. In this study, however, we have not attempted to assess readers' background knowledge in any way, concentrating instead on the domain of the text.

At the same time, an aspect of word meaning which writers provide to texts is word choice, or the selection of just the right lexical item to fit a particular sentence. In working with native-speaker subjects and their abilities to guess word meanings from context, it was a factor that needed to be taken into account. The lexical resources of English often provide writers with an array of choices. Moreover, stylistic conventions urge writers to make use of this broad menu. We realized that, in analyzing native speakers' ability to retrieve word meanings, we would push up against the boundaries of synonymy.

THE STUDY

Three central questions motivated the present study:

1. Can the elements which make up textual support be described in terms of natural texts selected at random?
2. How do L1 readers make use of textual support in producing lexical items which fit particular contexts?
3. What is the relationship between interactive reading theory and the utilization of textual support by readers?

Procedures

The initial phase of the study was undertaken with 21 adult, native speakers of American English, all with sufficient education and background (mostly undergraduate university students who were humanities and social science majors) to read newspaper articles dealing with popular science topics. The initial 21 subjects read the text entitled *Turtle May Be Clue to The Dinosaur's Demise* (see Appendix A). Subsequently, the same procedure was carried out with an additional 20 native-speaker, adult subjects of similar educational background. However, the second group of subjects read two other texts, *Back to Basics* (see Appendix B) and *In Search of a Perfect Calendar* (see Appendix C). All three texts are written for readers without specialized knowledge; in this genre (popular science writing) the writer tries to capture general readers' interest in topics that make use of science content.

The subjects were given a copy of the text with certain words deleted. This was not a traditional ratio-fixed cloze; neither was it a rational deletion cloze (Bachman, 1985). Rather, we used a cloze-like mechanism simply as a research probe. In most instances, the word deleted was a noun or verb; there were also a few adjective deletions. Function words such as definite and indefinite articles, particles denoting reference, and so on, were not deleted, since it was expected that native speakers' structural knowledge would be easily demonstrated through this type of cloze procedure. Further, they present a different type of problematic lexicon to L2 learners.

The cloze technique was chosen deliberately, since it inherently presses readers to seek textual support in order to retrieve words missing from a text. The task is obviously one of guessing from context, since it forces readers to use many of the strategies that would be put to use in normal reading whenever a word is blurred, erased, or unknown.

The deleted items were selected by having ESL teachers indicate words which they considered difficult for their nonnative students. Since these selections were under consideration for inclusion in a college-level ESL reading textbook, seeking information from teachers about the vocabulary load in each one had been part of the needs analysis phase of that materials preparation project. Teachers had been told to "mark the words that most of your intermediate/advanced students wouldn't know." Nation (1990), in summarizing the research on the effects of glossing, found ample evidence that experienced ESL teachers can, to a notable extent, read a passage and separate out the words that second-language students are likely to find difficult.

Our assumption then was that, if native speakers found certain items difficult to guess even in context, then textual support was very low. Further, we wanted to see what native speakers would do in such cases where textual support was low: would they be able to retrieve a word close in meaning, or might they be misled by unsupportive clues?

After teacher-selected items had been deleted, the cloze "test" was given to the college students. The 41 subjects were given as much time as they needed to fill in the blanks with words of their own choosing. For each item, they were asked to try and specify the clues which helped them choose the word they supplied. An analysis of the text, the completions provided by the subjects, and their self-reports helped us understand the process of "guessing from context" as it was utilized by this group of L1 readers.

ANALYSIS OF THE DATA

In our earlier work with word guesses supplied by both L1 and L2 readers (Dubin & Olshtain, 1987b), we suggested a continuum to describe the variation in the degree of textual support. At one end of the continuum were words which seemed to be easy guesses, since they had ample thematic and semantic support in the passage (both through coherence and cohesion features), while at the other end were words almost impossible to guess. For lack of a clear theoretical explanation for this variation, we decided to use the experimental data from that study to help us categorize lexical items into "high textual" and "low textual" support categories.

On the basis of the data analysis for the three texts, which included a total of 42 deletions, the words which were supplied by the subjects fell into three categories as follows:

Category One: High Textual Support

This category included 14 words from the 42 deletions (33%) and showed at least 35% exact retrieval of a word identical to the one deleted from the original text and usually 50% or better, and at least an additional 35% of close substitutions. Thus, less than 25% were inappropriate fillers for this category (except for some exceptions, which will be treated separately). Close substitution was defined as the range of related words that would appear in a dictionary or a thesaurus. The data for this category are shown in Table 9.1:

Table 9.1. High Textual Support

Deleted Word	Number in Text	Exact Retrieval	Close Substitute	Others
TEXT ONE: "Turtle May Be Clue to Dinosaur Demise"				
ancestors	(3)	43%	52%	5%
fossils	(6)	52%	48%	—
succumb	(10)	62%	38%	—
extinction	(11)	48%	—	52%
incubated	(16)	62%	38%	
TEXT TWO: "Back to Basics"				
chipped	(2)	35%	65%	—
shatter	(5)	45%	55%	—
extract	(6)	60%	40%	—
expensive	(9)	50%	25%	25%
molded	(10)	90%	10%	—
resistant	(11)	50%	30%	20%
TEXT THREE: "Search for a Perfect Calendar"				
affected	(4)	45%	20%	35%
resistance	(8)	65%	10%	25%
devices	(9)	35%	50%	15%

Discussion

Text One: Number (10) succumb. Although *succumb* appeared to be less familiar or more obscure than the others in this group, it seemed to have had the most textual support and was therefore easy to guess.

In an age when our own species, Homo Sapiens, ponders survival, it seems particularly important to find out what happened to the reptiles that dominated this planet for so long. Did they _____ to a single catastrophe? If so, what? Or did they survive by evolving into one or more of the species alive today?

To supply the proper filler, the reader needed to use a combination of all five elements suggested for textual support. In terms of world knowledge along with earlier information in the selection, the reader knew that dinosaurs existed in the distant past but not now. Within the sentence itself, there is a semantic clue: the word *catastrophe*, and a structural clue: the word to be supplied is the main verb of the sentence and needs to agree with the subject *they* referring to dinosaurs. A quick (and probably partly unconscious assessment) enabled L1 readers to come up with the exact missing word or a very close substitute for it.

Text One: Number (3) ancestors. This was another case of high support, since all five subtypes of textual support were present for the retrieval of this item:

> Some evolutionary biologists see a genetic shadow of their presence in modern-day lizards. Others suspect that warm-blooded, feathered dinosaurs were the _____ of living birds.

In terms of extratextual knowledge, the reader knows that the topic is animals that disappeared, specifically the dinosaurs mentioned in the very sentence for which they must give a filler. The relation between creatures existing in our time (modern-day) and the distant past (genetic shadow) is given in the paragraph. The word *genetic* also draws attention to the developmental connection. From the immediate environment it is obvious that the missing word is a noun in the plural form. In this case, readers supplied *ancestors* (43%), *precursors* (24%), *predecessors* (14%), *forerunners* (9%), and *forefathers* (4%).

Text Two: Number (6): extract. The completion of the proper word in this case is dependent on all five subtypes of textual support. The thematic information related to basic materials, specifically metals. The immediate context was supportive at the sentence and paragraph level for the completion needed:

> Finally, about 3,500 years ago, people found out how to _____ iron from ores.

The fact that 45% supplied the exact word *extract* is also due to the fact that earlier in the paragraph the same word had been used: "Metal . . . had to be extracted from . . . rocks" (information from self-reports). The other 55% of the readers missed this particular clue and relied mostly on their extratextual knowledge about metal and ores, supplying fillers such as *smelt* and *forge*.

Text One: Number (11) extinction. In Table 9.1, there is one instance which does not seem to belong in this category, since it does not adhere to the proposed norms: Only 48% of the readers supplied the exact retrieval, while 52% supplied inappropriate completions. The text, in this case, supplied a misleading clue:

_____ , the dying of a species, can result from a variety of causes

Readers gave unlikely fillers such as *obviously, actually, in fact, therefore*, and *sadly*. In this case, supplying the exact word depended crucially on a punctuation convention in English: readers who ignored the fact that the use of two commas here means that the phrase provided within the commas is in apposition to the concept provided in the blank did not get the right meaning. They reacted as though there was a comma after the missing word, but that the paragraph which followed was independent of it, ignoring the second comma. So, they chose a cohesive item as the filler. It seems that these subjects were not using appropriate bottom-up processing strategies in supplying the missing word. Most of those who gave an incorrect selection, in fact, reported that they had read the passage rather fast, filling in the first choice that came to their mind.

Text One: Number (6): fossils. Perhaps the best example for good textual support is in (6) *fossils*, for which respondents supplied 52% exact completion and 48% close words such as *bones, specimens*. The clues in the text are related to knowledge of the world, semantic information in the immediate text, and structural selection within the sentence.

It is also an example of lexical cohesion (reiteration), since the word *fossils* is mentioned earlier in the paragraph. The fact that paleontology is mentioned helps the reader make use of general knowledge of the world. The sentence within which the missing word is to be inserted has the verb phrase *were found* as its main verb; all these clues lead to successful guessing.

> As North America was settled, dinosaur fossils turned up in New England, Virginia, New York, and finally Wyoming, Utah, and Montana. The great age of paleontology happily overlapped with the westward movement. A few _____ were also found in Britain and the Gobi Desert, but none in as great quantities as in the American West.

Summary: Category One

High textual support items are those for which readers employed both top-down strategies including knowledge of the world, thematic support available in the text as a whole, and semantic support within the paragraph level, together with bottom-up strategies such as semantic support within the sentence and structural support, to the extent that it was available.

Category Two: Mid Textual Support

Mid-level support was defined as surrounding those words which most subjects could not retrieve precisely but were able to reach at least 40% success by supplying a close and acceptable filler, or a word which did not alter the meaning of the original text. The words in this category are shown in Table 9.2.

Table 9.2.   Mid Textual Support

Deleted Word	Number in Text	Exact Retrieval	Close Substitute	Others
TEXT ONE "Turtle May Be Clue to Dinosaur Demise"				
dominating	(1)	—	100%	—
vanished	(2)	—	90%	10%
unearthed	(5)	10%	43%	47%
dubbed	(9)	—	77%	23%
calamity	(13)	—	86%	14%
cataclysm	(15)	—	43%	67%
TEXT TWO "Back to Basics"				
treated	(7)	—	100%	—
isolate	(8)	—	47%	53%
TEXT THREE "Search for a Perfect Calendar"				
No words in this category				

Discussion

Because virtually none of the subjects were able to retrieve the exact word, we concluded that these were instances in which the author had made rather idiosyncratic choices, her own bull's eye word selections, which may be impossible to retrieve by anyone else (except by accident, as in the case of (5), *unearthed*) since the language has a storehouse of closely related expressions which fit quite well. In terms of overall guessing, we found, however, that this group had a high level of textual support, as indicated by the high percentages of well-chosen words supplied. Thus, although none of the subjects supplied the word (1) *dominating*, there were three other items supplied by the subjects, all excellent fillers for the same blank: *inhabiting* (57%), *roaming* (34%), and *wandering* (9%). These three alternatives were chosen, since they complied with both the global theme and the immediate textual support.

Text One: Number (1) dominating.

After _____ this planet for about 150 million years, the dinosaurs vanished.

The fact that the blank is followed by the words *this planet* guides readers to choose a verb which collocates with them. Further, the specification of the period of time in the rest of the sentence reinforces the need to use something from the family of words synonymous with *inhabit*. Finally, the structural requirements are for the form *verb + -ing*, since it is used in a time expression beginning with the word *after*.

Text One: Number (2) vanished. This is a case in which respondents were unable to hit the author's bull's eye but supplied choices such as *disappeared* and *perished*, logical fillers.

Text One: Numbers (5) and (9) unearthed and dubbed. These words present additional complications. Their contexts are less constraining and allow for other meanings in each case. For (5) *unearthed*, while only 10% supplied the actual word, 43% supplied good synonyms such as *discovered* and *found*. However, 47% supplied plausible fillers according to the text, but these words had different meanings from the one the author intended: *seen* (43%), and *studied* (4%). Similarly, in the case of *dubbed*, 77% offered fillers such as *called* (43%), *named* (24%), and *labeled* (10%), while others, recognizing the word *Mesozoic* as a period, used words such as *during* and *before*. In a way, their general knowledge might have led them astray here by creating more choices for their cloze filler than the author's original meaning.

Text Two: Number (7): treated. For the word *treated*, which has high textual support, subjects gave the following completions, all of which related to the context: *treated* (15%), *processed* (15%), *smelted* (15%), *heated* (15%), *refined* (10%), *fired* (10%), and four words, *forged, extracted, cured*, and *melted*, which made up 20% of the answers. In this case, the possibilities for filling the following blank,

Iron _____ properly becomes steel, which is particularly hard and tough.

were varied in terms of the verbs that could fit the context, the production of steel from iron. Based on their extratextual knowledge, readers suggested a whole array of possibilities which could all work, but they did not get the particular choice made by the author, which was, in this case, the more general term *treated*. This case is somewhat different from the two discussed above, *unearthed* and *dubbed*.

Three words in Table 9.2 seem to be outside the range of Category Two, since they exhibited more inappropriate fillers than allowed for in this category: *unearthed* (47%), *cataclysm* (57%), and *isolate* (53%). In *isolate* (8), Text Two, the specific semantic support at the sentence level, Semantic II, was missing, since it allowed a large range of possibilities for the omitted verb.

However, aluminum holds on so tightly to the other atoms in its ores that a great deal of energy must be used to _____ it, so it is more (expensive) than iron.

The word *energy* in the sentence could be misleading in the sense that it connects semantically and logically to *manufacture, produce, mold, bend, heat*, and so on, all of which could be logical fillers for the blank but do not have the meaning of *separation* that *isolate* does and are therefore not appropriate completions in terms of the original meaning of the text. Fillers such as *extract, separate,* and *abstract* were considered close substitutes. Therefore, in a case where the sentential-semantic information is not specific enough to lead to the meaning of the missing items, we considered it a case with no Semantic II support. The same is true for the cases of *cataclysm* and *unearthed.*

Summary: Category Two

The mid-category is in some respects similar to the high category, since the text provides ample support for a word close to the one intended by the author. But in all these cases, the author chose a unique element in a group of related words, and therefore there is random chance that readers might happen to choose the exact variant and hit the bull's eye.

Category Three: Low Textual Support

The low category consisted of words for which most L1 readers were unable to provide either the exact retrieval or a close substitute. Instead, they suggested a wide range of possibilities. It is our contention that, for this category, the text does not supply sufficient support for the specific meaning; in fact, it lacks constraints to the extent that a wide range of fillers might be supplied and still make sense. Table 9.3 presents the data for Category Three.

Table 9.3.   Low Textual Support

Deleted Word	Number in Text	Exact Retrieval	Close Substitute	Others
TEXT ONE "Turtle May be Clue to Dinosaur Demise"				
fate	(4)	5%	—	95%
idiosyncratic	(7)	—	—	100%
extinct	(8)	—	—	100%
debris	(14)	—	—	100%
TEXT TWO "Back to Basics"				
brittle	(1)	—	15%	85%
tough	(3)	—	—	100%
resisted	(4)	—	35%	65%
deterioration	(11)	5%	—	80%
derived	(13)	15%	—	85%
brittle	(15)	5%	5%	90%
TEXT THREE "Search for a Perfect Calendar"				
determine	(1)	15%	—	85%
adapt	(2)	15%	—	85%
grouping	(3)	10%	—	90%
precise	(5)	—	—	100%
reconciling	(6)	25%	—	75%
knowledge	(10)	10%	—	90%

Discussion

Among the words in this group were some that are globally related to the theme of the passage such as (4) *fate*, (12) *vanished*, and (8) *extinct*. Yet, it seems that the local context was so low in textual support in each case that L1 readers had no way of retrieving the deleted words.

The two occurrences of *vanished* are particularly interesting. While *vanished* (2) was placed in the mid textual support category, the second occurrence, *vanished* (12), is in the low textual support category. In the first instance (2), 100% of the completions suggested by the readers were close substitutes such as: *disappeared, died*, and *perished*. In the second instance (12), 40% of the completions were close substitutes such as *demised* and *extinct*, while the other 60% consisted of fillers such as *discovered, contacted, excavated*, and *aboriginal*, which could have all been possible fillers but did not coincide with the meaning of the original text. In fact, since the semantic support was missing, readers fell back on extratextual knowledge and supplied all these other possibilities based on the context of the paragraph which dealt with a theme quite different from that of dinosaurs, namely, "human inhabitants of Tasmania."

> Like the recently _____ human inhabitants of Tasmania, the dinosaurs could have been downed by disease.

Text Two: Number (1) brittle. The deletion of *brittle* (1) in Two presented subjects with two possible paths. The choices depended ultimately on the fact that the second paragraph in the passage had a sequence of deletions that were 5 to 10 words apart, making the completions interdependent of each other. Teachers who selected the deleted words that were used in the study claimed that often L2 readers are in exactly this situation. Namely, there are a number of words which they do not understand in a paragraph, and the interpretation may depend on the interaction between the words.

> But then about 5,000 years ago, people began using metal. It had advantages. Whereas rock was _____ (brittle) and had to be _____ (chipped) into shape; metal was _____ (tough) and could be beaten and bent into shape. Metal _____ (resisted) a blow that would _____ (shatter) rock, and metal held an edge when a stone edge would be blunted.

The analysis of the above passage revealed that many of the respondents in their self-reports thought that the first blank should be filled with an adjective that fits the quality of rock and so 75% chose words such as *hard, solid*, and *rigid*. These all worked well with the immediate environment, even after they filled in *chipped*, or *carved*, or *chiseled* in the second blank. Instead of *tough*, they came up with *pliable, flexible*, and *softer*. So, the interdependence between *brittle* and *tough* was maintained, but it was reversed in meaning.

The second occurrence of *brittle* (15) is quite different, since the deletion of this word leaves room for a very large spread of possibilities in the context:

Unfortunately, rock remains just as _____ now as it was during the Stone Age.

In fact, readers were so irritated by the openness of this item that 40% of them chose not to suggest a filler (self-reports), since they could not make up their minds as to what would be the best choice. Those given were: *hard, plentiful, problematic*, and so on.

Text Three: Number (5) precise. Text Three has an example in Category Three that can be accounted for as a thematically and semantically related word to the notion of a "perfect calendar": *precise* (5):

Along the road to the acquisition of this _____ knowledge, calendar makers devised various ways of reconciling. . . .

This blank can be filled by any adjective that is compatible with knowledge, for example, *scientific, universal, astronomical, relevant, celestial, cosmic, elusive, complex*, and so on. All of these possibilities can be considered potential fillers of the blank, since they fit both the immediate, local environment and the overall thematic frame at the global level.

Text One: Number (7) idiosyncratic. This word was particularly interesting, since the context around it did not contain even the slightest indication of what the adjective might be.

The first people to dig up the fossils could not possibly recognize what they were. But their great size did give pause. Through a(n) _____ interpretation of Scripture, some theologians advanced the belief that biblical animals had been monumental and they hailed these giant bones as remnants of Noah's animal passengers.

The words supplied covered a broad range and probably depended on the personal understanding of each subject regarding "theologian's interpretation of Scripture." Too, the context might have been misleading, allowing for considerable personal variation. It is interesting, however, that, within the wide range of responses, there were even some complete opposites. The list included items such as: *evangelical, liberal, creational, literal, subjective, tortured, loose, elaborate, misguided, detailed*, and *unusual*.

Text One: Number (8) extinct. While (8) *extinct* is thematically related to the topic of the article and appeared a number of times (with different morphological forms), because the immediate context was not supportive, there were a large variety of responses, all of which could actually fit the passage. One group related to the large size of the dinosaurs with completions suggested as follows: *giant, enormous*, and *huge*. Another group of words was related to the age or familiarity with the dinosaurs: *ancient, new, known, unknown, prehistoric,* and *fossilized*. In fact, both of the deleted adjectives in our cloze passage created problems for the readers, and it is probably the case that adjectives, in general, have fewer constraints placed in the text than do nouns and verbs.

> Paleontology advanced swiftly and soon the _____ animals were named dino-saurs, "terrible lizards," and classified as reptiles, ancestors of living snakes and turtles.

Summary: Category Three

The low category is one for which the immediate context is often contradictory in relation to the overall theme, lacking any specific constraints for the selection of meaning. It is mostly at the local level that the information is not limiting enough to enable the reader to assign specific meaning. Therefore, when respondents are asked to fill a blank for which there is low textual support, it is possible that every one will provide a different word. Sometimes the immediate environment is not only lacking support but may even be contradictory in relation to the overall theme and thus mislead the respondent.

CONCLUSION

Tables 9.4–9.6 show a summary of the findings in terms of the five components for textual support as determined by the authors for all of the texts, indicating high, mid, and low textual support.

The analyses indicated that, for lexical meanings to be retrievable, all of the components which had previously been hypothesized as constituting textual support must be present:

1. general, extratextual knowledge
2. thematic content
3. semantic information beyond the sentence and paragraph level
4. semantic information at the sentence level
5. structural information within the sentence or paragraph.

On the basis of responses from adult native speakers, a continuum of textual support is suggested as represented in the graph of Table 9.7, which also sets out the retrieval criteria used in this study. Note that range designations for the three categories necessarily imply overlapping areas.

Table 9.4.   Delineation of Textual Support for Each Word

		High Support			
Word	Extra-Textual	Thematic	Sem.I: Discourse/ Paragraph	Sem.II: Sentence Level	Structural Sentence Level
TEXT ONE					
(3) ancestors	x	x	x	x	x
(6) fossils	x	x	x	x	x
(10) succumb	x	x	x	x	x
(11) extinction	x	x	x	x	x
(16) incubated	x	x	x	x	x
TEXT TWO					
(2) chipped	x	x	x	x	x
(5) shatter	x	x	x	x	x
(6) extract	x	x	x	x	x
(9) expensive	x	x	x	x	x
(10) molded	x	x	x	x	x
(11) resistant	x	x	x	x	x
TEXT THREE					
(4) affected	x	—	x	x	x
(8) resistance	x	—	x	x	x
(9) devices	x	x	x	x	x

Table 9.5.   Delineation of Textual Support for Each Word

		Mid Support			
Word	Extra-Textual	Thematic	Sem.I: Discourse/ Paragraph	Sem.II: Sentence Level	Structural Sentence Level
TEXT ONE					
(1) dominating	x	x	x	x	x
(2) vanished	x	x	x	x	x
(5) unearthed	x	x	x	—	x
(13) calamity	x	x	x	x	x
(15) cataclysm	x	x	x	—	x
TEXT TWO					
(7) treated	x	x	x	x	x
(8) isolate	x	x	x	—	x
TEXT THREE					
No Examples					

Table 9.6.   Delineation of Textual Support for Each Word

	Low Support				
Word	Extra-Textual	Thematic	Sem.I: Discourse/Paragraph	Sem.II: Sentence Level	Structural Sentence Level
TEXT ONE					
(4) fate	x	x	—	—	—
(12) vanished	x	—	—	—	—
(7) idiosyncratic	—	—	—	—	—
(8) extinct	x	x	—	—	—
(14) debris	x	x	—	—	—
TEXT TWO					
(4) resisted	x	x	—	—	—
(11) deterioration	x	x	—	—	—
(13) derived	x	—	—	—	x
TEXT THREE					
(1) determine	x	x	—	—	x
(2) adapt	x	x	—	—	x
(3) grouping	x	x	—	—	x
(5) precise	—	x	—	—	x
(6) reconciling	—	—	—	x	x
(10) knowledge	—	—	—	—	x

Although texts can be quite different from each other, there is good reason to believe that the three categories of high, mid, and low would appear in any text. Further work on the hypothesis of textual support, using additional texts, could utilize the norms which were established in this study as base data. This study also indicated that a high level of exact retrieval can only result from a context that is high in textual support and has all five subtypes, or components. How-

Table 9.7.   Summary Table

High Textual Support	Mid Textual Support	Low Textual Support
Exact Retrieval Range: 35%–90%	0%–10%	0%–25%
Close Substitution Range: 10%–65%	40%–100%	0%–35%
Other Inappropriate Fillers Range: 0%–25%[1]	0%–60%	65%–100%

[1]*Extinction* is an obvious exception to this range or norm. However, please see pp. 185 and 186 for the discussion of this word which points out that some readers failed to use local clues, i.e., punctuation, and therefore this is an error of performance rather than of competence.

ever, when one or two of the components is weak, it often results in lower levels of agreement. See, for example, *expensive* in Tables 9.1 and 9.4.

It appears that, in the retrieval process, readers rely heavily on the immediate environment, and that local features are significant in making the final selection. It would be erroneous to believe that one can do quite well with global support alone, as indicated in Tables 9.3 and 9.6.

Although the study focused on native speakers, there are clear implications for L2 contexts as well:

1. Materials preparers and textbook writers who encourage word guessing without proper analysis of each lexical item need to be aware of the pitfalls of guessing when the context is not adequate for the purpose.
2. Teachers of ESL/EFL, similarly, must be able to analyze words for their inherent guessability within a textual context.
3. As used in this study, the cloze technique, along with its other uses, is a valuable mechanism for teasing out native speaker knowledge.

APPENDIX A
TEXT ONE
TURTLE MAY BE CLUE TO DINOSAUR DEMISE
by BettyAnn Kevles

The turtle and the dinosaur—the first diminutive in size, sea-dwelling and four-legged, the second gigantic, land-roving and bipedal—seem as remote from each other in function as they are in form. Yet research into the ways of turtles may explain the greatest mystery of the dinosaurs.

After dominating (1) this planet for about 150 million years, the dinosaurs vanished (2). Some evolutionary biologists see a genetic shadow of their presence in modern-day lizards. Others suspect that warm-blooded, feathered dinosaurs were the ancestors (3) of living birds. But neither iguana nor pelican resembles the dinosaur's great size.

Unique to its era, the fate (4) of the dinosaurs has perplexed scientists for more than a century. So complete was their disappearance that humanity was unaware of their existence until the 19th century.

Although their bones had been lying beneath the soil, quite literally for ages, no one had never unearthed (5) one before. As North America was settled, dinosaur fossils turned up in New England, Virginia, New York, and finally in Wyoming, Utah, and Montana. The great age of paleontology happily overlapped with the westward movement. A few fossils (6) were also found in Britain and the Gobi Desert, but none in as great quantities as the American West.

The first people to dig up the fossils could not possibly recognize what they were. But their great size did give pause. Through an idiosyncratic (7) interpretations of scripture, some theologians advanced the belief that biblical animals had been monumental and they hailed these giant bones as the remnants of Noah's animal passengers. (According to this theory, it was only the second time around, after the flood, that God shrank the animal world to its present proportions.)

Paleontology advanced swiftly and soon the extinct (8) animals were named dinosaurs, "terrible lizards," and classified as reptiles, ancestors of living snakes and turtles. The era in which they lived was dubbed (9) the Mesozoic.

With the acceptance of the concept of evolution, paleontologists began disputing the nature of these creatures. Were they simply enormous reptiles? Or were they, in fact, the ancestors of modern birds? Determining whether they were reptile or proto-bird might have a lot to do with solving the greater mystery: whatever happened to them?

In an age when our own species, Homo sapiens, ponders survival, it seems particularly important to find out what happened to the reptiles that dominated this planet for so long. Did they succumb (10) to a single catastrophe? If so, what? or did they survive by evolving into one or more of the species alive today?

Extinction (11), the dying out of a species, can result from a variety of causes. An enemy as small as a bacterium could have been the villain. Like the recently vanished (12) human inhabitants of Tasmania, the dinosaurs could have been downed by disease. Or, like the primate inhabitants of the disappearing rain forests, they could have been felled by clever hunters. Or they could have been done in by a great calamity (13).

This last approach got a boost recently when Berkley physicist Louis Alvarez suggested that the Earth suffered the impact of a huge asteroid that filled the skies with debris (14). Indeed, he has claimed to find proof of this theory in layers of rock near the town of Gubbio, Italy, where ancient layers of a rare metal, iridium, suggests a galactic origin.

A variation on this theme places the cataclysm (15) at the same time but from the bowels of the Earth. The eruptions of volcanos many times the size of Mount St. Helens would also have covered the earth with enough dust to lower the temperature by about 5 degrees centigrade for at least a year.

Which brings us to the turtles. We know that the dinosaurs, like turtles, laid eggs in the sand because nests filled with broken shells and the fossilized remains of baby dinosaurs have been unearthed in Montana. If they were reptiles like turtles, they also may have been heteromorphs, that is to say, their sex was not determined at conception genetically by the inclusion of an x or y chromosome, as it is in birds and mammals, but rather developed while they were being incubated (16).

Zoologists at the State University of New York in Buffalo have observed how sea turtles develop into males or females. Turtle eggs that lie in the sand at cool temperatures produce male turtles. And eggs that incubate at about 5 degrees higher produce females. Likewise, eggs hatched in plastic boxes at cool temperatures produced boy turtles, and warmer boxes netted girls.

If dinosaurs were like modern turtles, a sudden drop in temperature for even a short time may have simply eliminated all females from the species. Under stress, some female lizards that are alive today, reproduce hermaphroditically, that is, all by themselves. But male lizards cannot manage on their own.

The world of the dinosaurs may have ended initially with a bang, as volcanos erupted or an asteroid crashed. But then, as lonely males sought fruitlessly for mates, it may have simply faded away, with a whimper.

DELETED WORDS: TEXT ONE

1.	dominating	9.	dubbed
2.	vanished	10.	succumb
3.	ancestors	11.	extinction
4.	fate	12.	vanished
5.	unearthed	13.	calamity
6.	fossils	14.	debris
7.	idiosyncratic	15.	cataclysm
8.	extinct	16.	incubated

APPENDIX B
TEXT TWO
BACK TO BASICS

By Isaac Asimov

In prehistoric times the chief tool-making material was stone. In fact, that period is referred to as the Stone Age. There were advantages to stone: There was a lot of it. It could be had almost anywhere just for the picking up. And it lasted indefinitely. The pyramids still stand, and the rocks of Stonehenge are still there.

But then about 5,000 years ago, people began using metal. It has advantages. Whereas rock was brittle (1) and had to be chipped (2) into shape, metal was tough (3) and could be beaten and bent into shape. Metal resisted (4) a blow that would shatter (5) rock, and metal held an edge when a stone edge would be blunted.

However, metal was much rarer than rock. Metal occasionally was found as nuggets, but generally it had to be extracted from certain not very common rocks (ores) by the use of heat. Finally, about 3,500 years ago, people found out how to extract (6) iron from ores. Iron is a particularly common metal and is the cheapest metal even today. Iron properly treated (7) becomes steel, which is particularly hard and tough. However, iron and steel have a tendency to rust.

About 100 years ago aluminum came into use. It is a light metal and can be made even stronger than iron, pound for pound. What's more, it is even more common than iron and won't rust. However, aluminum holds on so tightly to the other atoms in its ores that a great deal of energy must be used to isolate (8) it, so it is more expensive (9) than iron.

In the Twentieth Century plastics came into use. They are light materials that are organic (that is, built of the same atoms that are found in living organisms). Plastics can be as tough as metals, can be molded (10) into shape, can be resistant (11) to water and to deterioration such as rust (12) and can come in all sorts of compositions so as to have almost any kind of property desired.

However, plastics usually are derived from the molecules in oil and gas, and oil and gas aren't going to last forever. When oil is gone plastics, for the most part, will be gone as well. Then, too, plastics are inflammable and liberate poisonous gases when burned.

Well, then, are there any other alternatives? How about getting back to basics, to the rocks that human beings used before they developed the sophisticated (14) way of life called civilization. Rock remains far more common and cheaper than either metal or plastics. Unlike plastics, rock doesn't burn; and unlike metal, rock doesn't rust. Unfortunately, rock remains just as brittle (15) now as it was during the Stone Age. What can be done about that?

[Text continues but since the remainder does not contain deleted words, it has been left out here.]

DELETED WORDS: TEXT TWO

1.	brittle	9.	expensive
2.	chipped	10.	molded
3.	tough	11.	resistant
4.	resisted	12.	rust
5.	shatter	13.	derived
6.	extract	14.	sophisticated
7.	treated	15.	brittle
8.	isolate		

APPENDIX C
TEXT THREE
4,000 YEAR SEARCH FOR A PERFECT CALENDAR
by Isabel R. Plesset

For thousands of years, people all over the world have pursued the unattainable objective of creating a perfect calendar. Calendar making is not a science, but it does require an understanding of the natural phenomena that determine (1) climate, the tides, the days and nights and seasons, to all of which living things on Earth must adapt (2). The calendar maker's job is to find ways of grouping (3) days to meet the needs of human beings.

As we now know, the basic problem is that there are 29.53059 days in a lunar month, and 365.242199 days in the solar year. If that seems like a mess, it doesn't change anything. The orbits of the Moon and the Earth, the rotation of the Earth on its own axis, the periods of the Moon's phases and the Earth's rotation around the Sun are in no way affected (4) by human perception of them.

Along the road to the acquisition of this precise knowledge, calendar makers devised various ways of reconciling (6) these irreconcilables (7), but as people became accustomed to each modification (8) over periods of centuries, they resisted each new change. This human resistance (9) to change in well-established patterns of life constituted a second great problem for the calendar makers.

Beginning about 2000 BC, the Stonehenge people of England created precise measuring devices (10) using enormous stones, but we have little idea of how they made use of their astronomical measurements. By that time, Chinese astronomers had a sophisticated knowledge (11) of the number of days in a solar year, but we don't know how they made these determinations. The calendar most widely used today for agriculture, for business and trade, and for historical purposes is the Gregorian calendar, but for other purposes, there are many other calendars.

1.	determine	7.	irreconcilables
2.	adapt	8.	modification
3.	grouping	9.	resistance
4.	affected	10.	devices
5.	precise	11.	knowledge
6.	reconciling		

REFERENCES

Asimov, I. (1985, April 2). Back to basics. *American Way,* p. 18.

Bachman, L. F. (1985). Performance on cloze tests with fixed-ratio and rational deletions. *TESOL Quarterly, 19* (3), 535–556.

Drum, P., & Konopak, B. C. (1987). Learning word meanings from written context. In M. G. McKeown & M. E. Curtis (Eds.), *The nature of vocabulary acquisition* (pp. 73–80). Hillsdale, NJ: Erlbaum.

Dubin, F., Eskey, D. & Grabe, W. (Eds.). (1986). *Teaching second language reading for academic purposes.* Reading, MA: Addison-Wesley.

Dubin, F., & Olshtain, E. (1987a, April). *Let's stop pushing vocabulary under the rug.* Paper presented at TESOL Convention, Miami.

Dubin, F., & Olshtain, E. (1987b, December). *The function of textual support in interpreting unknown lexical meanings.* Paper presented at AAAL Annual Meeting, San Francisco.

Eskey, D. (1986). Theoretical foundations. In F. Dubin, D. Eskey, & W. Grabe (Eds.), *Teaching second language reading for academic purposes* (pp. 3–22). Reading, MA: Addison-Wesley.

Gairns, R., & Redman, S. (1986). *Working with words.* Cambridge, UK: Cambridge University Press.

Goodman, K. S. (1967). Reading: A psycholinguistic guessing game. *Journal of the reading specialist, 4,* 13–26.

Haynes, M. (1984). Patterns and perils in second language reading. In J. Handscombe, R. Orem & B. Taylor (Eds.), *On TESOL '83* (pp. 163–176). Washington, DC: TESOL.

Huckin, T. N. (1988, March). *Avoiding potholes and red-herrings: The anatomy of guessing word-meanings in context.* Paper presented at TESOL Convention, Chicago.

Kevles, B. (1982, October 6). Turtle may be clue to dinosaur demise. *Los Angeles Times*, p. 42.

Nation, I. S. P. (1990). *Teaching and learning vocabulary*. New York: Newbury House.

Parry, K. J. (1987). Reading in a second culture. In J. Devine, P. L. Carrell, & D. E. Eskey (Eds.), *Research in reading in a second language* (pp. 61–69). Washington, DC: TESOL.

Plesset, I. (1983, December 20). 4,000 year search for a perfect calendar. *Los Angeles Times*, sec. III, p. 6.

Rumelhart, D. E. (1977). Toward an interactive model of reading. In Dornic (Ed.), *Attention and performance* (Vol. 1, pp. 573–603). New York: Academic Press.

Editorial Comments

The findings in this chapter are especially worth noting, since one of the main issues in this volume is how readers actually do guess the meanings of unknown words in texts. The use of cloze in this case assumes that the L1 subject already has the appropriate concept in his or her lexicon and must somehow determine the exact word-form which the author used based on the evidence in the text as well as whatever background knowledge the subject has. This is clearly not the same task as guessing at the meaning of a totally unknown word, even when one assumes the same type of textual evidence and prior knowledge. Therefore, these findings are not directly applicable to the process of guessing, which is mentioned so often in this volume. At the same time, there must be a relationship between these two cognitive procedures. One possibility is that subjects are more successful at cloze completion than they are at guessing, because of the assumption that they already know the words involved. This is obviously an area for further research.

On the other hand, this chapter does present good evidence that a text must have a high degree of both local and global information in order for subjects to be able to determine the exact word-form or even a close synonym. If this finding does extrapolate to the case of guessing unknown words, then the authors will have assisted materials writers who must take dimensions of context into consideration.

Another nice aspect of this study is its attempt to establish some sort of baseline based on native speaker performance (see also Haynes & Baker, Chapter 7, this volume). Follow-up studies with L2 learners might find the same basic trends but with lower accuracy.

One possible factor which makes this study difficult to interpret is that it gave the subjects rather short texts on presumably unfamiliar topics. As Parry points out in Chapter 6, a learner using a longer text and developing extensive background knowledge through coursework can often be successful, despite very limited L2 proficiency, in comprehending unknown vocabulary words.

Chapter 10
The Healthy Inadequacy of Contextual Definition

Mark J. Stein
BRS Software Products
Latham, NY

Contextual clues are crucial to second-language vocabulary acquisition and are both widely discussed in theory and used in everyday pedagogy. Contextual clues, however, often fail to narrow in on a word's meaning. The failure is one of language itself, and not of student or teacher. Three examples of how narrow context clues underdetermine meaning are given, examples involving (a) conceptual relevance and definition, (b) containment and hyponymy, and (c) cultural knowledge and individual beliefs. We provide a checklist for constructing more perspicuous contextual clues. Finally, we suggest that these more perspicuous clues are in many cases counterproductive. While perhaps aiding in vocabulary acquisition, they can hinder more general progress in reading; letting an L2 learner see where context fails also lets that learner see how cultural knowledge, text, and reader jointly construct meaning.

INTRODUCTION

Of the factors most important to academic achievement for second-language learners, vocabulary knowledge is often considered the most crucial (Saville-Troike, 1984). One common method of teaching vocabulary is to teach contextual definition. The student constructs intelligent guesses or hypotheses about the meaning of a word based on the grammatical and pragmatic context in which the word is found.

Clarke and Silberstein (1977) argue that contextual definition is the most crucial of vocabulary skills, and standard ESL pedagogies stress its importance (e.g., Dubin, Eskey, & Grabe, 1986). In this, L2 reading theory mirrors the concerns of both L1 reading theory (Goodman, 1967; Smith, 1982) and, more recently, theories of language acquisition by machines (Zernik, 1987). Though second-language textbooks differ on just what counts as contextual definition, they all use clues of one sort or another, often treating contextual definition as a central organizing theme (an outstanding example is found in Dubin & Olshtain, 1981).

But as Huckin (1987) and others have noted, contextual definition unfortunately does not often work for ESL students. Part of the problem is that the contextual clues themselves are largely insufficient to narrow in on a word's meaning. The language itself allows for many unavoidable possibilities in interpretation, often many more than wanted. What can be of use in this uncomfortable situation is for the ESL/EFL teacher to be more conversant in the ways in which contextual clues are insufficient, and to use that understanding in the teaching of vocabulary, reading, and cross-cultural communication skills. In this chapter, three examples of the insufficiency of contextual clues are presented, along with a checklist for teachers of how to productively make use of these inadequacies.

CONTEXTUAL CLUES CAN FAIL

A perspicuous starting point in the examination of contextual definition is found through Twaddell's (1963; discussed in Chastain, 1976) famous example:

(1) The clouds parted momentarily and the snow on the mountain-top *coruscated* in the rays of the rising sun.

We are supposed to determine from context that *coruscated* means "shone brightly." To say that we determine matters from context is to say that we can figure out the meaning of *coruscated* without ever in fact having seen that word before. We make intelligent guesses or hypotheses about the meaning of the word, based on the grammatical and pragmatic context in which the word is found. The word's meaning is discovered merely from what surrounds it, from the "textual support" (Dubin & Olshtain, Chapter 9, this volume) the word enjoys.

But how many who have never heard this word before will conclude that the word means "shone brightly"? Unfortunately, context yields many possible definitions for *coruscated,* among them "shone brightly," but also "melted," "changed consistency," and "changed color." The possible meanings are limited only by the reader's imagination and knowledge of the nonlinguistic world.

In an informal survey of 30 native speakers of English, only one had heard the word *coruscated* before. None admitted knowing the meaning of the word, and yet all but one readily offered a meaning from context when prompted.

Many offered more than one contextual definition. Fifty percent of those unfamiliar with the word guessed its meaning from context correctly, though 63% (25 of 40) of answers were incorrect. Thirty-seven percent hypothesized "melted," and an array of other meanings surfaced: "was illuminated by," "showed up," "crusted on top," and so on. Interesting also was the way that respondents typically viewed contextual definition as something quite distinct from both meaning and definition. The following conversation was typical:

Interviewer: Any idea what it means?
Respondent: None.
Interviewer: I mean from context, you know, the sentence.
Respondent: Oh, OK . . .

As ESL teachers, we attempt to make the grammatical and pragmatic mechanisms and clues of contextual definition clearer to our students. But whatever clues may be in Twaddell's example, these clues are clearly insufficient. A typical advanced intermediate ESL text (see, for example, Adams & Dwyer, 1982) will contain work on clues provided by such grammatical constructions as appositives, relative clauses, equative constructions, demonstrative *this, such,* and *such as,* adverbial modifiers, and conditional clauses; and all of these clues are regularly insufficient to unambiguously determine a word's meaning.

Contextual clues can fail. In fact, contextual clues do fail, and that they do fail is not particularly a failure of the (teacher or) student; rather, it is a failure of the language itself. Thus, a hope that once our students, by knowing the required grammatical rules or clues, will then be able to use them to figure out word meaning is a misguided hope. Would that life were so simple for our students, for often even the brighter ones fail to have any success with these contextual clues.

What the teacher can do in this uncomfortable situation, both in constructing new contextual clue examples, and in helping students through the examples in others' textbooks, is to be attuned to the particular ways in which contextual definitions fail. I offer three such examples, involving ways in which grammatical information underdetermines meaning. These examples involve the problems of (a) conceptual relevance and definition, (b) containment and hyponymy, and (c) belief and culture. Following this, I present a checklist that ESL teachers can use in evaluating their own and others' contextual definitions.

THE PROBLEM OF CONCEPTUAL
RELEVANCE/DEFINITION

Consider the following example:

(2) House seekers who look for only the perfect house to buy are never happy with nice, average, but imperfect homes. (Adams & Dwyer, 1982, p. 71)

If a student did not know the meaning of *seekers,* he or she could nevertheless surmise that a seeker is some sort of person who looks for something. This surmising makes use of knowledge concerning the head noun, *house seekers,* and the relative clause, *who look for only the perfect house to buy.* In this example it is crucial that the relative clause is used to give definitional information of the noun it modifies. Alternatively, we could say that the material in the relative clause is conceptually relevant to the noun, or that it is essential to the definition of the noun. And so, looking for a perfect house is essential to being a seeker.

The general semantic function of a relative clause is to combine the properties of a head noun and its embedded clause. Thus, the nominal *boy that I know* means something like "being an x such that x is a boy and I know x." Semantically, the relative clause need not in any way provide any definitional information about its head noun. For example "boy that is a boy" certainly provides no definition of boy. Hence, it is not by semantics alone that we know that the relative clause is providing definitional information. Conversationally, however, there are requirements that the relative clause be relevant to its head noun. Generally, it is good conversational behavior to avoid redundancy when talking to others. However, in cases where there is a likelihood that the hearer will not understand the head noun, where the speaker knows that the hearer will likely not understand the head noun, and where the hearer knows that the speaker knows that the hearer will likely not understand the head noun, standard Gricean principles (Grice, 1975) of conversational etiquette demand that any maxims to avoid redundancy be broken, and that the speaker be as redundant as is necessary to make the conversation work. In such cases, the relative clause will be used to give a definition of its head noun. Relative clause structure provides a clue to word meaning only when, in order to make the conversation work, the relative clause is used to form a definition. Unfortunately, there is nothing about the structure of relative clauses that demands that they be put to such a use.

Consider the following example. In this example, we try to use the relative clause as a contextual clue. We do not, however, find conceptually relevant or definitional information in that relative clause:

(3) House seekers who can get below average mortgages are never happy with nice, average, but imperfect homes.

A house seeker is not one who necessarily borrows money at the right cost. Consider a similar example:

(4) I like a medium steak that is pink on the inside. (Kimmelman, Krantz, Martin, & Seltzer, 1984, p. 98)

Assuming that the relative clause is used to define or characterize the head noun, we determine that medium steaks are the kinds of things that are pink. Depending on their beliefs about what makes for a good steak, some chefs would agree. Now, however, substitute *hickory smoked, larded with bacon,* or *pierced with tarragon* for *medium.* However strange the sentences, note the failure of the relative clause contextual clue to determine from context the meaning of *medium:*

(5) I like a medium steak that is hickory smoked on the inside.

THE PROBLEM OF CONTAINMENT

Words exist in a complex lexical network. In this network the meaning of one word may be contained in the meaning of another. Thus, the word *dog* contains within it the meaning of other words such as *animal* or *thing.* Let us call the relationship between *dog* and *animal* containment or hyponymy. Oftentimes students fail in contextual definition by determining that an unknown word means one of those other words found "higher-up" in the word's lexical network. The student figures out, for example, that *dog* means "thing."

An example:

(6) Adding a new computer system to an industry requires a great many adaptations. Workers frequently need retraining because of these changes. (Adams & Dwyer, 1982, p. 23)

We first make use of the contextual clue provided by the demonstrative *these,* and conclude that *adaptation* means "change."

This is fine, but of course, *adaptation* is just one sort of change. The word *change* is more all encompassing. Thus, the demonstrative, even if correctly applied, will at best show us that the word we wish to understand is a kind of, or instance of, the word following the demonstrative.

Consider another example:

(7) Martin was very unhappy about the financial *aspect* of his life. He tried to improve this important part of his life by getting a new job and renting a less expensive apartment. (Adams & Dwyer, 1982, p. 23)

Again we have a contextual clue, the demonstrative *this.* The meaning of *aspect* will somehow correspond to the words following *this,* in this case the nominal, *important part of his life.* But what then does *aspect* mean? Part? Important part? The second meaning is a bit more inclusive than the first. But which is the correct meaning? The contextual clue, the demonstrative, does not tell.

In this particular case, *aspect* simply means "part." But can we in general ignore that preceding adjective, and so avoid any problem of words or concepts contained within other words or concepts?

Again, we try to construct an example in which the clue does not work as advertised. Imagine a French student, unfamiliar with the word *beans*. She would want to figure out that beans are not merely legumes, but also legumes that characteristically wind their way upward:

(8) Jack loves beans. He first saw this climbing legume while heading skyward.

This example illustrates the general problem we have seen concerning superordination: How do we know whether what follows the demonstrative is equivalent to the word whose definition we are seeking, or the word whose definition we are seeking is merely an instance of or example of or kind of the thing following the demonstrative?

Within the theoretical linguistics literature, problems in lexical semantics such as the ones discussed here go under the heading of *hyponymy* (Cruse, 1986, p. 88). Within the Language for Special Purposes (LSP) literature, Swales (1983) has suggested that these problems of "lexical superordination" or "summary words" must be studied in far greater detail if LSP is to deal adequately with the need for vocabulary learning of its students.

THE PROBLEM OF BELIEF AND CULTURE

Consider a third example. In this example, grammatical clues may be insufficient, because to apply the clues one must make explicit use of cultural knowledge in the second language, a knowledge that students may not yet possess. Note that belief also comes into play in the previous sets of examples, though its influence there is far less pronounced.

Consider one example of the interaction of contextual definition and cultural knowledge:

(9) Whenever I see cars creeping along the highway in the middle of the day, I am sure that there is going to be an accident.

The adverbial *whenever* is the contextual clue, indicating that *creeping* in the first clause happens at the same time as the certainty of an accident in the second. The contextual definition we are meant to hypothesize is "slow moving."

This contextual definition is not forced by the structure of the sentence. The reader's beliefs and how they correspond with the beliefs of the target culture enter in the equation. If a person is part of a fast-moving and hurried culture, he or she is probably very uncomfortable seeing slow-moving cars, believing that these cars are more likely than not to cause accidents.[1]

In contrast, a person from a slow-moving, more lingering culture, or a person who is temperamentally a worrying type, may look at matters differently. When such people see cars speeding along, they worry that they should not be speeding along—surely danger accompanies such high speed. Under such assumptions—whether cultural or individual, whether reasonable or strange from a particular vantage point—one would understand *creeping* to mean "going at a good clip." By constructing other contexts, one can induce many other readings for the word *creeping,* among them, "clanging" or "standing."

In a quite significant sense, we could even use a person's behavior when confronted with such contextual definitions as a diagnostic of aberrant and idiosyncratic behavior or thinking on the one hand, or of cultural mores on the other. A person's use of contextual clues can point to the person's view of the world.

This interaction of belief and contextual definition is a particularly vexing problem, for typically we are not merely building up our students' vocabulary, but also introducing them to new belief systems of new communities and cultures. We thus can take neither vocabulary nor culture as given or theoretically prior, attempting to define one on the basis of the other. Carrell and Eisterhold (1983) have written about the ways that reading of a text is influenced by one's cultural knowledge and assumptions. They propose that students not be called upon to simultaneously manipulate both linguistic and cultural codes, and hence that readings be constructed that introduce new material only along one of these parameters. This suggestion does not bode well for contextual definition exercises, in which the two codes are quite intricately entwined.

A CHECKLIST

How does one make do in the imperfect world of contextual definition and clues? If the language itself (and not us, and not our students) underdetermines the meaning of words by means of contextual definition, why trust in contextual definition at all? Perhaps the most direct answer is that there is no getting around it. Not just second-language learners but all language users are confronted with unknown words in contexts only somewhat better known than the unknown words themselves. Examine the reading habits of a sophisticated first-language speaker, and you will see that he or she seldom uses a dictionary. This ability to "get-on" with the reading of a text is a skill that we must impart to our students.

That there is no getting around contextual definition still does not make us more comfortable in its daily use and in its place in our pedagogy. I suggest that the best way to confront the problem is to face it head on; to be aware of the clues themselves, and of the places where any particular clue will fail; hence also, to be prepared for certain sorts of student mistakes and to revise exercises at points where we find no advantage in seeing students consistently fail. Of course, many times we will want students to fail. A failure in the *creeping* sentence above might lead quite directly from a rather mundane discussion of grammar to a more engaging discussion of varying attitudes towards speed and time and safety.

The following checklist could be tried in constructing contextual definition sentences:

1. Construct a sentence with the unknown word and some contextual specification of that word.
2. Determine what contextual clue or rule is being appealed to in the sentence. Reasonable grammatical structures to look for are appositives, relatives clauses, equative constructions, demonstratives, adverbial modifiers, and conditional clauses.
3. Construct a sentence very similar to the original contextual clue sentence, in which the contextual clue is a blatant failure.
4. Once the blatantness of that failure is seen, and if you deem it appropriate, build in extra information into the context of the original sentence, thus relieving the burden such a contextual clue will place on the student.

These four steps are not always applied in strict order. Thus, Step 2 may apply before Step 1 if one is explicitly trying to write an exercise dealing with a particular grammatical construction. Here's an example of how these four steps work:

Step 1. I have a sentence. The sentence has a word in it that will likely be unknown to the student:

(9) Whenever I see cars creeping along the highway in the middle of the day, I am sure that there is going to be an accident.

Step 2. I determine the rule/clue: The adverbial *whenever* is the contextual clue, indicating that *creeping* in the first clause happens at the same time as the certainty of an accident in the second. Depending on the sophistication and present needs of the class, I might or might not eventually choose to explain this rule to them in terms of the grammatical vocabulary of subordinating conjunctions, temporal clauses, and so on.

Step 3. I break the rule. Or rather, I use the rule not to achieve my stated goals of encouraging contextual understanding of unknown words: My goal was to get the student to see that *creeping* means ''to move slowly.'' So, I try to construct a sentence in which the *whenever* clue doesn't yield the right result. Consider two such attempts:

(10) Whenever I see cars *zooming* along the highway in the middle of the day, I am sure that there is going to be an accident.

Here, the contextual clue is the same, and yet the word in italics has the opposite meaning. Seeing the ease with which (10) was constructed, I am very quickly brought to see how individual beliefs or cultural assumptions are embedded in the original sentence. Such information could be of great interest and use to my students.

Here is a second example:

(11) Whenever I see cars creeping along the highway in the middle of the day, I thank God for my old Model-T.

Here, the word to be contextually defined remains the same, the contextual clue, *whenever,* remains the same, and yet it seems most difficult to see what the sentence is saying *creeping* means. Does the writer of the sentence feel a certain camaraderie with those creeping along the highway, or does the driver feel aloof and superior? Once again, interesting questions of cultural assumptions and individual beliefs are raised.

Step 4. I use the idea behind the misbegotten sentences in Step 3 to repair the original sentence. Here are two possible repairs:

(12) Whenever I see cars creeping along the highway in the middle of the day, I am sure that there is an accident . . . (or road construction somewhere ahead of me) (Adams & Dwyer, 1982, p. 97)

Note that, in this sentence, the *is going to be* of (9) is replaced by the simple *is* of (12). Though the relationship between the creeping of a car and the likelihood of future accidents is open to individual and cultural difference, the relationship between the creeping of a car and the actuality of a present accident is far more direct: Slowed cars mean that an accident has occurred. Adams and Dwyer have clearly constructed a far better contextual definition sentence in (12) than I, for expository purposes, have constructed in (9). (12) avoids much of the uncertainty of (9).

Here is another possible repair:

(13) Whenever I see cars creeping along the highway in the middle of the day, I am sure that there is going to be an accident. I think it is just terrible that they let all those slow-moving cars travel on our California superhighways.

Though the author's beliefs about car speed are unclear in the first sentence of (13), the second sentence, with its demonstrative *those slow-moving cars,* has served to narrow down the range of possible interpretations.

After teachers have gone through this checklist, they may decide not to fix up their original sentence. There is much to be said for this obstinance. There is a certain healthiness in the failure of contextual clues. Their failure is often an entry point into the beliefs and assumptions of another individual or culture. And while students may appreciate certainty in the early stages of their second-language vocabulary acquisition, ultimately they will want to achieve a more sophisticated literacy—a literacy in which it is in the very nature of language that meaning is not totally fixed in the text itself, but is rather something constructed by a reader, with the help of the text, and with the help of the culture.

REFERENCES

Adams, J., & Dwyer, M. A. (1982). *English for academic uses.* Englewood Cliffs, NJ: Prentice-Hall.

Carrell, P. L., & Eisterhold, J. C. (1983). Schema theory and ESL reading pedagogy. *TESOL Quarterly, 17* (4), 553–574.

Chastain, K. (1976). *Developing second language skills: Theory and practice* (2nd ed.). Chicago: Rand McNally.

Clarke, M. A., & Silberstein, S. (1977). Toward a realization of psycholinguistic principles in the ESL reading class. *Language Learning, 27* (1), 135–154.

Cruse, D. A. (1986). *Lexical semantics.* Cambridge, UK: Cambridge University Press.

Dubin, F. & Olshtain, E. (1981). *Reading by all means.* Reading, MA: Addison-Wesley.

Dubin, F., Eskey, D. E., & Grabe, W. (1986). *Teaching second language reading for academic purposes.* Reading, MA: Addison-Wesley.

Goodman, K. S. (1967). Reading: A psycholinguistic guessing game. In H. Singer & R. Ruddell (Eds.), *Theoretical models and processes of reading* (2nd ed., pp. 497–508). Newark, DE: International Reading Association.

Grice, H. P. (1975). Logic and conversation. In P. Cole & J. Morgan (Eds.), *Syntax and semantics 3: Speech acts* (pp. 41–58). New York: Academic Press.

Huckin, T. N. (1987). The use of discourse patterning in foreign-language reading and vocabulary acquisition. *DELTA, 2* (1), 57–75.

Kimmelman, J., Krantz, H., Martin, C., & Seltzer, S. (1984). *Reading and study skills: A rhetorical approach.* New York: Macmillan.

Saville-Troike, M. (1984). What really matters in second language learning for academic achievement? *TESOL Quarterly, 18*(2), 199–220.

Smith, F. (1982). *Understanding reading: A psycholinguistic analysis of reading and learning to read.* New York: Holt, Rinehart and Winston.

Swales, J. (1983). Vocabulary work in LSP—a case of neglect? *Bulletin CILA 37,* Neuchatel.

Twaddell, F. (1963). Foreign language instruction at the secondary level. *Teacher's manual: Espanol: Hablar y leer.* New York: Holt Rinehart & Winston.

Zernik, U. (1987). *Strategies in language acquisition: Learning phrases in context.* Unpublished doctoral dissertation, Department of Computer Science, UCLA.

ENDNOTES

1. There is a further indeterminacy in the sentence. The *bare-plural cars* possesses no overt quantifier, and so may be understood as meaning either ''some cars,'' ''all cars,'' or ''cars in general.'' Each of these possible interpretations would help shape a different overall meaning for the sentence.

Editorial Comments

Many language teachers and materials developers who are convinced of the importance of guessing vocabulary from context try to help their students by giving them pedagogical materials with clear linguistic clues to unknown words (i.e., local context clues in the same sentence). In this thought-provoking chapter, Stein argues against this practice. He points out that everyday reading materials do not usually include such perspicuous clues, and that, if we want to help our students become more sophisticated both in learning new vocabulary and in reading, we should teach them how to cope with the inexplicitness of natural language.

How exactly should we do this? Stein does not provide a full prescription, but he does suggest that we encourage learners to draw on the beliefs and assumptions of the culture in which the text is produced. Although this is a very broad sense of "context," one that would be difficult for many nonnative-language teachers to master, Stein makes a good case for using it in the teaching of reading and vocabulary learning. (See also Steffensen, Joag-Dev, & Anderson, 1979; Carrell, 1981; Johnson, 1981, 1982; Adams, 1982; and Bensoussan, 1986, for research supporting the view that cultural knowledge facilitates word guessing and reading comprehension.)

But it is important, we think, not to push the argument too far, for if cultural knowledge is used inappropriately, it can actually lead students astray. In the study of Haynes and Baker (Chapter 7, this volume), for example, L1 and L2 readers were given text-embedded words that were explicitly defined as technical terms in the text. Yet in many cases, these readers drew on their prior knowledge (experiential or lexical) and ignored these stipulated definitions, giving incorrect nontechnical definitions instead. That is, they opted for sense selection over the more cognitively demanding but more appropriate (in this case) sense creation.

Thus, it would be a mistake to encourage learners to depend too heavily on cultural knowledge. As Stein himself notes, skilled guessing requires both attention to the larger context and attention to the language of the text.

References

Adams, S. J. (1982). Scripts and the recognition of unfamiliar vocabulary: Enhancing second language reading skills. *Modern Language Journal, 66,* 155–159.

Bensoussan, M. (1986). Beyond vocabulary: Pragmatic factors in reading comprehension—culture, convention, coherence, and cohesion. *Foreign Language Annals, 19,* 399–407.

Carrell, P. L. (1981). Culture-specific schemata in L2 comprehension. In R. Orem & J. Haskell (Eds.), *Selected papers from the Ninth Illinois TESOL/BE Annual Convention and the First Midwest TESOL Conference* (pp. 123–132). Chicago: TESOL/BE.

Johnson, P. (1981). Effects on reading comprehension of building background knowledge. *TESOL Quarterly, 16,* 503–516.

Johnson, P. (1982). Effects on reading comprehension of language complexity and cultural background of text. *TESOL Quarterly, 16,* 169–181.

Steffensen, M. S., Joag-Dev, C., & Anderson, R. C. (1979). A cross-cultural perspective on reading comprehension. *Reading Research Quarterly, 15,* 10–29.

IV
Research with Innovative Instructional Approaches

Chapter 11
High Frequency Vocabulary and Reading Proficiency in ESL Readers

James Coady
Department of Linguistics
Ohio University
Athens, OH

**Jeff Magoto,
Philip Hubbard,
John Graney,
and Kouider Mokhtari**
Ohio University

This chapter is based on the proposition that there is a positive and significant relationship between knowledge of high-frequency vocabulary and reading proficiency. It is claimed that high-frequency vocabulary can be learned efficiently through computer-assisted learning, and that such increased proficiency in the high-frequency vocabulary of English will lead to an increase in reading proficiency. Two different experiments were carried out with positive results.

This study is complementary to two recent trends in language learning research and teaching methodology. First, there is the trend in the area of reading to focus on interactive text processing, that is, the interaction between top-down and bottom-up processing of the text and the formal and content schema (background knowledge) which the reader brings to bear on the text (Alderson & Urquhart, 1984; Carrell, Devine, & Eskey, 1984; Barnitz, 1985). Second, there is the growing awareness of the roles that effective metacognitive strategies play in the reading event, for example, strategies for inferring the meanings of unknown words from context (Block, 1986; Carrell, 1989a,b; Barnett, 1988). Our study focuses on the relationship of vocabulary knowledge to reading proficiency in a way that, on the one hand, complements these trends, and yet, at the same time, suggests some new directions for research in the areas of both reading and vocabulary.

The significant contribution that vocabulary knowledge or the lack thereof makes to success in reading in L1 has received surprisingly little attention in recent research (see Chapter 1, this volume). Moreover, to the extent that vocabulary has been specifically addressed in second-language learning research and teaching methodology, there has been a tendency to assume either that it will develop automatically through exposure to and interaction with "comprehensible input" (Krashen, 1985), or that the student's learning of vocabulary will be accomplished "naturally" through development of the skill of inferencing. In both cases the assumption seems to be that vocabulary is not a significant problem, because it will be effectively learned through context without any special effort. In short, the current approaches to second-language acquisition, with their emphasis on communicative methods of learning, assume that vocabulary will be learned naturally, with little or no overt instruction. However, as can readily be seen in other chapters in this book (Haynes, Stein, Holmes & Ramos; Haynes & Baker; and Huckin & Bloch) the naturalistic approach to vocabulary acquisition is quite problematic.

The impetus for this research project came from a paper by Coady, Carrell, and Nation (1985) in which we outline a theory of vocabulary acquisition for second language learners. This theory is specifically concerned with acquisition through the medium of reading and is based on the notion of lexical entries as schemas. Central to our theory is the claim that the lexical items encountered by second-language learners at any given stage of their language development can be divided into three categories: (a) words whose forms and common meanings are recognized automatically irrespective of context (sight vocabulary), (b) words whose forms and meanings are to some degree familiar to the learner but are recognized only in context, and (c) words whose forms and, often, meanings as well are unknown to the learner and whose meanings must therefore be inferred from the context, looked up in a dictionary, or left uncomprehended. It is assumed that the majority of sight vocabulary will consist of high-frequency words, due to the effect of repeated exposure.

Recent research in second-language learning has been concerned about the information-processing load of language use (Levelt, 1977; McLaughlin, Rossman, & McLeod, 1983; O'Malley, Chamot, & Walker, 1987). Schneider and Shiffrin (1977) propose a two-way theory of human language processing that consists of automatic and controlled processing. *Automatic processing* is the activation of already learned elements in long-term memory. These elements are activated by appropriate input and implemented without conscious attention. *Controlled processing,* on the other hand, is a temporary activation of a series of elements which requires conscious attention. Because of the limitation of short-term memory capacity, the amount of information which humans can cognitively manipulate at one given point in time by means of controlled processing is limited. It is hypothesized that, through repetition, elements which currently require controlled processing can become automatic. Once such subtasks have become automatized, they require less cognitive capacity, and therefore more time is available for other tasks.

One consequence of controlled processing is a significant limitation on the amount of higher level processing, such as that by which the meaning of an unknown item is inferred from context and eventually learned. Citing Perfetti and Lesgold (1977, 1979), who argue that context cannot be taken advantage of fully if the reader's word recognition efforts are slow and labored, Coady et al. conclude the following:

> Poor readers do not have enough sight vocabulary to take advantage of the context. This suggests that ESL readers must also have sufficient sight vocabulary in order to be able to read successfully and especially to be able to recognize words in context. (p. 10)

While it is still unclear what would constitute "sufficient sight vocabulary," conclusions from a word frequency count by Carroll, Davies, and Richman (1971) suggest that, if a learner knew the meanings of only the most frequent 2,000 words of English, he or she would know more than 80% of the vocabulary on an average page of text (at least at the 9th-grade level). Thus, if students controlled these 2,000 words as sight vocabulary, they would be much more likely to be able to make use of context in determining the meanings of the lesser known or unknown lower frequency words.

Assuming that highly frequent vocabulary represents highly frequent concepts, for example, *sleep, storm, stone,* it is quite likely that the learning of such vocabulary places a much smaller cognitive demand on the learner than the learning of many lower frequency words, for example, *sleigh, smug, spangle.* In the area of content words, highly frequent concepts are more likely to be universal, so the learner will be well served initially by attaching an English label to an already existing native-language schema rather than building an entirely new schema. Thus, initially at least, the emphasis for the L2 learner would need to be on acquisition of the form of the word rather than its meaning. This approach is probably not as successful in terms of the productive use of vocabulary, because of collocational differences between languages, for example, "he stormed into the room." But it does seem to be a useful acquisition strategy in the beginning for improving the receptive skill of reading. Moreover, this strategy turns out to be very natural, and one which is used frequently by beginning language learners. For ultimate success in language learning, however, it is crucial that the learner be aware of the provisional nature of this early hypothesis about the schema equivalence of content words, and gradually modify the preliminary L2 schema entries as the target words are encountered in authentic texts.

In summary, then, our claim is that computer-assisted instruction in high-frequency vocabulary items will increase the amount of sight vocabulary in the experimental group, which will as a result show greater gains on a reading proficiency test than the control group which will not have received such vocabulary instruction. Here are the results of the first study designed to test this claim.

EXPERIMENT 1

The initial experiment in this study was carried out over an 8-week period, with 22 subjects in the experimental group and 20 in the control group. All subjects were studying English full time in a university academic preparation program. They were given pre- and posttests in vocabulary and reading comprehension. The vocabulary test was a 36-item multiple choice synonym test derived from West's (1953) General Service List. The reading test was the Degrees of Reading Power (DRP) exam from the CEEB, form CP-1B, designed for native speakers, which we have found to correlate highly with ESL teachers' evaluations of reading skill. It is a 63-item multiple-choice rational cloze test based on passages of increasing difficulty, with no time limit.

The control group received no systematic treatment in vocabulary other than the regular instruction in English they were receiving along with the experimental group. The experimental group studied the Keyword Vocabulary Lessons, which are a template program for teaching units of 20 words each on Apple IIE computers. The 1,200 words chosen were selected from the 600–2,000 frequency range on the General Service List. After an initial training session, the subjects used the vocabulary program independently.

After loading the desired lesson, the student would see a list of the 20 words in it and could then select a word to view by moving the cursor in front of it and pressing return. For each word, a short definition and an example sentence were given, covering the most common meaning of the word. Since the goal was receptive rather than productive vocabulary, it was assumed that, once a core meaning had been learned for the word, many of the other possible meanings for it would be further deciphered, understood, and learned when encountered in context. When the word, definition, and example sentence were displayed, there was a line called the *keyword line* where the subject could type in a personal mnemonic, based on the keyword technique (see Stoller & Grabe, this volume), or anything else, such as a synonym or translation, up to 30 characters.

Subjects in the experimental group were given a training session in the use of the program and instruction in the keyword technique as described by Pressley, Levin, and Delaney (1982) and Pressley, Levin, and McDaniel (1987). Briefly, the keyword technique is a mnemonic procedure whereby a learner likens the new word to a phonetically similar word in the L1 and then visualizes an image linking the two. For example, a Spanish speaker learning the word *payment,* using this technique, would first look for a Spanish word similar in sound, such as *pimiento* (''red or green pepper''). Having done so, the next step would be to create a mental image linking the two, such as an image of two hands exchanging a couple of peppers for a dollar. Pressley et al. claim, on the basis of over 50 studies, that the keyword technique is more effective than simple rote learning. Note that the keyword method emphasizes the form of the word which is important for long-term retention; and, moreover, it is interactively generated, as is a student-generated test file.

The program offered the subjects two kinds of tests: practice tests, which they could take as often as they wanted and could exit from at any time, and final tests, which they could only take once for each 20-word unit. Both tests were multiple choice, consisting of the definition followed by the correct answer and distractors. The distractors were taken from a pool consisting of the other words in the unit and the words from the immediately following unit. The practice test format was three-item multiple choice, and the final test format was five-item; both tested the subject on all 20 words in the unit. The tests were randomly generated, so that no two were likely to be identical with respect to the order of the items, the selection of distractors, or the placement of the correct answer. The student was not forced to complete the practice test and could quit at any time.

A review file was kept containing words which were difficult for the subjects. Words were added to the file in two ways: subjects could select the words themselves to add to the file, and any words missed on a final test were automatically added to the file. The subjects could see the entries in the review file at any time, and if the file contained 20 or more words, they could select 20 words and create a review unit which could then be used for testing like a regular unit.

Each subject was given three disks of 20 units each, for a total of 1,200 words. Records were kept in a number of categories: number of times a unit was accessed, number of times the entry of words in a unit was viewed, number of keyword changes, number of practice tests in a unit (and the scores), scores on final tests, number of words added to the review unit, and number of times the review unit was accessed.

It is important to note that, when using the program, subjects had complete control over all the components in the lesson. They made the decisions concerning which words to view, when to use the keyword option, when to take practice and final tests, and when to review. In fact, it was possible to complete the unit by jumping to the final test without ever viewing any of the definitions. We assumed that, since many of the words in a given unit would already be familiar to the subjects, it would be counterproductive to force them through the lessons in a lockstep fashion. We will discuss this issue of student-controlled CALL lessons later in the chapter.

After the initial training session, the vocabulary program was used by the subjects independently. Each subject was required to go to the computer lab for 1 hour a week over an 8-week period. There was no attempt to work with this specific group of words either in class or outside of class using any other supplementary materials.

Let us now turn to a more extensive description of the GSL Vocabulary Program itself.

ACTIVITY TYPE: a multiple-choice drill and practice format

LEARNING STYLE: receptive and individualized, with a mnemonic technique

PROGRAM FOCUS: mastery of high-frequency vocabulary

LEARNER FOCUS: rapid learning and reviewing; motivation dependent upon students recognizing the importance of these words to their reading proficiency.

PROGRAM DIFFICULTY: simple on-screen instructions. Speed of presentation and practice is student controlled. Answers must be exact matches, with no hints or explanations. Missed words are loaded into review list. Feedback is clear and encouraging.

LANGUAGE DIFFICULTY: dependent on students' previous knowledge of vocabulary, and, somewhat, their grammar control. Definitions and examples written at or below students' assumed vocabulary level.

CLASSROOM MANAGEMENT: designed to be used individually either during or outside class time. Students have "personal" data disks to optimize the individualized learning aspects and to enable them to carry out efficient monitoring of their own progress.

METHODOLOGY: based on traditional explicit learning wherein the student selects list of words, looks up and studies the ones not known, and, finally, takes a series of quizzes to demonstrate mastery.

JUSTIFICATION FOR EDUCATIONAL OBJECTIVES: With the emphasis on the communicative approach has come an unfortunate decline in the systematic teaching of vocabulary. It is the authors' conviction that a core vocabulary is essential before effective reading can take place. Frequency lists are used as a criterion for vocabulary selection.

JUSTIFICATION FOR USING THE COMPUTER: The computer is an ideal instrument, due to its individualizing capabilities: students work on what they want to, when they choose to, and at the pace they prefer. During optional previews and practice quizzes, the students choose which words to practice or mark for further review. Students have the option to enter translations, "keywords," or notes on their personal data disks.

RECORD KEEPING CAPABILITIES: students have automatic records of lessons completed and the words giving them difficulty. Program automatically cycles words which have been missed on final quizzes into the review lessons. Records are also available to the teachers.

JUSTIFICATION FOR PROGRAM DESIGN: This program design enhances explicit learning in three ways: (a) It controls input to facilitate rapid progress. Definitions are presented in terms of the students' existing vocabulary. (b) When the students enter translations, "keywords", or notes, it increases the likelihood of deeper processing as they must stop and think before writing. (c) It provides immediate feedback at the end of quizzes and final tests with the option of further practice only on those words presenting difficulty.

RESULTS AND DISCUSSION

The means and standard deviations on the reading comprehension and the vocabulary test scores are presented in Table 11.1. The data were analyzed using two way repeated measures ANOVAs using Group (Vocabulary vs. Control) and Time (Pretest vs. Posttest) as independent variables with repeated measures on Time (see Tables 11.2 and 11.3). The main effects of Time were found significant [$F(41,1) = 52.92, p < .001$)]. The Group by Time interaction was also found significant [$F(41,1) = 9.55, p < .005$]. These results indicate (a) that computer-assisted instruction does indeed facilitate vocabulary acquisition in L2; and (b), more importantly, that this vocabulary gain has a significant positive effect on reading comprehension. It is an especially noteworthy finding that such a small amount of time spent on vocabulary study should result in such a significant improvement in reading proficiency.

Table 11.1. Means and Standard Deviations for Reading and Vocabulary Tests for Control and Vocabulary Groups

	Control		Vocabulary	
	M	*SD*	*M*	*SD*
Reading Comprehension[a]				
Pretest	20.90	15.56	15.32	6.56
Posttest	27.05	16.01	28.18	6.92
Vocabulary[b]				
Pretest	22.10	7.09	22.23	6.40
Posttest	24.10	7.20	27.18	4.80

[a]maximum score is 63
[b]maximum score is 36

Table 11.2. Summary of ANOVA for Reading Test Scores

Source	DF	SS	F	R > F
Subjects	41	10677.95		
Time	1	1893.67	93.91	.0001
Group × Time	1	236.10	11.71	.0014

EXPERIMENT 2

The following Fall, an attempt was made to replicate this study, since, as was noted before, the results were indeed contrary to some contemporary views of the importance of frequency in vocabulary acquisition. Moreover, the significant impact of this vocabulary knowledge on reading proficiency was a very important finding that deserved further investigation. Thus it appeared to be not only appropriate but necessary to carry out a follow up study. New tests were administered to the experimental group that were designed to be even more sensitive to the hypothesized gains. First, a new 60-item vocabulary test was constructed that sampled the words taught in the Keyword Vocabulary Lessons systematically but randomly. Second, another version of the DRP was used that encompassed a lower range of reading achievement, thus allowing some of the weaker students to better demonstrate their gains. Unfortunately, it became impossible to form a control group, because the previous success with the materials had so enhanced their reputation that virtually all the students in the program wished to use them. It did not seem ethical to deny the students access to these materials, and so the experiment was carried out without a control group. This unfortunately limits the value of the study, but since the results were so clearly in line with the previous study and supported its findings, they will be reported.

Because it was a repeated measure design matched T-tests were conducted on the pre- and posttest scores in both areas. The results showed a difference significant at the .05 level in both cases (see Table 11.4). Consequently, although there was no control group in this experiment, there was statistical significance on the treatment.

Other important evidence as to the success and validity of the instructional materials came from a questionnaire which the students filled out about the materials and which is briefly summarized in Table 11.5.

Table 11.3. Summary of ANOVA for Vocabulary Test Scores

Source	DF	SS	F	R > F
Subjects	41	3147.20		
Time	1	253.34	52.92	.0001
Group × Time	1	45.73	9.55	.0036

Table 11.4. Means

Reading Comprehension	
Pretest Mean	20.02
Posttest Mean	30.18
	(+10.16)*
N = 37	

Vocabulary	
Pretest Mean	41.82
Posttest Mean	47.45
	(+5.63)*
N = 35	

*$p > .05$

Note that the overwhelmingly positive response of users of this vocabulary program, along with the impossibility of continuing to have a control group, indicates the motivational power of this mode of learning vocabulary.

In sum, the same general pattern of significant results was found. Thus the two studies combined demonstrated clear and positive research findings in support of this pedagogical approach in general. However, the relationship between vocabulary knowledge and reading comprehension still needs to be further examined before it can be claimed that the association is clearly supported. We do believe, however, that the results of these studies are positive enough to support the following pedagogical recommendations:

1. It is worthwhile spending valuable instructional time on the 2,000 most frequent words in English.
2. Since individuals will know differing subsets of this vocabulary, individualized instruction is a very feasible mode of instruction.
3. Computers can be utilized for such instruction.
4. Pedagogical emphasis on this vocabulary can result in increased reading proficiency.

Table 11.5. Student Survey

	The Percentage of Those Who Answered Agree or Strongly Agree
The program helped me to learn vocabulary	90%
The program was enjoyable to use	90%
The program helped me with my reading	83%
I wish there were more computer programs for reading and vocabulary	90%

REFERENCES

Alderson, J. C., & Urquhart, A. H. (Eds.). (1984). *Reading in a foreign language.* New York: Longman.

Barnett, M. A. (1988). Reading through context: How real and perceived strategy use affects L2 comprehension. *Modern Language Journal, 71,* 15–162.

Barnitz, J. G. (1985). *Reading development of nonnative speakers of English.* New York: Harcourt Brace.

Block, E. (1986). The comprehension strategies of second language readers. *TESOL Quarterly, 20,* 463–494.

Carrell, P. L., Devine, J., & Eskey, D. (Eds.). (1984). *Interactive approaches to second language reading.* New York: Cambridge University Press.

Carrell, P. L. (1989a). Metacognitive awareness and second language reading. *Modern Language Journal, 73,* 121–134.

Carrell, P. L. (1989b). Metacognitive strategy training for ESL reading. *TESOL Quarterly, 23*(4), 647–678.

Carroll, J. B., Davies, P., & Richman, B. (1971). *The American heritage word frequency book.* Boston: Houghton Mifflin.

Coady, J., Carrell, P., & Nation, P. (1985). *The teaching of vocabulary in ESL from the perspective of schema theory.* Milwaukee: Midwest TESOL.

Krashen, S. D. (1985). *The input hypothesis: Issues and implications.* New York: Longman.

Levelt, W. J. M. (1977). Skill theory and language teaching. *Studies in Second Language Acquisition, 1,* 53–70.

McLaughlin, B., Rossman, T., & McLeod, B. (1983). Second language learning: An information-processing perspective. *Language Learning, 33,* 135–58.

O'Malley, J. M., Chamot A. U., & Walker, C. (1987). Some applications of cognitive theory to second language acquisition. *Studies in second language acquisition, 9,* 287–306.

Perfetti, C. A., & Lesgold, A. M. (1977). Discourse comprehension and sources of individual differences. In M. Just & P. Carpenter (Eds.), *Cognitive processes in comprehension* (pp. 141–183). Hillsdale NJ: Erlbaum.

Perfetti, C. A., & Lesgold, A. M. (1979). Coding and comprehension in skilled reading and implications for reading instruction. In L. B. Resnick & P. A. Weaver (Eds.), *Theory and practice of early reading* (pp. 57–84). Hillsdale, NJ: Erlbaum.

Pressley, M., Levin, J. R., & Delaney, H. (1982). The mnemonic keyword method. *Review of Educational Research, 52*(1), 61–91.

Pressley, M., Levin, J. R., & McDaniel, M. A. (1987). Remembering versus inferring what a word means: Mnemonic and contextual approaches. In M. G. McKeown, & M. E. Curtis (Eds.), *The nature of vocabulary acquisition* (pp. 107–128). Hillsdale, NJ: Erlbaum.

Schneider, W., & Shiffrin, R. M. (1977). Controlled and automatic human information processing: I. detection, search, and attention. *Psychological Review, 84,* 1–66.

West, M. (1953). *A general service list of English words.* London: Longman, Green & Co.

Editorial Comments

This chapter combines a solid theoretical foundation concerning the role of automaticity in successful reading (according to interactive models) with exploration of computer-assisted vocabulary instruction. The persuasive theoretical argument is followed up with statistical findings that suggest that practice with high-frequency L2 vocabulary does benefit reading. Further persuasion comes in the form of survey results and discussion of patterns of lab use, both indicating the powerful motivational attraction of the software program described here.

The 2,000 high-frequency words taught in this program are likely to be familiar to most L1 learners once they have completed initial reading instruction in the first few grades of elementary school; it is specifically lower level L2 learners who need practice with these words to develop automatic recognition of their printed form. Still, the principle of giving individualized practice with useful new vocabulary in a motivational computerized environment probably applies equally well to L1 readers. Similar programs could be useful in learning vocabulary of academic environments, particularly for weaker developmental readers who may not have sufficient literacy experience with subtechnical vocabulary encountered in college (see Nation, 1990, for a discussion and list of subtechnical vocabulary).

The researchers have included two types of pre- and posttests in their design: vocabulary and reading comprehension. This has the potential of revealing effects of computer-assisted vocabulary instruction. Does such an instructional program merely build vocabulary or does it improve reading comprehension as well? Future studies of this type should consider in addition the element of reading speed, for it is possible that effects of automatic vocabulary recognition at lower L2 proficiency levels would be even more obvious with changes in reading speed than with changes in comprehension. Also, it would be useful to have individualized records of lab use so that effects of different amounts of time spent with the program could be measured.

For teachers and curriculum designers seeking model computer programs to complement classroom learning, the description in this chapter of the design of the computer program in vocabulary learning will be of great interest. The authors provide convincing theoretical and practical justification for several aspects of the program: its emphasis on teaching of core meanings, its opportunity for students to type in their own mnemonics (based on the keyword approach), its options for learners to take various open-exit practice "tests" before taking a final test on a given set of words, and its provision of an individualized review file of words missed on tests or words selected by students to be included in the file. Though this program gives low-level content, it appears to generate strong motivation, because it provides opportunities for deeper processing through productive interaction as well as giving the user considerable control in over task selection (see Dever, 1986, for further discussion of the distinctions between content and task in computer assisted reading instruction).

References

Dever, S. Y. (1986). Computer Assisted Reading Instruction (CARI). In F. Dubin, D. E. Eskey, & W. Grabe (Eds.), *Teaching second language reading for academic purposes*. Reading, MA: Addison-Wesley.

Nation, P. (1990). *Teaching and learning vocabulary*. New York: Newbury House.

Chapter 12
Procedural and Declarative Knowledge in Vocabulary Learning: Communication and the Language Learner's Lexicon

Peter J. Robinson
University of Hawai'i at Mānoa
Department of ESL
Honolulu, HI

The traditional approach to vocabulary building is to concentrate on developing familiarity with the definitions of increasingly low-frequency words. In contrast this chapter takes a procedural perspective on vocabulary development. The declarative knowledge *that* words have particular meanings, and the procedures we typically employ for realizing or achieving this declarative knowledge, are distinguished. It is argued that such procedures form part of our procedural knowledge of *how* to negotiate and require ability in the production and comprehension of a reduced set of frequently occurring core words. After discussing criteria for linguistically identifying such core words, it is then argued that a communicative view of the interactive nature of lexical negotiation requires us to focus pedagogically as much on core word procedures as we do on the more narrowly defined declarative meanings which specialist words have. A suggestion for a framework which can be used in developing materials to promote procedural lexical competence is made which adapts Canale and Swain's (1980) checklist of the four dimensions of communicative competence. Exercise types are then presented that exemplify how these dimensions could be covered lexically, as a prelude to task-based vocabulary learning extensions.

CORE VOCABULARY AS PRODUCT AND AS PROCESS

The idea that there is a core vocabulary available to second-language learners has long been attractive to those researchers concerned with the grading and sequencing of language items as a basis for syllabus design, since items identified as core are obvious targets for initial or early presentation in syllabuses of the *synthetic*, not the *analytic* type (see Nunan, 1989, for this distinction). Much of this research has been predicated on the assumption that syllabus design is primarily a specification of language items or linguistic content (e.g., West, 1953; Wilkins, 1977; Sinclair & Renouf, 1988; Willis, 1990). Accordingly, most previous studies of the relationship between general, core, and specific, noncore, words have concentrated on the extent to which lexical items can be systematically distinguished from one another, and the various semantic and grammatical differences between core and noncore words have been itemized, for example, the relationship between coreness and superordinacy, or between core words and neutral tenor of discourse, or marked and unmarked levels of specificity (see the tests in Stubbs, 1986; Carter, 1986; the work of Halliday, 1978, on tenor; Cruse, 1977, on specificity). Such studies tend to treat core words as a special *kind* of vocabulary (though the emphasis in Halliday's and Cruse's work is on the communicative function served by neutral tenor, and unmarked choices of specificity) and attempt to distinguish them as a *product* from more specific, technical words. This is particularly so in the attempt of Stein (1978) to fix a nuclear vocabulary on semantic grounds, which can serve as a component of the nuclear English that Quirk (cited in Carter, 1986) has envisioned as being as "culture free as calculus." Gernsbacher, Givon, and Yang (1990), taking this product-oriented view to its extreme, have claimed that core words are stored in different parts of the brain, while Tulving (1984) suggests they are associated with episodic, as opposed to semantic, memory.

The concern of this chapter, though, is with how such words are *used* in the *process* of discourse negotiation, as part of the means available to teacher and learner for deploying strategies to overcome problems in communication. This reflects a wider conviction that attempts to locate potentially useful distinctions between words, which result in reduced or staged vocabularies for language learners, within a framework which takes little account of their actional nature in discourse is fundamentally mistaken. In fact the preoccupation with a lexicon itself (Fromkin, 1987), with the modular organization of "words in the mind" (Aitchison, 1987) obscures the fact that our access to such a repository must consist largely of the study of words in the air, or in the text. Yet the framework necessary to aid the description and observation of the discourse properties of lexis remains largely undeveloped (though see Winter, 1977, 1978; McCarthy, 1988; Brazil, 1985; Halliday & Hasan, 1977; Hasan, 1984; Thomas, 1985). Perhaps this static repository metaphor for the lexicon, familiar from many current theoretical frameworks like Lexical Functional Grammar (Bresnan, 1982; Pinker, 1984), Generalized Phrase Structure Grammar (Gazdar & Pullum, 1981), and the like, has exerted a covert influence on language teachers' attempts to conceptualize the problems involved in developing lexical competence.

But to represent the language learner's, and language user's, lexicon as a box into which we can put things is inadequate at best, and, at worst, a misrepresentation that creates confusion. The lexicon is also fluid and a medium through which meanings are carried and negotiated. In other words, this chapter's claim is that the debate about the development of lexical competence has focused on developing the learner's declarative knowledge *that* relations exist between words (see Crow & Quigley, 1986; Rudzka, Channell, Putsys, & Ostyn, 1982, 1985, for work on semantic field theory), or *that* words have static meanings, and largely ignored issues relating to the procedural knowledge a learner must have of *how* to realize these relations and meanings as use in actional contexts. See Anderson (1980) for a summary of the distinction between declarative and procedural knowledge, and Widdowson (1983), Faerch and Kasper (1983, 1984), and Prabhu (1987) for various pedagogic and research applications of the terms.

Here, for example, is Nation's schema (1984) for representing what is involved in knowing a word (see Table 12.1):

Many vocabulary teaching materials seem to concentrate on developing a number of these aspects of receptive and productive knowledge in relation to words on a particular list, often overemphasizing some, like conceptual knowledge, at the expense of others, like word-form, both graphological and phonological, as Dussere (1988) has recently pointed out. But to what extent do such materials also attempt to develop pragmatic ability in the use of such words? And is Nation's categorization adequate within a communicative orientation to lexical development? This chapter will propose a rather different set of categories for grouping lexical knowledge, based on Canale and Swain (1980) and Canale (1983).

The following diagram (Figure 12.1) shows the relationship of the different terms used so far. Communication, it can be seen, involves the conversion of knowledge into skill, that is, the mobilization of both declarative and procedural knowledge in time-constrained, goal-oriented discourse. Communicative competence, of course, includes not only the idealized declarative knowledge we have of word meaning, but the procedural knowledge we draw on in converting that knowledge to performance.

Let us look first, though, at the properties of some words that are particularly important to the ability to do things in discourse via the exercising or application

Table 12.1. Receptive and Productive Aspects of Word Knowledge

form	spoken form	R	What does the word sound like?
		P	How is the word pronounced?
	written form	R	What does the word look like?
		P	How is the word written and spelled?
position	grammatical patterns	R	In what patterns does the word occur?
		P	In what patterns must we use the word?
	collocations	R	What words or types of words can be expected after the word?
		P	What words or types of words must we use with this word?
function	frequency	R	How common is the word?
		P	How often should the word be used?
	appropriateness	R	Where would we expect to meet this word?
		P	Where can this word be used?
meaning	concept	R	What does the word mean?
		P	What word should be used to express this meaning?
	associations	R	What other words does this word make us think of?
		P	What other words could we use instead of this one?

Note: R = Receptive knowledge, P = Productive knowledge

of communication strategies like paraphrase, substitution, and circumlocution identified by Faerch and Kasper (1983) and summarized in Ellis (1985). Having looked at the pragmatic properties of such core words, we will then move to describing aspects of lexis that can be developed within the framework suggested by Canale and Swain. In this way the relationship between procedural and declarative knowledge, and implications for vocabulary teaching, will be shown.

ACKNOWLEDGING PROCEDURALITY

The procedural, enabling facility some words have is a criterion for selecting them to be used in some dictionary definitions, for example, those in the *Longman Learner Dictionary* (see Whitcut, 1988, for an interesting discussion of the lexicographic rationale for using a reduced vocabulary, and Robinson, 1990, for psycholinguistic support). This enabling facility is a feature too of the subtech-

Figure 12.1. Dimensions of Communicative Competence

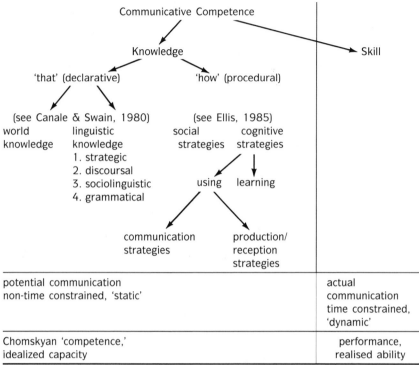

potential communication non-time constrained, 'static'	actual communication time constrained, 'dynamic'
Chomskyan 'competence,' idealized capacity	performance, realised ability

nical language used in the oral explanation of difficult, technical concepts. Hutchinson and Waters (1981) have demonstrated the problems learners face in coping with these words. They claim that it is not the performance repertoire of a technical, specialist vocabulary that is called on in giving and understanding technical classroom explanations, but:

> the ability to recognize the glossing techniques whereby teachers introduce specific terms, and the ability to ask questions when an explanation is not given. But the basic resource of both these strategies is a fund of general vocabulary in which the explanation will be expressed. (pp. 6–7)

These general words are thrown up, together with more specific words, in any frequency count of a specific language area or "field of discourse" in Hallidayan terms (1978; Benson & Greaves, 1981). For example, Table 12.2 is an extract from Friel's (1979) verb frequency count of legal texts in which both general and specific words occur together.

Table 12.2.   A Frequency Count of Verbs Used in English Legal Texts

1. be
2. have
3. commit
4. make
5. give
6. clause
7. do
8. say
9. take
10. find
11. try
12. think
13. provide
14. arrest
15. come
16. follow
17. apply
18. kill
19. know
20. appear

From "A Verb Frequency Count in Legal English," by M. Friel, *ESPMENA*, 1(1), p. 26. Copyright © 1979. Reprinted by permission.

Identifying Specificity

The specific words give text what Benson and Greaves (1981) call "institutional focus;" for example, the word *commit* in the list above occurs regularly in texts associated with legal subjects. Note, though, that it is of almost the same frequency in the legal texts used in Friel's sample as *do,* which is a word of much wider potential application. Frequency counts of specific subject areas thus fail to distinguish clearly between specific and general words. However, across subject areas, adopting the criteria of "range" (Mackey, 1966; Nation, 1984), words like *do* regularly occur, while *commit* is much less common. General words can be further identified by applying the criteria of "coverage," the ability they have to take on a variety of different meanings. It is this feature that will be focused on, and it is what Widdowson refers to when he calls words like *do* procedural; that is, they take on the "indexical" values particular contexts attribute to them, while having little independent meaning themselves (Widdowson, 1983, pp. 92–95). The index, as Widdowson makes clear, following Pierce (see Lyons, 1977, p. 99), is the referring function of the sign in context, where it operates to realize relevant schemata, as opposed to the structuring function of the sign as symbol, which operates to realize relevant systemic knowledge. When words are used indexically, they refer the addressee out to the context of situation for the value they have; when used symbolically, as in many teaching materials, they draw attention to their own properties as structural elements defined by their relations with other symbols within a system.

Lexical and Indexical Words: Sense, Structure, and Signification

In the following example the word *do* is used to substitute for both *button up* and *uncork,* respectively, and its interpretation in each case is dependent on knowledge of the relevant schema or frame of reference established by the context:

- If you are going to *do* it, *do* it properly. (spoken by a mother to her child as he buttons up a shirt)
- Here, let me *do* it. (spoken after an unsuccessful attempt to uncork a bottle of wine)

It may be that confusion arises between the speakers over what in the immediate environment is being referred to, for example:

- I wish you wouldn't *do* that.
- What, smoke?
- No, flick your ash all over the floor.

In this case *do* can receive more than one interpretation, as of course, it must do in question forms:

- What shall I *do* now?

where the reply must contain a specific verb to fill in the indexical gap left by *do*:

- Rinse the beans.
- Saute the potatoes.

Alternatively, the object can specify the indexical meaning of *do* indirectly, though this can be ambiguous;

- What shall I *do* now?
- Do the potatoes!
- Peel them?
- No, wash them first.

"Doing the potatoes" refers to a whole host of activities that can be performed on them. Contrast these problems with the specificity of *anaesthetize* in:

- "Whom shall I anaesthetize next?"

or *peel* in:

- "What shall I peel now?"

A consequence of the high indexicality of *do,* then, is that it is nonmonotonic (or multitracked, enabling the user to go back and change assumptions which originally took a wrong track; see Doyle, 1979) with regard to specifying a frame of reference. This means it is possible to revise existing assumptions about what action is being carried out when *do* is used. However, highly schema-specific *anaesthetize* is monotonic and carries with it a fixed set of assumptions about the action referred to. Metaphor is based on assumptions about shared knowledge of features, which are transferred to a second object. "I'm going to anaesthetize John," spoken in a bar, might be taken to mean, "put to sleep with a strong drink"; spoken by a child with a sewing needle, it takes on a different meaning, because different assumptions about features of *anaesthetize* are being transferred. *Do* isn't much use as a metaphor, though, because there are few assumptions about its meaning that can be fixed, and so shared, except +action. There are, of course, grammatical features, like +verb and +present tense, and these, as Widdowson (1984) shows in his analysis of cummings's poem[1]:

> anyone lived in a pretty how town
> with up so floating many bells down
> spring summer autumn winter
> he sang his didnt he danced his did

can be material out of which to construct metaphor. In this case *did* carries the features of +past and +verb but transfers them to the context of noun in the syntactic structure of the sentence. No noun has the features +past time and +process, but nothing else. Widdowson concludes:

> cummings creates a noun which has those features, 'did'; we might paraphrase the expression 'he danced his did' as something like 'he danced his way through all his activities in the past'. (1984, p. 11)

In summary, *do* is highly indexical and nonmonotonic schematically. It also has little lexical content, and this, generally, means it is less likely than words with more lexical content to be used metaphorically. There appear to be few assumptions we can make about the context-free features it has except, as noted above, +action, +verb, and +present. This is the reason it also has high symbolic value as an exemplar of those grammatical categories which are important to structuring the grammatical system, like tense, and part of speech. We can also add that words like *do, it, she,* and so on, appear to be "iconic" (Haiman, 1985), the third function of the sign distinguished by Pierce. The icon is the resembling function of the sign, and signs are icons where there is some perceptual similarity between the signifier and the signified. In other words, the form of the signifier is motivated by the signified, as with onomatopoeia, and the relationship is not completely arbitrary. So, to the extent that *do* is schematically empty out of context (apart from the minimal features of +action, etc.), it could be thought of as a semantically reduced, or little word, and this aspect of delexicality is indeed represented iconically in that such words are usually small, and much smaller on average than lexical words like, typically, *anaesthetize.* This may give them greater saliency for L1 and possibly L2 learners, particularly with regard to the extraction of variable units in morphosyntactic frames using those operating principles described by Peters (1983, 1989). Technical words, then, tend to be larger, and one obvious reason for this is that lexical words are much more morphologically productive and so have inflections which increase their size. In this way the smaller size of the tokens for procedural words is an example of iconicity (Haiman, 1985) resembling their reduced lexicality.

A further observation about procedural words and specific words is that the former contract no clear collocational restrictions. For example, *strong* and *tea* collocate, or co-occur quite regularly, just as *powerful* and *car* also collocate. But this is not reversible. *Powerful* and *tea* do not co-occur or collocate significantly; and neither do *strong* and *car* (see Halliday, 1966; Sinclair, 1966, 1986; McIntosh, 1962). The reason procedural words do not have clear, or *narrow,* collocational restrictions is that they are extremely mobile and occur in many environments with many other words. Their collocational distribution is *wide* and unfixed. Lexical words like *strong* and *powerful,* of course, with a narrower range of distribution, do collocate significantly and this is the basis of analyses of "field of discourse" in the Hallidayan sense (Benson & Greaves, 1981).

Let us now bring this group of distinctions together in diagrammatic form so as to illustrate more clearly the differences between general and specific (procedural and schematic) words (see Table 12.3). Procedural words would be located to the left of this series of clines.

The examples *do* and *anaesthetize* have been placed in relation to each of the clines above. Of course, these clines can also be used to distinguish supposedly grammatical words from lexical or full words. The clines also correspond to the function procedural words have on three separate planes, (a) the semiotic, (b) the semantic, and (c) the syntactic (see Robinson, 1987a, 1989).

Sinclair and Renouf (1988) have recently named the class of indexical verbs like *do* "delexical," and, based on large computer concordances of text, they identify a large number of these verbs and their auxiliary supportive function. They appear most commonly in the context of other words whose meanings they adopt. "Textual evidence shows the extent to which the phenomenon of delex-

Table 12.3. Characteristics of Procedural and Schematic Words

Procedural (grammatical words)	Schematic (content words)
a) high indexicality .... (nonmonotonic) (schema-free)	low indexicality (monotonic) (schema-specific)
b) low lexical content .... (few fixed features)	high lexical content (many fixed features)
c) wide distribution .... (no clear collocations)	narrow distribution (clear collocations)
e.g., *do*	e.g., *anaesthetize*

icality occurs. The primary function of *make,* for example, is to carry nouns like *decision, discoveries, arrangements,* thereby offering the alternative phraseology, "make your own decisions, to decide on something," and so on (p. 151).

This, then, presents a pedagogical issue, for although these delexical words are undoubtedly useful to the learner as a resource for conveying the meanings of more specific words, their very generality often causes the learner problems. For example, given Sinclair and Renouf's comment, how do you teach the range of uses and contexts of a word like *make,* and its consequential range of collocates: "make a million, make a decision, make a cake, make a promise," and so on?

One possibility is through teaching words like *decision* and *cake.*

- What does cake mean?
- Well, you make a cake, like this . . .
- What does make mean?
- Well, you make a cake or a decision . . .

And so procedural and specific words mutually feed off and support each other. While appearing to have different distributional characteristics, then, procedural and specific words are in a complementary relationship with each other. Empty, procedural words realize the schematic meanings specific words have, while the contentive and lexical specific words demonstrate the capacity general words have for doing just that.

ASSERTING AND ASSIMILATING MEANINGS

One could say that the meanings of *do* or *make* are "potential," while those of *decision, commit, anaesthetize,* etc. are more "schematic" and associated with typical event structures or scenes. Now these two sorts of meaning are involved typically in any negotiation, particularly those in the technical classroom. The effort of one participant is often to fix, or explain, what he or she means by finding the "right word," as it were, while the other, more suppliant partner tries to "see" what he or she means. In other words, one tries to assert a meaning while the other tries to break what is said down into more manageable or familiar units so as to assimilate them. Often the teacher is called on to perform both jobs at once, and so she offers the asserted meaning, and then, in the face of real or anticipated incomprehension, she breaks it up so as to make it assimilable. Here is a concocted example of procedural vocabulary at work, realizing these procedures for making sense. The declarative knowledge or meaning being asserted is *anaesthetic*. The procedural words used to break this down include, *put, someone, make, them,* and so on.

learner	*teacher*
	and some drugs can also be used as anesthetics, like. . .
umm . . . what is anaesthetic?	
	oh er . . . when you put someone to sleep, you make them go to sleep before an operation
sleep?	
	yes, you anaesthetize them . . . you give them a drug or anaesthetic that makes them sleep . . . so they have no pain . . . you make them sleepy

Incidentally, this example also serves to illustrate the point Allwright, Pit Corder, and Rossner have made recently when they comment:

> Learners in class seem to focus their energies on lexis and ask questions about it, and possibly get all sorts of grammatical help via the lexis . . . if we study the processes by which lexis is acquired, we may get closer to the way grammar is acquired. (1986, p. 187)

In the exchange above we can see the teacher illustrating two sorts of grammatical information for the learner. There is the derivational link between the noun *anaesthetic,* and the verb *anaesthetize,* which the teacher illustrates by providing relevant frames for each part of speech:

- you anaesthetize them
- give them a drug or anaesthetic

and this process is analogous to the parent's repetition of learner units, and variation of elements within those units, which Peters (1983) has suggested are useful for the language learner (in L1 or L2) to perform the analytic process of

Figure 12.2. The Relationship Of Communication Strategies To Strategies for L2 Learning

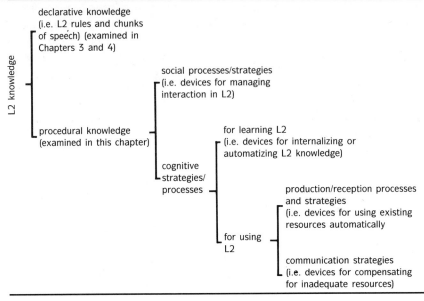

From *Understanding Second Language Acquisition,* by R. Ellis, p. 165. Copyright © 1985 by Oxford University Press. Reprinted by permission.

"fission" on, thereby gaining structural information about individual elements and larger patterns (see Robinson, 1986, 1990a, 1990b). The second sort of grammatical information is the provision of a frame or pattern for the verb. By giving the example "you anaesthetize them," the teacher demonstrates that, typically, the verb requires animate subject and object NPs. We can see, then, that this small exchange could illustrate the process whereby the learner begins to develop or confirm hypotheses about the verb valency or the grammatical dependencies between the verb and its frame, as well as about the derivational link between the noun-form and the verb-form of *anaesthetize* (see also Ard & Gass, 1987; Pinker, 1989, on learning grammar via lexis).

Procedural vocabulary is essential to this process. It not only provides the means for negotiating the lexical meaning of *anaesthetic* via such words as *put, someone, make,* and *go to sleep,* but it is also used to provide fillers for the grammatical slots in a frame that the learner is potentially seeking to analyze and make generalizations about. For example, the use of *you* and *them* as subject and object placeholders is particularly important here.

In this way the learner simultaneously makes sense and structure via the contexts provided by the negotiation of the meaning of *anaesthetic*. This process involves, as illustrated, the assertion and the assimilation of meaning. Two sorts of knowledge are involved, the declarative knowledge which the teacher is asserting (that an anaesthetic is used to make you sleep), and the procedural knowledge of how to make this assimilable for the learner using a reduced vocabulary. The fact that such a reduced indexical vocabulary is there in the language system is probably a systemic reflex of these negotiating procedures born of the need to have such a resource to enable the processes just described to operate. The vocabulary, in other words, is a reflex of its use.

This means then, that the core vocabulary exemplified via *do* is important both at the level of communication strategies (which relate to the ability to use language) and at the level of the cognitive strategies and processes underlying them, for understanding language structure. This can be seen in the initial figure in this chapter, as well as in Figure 12.2 (from Ellis, 1985, p. 165).

KNOWLEDGE "THAT" AND KNOWLEDGE "HOW": MATERIALS AND METHODOLOGY

The issue of concentrating on a core vocabulary and the development of procedural knowledge seems to be largely methodological, since it involves the contrivance of contexts for asserting and assimilating meaning that serve to realize the values of the two sorts of words identified as general and specific. Let us now turn to the issue of materials and exercise types which can serve as the vehicle for such an approach to focus on in the classroom.

First, a distinction is often made between the vocabulary-learning demands of students of ESP and those in more general courses in EFL or ESL. Where does the difference lie? ESP contexts provide ready-made schemata, and corresponding groups of specific words, which can be realized procedurally (Widdowson, 1983, p. 95). This does not mean, though, that the declarative acquisition of content, adopting the lexicon as letterbox metaphor, should be the overall preoccupation of ESP courses. If procedural ability is not developed, how does the learner cope with unforeseen and unforeseeable problems in understanding the use of semitechnical vocabulary? We cannot hope to provide the learner with all the meanings he or she will ever need. More importantly, we cannot anticipate the different ways the learner will use the words in discourse. We must develop the ability to establish meaning, and not simply the ability to bring a ready-made meaning complete to a context. McCarthy (1988) has recently made the same points. Meanings are existential and relate to the here-and-now of the discourse. They are the means whereby speakers in conversation come to view the "possible worlds" (Robinson, 1988a, 1992) from which each views the interaction, and thereby come to convergence in understanding. For example, McCarthy has shown that abstract, decontextualized semantic relationships like synonymy are particular to an interaction and do not preexist it. He proposes that, within pragmatics, we relabel the relationship of synonymy as "equivalence" to show that a word's:

> usefulness as an equivalent to another item is a local, existential value . . . which is different in kind from statements made in a decontextualized structural description of the lexicon. (1987, p. 183)

Equivalences are negotiated in discourse by establishing a paradigm which the other speaker may accept, or reject. A prominent stressed syllable marks the speaker's choice of item as selective (Brazil, 1985), and second speakers can either accept the meaning this item selects or renegotiate by offering their own choice as selective in the paradigm by stressing the lexical item. When they do this, they signal that they are adding some extra increment of sense to the first speaker's choice or contribution. For example:

A: so you VISITed the BIG ISland

In this case *visited* and *big island* are each prominent, and therefore marked as selective for sense.

B: YES, and we took in MAUI TOO

The second speaker accepts the sense of *visited,* and therefore the choice of *took in* is nonprominent, signalling that they are synonymous and occupy the same sense paradigm. However, the speaker could quite easily have marked the contribution as selective, by giving it prominence:

B: YES, and we TOOK IN MAUI

In this case the speaker adds to, or redefines, the meaning of *visited* offered by the first speaker, perhaps to show the desire to add an extra dimension of temporariness than *visited* expresses. The declarative knowledge we have of sense relations like synonymy, antonymy, etc. is a provisional, meaning bank, or base competence, to be drawn on in discourse. Such relations are subject to negotiation, they do not preexist it (Robinson, 1992).

But the arguments against an over-preoccupation with declarative knowledge are not simply that it leaves the language learner with a static monolithic lexicon and little procedural competence in language use, but that—as shown earlier—if the opportunities to negotiate meaning via assertion and assimilation are not available in the classroom, the learner is deprived of the means of learning the grammatical, structural information via the negotiating process. It is of course true that, with the specialist language of medicine, for example, some words do retain an impermeable, static sense regardless of context, words like *anaesthe-*

**Table 12.4.   Methods For Presenting Medical Vocabulary
At Kuwait University**

1. Words given in sentences that make their meaning clear.
   e.g., *Synergetic* drugs are drugs that work together to increase each other's effects. The three muscles that work together to flex the forearm are called synergetic muscles.
2. A list of words with meanings:
   e.g., *nasomental*—pertaining to the chin and nose.
   ankylostoma—lockjaw
3. The use of word roots or groups of related words.
   e.g., *path (o)*—disease
   pathologist
   pathology
4. Sometimes the responsibility for identifying and looking up new words has been left to you.

From "The Acquisition of Technical Vocabulary," by D. Adams-Smith, *ESPMENA*, 1(1), p. 26. Copyright © 1979. Reprinted by permission.

tize, synergetic, and so on. But to treat all vocabulary development as analogous to the processes involved in learning such words is a misrepresentation. Note Diana Adams-Smith's summary of her methods of presenting new vocabulary to second-year premedical students at Kuwait University in Table 12.4 (Adams-Smith, 1979, p. 26).

The above arguments suggest the need for a pedagogic framework within which to provide coverage of the procedural aspects of lexical competence, and to focus the teacher and learner in their twin enterprises of asserting and assimilating meanings. The following suggestion is a contrivance that aims to be useful by serving these ends, and also to provide the basis for a wider variety of exercise types than are commonly found in many vocabulary-teaching materials, where the preoccupation is often with variations on the simple gap-and-filler type formula, or the matching of words and sentences in the manner suggested by Adams-Smith's summary above.

LEXICAL AND COMMUNICATIVE COMPETENCE

Canale (1983) describes *communicative competence* as "the underlying systems of knowledge and skill required for communication" (1983, p. 5; Canale & Swain, 1980). He distinguishes between four areas of this competence. *Grammatical competence* is concerned with the user's mastery of the language code, vocabulary and linguistic semantics:

> it is still not clear that any current theory of grammar can be selected over others to characterize this competence. (1983, p. 7)

All of the three current syntactic theories surveyed by Sells (1985) have a much larger lexical component than was included in the transformational models of 20 years ago. Wasow comments in the postscript to Sells:

> It is interesting that contemporary syntactic theories seem to be converging on the idea that sentence structure is generally predictable from word meaning, for this seems to be close to the naive view of a great many non-linguists. (Sells, 1985, p. 204)

Naive or not, the traditional wedge driven between syntax and lexis seems increasingly insubstantial, and to be a theoretical obstacle to those like All-wright, who seem to view the acquisition of structure as simultaneous, or consecutive to the acquisition of lexical knowledge. A lexically based grammar seems more likely to be most closely attuned to the learner's perceptions of how the "units of acquisition" (Peters, 1983) are to be broken down and stored as "frame patterns" (Robinson, 1986, 1990a; Hudson, 1984, 1986; Pinker, 1984, 1989).

Sociolinguistic competence is involved in decisions about appropriateness of language to context, at the levels of both meaning and form: for example, whether it is appropriate to complain in a given situation, and whether to do so formally or informally (meaning), and given that it is appropriate, how the formal or informal complaint is realized (form). Since this involves decisions about when and how to interact, it spills over into *discourse competence*—the ability to construct, and maintain in negotiation, properly cohesive and coherent talk and text.

Strategic competence is involved in decisions about how to repair break-downs in communication, or decisions about how to enhance the message. Reformulations, for example, can serve either purpose, both as a way of presenting your co-speaker your assessment of his or her gist or propositional meaning (Heritage & Watson, 1979), or "upshot," the illocutionary meaning of the utterance. More is involved in each component than this brief summary suggests, and each component interacts with the others in any message. The purpose in identifying them separately has been to give broad coverage to the range of abilities involved in developing lexical-communicative competence.

Where particular groups of students are involved, with particular needs, the coverage given to each of these aspects can be restricted to some extent. For example, at the University of Bahrain where the materials below were used, two groups of students, engineers and business students, are likely to be involved in using English in different settings, to different addressees, and on different topics, and so on. This would affect the characterization of sociolinguistic performance we might wish to prioritize in their learning materials.

Similarly, the situation of these students during an orientation year, prior to beginning full-time studies on specific degree courses, means that we might identify specific performance manifestations of strategic competence as most immediately relevant to their future role as students. Examples of relevant activities include asking for clarification by reformulating content, using reference sources to check understanding, and coping with background noise while taking part in a laboratory session (Canale, 1983, pp. 22–25). These performance manifestations of the underlying competencies we are aiming to develop are motivating, because they are felt to be directly relevant and can be seen as providing authenticating contexts for validating such competencies (Robinson, 1987b).

A further point needs to be made about learning styles. There is obviously a plurality of learner preferences as regards modes of studying vocabulary. Some like to learn lists, others do not enjoy active dictionary work, while yet others enjoy sifting through stories, or more technical literature in English, and identifying lists of unknown words. Some like to pepper their speech or written work with newly acquired vocabulary as a way of trying it out, while others are more cautious and less eager to convert their passive knowledge into tokens in discourse. With this in mind we need to ensure that vocabulary development materials provide as diverse a range of exercise types as possible. Some materials and resource books do attempt to provide such diversity (Rinvolucri & Morgan, 1986; McCarthy, MacLean & O'Malley, 1986; Gairns & Redman, 1986; Nation, 1984). Others seem much less varied and more preoccupied with one technique, such as Crow (1986) with the keyword approach, or Rudzka et al. (1982, 1985) with the use of componential and collocational grids, or Barnard (1982) with the semiautomatic filling in of words in long stretches of artificial and contrived text on the assumption that this helps the learner to contextualize the word he or she is filling in. Many materials, then, do seem to be based on one view of what it is to learn vocabulary, but the implication underlying the following materials is that there is no one way that is suitable to all learning styles, and that materials need to attempt to present as diverse a range of exercise types as possible to accommodate this plurality.

Since the learning predisposition in Bahrain is, in a sense, Koranic, with the consequent emphasis on rote memorization, the Bahraini students were provided with a lot of exercises that test vocabulary learned in this way. For example, there are many multiple choice quizzes with the emphasis on all-or-nothing answers. Many frames or definitional phrases are recycled in computer lessons, and students learn them by heart. It is not the only way, or even a good way, to learn the aspects of vocabulary use discussed above, and for the reasons given, but there is a point in providing this sort of exercise to students as a starting point for extension exercises which draw on a declarative meaning-bank, and also as a way of creating a sense of security or continuity in their learning environment.

CONTEXTUALIZING: SOCIOLINGUISTIC COMPETENCE
AND WORD SETS

This artificial fixation of meaning, then, must be balanced by a procedural orientation to establishing word meaning in fluctuating contexts. This is the idea that lies behind many of the word-set exercises which are much more heavily dependent on teacher elicitation and aim to encourage learners to imagine possible worlds in order to contextualize presented lexis. For example, they are asked to identify some word as belonging to a particular register that will lead them to access a relevant schema and then build lexical sets in relation to particular fields. These exercises are therefore very open ended and draw on interpretative procedures. But they do assume that the declarative base, the provisional definition, has been fixed in place first, perhaps in the manner described above, through the completion of definition frames. In this way we move from the declarative and definitive:

When we *subtract* an amount we take it away from a larger amount.
When we *trade* with another country we sell goods to them.
A *balance* is an instrument for measuring weight.

to the procedural and fluctuating word-set activities (see Figure 12.3).

In using this exercise students are put in groups to discuss possible answers, then asked to report back to the whole class. Sometimes they are asked to justify what seem to be unusual choices or decisions; for example, how could (a) be about a birthday? (A rich Sheikh could be buying his son an oilfield or a large company). How could (b) be about a meal? (It could involve complaints about the bill in a restaurant). The important thing is to exploit as much as possible the leeway this exercise type provides students for imagining possible worlds or contexts which can justify their choices. Get them to explain as fully as they can, and get the rest of the class or group to act as a sort of jury, passing verdicts on how feasible each justification is. A lot of useful oral practice is generated in this way, and it has the attraction of "puzzle value."[2]

At a beginner level the basic word-set idea can be presented through "odd-one-out" exercises in which the learner has to identify which word doesn't belong with a particular schematic group, for example, is not a "cooking" word, or a "weather" word, and so on.

In the following word-set exercise, there are no absolutely correct answers to the questions; they are ways of making conscious the activity of sorting words into schemas and attributing frames of reference. These are what is meant by "word-sets," the idea being that the frame of reference suggested by the title will constrain the selection of likely words. This exercise involves top-down word-setting, from titles to words, as opposed to the activity above, where they are given some words and have to construct the setting in a bottom-up fashion (see Figure 12.4).

Figure 12.3. Word Sets-Letters

Do you remember the introductory reading exercise we did when we had to decide what the purpose of a text was and who the intended reader was? There were many things in the text to help you. One thing that can help you is the vocabulary. Here is a puzzle. *There is more than one answer that might be correct.* Look at the word below, from unit 3. Imagine they have been used in a letter. Can you decide who the intended reader of the letter might be, and what the letter might be about, and what the purpose of the letter might be? *Tick the boxes you think might be correct.*

a) Dear . . .   position

    check

      a basis   Europe

trade with

   total   fifty million

INTENDED READER

a footballer
an economics student
a politician
a physics student
a shopkeeper

THE PURPOSE IS

to persuade
to advertise
to give information
to warn
to amuse
to complain

THE LETTER IS ABOUT

making soup
the World Cup
the price of oil
buying a company
poetry
a birthday

b) Dear . . .
    inconvenient
  incorrect   total
a kind of
      problem
subtract
    necessary
  check
     convenience

INTENDED READER

a computer programmer
a shopkeeper
a teacher
a bank manager
a car dealer
your grandmother

THE PURPOSE IS

to persuade
to amuse
to warn
to complain
to teach
to advertise
to agree

THE LETTER IS ABOUT

a wedding
a bill
your salary
a new car
Arabic history
a meal
a holiday

Both of these exercises, then, apart from generating a lot of oral production through justifying choices, agreeing and disagreeing, are lead-ins to other skills areas, the first to writing letters and activities aimed at encouraging learners to

Figure 12.4. Word Sets-Predicting Content from Title

a) Here are the titles of two pieces of writing.

How To Use This Dictionary   *OPEC Meeting Successful*

Where would you expect to find each of these? What are their *sources?* Who might the *intended reader* be? Making guesses like this before you read is called *predicting.*

Look at the group of words from unit 5 below, and decide which words *could* be used in each text and then write them in the boxes. Some words may be used in both texts, and others might only be used once.

HOW TO USE THIS DICTIONARY   OPEC MEETING SUCCESSFUL

classify various
abbreviation economic
intense purpose limit
knowledge generally
political tube exist
situation practice
produce relationsip

b) Now look at words from other units we have done. Which words do you think would be used in texts with these titles?

THE PLANETS   CAUSEWAY OPENS TODAY*

*The causeway referred to here was opened between the island of Bahrain and the mainland of Saudi Arabia in early 1987.

adopt appropriate models of their intended reader (Robinson, 1987a), the second to prediction exercises which aim to develop purposive reading strategies (Gairns & Redman, 1986; Robinson, 1987b).

ASSOCIATING: GRAMMATICAL COMPETENCE AND WORD NETS

The above contextualizing activities take place in relation to word-sets which result from learner projections of possible shared sociolinguistic settings. They therefore draw on and help to develop awareness of the conventions regulating participation in standardized speech events, that is, how a particular *addresser* addresses a particular *addressee* to achieve a particular *purpose* through a particular *channel* like a written letter (Hymes, 1971; Malamah-Thomas, 1986). In so doing they help to develop the sociolinguistic dimension of communicative competence. However, other relations between words are more cognitive and private, "intraorganism," not "interorganism," relations, as Halliday (1975) has said. These relations are independent of any conventions regulating participation in specific speech events, and the word-net exercises aim to develop the learner's network of private psychological associations. See Blum-Kulka and Levenston (1979) for their views on the contribution made by knowledge of sense relations like synonymy, antonymy, and so on, to the learner's developing semantic competence in the second language. Here (Figure 12.5) is an example of a word-net:

Figure 12.5.   A Word Net For 'Plentiful' and 'Scarce'

Plentiful and *scarce* are _____ . Look at the word net below for plentiful things in Bahrain. Try to complete it by adding as many words for things that are plentiful as you can.

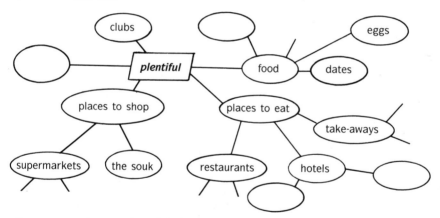

Now can you do a word net for things that are *scarce* in Bahrain?

Here *plentiful* and *scarce* are introduced as antonyms or opposites, and the learner has to add to the network. The covert organization of this net involves attaching the central adjective to generic nouns, places to eat, and so on, which are the superordinates of more specific exemplars. The net is therefore structured, but this is not the focus of the exercise at the early stages. The aim is simply to encourage the learner to add words. At a secondary stage we return to the nets and use them as a basis for written production of the vocabulary. Here we try to make the structural principles underlying the organization of the net more overt by adding symbols like this (Figure 12.6):

Figure 12.6. A Structured Word Net

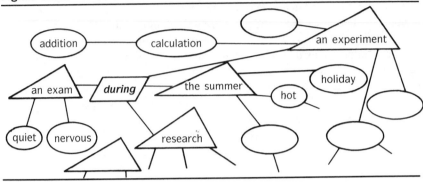

We can then elicit and demonstrate relations of dependency between the words (Hudson, 1980; Matthews, 1981). These dependencies are either of a structural semantic nature, that is, superordinate to hyponym, or grammatical nature, involving developing awareness of parts of speech. This is the basis of building simple sentence patterns:

> *During* an *exam* the room is very *quiet* and I feel *nervous*. Now try to use the words *you* have added to the net in your sentences. Write some examples here.
>
> 1. ————————————————————————————.
> 2. ————————————————————————————.
> 3. ————————————————————————————.

In this way lexical knowledge can be shown to lead to grammatical awareness in the way referred to earlier. This is one way of learning grammar via lexis. It makes overt what Allwright (1986) has identified as the learner's covert acquisition of grammatical information via the procedure of asking questions about words, and returns us to the discussion earlier about the relation of procedural to schematic words and the acquisition of sense and structure.

STRATEGIC COMPETENCE: SUBSTITUTION AND PARAPHRASE

Of relevance here is the knowledge of how to act on the provisional sense relations discussed earlier, hyponymy and superordinacy, synonymy and antonymy, and so on, to perform achievement strategies like substitution and paraphrase, for example:

I: Substitution
NS: do you have any animals—
L: (laugh) yes—er—er that is er—I don't know how I say that in English—[. . .]

NS: I think they must be rabbits—
L: er what
NS: rabbits—
L: rabbits—
NS: yer rabbits [. . .]
NS: does it—sleep on—in your room
L: er my—my animals—
NS: mm your animal

2:    *Paraphrase*
L: [. . .] some people have a car—and some people have a er bicycle—and some people have a er—erm—a cycle there is a motor
NS: oh a bicycle—with a motor. (Faerch & Kasper, 1983, p. 49)

In the first example the learner (L) is substituting a superordinate introduced earlier by the native speaker (NS), *animals,* for *rabbit.* In the second example the learner is paraphrasing, in the absence of a knowledge of the target item *motorbike.* Both examples could be the basis of cloze tests for learner completion, with the substituted and paraphrased items deleted. This would be a way of drawing attention to the particular strategy and its formal realizations. The clozes could be on either written or spoken text. Variations in planning time (Crookes, 1990) allowed learners before they respond could be manipulated; that is, decreasing amounts of planning time could be allowed on successive clozes, and this could promote automatization of the knowledge (McGlaughlin, 1990; Schmidt, 1990).

While such strategies could be said to help the learner, or language user, make the propositional content of the message clear, they can also be used, as Thomas (1985) has shown, as ways of exerting power over an interlocutor on what Halliday would call the interpersonal dimension of the discourse. For example, after a long conversation with a subordinate police constable, the police inspector sums up, or paraphrases, like this:

Inspector: Are you suggesting there's a bit of a conspiracy to put the skids under you?
Constable: . . . conspiracy, I can't say that, sir.

where the inspector makes use of the pragmatic tactic of reformulating using *conspiracy*—which implies wrongdoing—thus making the subordinate back down, because he doesn't have the power to accuse his superior of wrongdoing directly. Such tactics can be effectively countered, though, where the relationship between the participants is more equal, as in this example:

Politician: I don't deny that the Government is right to put security at the top of their priorities . . . But on the other hand they could have handled it better.
Interviewer: Are you saying that they cocked it up?
Politician: You said that. What I said was . . . (Thomas, 1985)

Whether we teach such strategies directly or not, the knowledge of the words they draw on, such as, that *conspiracy* implies illegality, or that *cocked it up* is a pejorative variant on *made a mistake,* are certainly examples of the kinds of lexical knowledge advanced learners are interested in developing, and it seems sensible to teach them in scenarios which draw on the related procedural knowledge of how to reformulate in strategically appropriate circumstances.

DISCOURSE COMPETENCE: COHESION, COHERENCE, SPECIFICITY, AND IMPLICATURE

Finally, a discourse perspective on lexical competence returns us to the issues raised by McCarthy (1984, 1988) of the need to develop awareness of the role of intonation in signalling equivalence, and of the way in which, during conversational negotiation, the static, structural semantic relations of superordinacy, synonymy, are in a much more fluid relationship to each other (*emergent* as opposed to *a priori,* in the terminology of Hopper, 1987). We can do no more than touch on these issues here. There is the important area of choice of level of specificity (Cruse, 1977, 1986) in which deviance from a core, unmarked level of specificity generates additional implicatures (Grice, 1975). For example, as Cruse observes, the basic-level concept is most often the neutral level of specificity; for example, in the case below, *dog* is a more basic concept than that of *animal* or *alsatian.* He explains that the fact that an animal is a dog is more likely to be important than the fact that the dog is an alsatian, or that an alsatian is an animal. See Brown (1973) concerning basic-level concepts. *Dog* is therefore the unmarked choice:

- Where are you going dear?

	alsatian,	
- I'm going to take the	dog,	for a walk.
	animal	

The choice of a markedly over- or underspecific word generates additional implicature. In the case of *alsatian* it implies more than one dog; in the case of *animal,* it implies dislike. Mehrabian (1971) has also pointed to the link between choice of specific items and degrees of "liking":

	Chevrolet	
- Tom let me drive his new	car	today.
	vehicle	

Figure 12.7.   An Intensity Scale

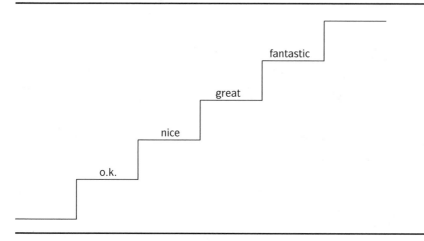

The more specific term indicates greater enthusiasm. Apart from the issue of synonymy and prominence discussed earlier:

- I didn't think it was very SUBTLE, the way he handled it.
- It was BLATANT.

where prominence signals the creation of a new sense paradigm by one speaker, there are issues relating to the role of sense relations in lexical take up (see Figure 12.7):

- I thought the film was great tonight.
- Yes, it was   fantastic.
                         nice.
                         o.k.

where choice of an item from above, or below, the initially offered item on an intensity scale has communicative consequences. Again, superordinacy, or underspecificity, appears to be used to communicative effect in this example of encapsulation:

- I hope you got the bananas I asked for.
- Yet I got your FRUIT, but I forgot the cigarettes.

It not only establishes cohesion, but it also indicates a certain disdain or downplaying of importance for fruit versus cigarettes.

    In written text the role of sense relations is important in establishing cohesion, for example (Figure 12.8):

Figure 12.8. Sense Relations and Cohesion

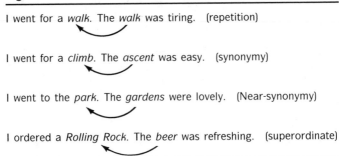

I went for a *walk*. The *walk* was tiring. (repetition)

I went for a *climb*. The *ascent* was easy. (synonymy)

I went to the *park*. The *gardens* were lovely. (Near-synonymy)

I ordered a *Rolling Rock*. The *beer* was refreshing. (superordinate)

The proforms like *do, you, them,* and so on, identified earlier as of procedural use are also important in establishing what Hasan (1984) calls *identity chains* of reference in written text. These are distinct from the sorts of chain that "reflect the composition of semantic fields which lie outside the text." These she calls *similarity chains,* and they are invoked, for example, by the use of *off-form* and *depression* in the following example, (Figure 12.9), by virtue of the schematic knowledge we have of illness:

Figure 12.9. Identity and Similarity Chains

Identity Chains   **Similarity Chains**

The Steelers are a great team. They won four

superbowl championships in the seventies. Their record is

still envied by other teams. However the club has been going

through a depression recently. The quarterbacks have been off-form

and the management has been under pressure too.

The use of words in signaling the structure of texts is also important; Winter (1977) has identified a number of items that seem to signal when these stages are being realized in the text (Hoey, 1984; Jordan, 1984; Robinson, 1988b, 1988c). Crombie (1985) gives us an example of the situation, problem, solution, evaluation macrostructure. Consider the structure signalling role of the words *proposed, problem, attempted,* and *advantage* in this text (Figure 12.10):

Practice in identifying and using such words can be particularly useful to students who have to read many academic articles, and who therefore want to be able to identify the problem and suggested solutions in abstracts like these (Figure 12.11).

Figure 12.10. Lexical Signallers of Text Macrostructure

DISCOURSE
ELEMENTS

Situation	Pauling and Corey have *proposed* a model for the structure of D.N.A. Their model consists of three inter-twined chains, with the phosphates near the fibre axis and the bases on the outside.
Problem	The *problem* is that their model fails to identify the forces which could hold the structure together.
Solution	We have *attempted* to solve this problem by proposing a radically different structure which has two helical chains each coiled around the same axis and in which the two chains are held together by the purine and pyramidine bases.
Evaluation	Our model has two *advantages*. It accounts for the structural cohesion and it suggests a possible copying mechanism for the genetic material.

Figure 12.11. Lexical Signallers In Two Journal Article Abstracts

ON THE ROLE OF THE OBLIGATORY CONTOUR PRINCIPLE IN PHONOLOGICAL THEORY

DAVID ODDEN

Ohio State University

In autosegmental phonology, a sequence of adjacent identical tones can be represented (a) as a single tone mapped onto multiple vowels, (b) as a one-to-one mapping between multiple tones and vowels, or (c) as a combination of these extremes. The Obligatory Contour Principle (OCP) has been *proposed* as a constraint which restricts tonal representations to a one-to-many mapping between tones and vowels. It is *argued* here that the strongest form of the OCP is falsified by a number of languages which distinguish single vs. multiple tones associated with a sequence of vowels. The language-particular violations of the OCP constitute a *strong argument* for the full power of autosegmental phonology.*

INALTERABILITY IN CV PHONOLOGY

BRUCE HAYES

University of California, Los Angeles

Geminate consonants and long vowels frequently *resist* the application of rules that would a-priori be expected to apply to them; i.e., they are frequently 'inalterable.' This article *argues* that by invoking the theory of CV Phonology, it is often *possible to predict* which phonological rules are unable to affect long segments. The prediction follows from rather minimal assumptions about how rules apply to forms.*

(from *Language, 62*(2),pp321,353)

The ability to use words like *proposed, argued,* and *possible to predict* in the extracts above, which are much less schema specific than words like *autosegmental, geminate,* and *pyramidine,* etc., is an aspect of procedural ability in the construction and interpretation of written discourse. Let us conclude by returning to this distinction.

CONCLUSION: THE LEXICON AS MEANING POTENTIAL

The aim in this chapter has been to distinguish between the declarative and procedural dimensions of vocabulary knowledge. It has also been suggested that these dimensions are reflected in the existence of two types of words, highly specific or technical lexical words, and the more general delexical words.

The claim is that vocabulary materials in the past may have overemphasized the declarative, static meaning that attaches to a technical word, while ignoring procedural aspects of vocabulary learning. This may have been because technical words, for example, are often seen as more directly relevant to learners in specific areas, and consequently they are focused on because they are more motivating, or have more face-validity. However, such words provide contexts for the development of assimilation procedures involving more general, basic words. Hutchinson and Waters (1981) claim that it is proficiency in such everyday words that is most important to technical subject students of English.

Knowing how to use procedural words to negotiate the meaning of more technical, specific words is essential to learners if they are to engage in fruitful classroom communication, involving the twin activities of asserting and assimilating meaning. Some arguments have been given for seeing this debate over the sense of words as crucial to the acquisition of structural knowledge, for learning grammar *through* lexis; in other words, the learner's procedural ability in the use of communication strategies will have direct consequences for the operation of his or her cognitive strategies, which are directed at learning the grammatical structure of language—both sets of strategies tending to focus, in their differing ways, on a reduced core of highly indexical words.

The approach to vocabulary development outlined here places the ability to engage such negotiating procedures at the heart of successful communication and language learning. A framework was proposed for developing awareness of this potential based on Canale and Swain's checklist of the four dimensions of communicative competence. The example exercise types are diverse, have as an organizing principle the need to conjoin declarative and procedural knowledge of lexis, provide contexts for exchanges and discussion, and develop awareness of the structural relations between words. As such, these exercises and the larger framework provide a basis for the organization and presentation of lexis in tandem with the realization of the meaning potential words have in actual classroom negotiations. It is only through negotiation, assertion, and assimilation that learners can authenticate the awareness they have of lexical grammar, lexis in discourse, and lexical strategies by converting it to the actual procedures used in attempting to bring the possible worlds of participants in discourse to convergence—thereby achieving temporary communication, and more permanent language learning.

REFERENCES

Adams-Smith, D. (1979). The acquisition of technical vocabulary. *ESPMENA Bulletin, 1*(1). 18–25.

Aitchison, J. (1987). *Words in the mind.* Oxford: Basil Blackwell.

Allwright, R., Pit Corder, S., & Rossner, R. (1986). Talking shop: Pit Corder on applied linguistics and language teaching. *ELT Journal, 40*(3), 185–191.

Anderson, J. R. (1980). *Cognitive psychology and its implications.* San Francisco: Freeman.

Ard, J., & Gass, S. (1987). Lexical constraints on syntactic acquisition. *Studies in second language acquisition, 9*(2), 233–253.

Barnard, H. (1982). *Advanced English vocabulary (Workbooks 1–5).* Rowley, MA: Newbury House.

Benson, J. D., & Greaves, W. (1981). Field of Discourse: Theory and applications. *Applied Linguistics, 2*(1), 38–49.

Blum-Kulka, S., & Levenston, E. A. (1979). Universals of lexical simplification. *Language Learning, 28,* 399–416.

Brazil, D. (1985). *The communicative value of intonation in English* (Discourse Analysis Monograph no. 8). Birmingham: ELR.

Bresnan, J. (Eds.). (1982). *The mental representation of grammatical relations.* Cambridge, MA: MIT Press.

Brown, R. (1973). *A first language: The early stages.* Cambridge, MA: Harvard University Press.

Canale, M. (1983). From communicative competence to language pedagogy. In J. Richards & R. Schmidt (Eds.), *Language and communication* (pp. 2–27). London: Longman.

Canale, M., & Swain, M. (1980). Theoretical bases of communicative approaches to second language teaching and testing. *Applied Linguistics, 1*(1), 1–47.

Carter, R. (1986). Core vocabulary and discourse in the curriculum. *RELC Journal, 17*(1), 52–70.

Carter, R. (1987). *Vocabulary: An applied linguistic perspective.* London: Allen & Unwin.

Crombie, W. (1985). *Discourse and language learning: A relational approach to syllabus design.* Oxford: Oxford University Press.

Crookes, G. (1990). Planning time and interlanguage variation. *Studies in Second Language Acquisition, 12*(1), 1–22.

Crow, J. T. (1986). *Vocabulary development: The keyword approach.* New York: Prentice-Hall.

Crow, J. T., & Quigley, J. R. (1986). A semantic field approach to passive vocabulary acquisition. *TESOL Quarterly, 19*(3), 497–514.

Cruse, D. A. (1977). The pragmatics of lexical specificity. *Journal of Linguistics, 13,* *155–164.*

Cruse, D. A. (1986). *Lexical semantics.* Cambridge, UK: Cambridge University Press.

Doyle, J. (1979). *A truth maintenance system* (A. I. Laboratory Memo No. 521). Cambridge, MA: MIT.

Dussere, C. (1988). *A review of the literature on vocabulary teaching and learning.* Term Paper, Linguistics 205, University of Pittsburgh, Department of General Linguistics.

Ellis, R. (1985). *Understanding second language acquisition.* Oxford: Oxford University Press.

Faerch, C., & Kasper, G. (Eds.). (1983). *Strategies in interlanguage communication.* London: Longman.

Faerch, C., & Kasper, G. (1984). Pragmatic knowledge: Rules and procedure. *Applied Linguistics, 5,* 214–226.

Friel, M. (1979). A verb frequency count in legal English. *ESPMENA Bulletin, 1*(1), 18–22.

Fromkin, V. (1987). The lexicon. *Language, 63*(1), 1–22.

Gairns, R., & Redman, S. (1986). *Working with words.* Cambridge, UK: Cambridge University Press.

Gazdar, G., & Pullum, G. (1981). Subcategorization, constituent order and the notion 'head'. In M. Moortgat (Ed.), *The scope of lexical rules* (pp. 107–123). Dordrecht: Foris.

Gernsbacher, M. A., Givon, T., & Yang, L. (1990). *The processing of second language vocabulary: From attended to automated word-recognition.* Unpublished manuscript, University of Oregon, Institute of Cognitive and Decision Sciences.

Grice, P. (1975). Logic and conversation. In J. Morgan (Ed.), *Syntax and semantics vol. 3: Speech acts* (pp. 41–58). New York: Academic Press.

Haiman, J. (1985). *Natural syntax.* Cambridge, UK: Cambridge University Press.

Halliday, M. A. K. (1966). Lexis as a linguistic level. In J. Bazell (Ed.), *In memory of J. R. Firth* (pp. 148–162) London: Longman.

Halliday, M. A. K. (1975). *Learning how to mean.* London: Edward Arnold.

Halliday, M. A. K., & Hasan, R. (1977). *Cohesion in English.* London: Longman.

Halliday, M. A. K. (1978). *Language as a social semiotic.* London: Edward Arnold.

Hasan, R. (1984). Coherence and cohesive harmony. In J. Flood (Ed.), *Understanding reading comprehension* (pp. 181–219). Newark, DE: International Reading Association.

Heritage, J. C., & Watson, D. R. (1979). Formulations as conversational objects. In G. Psathas (Ed.), *Everyday language: Studies in ethnomethodology* (pp. 121–148). New York: Irvington.

Hoey, M. (1984). *On the surface of discourse.* London: Allen & Unwin.

Hopper, P. (1987). Emergent grammar and the 'a priori' postulate. In D. Tannen (Ed.), *Context: Connecting observations and understanding* (pp. 117–134). Norwood, NJ: Ablex Publishing Corp.

Hudson, R. (1980). Constituency and dependency. *Linguistics, 18,* 179–198.

Hudson, R. (1984). *Word grammar.* London: Basil Blackwell.

Hudson, R. (1986). Frame linguistics, frame semantics, frame . . . *Quaderni Di Semantica, VII*(1), 85–101.

Hutchinson, T., & Waters, A. (1981). Performance and competence in ESP. *Applied Linguistics, 2*(1), 32–47.

Hymes, D. (1971). *On communicative competence*. Philadelphia: University of Philadelphia Press.

Jordan, M. (1984). *The rhetoric of everyday English texts*. London: Allen & Unwin.

Lyons, J. (1977). *Semantics* (2 vols.). Cambridge, UK: Cambridge University Press.

Mackey, W. (1966). *Language teaching analysis*. London: Longman.

Malamah-Thomas, A. (1986). *Classroom interaction*. Oxford: Oxford University Press.

Matthews, P. H. (1981). *Syntax*. Cambridge, UK: Cambridge University Press.

McCarthy, M. J. (1984). A new look at vocabulary in EFL. *Applied Linguistics, 5*(1), 12–22.

McCarthy, M. J. (1988). Some vocabulary patterns in conversation. In R. Carter & M. J. McCarthy (Eds.), *Vocabulary and language teaching* (pp. 181–200). London: Longman.

McCarthy, M. J., MacLean, A., & O'Malley, P. (1986). *Proficiency plus*. London: Basil Blackwell.

McGlaughlin, B. (1990). Restructuring. *Applied Linguistics, 11*(2), 113–128.

McIntosh, A. (1961). Patterns and Ranges. *Language, 37*(3), 325–338.

Mehrabian, A. (1971). *Silent messages*. Belmont, CA: Wadsworth.

Nation, I. S. P. (1984). *Teaching and learning vocabulary* (Occasional Paper No. 7). Wellington, New Zealand: University of Wellington.

Nunan, D. (1989). *Syllabus design*. Oxford: Oxford University Press.

Peters, A. (1983). *The units of language acquisition*. Cambridge, UK: Cambridge University.

Peters, A. (1989, October). *From schwa to morpheme: The child's development of grammatical structure*. Paper presented at the Linguistics Department Seminar, University of Hawaii at Manoa, Honolulu.

Pinker, S. (1984). *Language learnability and language development*. Cambridge, MA: Harvard University Press.

Pinker, S. (1989). *Learnability and cognition: The acquisition of argument structure*. Cambridge, MA: MIT Press.

Prabhu, N. S. (1987). *Second language pedagogy*. London: Longman.

Rinvolucri, M., & Morgan, J. (1986). *Vocabulary*. Oxford: Oxford University Press.

Robinson, P. J. (1986). Constituency or dependency in the units of language acquisition? *Lingvisticae Investigationes, 10*(2), 417–437.

Robinson, P. J. (1987a, April). *Towards a lexical-functional syllabus for ESL*. Paper presented at the 21st TESOL Conference, Miami, U.S.A.

Robinson, P. J. (1987b). Authenticating contexts for study skills. *RELC Guidelines, 9*(1), 51–60.

Robinson, P. J. (1988a). Possible worlds in the discourse lexicon. Proceedings of the Twelfth Annual Penn Linguistics Colloquium, University of Pennsylvania Linguistics Club. *Penn Review of Linguistics, 12,* 55–79.

Robinson, P. J. (1988b). Components and procedures in vocabulary learning: Grids, prototypes and a procedural vocabulary. *Interface, 2*(2), 17–29.

Robinson, P. J. (1988c). A Hallidayan framework for vocabulary teaching. *International Review of Applied Linguistics, XXVII*(3), 228–239.

Robinson, P. J. (1989). Procedural vocabulary and language learning. *Journal of Pragmatics, 13*(4), 523–546.

Robinson, P. J. (1990a). Metaphors for the description of acquisition data. *International Review of Applied Linguistics XXIX*(4), 273–294.

Robinson, P. J. (1990b). *Modeling the acquisition of the locative alternation; connectionism, learnability and the acquisition of argument structure.* Unpublished manuscript, University of Hawaii at Manoa, Department of English as a Second Language.

Robinson, P. J. (1990c). *The comprehensibility of core vocabulary for second language learners.* Unpublished manuscript, University of Hawaii at Manoa, Department of English as a Second Language.

Robinson, P.J. (1992) Discourse semantics, interlanguage negotiation and the lexicon. *University of Hawai'i Working Papers in ESL, 11*(2) 1–33

Rudzka, B., Channell, J., Putsys, Y., & Ostyn, P. (1982). *Words you need.* London: MacMillan.

Rudzka, B., Channell, J., Putsys, Y., & Ostyn, P. (1985). *More words you need.* London: MacMillan.

Rutherford, W. (1987). *Grammar and second language teaching.* London: Longman.

Schmidt, R. W. (1990). The role of consciousness in second language learning. *Applied Linguistics, 11* (2), 129–159.

Sells, P. (1985). *Lectures on contemporary syntactic theories.* Stanford, CA: CSLI.

Sinclair, J. (1966). Beginning the study of lexis. In J. Bazell (Ed.), *In memory of J. R. Firth* (pp. 410–430). London: Longman.

Sinclair, J. (1986). *First throw away your evidence.* Working paper, University of Birmingham.

Sinclair, J., & Renouf, A. (1988). A lexical syllabus for language learning. In R. Carter & M. J. McCarthy (Eds.), *Vocabulary and language teaching* (pp.140–160). London: Longman.

Stein, G. (1978). Nuclear English: Reflections on the structure of its vocabulary. *Poetica, 10,* 64–76.

Stubbs, M. (1986). Language development, lexical competence and nuclear vocabulary. In K. Durkin (Ed.), *Language development in the school years* (pp. 56–76). London: Croom Helm.

Thomas, J. (1985). The language of power: Towards a dynamic pragmatics. *Journal of Pragmatics, 9*(2), p. 263–281.

Tulving, E. (1984). Precis of "Elements of episodic memory". *The Behavioural and Brain Sciences, 7,* 223–268.

West, M. (1953). *A general service list of English words.* London: Longman.

Whitcut, J. (1988). Lexicography in a simple language. *International Journal of Lexicography, 1*(1), 49–55.

Widdowson, H. G. (1983). *Learning purpose and language use.* Oxford: Oxford University Press.

Widdowson, H. G. (1984). *Explorations in applied linguistics 2.* Oxford: Oxford University Press.

Wilkins, D. A. (1977). *Notional syllabuses.* Oxford: Oxford University Press.

Willis, D. (1990). *The lexical syllabus: A new approach to language teaching.* London, Glasgow: Collins ELT.

Winter, E. A. (1977). A clause relational approach to English texts: A study of some predictive lexical items in written discourse. *Instructional Science, 6*(1), 1–92.

Winter, E. A. (1978). Replacement as a fundamental function of the clause in context. *Forum Linguisticum, 1*(2), 95–134.

ENDNOTES

1. From ''Anyone Lived in a Pretty How Town,'' by e e cummings, in *Collected Poems 1913–1962*. Reprinted by permission of Grafton Books, part of Harper Collins Publishers.
2. Provisional answers to this exercise are: (a) Reader—could be economics student, politician, but not footballer, physics student. *Trade* and *total* seem to indicate that the field and register are those of economics. It could be about the price of oil, buying a company. The purpose could be any of those given, except to amuse; perhaps *warn* seems most likely considering *check*. (b) Reader—could be any of those given, except the grandmother. It could be about any of them except Arabic history or a wedding (unless the wedding involves a bill for the reception). The purpose could be warning, teaching, or most likely complaining, because of the negativity of *inconvenient, incorrect,* and the imperative *check*.

Editorial Comments

Robinson provides us with a much needed shift in emphasis toward viewing the lexicon as fluid and dynamic rather than static and fixed. The crux of his proposal is that the acquisition of the meaning of a great many technical words (low-frequency vocabulary) is negotiated through the use of procedural vocabulary. Therefore students need to be taught how to use this procedural vocabulary in order to effectively learn the declarative vocabulary. Moreover, he emphasizes that these actually feed off of and support each other in a mutual manner so that one learns the meaning of one through the other.

It is especially valid in the context of a communicative curriculum to teach students how to develop pragmatic abilities in vocabulary acquisition. Note that this proposal would appear to be in direct opposition to those who argue for the utility of focussing on a reduced vocabulary in the initial stages of acquisition (see Coady et al., Chapter 11, this volume). However, as Robinson's example exercises make clear, there is a need to communicate declarative meanings to students in a relatively straightforward manner before extensive use of the more procedurally oriented exercises.

Robinson also argues that as one learns to negotiate the lexical meaning there is a corresponding acquisition of the grammatical interrelationships. This is an extremely interesting argument not only because it is in agreement with contemporary grammatical theories which are much more word-based, but also because it sheds light on how students can learn grammar "automatically" while paying attention to meaning, a phenomenon which has long been a puzzling aspect of L2 acquisition.

One question which arises is whether these procedural words are universal in their function and type across all languages. In other words, might there be significant differences in the role and function of procedural vocabulary from a given L1 to another L2? This is an issue which merits further research.

One important aspect of the exercise types which Robinson presents is that they would appear to necessitate a highly experienced and/or competent teacher because they imply a good deal of expertise at managing classroom interactions in order to make the exercises effective. It would also seem that the students would have to be fairly advanced in order to communicate fluently when they "imagine possible worlds in order to contextualize presented lexis." Thus the ultimate value of the exercises he cites is as models. Teachers will need to create their own exercises as appropriate to their own teaching situations. Nevertheless, the exercises provide useful examples of the general principles which Robinson has presented.

Chapter 13
Factors Affecting the Acquisition of Vocabulary: Frequency and Saliency of Words*

Cheryl Brown
Linguistics Department
Brigham Young University
Provo, UT

Although most ESL scholars recognize the importance of vocabulary, little is known about what causes words to be learned. This chapter reports on research studying four such factors: (a) overall word frequency, (b) specific context word frequency, (c) instructional focus saliency, and (d) gap in concept saliency. Over 100 ESL students were pre- and posttested on 180 words with various frequency levels in a specific context (a *Raiders of the Lost Ark* videodisc program) and the general context. Some words received focus in the program exercises; some represented "gaps" where concepts were seen but word forms for the concepts were not seen nor heard in the movie until they appeared in exercises or glosses. The posttest results showing the number of students who acquired each word were then analyzed to reveal the relationships between the word's acquisition and its frequency in *Raiders,* its general frequency, its saliency in the program exercises and glosses, and its visual gap. Results suggest that visual gap, followed by appearance of the word form in exercises and then again later in the spoken script, produced the greatest gains.

* I would like to express appreciation to Drs. Del T. Scott and H. Gill Hilton of the Brigham Young University Statistics Department for their advice and help with the statistics in this study.

Anyone involved in the teaching of languages is well aware of the importance for students to acquire words. In fact teachers know that many students view language learning *as* learning vocabulary. Although few teachers themselves would be willing to accept this simplistic view openly and in print, all teachers, as well as the public in general, acknowledge the primacy of vocabulary in language learning in other more subtle ways. As Higgins and Johns (1984) have pointed out,

> The lexical inventory tends to be treated as dominant. If a speaker uses only English words but puts them into German word order, we will usually think of him as speaking 'bad English' rather than 'bad German'. . . . A speaker who uses German sounds in rendering English sentences is speaking 'English with a German accent,' not 'German with English grammar and lexis.' (p. 13)

Also, although teachers do not accept the simplistic view of some students that vocabulary learning *is* language learning, there has been considerable focus recently on the importance of vocabulary and how it is learned (see Cohen & Aphek, 1980; Nation, 1982; Allen, 1983; Harvey, 1983; Stieglitz, 1983; Bensoussan & Laufer, 1984; Haynes, 1984; Meara, 1984; Gairns & Redman, 1986; Laufer, 1986; Morgan & Rinvolucri, 1986; Carter, 1987; Hague, 1987; and Carter & McCarthy, 1988).

As we focus on the learning of vocabulary, it becomes obvious that all words presented in the environment to learners are not learned or acquired[1] equally. (See Parry, 1988, for example, for evidence of the differences in how encountered words are or are not acquired.) Because of this unevenness in how words are acquired, the question naturally arises as to what is producing the unevenness. What characteristics of individual words make the difference in the extent to which and the ease with which words are acquired?

POSSIBLE FACTORS AFFECTING ACQUISITION

Frequency of occurrence

Several factors have been suggested as contributing to the differential acquisition of vocabulary. One such factor is frequency of occurrence. Nagy and Herman (1987) have argued that "even a single encounter with a word in context" could help move it "a little bit higher on the scale of knowledge" (p. 25), and Sternberg (1987) points out that "multiple occurrences of an unknown word increase the number of available cues and can increase the usefulness of individual cues if readers integrate information obtained from cues surrounding the multiple occurrences of the word" (p. 92). There has been some disagreement about precisely how many encounters with a word would be sufficient to ensure its acquisition, but most researchers put it somewhere between 6 and 12 (Jenkins & Dixon, 1983). The number of encounters necessary is modified somewhat by the variety of contexts in which the word occurs, as well as by its saliency.

Saliency

Saliency, or the importance of a word, is a second factor which has been claimed as influential in whether a given word will be acquired or not. There are several ways which words can come to have saliency. Although frequency of occurrence is one of these (Brown, 1985), for the purposes of this chapter, frequency is treated as a separate factor and only other means of producing importance are examined under the heading of saliency.

One of these other ways in which words can become salient is instructional focus. If a teacher explicitly teaches a word, gives the word on a list to be learned, or has students do exercises using the word, learning of the word generally increases. Although there is still much argumentation about what kind of instruction is best, there is a general consensus that instruction does facilitate the learning of words (Calfee & Drum, 1986; Stahl & Fairbanks, 1986; Beck, McKeown, & Omanson, 1987; Chall, 1987; Drum & Konopak, 1987; Graves, 1987).

Words also become salient if they are vital to the message being communicated. With regard to this issue, Sternberg (1987) states,

> if a given unknown word is judged to be necessary for understanding the surrounding material in which it is embedded, the reader's incentive for figuring out the word's meaning is increased. If the word is judged to be unimportant to understanding what one is reading (or hearing), one is unlikely to invest any great effort in figuring out what the word means. (p. 93)

Hatch, Flashner, and Hunt (1986) discuss the importance of this kind of salience as part of their Experience Model of language learning. They point out how experience may cause learners to recognize that they do not have a particular piece of linguistic information (for example, a word) that they need in order to communicate. That is, learners recognize a gap (Hatch, et al. call it an "empty box") in their knowledge. In future experience learners may encounter (hear or read) the piece of linguistic information they had needed. Because the learners' gap was recognized through the previous experience, the linguistic information now being heard or read is "salient" and has a greater potential for being acquired.

Besides the factors mentioned here, there are numerous other factors—for example, phonology (Levenston & Blum, 1977; Celce-Murcia, 1978; Schwartz & Leonard, 1982; Stoel-Gammon & Cooper, 1984) and part of speech (Gentner,

1982; Sternberg, 1987; Yun, 1989)—which might be making a difference in whether certain vocabulary is acquired by learners or not. It is hoped that, as research expands, all of the factors, and the way they interact with each other, will be examined in order to get a full picture of how and why words are acquired.

RESEARCH QUESTIONS FOR THIS STUDY

The particular study that this chapter reports focused on only two main factors—frequency and saliency—and on only some of the possible subcategories of those factors.

Two aspects of the frequency issue were considered. The first aspect was whether the frequency of a word within a particular context which learners were known to encounter, such as within a particular book or movie, would make a difference.

The second aspect of the frequency question was one of general frequency. Would just knowing how often a word occurred in the language in general allow a more accurate prediction of whether the word would be acquired or not? In other words, is there any correlation between how often a word appears in the language in general and whether it is acquired by learners?

With regard to saliency, several issues could be considered, but in this study, only two were examined. One was the issue of focus in exercises. If a word which learners read or hear receives focus in instructional materials—exercises or glosses, for example—will the learners be more likely to acquire the word?

The second issue has to do with "gapping" of the sort discussed by Hatch et al. (1986). If learners have experienced a need for a word form before they encounter it, will they acquire the word more readily when that opportunity is presented?

With these issues in mind, then, the research questions guiding this research were the following:

1. Does word frequency affect the acquisition of words?
    1a.   Does frequency in a particular context make a difference?
    1b.   Does general frequency make a difference?
2. Does word saliency affect the acquisition of words?
    2a.   Does saliency created by focus in exercises or glosses make a differ-ence?
    2b.   Does saliency created by "gapping" make a difference?

RESEARCH DESIGN

Materials

In order to answer the research questions about frequency and saliency, it was necessary to have a set of words which could be tested with a group of second-language learners. Most studies examining the effect of frequency on word learning have centered on written contexts, where frequency counts could be done relatively easily; oral contexts have been neglected because of the difficulty in getting any kind of record of what words learners encounter orally. Even if only the words used in the classroom are examined, the task is formidable to researchers, as they must record, transcribe, and sort all of the words. In the case of this study, a boon was found in that ESL learners at the Brigham Young University English Language Center (an intensive ESL preuniversity program) were using an interactive videodisc program developed by Probst and Bennion (1986) that was based on the movie *Raiders of the Lost Ark*. The script of the movie had already been transcribed, and it was, therefore, easy to get a good frequency count of the words as they were used in the specific context of the movie.

The interactive videodisc program was also useful for this study, because it had been devised with exercises. With the videodisc program students have several options as they watch the 33 scenes in the movie. They may watch one scene and go on immediately to the next scene, or they may watch and then ask for an accompanying on-screen written version of the script. They may also ask for a gloss on screen of certain key words which were used in the scene, or they may do exercises which ask questions about the scene. The exercises generally consist of fill-in-the-blank sentences with phonologically similar words or phrases offered as options, such as:

Indiana Jones didn't want _____ . (money/many)

There are also a few short answer questions (e.g., What obstacles did Jones have to overcome to get the idol?) and an occasional matching or grouping question (e.g., List the problems that Jones faced in getting out of the map room).

Word Selection

In order to answer the questions about specific frequency and general frequency, it was necessary to have a sample of words which exhibited a wide range of frequencies both in the specific context (*Raiders of the Lost Ark*) and in the general context of the language as a whole as determined by word-frequency counts. In order to answer the questions about saliency, it was necessary to have a sample of words that exhibited a difference in focus received and gaps produced.

The frequency issue was handled by getting a frequency print-out of all of the words in *Raiders of the Lost Ark*. This print-out was divided into 15 frequency levels, as shown in Table 13.1.

The levels were divided in this manner for two reasons: (a) in order to have a clear picture in the 6- to 12-occurrence area (the area covering the number of occurrences which the literature had suggested was necessary for acquisition),

Table 13.1. Frequency Levels in *Raiders of the Lost Ark*

Level	Occurrences in Raiders
1	1
2	2
3	3
4	4
5	5
6	6
7	7
8	8
9	9
10	10
11	11–12
12	13–15
13	16–20
14	21–30
15	30+

and (b) in order to have as equal as possible the number of words (types) falling within each of these levels. (As anyone knows who deals with corpus frequency counts, most words occur few times, so the lower frequency levels had more words in them.)

Once the words were divided into the 15 levels, a random sample of about 15 words was taken from each level. The absolute frequency of occurrence from *Raiders* was then converted to an adjusted frequency of occurrences per million words. The words selected through this process provided a wide range of frequency from the specific corpus.

In order to get an equivalent range of frequency from a general corpus, the Brown University corpus (Francis & Kučera, 1982) was used. Although this corpus was not ideal, because it was not an oral corpus and because it came from data gathered in 1961, it was judged better than other available choices for several reasons. First of all, it was not limited to language from a specific field of study, such as psychology, as some corpora are. Second, with approximately 1,014,000 words, it was larger than most corpora. Third, it was not limited to the language of children, as many corpora are.

The Brown corpus was divided into 15 levels equivalent (in number of occurrences per million words) to the 15 levels used in the *Raiders* corpus. Then, sufficient words were randomly selected from each level of the Brown corpus until 10 words could be used to provide the following differentiation:

1. Two words *not* occurring in *Raiders,* but occurring in the Brown corpus.
2. Two words occurring more frequently in Brown than in *Raiders.*
3. Two words occurring almost equally in Brown and in *Raiders.*
4. Two words occurring more frequently in *Raiders* than in Brown.
5. Two words *not* occurring in Brown, but occurring in *Raiders.*

Because there were 15 frequency levels, 10 words selected from each frequency level in the manner described provided a total of 150 words.

Once these 150 words had been chosen, 30 additional words were selected so that there would be at least 20 in each category of saliency being studied. In order to do this, the 150 words selected were analyzed to see, first of all, what focus they had in the *Raiders* program. The major issue at the time of selection was whether the words appeared in the exercises or glosses, or didn't. With regard to gapping, words were analyzed to see if they appeared first in the exercises rather than the script. When this occurred, it generally meant that learners had seen some representation of a concept visually in the film but would not hear or see the word until they reached it in the exercises (e.g., the learners might see a shovel being used, but the word *shovel* would not be heard nor seen until encountered in the exercises). It was assumed that, if a learner was not familiar with the word, an "empty box" or gap would have occurred, as the concept had been encountered but the word form had not.

An attempt was made in the original selection of the 30 additional words to ensure that there were at least 20 words fitting in each of the four "saliency" categories of focus and gap: (a) no focus and no gap (the word was used in the script before it appeared in the exercises and it only appeared in the exercises as an incidental word, not a glossed word and not an answer to one of the exercises); (b) focus and no gap (the word appeared in the script before it appeared in the exercises, and it was focused on in the exercises by being glossed or by being the answer to one of the exercise items); (c) gap and no focus (the word was used in the exercises before it was used in the script, and in the exercises the word was used incidentally, not glossed and not as an answer to an exercise question); and (d) both focus and gap (the word appeared in the exercises before it appeared in the script, and it was focused on in the exercises by being glossed or by being the answer to one of the exercise items).

At the time of data analysis, preliminary examination of the data raised questions about whether words focused on in a gloss and words focused on as an answer to an exercise could be considered to be a uniform group of words. Preliminary examination also suggested that there might be a difference in the way words with a gap were learned, depending on whether or not the words were used later in the script after their appearance in the exercises. The questions raised in the preliminary examination prompted the redividing of the words into nine categories rather than the original four. The nine categories were: (a) No focus and no gap (the word was used in the script before it appeared in the exercises, and it only appeared in the exercises as an incidental word, not a glossed word and not an answer to one of the exercises); (b) Focus in answer, but no gap (the word was used in the script before it appeared in the exercises, and then it appeared in the exercises as an answer to a question); (c) Focus in gloss, but no gap (the word was used in the script before it appeared in the exercises, and then it appeared in the exercises with its meaning glossed in); (d) No focus but gap with word in exercise/gloss only (the word was used in the

Table 13.2. Sample of Words Used in Study Including Their General and Specific Frequency as well as Codes for Focus and Gapping

	Word	Level* in		Occurrences		Adjusted Frequency		Gap/Focus
		Ra	Br	Ra	Br	Raiders	Brown	
001	shouts	05	01	005	00085	00293.1176	00083.8264	05
002	each	08	12	008	00878	00468.9880	00865.8836	01
003	worth	09	02	009	00091	00527.6117	00089.7436	03
004	let	10	07	010	00418	00586.2350	00412.2316	01
005	happened	11	05	011	00285	00644.8887	00281.0651	01
006	windshield	02	01	002	00006	00117.2470	00005.9172	07
007	idol	13	01	019	00010	01113.8469	00009.8619	03
008	time	14	15	029	01915	01700.0821	01888.5602	01
009	script	15	01	033	00012	01934.5762	00011.8343	01
010	without	06	10	006	00583	00351.7411	00574.9507	01
011	let's	04	01	004	00069	00234.4941	00068.0473	01
012	requires	00	06	000	00340	00000.0000	00335.3080	01
013	bronze	03	01	003	00012	00175.8706	00011.8343	01
014	recently	00	02	000	00123	00000.0000	00121.3026	01
015	incurred	01	01	001	00016	00058.6235	00015.7791	07
016	honor	01	02	001	00117	00058.6235	00115.3846	07
017	markings	10	01	010	00003	00586.2352	00002.9586	03
018	course	00	09	000	00527	00000.0000	00519.7274	01

019	trap	06	01	006	00037	00351.7411	00036.4892	06
020	such	05	14	005	01303	00293.1176	01285.0099	02
021	lecture	01	01	001	00036	00058.6235	00035.5030	07
022	end	03	09	003	00563	00175.8706	00555.2306	01
023	ahead	02	02	002	00109	00117.2470	00107.4958	07
024	effort	01	05	001	00272	00058.6235	00268.2464	07
025	pistol	07	01	007	00031	00410.3646	00030.5720	08
026	intoxicated	02	01	002	00002	00117.2470	00001.9724	08
027	whip	12	01	015	00040	00879.3528	00039.4477	03
028	heavy	00	02	000	00110	00000.0000	00108.4820	01
029	upon	00	08	000	00495	00000.0000	00488.1690	01
030	live	09	09	009	00523	00527.6115	00515.7826	01

*This level has reference to the levels shown in Table 13.1 which were established and used in the initial selection of the test words.

Gap/Focus Key
01 = No focus and no gap
02 = Focus in answer, but no gap
03 = Focus in gloss, but no gap
04 = No focus, gap with word in exercise/gloss only
05 = Focus in answer, gap with word in exercise/gloss only
06 = Focus in gloss, gap with word in exercise/gloss only
07 = No focus, gap with word in exercise/gloss first and script later
08 = Focus in answer, gap with word in exercise/gloss first and script later
09 = Focus in gloss, gap with word in exercise/gloss first and script later

Abbreviation Key
Ra = Raiders corpus
Br = Brown corpus

exercises before it was used in the script, never appearing in the script later, and in the exercises the word was used incidentally, not glossed and not as an answer to an exercise question); (e) Focus in answer, gap with word in exercise/gloss only (the word was used in the exercises as an answer to a question, but never appeared in the script); (f) Focus in gloss, gap with word in exercise/gloss only (the word was used in the exercises before it was used in the script, never appearing in the script later, and in the exercises it appeared with its meaning glossed in); (g) No focus, gap with word in exercise/gloss first and script later (the word was used in the exercises before it was used in the script, but then it appeared in the script later, and in the exercises the word was used incidentally, not glossed and not as an answer to an exercise question); (h) Focus in answer, gap with word in exercise/gloss first and script later (the word was used in the exercises before it was used in the script, but then it appeared in the script later, and it appeared in the exercises as an answer to a question); and (i) Focus in gloss, gap with word in exercise/gloss first and script later (the word was used in the exercises before it was used in the script, but then it appeared in the script later, and it appeared in the exercises with its meaning glossed in).

Table 13.2 shows 30 of the selected words and indicates how they were analyzed with regard to specific frequency, general frequency, focus, and gap.

Because the words had been redivided into nine categories instead of the original four, there were not 20 words in each of the categories. Table 13.3 shows the number of words out of the 180 words tested which fit in each of the gap and focus categories.

Table 13.3. Number of Words on Test for Different Focus and Gap Levels

	No Focus	Focus in Answer	Focus in Gloss	TOTAL
No gap	83	20	28	131 (Gap 1)
Exercises only	20	18	1	39 (Gap 2)
Exercises first	1	4	5	10 (Gap 3)
TOTALS	104	42	34	180
	(Focus 1)	(Focus 2)	(Focus 3)	

Vocabulary Test

Once the 180 vocabulary words were selected, an exam was written to test them. The exam consisted of 180 multiple choice items (one for each word). Each item consisted of a sentence stem with the test word(s) underlined and four options (possible paraphrases or synonyms for the underlined words). The test words were used in the stem sentences in the same sense they were used in *Raiders* (if the words occurred in *Raiders*). However, the context was quite bare for the words and would provide few clues if the students did not know the words well, as can be seen in the following two examples:

What is your favorite *program*?
　　a. career　　b. show　　c. professor　　d. problem

That is *correct.*
　　a. corrupt　　b. happening　　c. right　　d. unexpected

Generally, at least one of the distractors for each item had a graphological or phonological similarity to the test word. For instance, in the examples given above, *problem* bears some graphological and phonological similarity to *program,* and *corrupt* bears some graphological and phonological similarity to *correct.* While some testing experts would say that this is mixing issues in a vocabulary test, previous work (as discussed above) has shown that phonology might affect the acquisition of words. While the phonology issue was not treated in this particular part of the study, it is being analyzed and will be discussed in future papers.

Four versions of the test were prepared with the items in a different order on each. This was done to lessen the effect that students' tiring might have on the test results.

Subjects

The learners who participated in this study were all students at the Brigham Young University English Language Center (ELC). The ELC is basically a preuniversity intensive course with five levels. Students from all levels participated in the study. There were 112 students who participated in some part of the study. However, only 85 students were present for all of the pretesting and posttesting for this particular part of the study, so most of the data reported came from those subjects. In that subject group, there were 38 native Spanish speakers, 39 Japanese speakers, 2 Chinese speakers, 2 Thai speakers, 2 Indonesian speakers, and 1 French and 1 Korean speaker. There were 33 males and 52 females.

Procedures

All students were given the pretest as a group the third week in September, before they began working with the *Raiders of the Lost Ark* videodisc program. The test forms were color coded and handed out so that students at the same level and from the same language group received a variety of versions of the test. As part of another study on ways of testing vocabulary, students were asked to translate the underlined words in the first 45 items into their native language. Then they were asked to complete the entire 180-item multiple choice test. All students were required to remain until they had completed the test or had worked on it for 2 hours (whichever came first). Most students completed the test within 2 hours. However, those who did not were allowed to leave or to finish the test according to their own desires.

Students then pursued their regular courses of study at the ELC. Students were taught how the *Raiders* program worked in their individual classes and then used it as they desired in the computer lab. Records were kept of who used the program and how much during the term.

The posttest (which was identical to the pretest) was given the third week in November, before the students' finals began. Each student received the same version of the test that he or she had had on the pretest, so that the same items would be more likely to be affected if tiring occurred. Once again, students were asked to translate the first 45 underlined words and then to do the 180-item test in the usual manner. Students were told that whoever showed the most gain from the pretest would be rewarded with a compact disk of his or her choice. Almost all students finished the test within the 2-hour period, and those who did not remained until they had completed it.

Data Analysis

Gain scores for each word were calculated by subtracting the number of students who got the word correct on the pretest from the number who got it correct on the posttest. If students had not completed the pretest, only those words which they had actually tried on the pretest and either answered incorrectly or left blank were counted as missed. The gain scores were then run as the dependent variable in the statistical tests.

Analyses of covariance and variance[2] were run using the pretest scores, the general frequency of the words, and the specific frequency of the words as covariates and those factors, plus gap, focus, and gap by focus as independent variables. Putting the pretest score in as a covariate pulled out the effect of prior knowledge so that actual learning during the treatment period, and not just overall knowledge, was measured. The covariance of general frequency with gain, and of specific frequency with gain, was used to show the relationship of these two frequencies with gain and tell whether either frequency had any relationship with a word's being learned. While cause and effect could not be claimed from high correlations (that is, a high correlation would not necessarily prove that high frequency causes high gain), a lack of correlation would cause serious doubts about the existence of any cause and effect. The statistics were run using VMS-SAS, Version 5.16 (SAS, 1988). For all tests, a probability level of .05 was used to decide if the factors were significant or not.

RESULTS AND DISCUSSION

Overall, there was an average gain of 13.622 for each word. That means that, on the average, 13 more students knew each word on the posttest than knew it on the pretest. The range of gains was from 1 (one more student knew the word on the posttest than knew it on the pretest) to 29 (29 more students knew the word on the posttest than knew it on the pretest).

As far as students went, their gain scores ranged from 2 (the student knew only two more words on the posttest than on the pretest) to 82 (the student knew 82 more words on the posttest than on the pretest). The original analysis of covariance, as described in the research design section of this chapter, produced results which raised some questions of concern. Table 13.4 shows the results of the original analysis of covariance.

As can be seen in Table 13.4, the pretest was a significant factor, as measured by the analysis of covariance. If a student already knew a word on the pretest, he or she could not show a gain on that word; in other words, there was a "ceiling effect"—words which were already known by most students could not be learned by as many students as words which were known by fewer students, so scores on those words would necessarily be low. As would be expected, therefore, the pretest score for the words showed a negative correlation with the gain scores, and that correlation was significant. This analysis of covariance also showed gap to be significant, but there was no significant effect for focus nor gap by focus.

However, caution had to be exercised at this point, because, when the relationship of pretest to gain scores was plotted on a scattergram, the data proved to be curvilinear. This being the case, it was necessary to find a way to neutralize

Table 13.4. Analysis of Covariance for Gain Scores by All Factors

Source	df	Adjusted SS	F-ratio	Significance
Between				
Covariates				
Pretest	1	1218.956	64.27	0.0001
General Frequency	1	29.068	1.53	0.2174
Specific Frequency	1	6.787	0.36	0.5505
Independent Variables				
Focus	2	27.819	0.73	0.4818
Gap	2	128.698	3.39	0.0359
Focus X Gap	4	40.766	0.54	0.7085
Within	168	3186.176		

the effect of the pretest data and then see if other factors were significant. One way to do such a neutralization is to include a mathematical term in the statistical model which would represent the data. In this case the curvilinearity of the pretest data was a very normal "mound," so a quadratic term (that is, the pretest X the pretest) could be placed in the model (along with the linear term—simple pretest scores) to represent the pretest, and significance of the other factors could be tested. (See Draper & Smith, 1981, for a more thorough discussion of this procedure.) Therefore, a second analysis of covariance was run using the pretest scores, the general frequency of the words, the specific frequency of the words, and the quadratic term for the pretest as covariates; these factors and gap, focus, and gap by focus were again used as independent variables. When gap by focus still proved to be nonsignificant, a third analysis was done eliminating that factor, so that main factor effects would be clearer. Table 13.5 shows the results of that analysis.

As can be seen in Table 13.5, the linear term for pretest still proves to be a significant factor. Part of the reason for that significance is explained above by the ceiling effect. The quadratic term for the pretest also proves to be significant. This is a harder variance to explain, as it is probably the result of more than one thing. The scatterplot shows that, for two kinds of words, gains were low. Those kinds of words were: (a) words which the majority (more than two-thirds) of the students knew on the pretest, and (b) words which few (fewer than one-third) of the students knew on the pretest. The reason for the low gains on the first kind of words may be attributed, as already explained, to the ceiling effect (words already known by most students cannot show high gain scores). The reason for the low gains on the second kind of words may be connected with the issue of input and the opportunity to hear the words. If fewer than one-third of the students know a word, it is not as likely to be used at all in the social milieu of the English Language Center (where these students spent 5 to 7 hours a day), or to be used very often. Consequently, fewer students increase in their knowledge

Table 13.5. Analysis of Covariance for Gain Scores by All Factors Including the Quadratic Term for Pre-Test

Source	df	Adjusted SS	F-ratio	Significance
Between				
Covariates				
Pretest	1	665.121	52.91	0.0001
Pretest 2 (Quadratic)	1	1077.482	85.72	0.0001
General Frequency	1	53.728	4.27	0.0402
Specific Frequency	1	28.232	2.25	0.1358
Independent Variables				
Focus	2	23.489	0.93	0.3948
Gap	2	132.088	5.25	0.0061
Within	171	2149.460		

of the word to the point that they can select a correct definition of it. If this reason is true, it would parallel gains in other kinds of skills. One becomes a better tennis player by playing with persons who are slightly better than one in different aspects of the game; one learns words by language playing (interacting) with persons who use more or different words than one does. The scatterplot of gains with pretest scores show that words that are known by about 40% to 60% of the people in an environment are words which are more likely to be learned by others in the environment. This "social milieu hypothesis" for vocabulary learning would need to be tested in other ways before total acceptance.

THE FREQUENCY ISSUE

It should be noted, also, that this social milieu hypothesis may have some bearing on the original questions about frequency. One of the research questions asks if frequency in a specific context influences the acquisition of a word. This study examined the specific frequency of use of words in the interactive movie and videodisk program which the students were using. It did not examine the specific frequency of use in this particular social milieu (the English Language Center) or in any other specific aspects of the students' lives. It was assumed that the general frequency would be close to the frequency of the words in the students' general lives.

Table 13.5 shows the results of the tests of frequency which were performed. As can be seen, general frequency (the frequency in the Brown corpus) but not specific frequency (the frequency in *Raiders*) reaches significance. Table 13.6 shows the pre- and posttest correlations between the number of students who knew the words and their frequency in the two corpora.

Although both correlations seem to be fairly low numbers, general frequency has a higher correlation than specific frequency with the words known. The specific frequency correlation, in fact, is really very close to zero, showing *no* relationship between the frequency in a specific context—the *Raiders* script— and the students' knowledge of a word. While the general frequency correlation is also low, it is significant at the .05 level. How often a word occurs in general does seem to have a relationship with whether it is learned, even if that relationship is not an especially large one.

Table 13.6. Correlations of Test Scores and Word Frequencies

	Pre-test	Post-test
General frequency	.204*	.201*
Specific frequency	.079	.063

*Significant at the .05 level (178 df)

Table 13.7. Words with the Highest Gains

Word	Gain	Raiders' Frequency	Word	Gain	Raiders' Frequency
hocus-pocus	29	02	windshield	24	02
chanting	26	01	ambush	23	05
blow	25	17	obtainer	23	03
covenant	25	10	secret	23	02
then	24	14	movement	23	00

THE SALIENCY ISSUE

The overall idea of salience and its effect on vocabulary acquisition becomes quite strong as one examines the words that had the highest gain scores. These are given in Table 13.7.

Almost all of the words with the highest gain scores are words which are central to the story in *Raiders*. Noticeable also is the fact that few of the words on this list would be likely to be vital and/or encountered much in the learners' day-to-day life. Students may have use for *blow* or *secret,* but they are very unlikely to need *chanting, ambush,* or *obtainer.* The low frequency of occurrence in the specific context of most of these words is also phenomenal. While nothing is actually proven on the basis of such a list as shown in Table 13.7, the list does suggest very powerfully the strength of context salience for the acquisition of words.

Salience from Focus

Table 13.8 gives the mean gain scores for the three different levels of focus and the three different levels of gapping. They are included here as they are the average of the actual number of students who learned the words. Because there was an uneven number of words in the various cells, the analysis of covariance was done using least squares means. These means have been adjusted for differences in numbers of words in the various categories, a step which is necessary for more accurate statistics on uneven data (see Cochran, 1940, 1943; Koch & Landis, 1977). Table 13.9 gives the least squares means for the same levels of focus and gap presented in Table 13.8.

Although most of the means of the gain scores increase as we move from no focus to focus in the gloss as can be seen in both Tables 13.8 and 13.9, focus in the program was *not* a significant factor in word acquisition, as was seen in Table 13.5. In other words, whether a word appeared as an answer in the exercises or as a focus in the glossary did not make a significant difference in whether the word was acquired.

Table 13.8. Mean Gain Scores on Words with Different Levels of Focus and Gap

	No Focus	Focus in Answer	Focus in Gloss	TOTAL
No gap	12.373	13.900	14.500	13.061 Gap 1
Exercises only	13.400	14.333	15.000	13.872 Gap 2
Exercises first	15.000	18.500	22.200	20.000 Gap 3
TOTALS	12.596	14.524	15.647	13.622
	Focus 1	Focus 2	Focus 3	

Table 13.9. Least Squares Mean Gain Scores on Words with Different Levels of Focus and Gap

	No Focus	Focus in Answer	Focus in Gloss	TOTAL
No gap	13.219	13.150	13.723	13.364 Gap 1
Exercises only	12.791	14.464	15.284	14.180 Gap 2
Exercises first	12.799	16.799	19.233	16.277 Gap 3
TOTALS	12.936	14.805	16.080	13.622
	Focus 1	Focus 2	Focus 3	

It may be that focus really does not make a difference. However, some caution in drawing that conclusion seems advisable. In the first place, with the exception of what happens when there is no gap, there is a definite consistency in the increase in the mean gain scores as one moves from no focus to focus in the gloss. And secondly, in this particular study we do not have records on how much the students actually used the exercises or glosses. Further study assuring the use of these tools, or at least tracking the amount of time spent with each or the number of times the program users used each, would be necessary before definite conclusions could be made. All that can be said on the basis of this study is that, given a program where students may choose to use the exercise or the gloss or not, having a word focused on in either of these ways does not seem to make a difference.

Salience from Gap

As can be seen in Table 13.5, gap *did* seem to make a difference in whether words were acquired or not. Also as can be seen from Tables 13.8 and 13.9, the increases were consistent as one moves from no gap, through a gap filled by a word in the exercises only, to a gap filled by a word in the exercises first with the word used later in the script again. However, a post hoc comparison revealed that the significant difference came only for the third condition. In other words,

Table 13.10. Gain Scores for Words with Appearance in Exercises First and in Script Later

truck	Noun	12	basket	Noun	20
temple	Noun	15	ambush	Noun	23
stands	Verb	15	secret	Adj	23
shouts	Noun	19	blow	Verb	25
trap	Noun	19	hocus-pocus	Noun	29

there is a significant difference in the amount of vocabulary gained when a gap is created by having a meaning demonstrated in some way without giving a term for it, then having the term given (in this case this was done in writing in the exercises), and finally having the term used again. Only 10 words of the 180 on the test were used in *Raiders* in this particular way. Table 13.10 lists those words and the gain scores for them.

One thing which could be interesting to pedagogues about the words given in Table 13.10 is the fact that the words were not all used as nouns in the *Raiders* program. The list includes verbs and an adjective as well. This suggests that "gaps" can be created for these other parts of speech as well as for the more "picturable" nouns.

The fact that this kind of gapping makes a difference holds implications for vocabulary instruction. It suggests that increase in vocabulary acquisition will result if teachers can find a way to create a need (a gap in the student's knowledge which the student recognizes) for a word (e.g., possibly by using pictures as they prepare students for reading assignments) and then having that word accessible as the filler for the gap somewhere in the assignment. Finally, the teacher would need to be sure that the students have the opportunity to encounter the word again soon in a meaningful context. It suggests the need for good visual contexts—pictures, videos, movies, and so on —as well as recycling or spiraling in the same vocabulary within a very short time. Obviously, interactive videodisc programs, such as the one used in this study, seem to provide the visual contexts and can be designed to provide the recycling quite easily, but they do not have to be the only means by which the principles learned here can be applied.

CONCLUSIONS, IMPLICATIONS, AND SUGGESTIONS FOR FURTHER RESEARCH

This research has made it clear that there are several areas which could profit from future research. For one thing, it would be advantageous to know specifically how students used the *Raiders* program. An informal analysis of the computer lab assistant's record revealed that the student learning the most words was also the student who spent the most time with the program. However, knowing which parts of the program each student used and for how long, as well as knowing how much time each student spent overall, would be very helpful. If this information were available, the actual relationship of the various levels of focus and gain would be clearer.

Further information about use of words in the general context or social milieu might also be helpful. It is highly possible that general frequency interacts with saliency factors in a way which this present study has not been able to tease out.

Furthermore, the possible effects of phonology of words or part of speech on vocabulary acquisition should be studied. The same data collected and reported in this study are currently being reexamined and reanalyzed with regard to these two factors. Furthermore, all effects of these or any other word factors should be examined as they interact with student background factors. It is possible that many of the issues mentioned in this chapter, including those of frequency and phonology, affect students from different language backgrounds differently.

Although further research is needed in many areas, this study has provided evidence to support the following points about factors which affect vocabulary acquisition:

1. General frequency does seem to make a difference in whether a word is acquired or not. Exactly how this works is not clear. Specific frequency in materials does not seem to make a difference. However, specific frequency in the social setting may. Words which were known in the beginning by about one-third to two-thirds of the students who shared this environment were the words which were most learned.
2. Words which are important (salient) in a specific context are more likely to be acquired regardless of frequency.
3. Learners are more likely to learn a word for which they have a concept prior to seeing or hearing the word form. This is especially true if the learners have the opportunity to experience the word form again in context after the initial encounter.

Although this current study is not definitive in many areas, it does provide a model which can be followed in future studies, and it does suggest ideas, such as "gapping" and frequency in the social milieu, which seem deserving of further exploration. It is obvious that there is still much to learn about vocabulary acquisition. Just as word acquisition is important to language learners, knowledge about word acquisition is important to language pedagogues. For that reason it is hoped that the current studies will definitely not be the last word on words.

REFERENCES

Allen, V. F. (1983). *Techniques in teaching vocabulary.* New York: Oxford University Press.

Beck, I., McKeown, M., & Omanson, R. (1987). The effects and uses of diverse vocabulary instructional techniques. In M. McKeown & M. Curtis (Eds.), *The nature of vocabulary acquisition* (pp. 147–163). Hillsdale, NJ: Erlbaum.

Bensoussan, M., & Laufer, B. (1984). Lexical guessing in context in EFL reading comprehension. *Journal of Research in Reading, 7,* 15–32.

Brown, C. (1985, March). *Using introspection to analyze the reading processes of advanced ESL speakers.* Paper presented at the Intermountain-TESOL Conference, Provo, UT.

Calfee, R., & Drum, P. (1986). Research on teaching reading. In M. Wittrock (Ed.), *Handbook of research on teaching* (pp. 804–849). New York: Macmillan.

Carter, R. (1987). *Vocabulary: Applied linguistic perspectives.* London: Allen & Unwin.

Carter, R., & McCarthy, M. (1988) *Vocabulary and language teaching.* New York: Longman.

Celce-Murcia, M. (1978). The simultaneous acquisition of English and French in a two-year-old child. In E. M. Hatch (Ed.), *Second language acquisition: A book of readings* (pp. 38–53). Rowley, MA: Newbury House.

Chall, J. (1987). Two vocabularies for reading: Recognition and meaning. In M. McKeown and M. Curtis (Eds.), *The nature of vocabulary acquisition* (pp. 7–17). Hillsdale, NJ: Erlbaum.

Cochran, W. G. (1940). The analysis of variance when experimental errors follow the Poisson or binomial laws. *Annals of Mathematical Statistics, 11,* 335–347.

Cochran, W. G. (1943). Analysis of variance for percentages based on unequal numbers. *Journal of the American Statistical Association, 38,* 287–301.

Cohen, A., & Aphek, E. (1980). Retention of second language vocabulary over time: Investigating the role of mnemonic associations. *System, 8,* 221–235.

Draper, N., & Smith, H. (1981). *Applied regression analysis* (2nd ed.). New York: John Wiley & Sons.

Drum, P., & Konopak, B. (1987). Learning word meanings from written context. In M. McKeown & M. Curtis (Eds.), *The nature of vocabulary acquisition* (pp. 73–87). Hillsdale, NJ: Erlbaum.

Francis, W. N., & Kučera, H. (1982). *Frequency analysis of English usage: lexicon and grammar.* Boston: Houghton Mifflin Company.

Gairns, R., & Redman, S. (1986). *Working with words: A guide to teaching and learning vocabulary.* New York: Cambridge University Press.

Gentner, D. (1982). Why nouns are learned before verbs: Linguistic relativity vs. natural partitioning. In S. Kuczaj (Ed.) *Language development* (Vol. 2). Hillsdale, NJ: Erlbaum.

Graves, M. (1987). The roles of instruction in fostering vocabulary development. In M. McKeown & M. Curtis (Eds.), *The nature of vocabulary acquisition* (pp. 165–184). Hillsdale, NJ: Erlbaum.

Hague, S. (1987). Vocabulary instruction: What L2 can learn from L1. *Foreign Language Annals, 20,* 217–225.

Harvey, P. (1983). Vocabulary learning: The use of grids. *ELT Journal, 37,* 243–246.

Haynes, M. (1984). Patterns and perils of guessing in second language reading. In J. Handscombe, R. Orem, & B. Taylor (Eds.), *On TESOL '83: The question of control* (pp. 163–176.) Washington, DC: TESOL Publications.

Hatch, E., Flashner, V., & Hunt, L. (1986). The experience model and language teaching. In R. R. Day (Ed.), *Talking to learn: Conversation in second language acquisition* (pp. 5–22). Rowley, MA: Newbury House.

Higgins, J., & Johns, T. (1984). *Computers in language learning.* Aylesbury, UK: Collins ELT and Addison-Wesley.

Jenkins, J. R., & Dixon, R. (1983). Vocabulary learning. *Contemporary Educational Psychology, 8,* 237–260.

Koch, G. G., & Landis, J. R. (1977). The measurement of observer agreement for categorical data. *Biometrics, 33,* 159–174.

Koch, G. G., Landis, J. R., Freeman, D. Y., & Lehnen, R. G. (1977). General methodology for the analysis of experiments with repeated measurements of categorical data. *Biometrics, 33,* 133–158.

Laufer, B. (1986). Possible changes in attitude towards vocabulary acquisition research. *IRAL, 24*(1), 69–75.

Laufer, B., & Bensoussan, M. (1984). Meaning is in the eye of the beholder. *English Teaching Forum, 22,* 10–13.

Levenston, E. A., & Blum, S. (1977) Aspects of lexical simplification in the speech and writing of advanced adult learners. In S. P. Corder & E. Roulet (Eds.), *The notions of simplification: Interlanguages and pidgins and their relation to second language pedagogy: Actes de 5eme Colloque de Linguistique Appliquee de Neuchatel, 20-22 Mai 1976* (pp. 51–71). Geneva: Librairie Droz.

Meara, P. (1984). The study of lexis. In A. Davies, C. Criper, & A. Howatt (Eds.), *Interlanguage* (pp. 225–235). Edinburgh: Edinburgh University Press.

Morgan, J., & Rinvolucri, M. (1986). *Vocabulary.* New York: Oxford University Press.

Nagy, W. E., & Herman, P. A. (1987). Breadth and depth of vocabulary knowledge: Implications for acquisition and instruction. In M. McKeown & M. Curtis (Eds.), *The nature of vocabulary acquisition* (pp. 19–36). Hillsdale, NJ: Erlbaum.

Nation, I. (1982). Beginning to learn foreign language vocabulary: A review of the research. *RELC Journal, 13,* 14–36.

Parry, K. (1988, March). Paper presented at the Applied Linguistics Interest Section Academic Session, TESOL, Chicago, IL.

Probst, G., & Bennion, J. (1986). Interactive videodisc courseware for *Raiders of the Lost Ark.* Provo, UT: Interactive Instruction.

SAS Institute. (1988). *VMS-SAS, Version 5.16.* Cary, NC: SAS Institute.

Schwartz, R. G., & Leonard, L. B. (1982). Do children pick and choose? An examination of phonological selection and avoidance in early lexical acquisition. *Journal of Child Language, 9,* 319–336.

Stahl, S., & Fairbanks, M. (1986). The effects of vocabulary instruction: A model-based meta analysis. *Review of Educational Research, 56,* 72–110.

Sternberg, R. J. (1987). Most vocabulary is learned from context. In M. G. McKeown & M. E. Curtis (Eds.), *The nature of vocabulary acquisition* (pp. 89–105). Hillsdale, NJ: Erlbaum.

Stieglitz, E. (1983). A practical approach to vocabulary reinforcement. *ELT Journal, 37,* 71–75.

Stoel-Gammon, C., & Cooper, J. A. (1984). Patterns of early lexical and phonological development. *Journal of Child Language, 11,* 247–271.

Yun, Z. (1989). *The effect of part of speech on the acquisition of vocabulary from context.* Unpublished Master's thesis, Brigham Young University, Provo, Utah.

ENDNOTES

1. Because of the work of Krashen, many people differentiate between *learning* and *acquisition,* using the former term for what second language learners do consciously and/or in formal educational settings, and the latter term for what they do subconsciously and/or in informal settings. For the purposes of this paper, the nouns *acquisition* and *learning,* and their companion verb forms, *acquire* and *learn,* will be used to refer to coming to know the meaning of words whether done consciously or subconsciously and whether done in formal or informal situations. While the papers in this volume and elsewhere point out that such acquisition is a gradual process and may involve various gradations in "knowing" the meaning of a word, the acquisition terms will be used in their lay sense until operationally defined in the section of this chapter dealing with the research design of the study.
2. A traditional chi-square treatment could not be used because of the nature of the data, even though some would regard them as frequency data. Rather, an analysis of covariance was used as being the safer technique. Arguments for using this procedure were established by Cochran (1940, 1943) and have been extended by Koch, Landis, Freeman, and Lehnen (1977) and Koch and Landis (1977).

Editorial Comments

This chapter reports on video context, yet for two reasons belongs appropriately in this volume about reading. First, it is somewhat easier in a video context than in written text to suggest word-meanings before the word-forms are presented. Thus this research with video offers a useful point of comparison with most of the research in section II of this volume using written text for contextual inference. Indeed, Brown's discovery is of great interest to us: that words seem more likely to be remembered when the concepts are first evoked in context, before the word-form appears. This suggests that *it is beneficial for learners if meaning precedes word-form,* that is, if learners experience first the concept and thus develop a need for the word-form which labels that concept. Such primacy of conceptual organization in the acquisition of word meaning has long been argued by scholars of child language acquisition (e.g., MacNamara, 1972; Bowerman, 1977). It is possible that video can more readily create this beneficial type of "gap" between concept and form than can a written text. A related study, Omanson's (1985) analysis of vocabulary learning from reading, has indicated that, when an unfamiliar word-form is encountered, it tends to become an empty slot in a given proposition rather than immediately evoking a synonym or guess about meaning. Thus, video instruction may be superior to text presentation, at least for some types of new words. The fact that only two appearances of the word-form were necessary once the concept had been activated is reminiscent of Carey's (1978) findings about "fast-mapping" during L1 children's rapid acquisition of new vocabulary.

A second reason for including Brown's research here involves the importance of visual word-form for vocabulary learning. Brown's results suggest that vocabulary learning takes place most readily when conceptual activation is followed later by a written word-form, which in turn is followed up by another use of that word-form in the video context. Thus learners exposed to on-screen representation would derive benefit from subsequent reading which most likely focussed attention for a brief period of time on the word-form as well as on meaning. Brown's study suggests to us the power of the written word for cementing vocabulary learning.

Brown's chapter also draws more very useful distinctions about lexical usage. She defines clearly traditional word frequency, frequency in a specific context, and various types of saliency. Like Parry (Chapter 6), the last part of Haynes and Baker (Chapter 7), and the translation analysis of Huckin and Bloch (Chapter 8), Brown focuses on attributes of words as a means of understanding how learning takes place successfully. However, unlike these other researchers, Brown analyzes learnability in a statistical manner using preestablished categories of frequency and saliency. Thus Brown's work offers another model approach to be followed by researchers of vocabulary acquisition. And it demonstrates that this approach can lead in an inductive manner to new and useful understandings of how instructional sequence can facilitate word learning.

Brown's work is not without its difficulties, however. This chapter basically describes the video resource, leaving unanswered questions about the details of student use. Had students who learned those words actually used the follow-up exercises? How many times had they watched the relevant portions of the video? Did they use any sort of writing or other mnemonic while learning this new vocabulary? As with Coady et al.'s Chapter 11, we feel the need for tighter record keeping on individual student use of interactive materials. We look forward to more detailed reports of this learning system which include individual student data. This will enable us to make firm pedagogical recommendations about the sequencing of concepts and word-forms for maximum learnability.

Secondly, we need to caution readers that Brown's approach tends to oversimplify "acquisition" by using single multiple choice items to test vocabulary learning. As has been stressed by Beck and McKeown (1991), among others, distractors on multiple choice tests may cause learner confusion and erroneous estimates of learner word knowledge; the limitations of such measurement approaches are even more apparent when word "acquisition" is reconceptualized as a rich, incremental process of concept elaboration (see especially Parry, Chapter 6).

References

Beck, I., & McKeown, M. (1991). Conditions of vocabulary acquisition. In R. Barr, M. Kamil, P. Mosenthal, & P. D. Pearson (Eds.), *The handbook of reading research* (Vol. 2). New York: Longman.

Bowerman, M. (1977). The acquisition of word meaning: An investigation of some current conflicts. In N. Waterson & C. Snow (Eds.) *Proceedings of the Third International Child Language Symposium.* New York: Wiley.

Carey, S. (1978). The child as word learner. In M. Halle, J. Bresnan, & G. A. Miller (Eds.), *Linguistic theory and psychological reality* (pp. 264–293). Cambridge, MA: MIT Press.

Macnamara, J. (1972). Cognitive basis of language learning in infants. *Psychological Review, 79*(1), 1–13.

Omanson, R. C. (1985). Knowing words and understanding texts. In T. H. Carr (Ed.), *The development of reading skills* (New Directions for Child Development, No. 27). San Francisco, CA: Jossey-Bass.

V
Points of Departure for Future Research and Teaching

Chapter 14
Summary and Future Directions

Thomas Huckin & Margot Haynes

The preceding chapters all point to the thoroughly interactive nature of second-language reading and word guessing. These two interrelated activities are neither mainly "top-down" nor "bottom-up" but a delicate balance of both. In this concluding chapter, we will summarize the argument for a balanced interactive view and then describe some of the implications it has for teaching and further research.

The argument begins with the pedagogical assumption that our ultimate goal in teaching learners a second language is to help them reach near native-speaker competence in certain applied linguistic skills. (For many, the primary such skill is reading.) One can easily imagine alternative goals, such as learning just enough of a language to survive in a foreign country as a tourist; in such cases, alternative methods (such as using a phrase book) might well be preferred. But in the typical second-language classroom at schools and colleges, more ambitious, long-term goals are usually pursued. If second-language learners wish to read advanced academic or professional reading material competently with full understanding, they will have to develop a vocabulary similar in size to that assumed by the writers of those materials—in most cases, more than 40,000 words (Nagy & Herman, 1987).[1]

Given the goal of reaching near native-speaker competence, it seems reasonable to assume that L2 learners should try to emulate L1 learners. How do native speakers learn more than 40,000 words? As many first-language researchers have noted (see Chapters 1–2), direct item-by-item teaching of vocabulary in formal educational settings can account for only a small fraction of the tens of thousands of words that native speakers come to know. Thus, the "default" explanation is that native speakers must gain the bulk of their word-knowledge through contextual guessing. Now if L1 learners rely heavily on context to develop their knowledge of words, the argument goes, so too should L2 learners. For the past 20 years or so, this L1/L2 analogy has been the primary rationale for a predominantly "top-down" approach to L2 vocabulary learning.

But as a number of the studies in this book have made clear, the use of contextual guessing by L2 learners is distinctly problematic. First, it is not uncommon for L2 learners to misrecognize word-forms. In Haynes's 1984 study of 63 nonnative speakers and in Huckin and Bloch's three case studies (see also Laufer 1988), misrecognition caused readers to short-circuit the contextual guessing process. That is, if readers thought they recognized a word-form, they would simply access the standard meaning for that form and not look to the context for confirmation. Thus, word-form recognition plays a crucial role even before contextual guessing begins, simply in alerting the reader to the *need* to guess.

Second, L2 learners sometimes misuse context clues due to impoverished vocabulary knowledge. This problem is underscored especially in the Haynes and Baker study, where stipulated definitions of target words were sometimes unusable by nonnative speakers because the definitions themselves contained words like *jagged, slices,* and *tears* that were unknown to them.

Third, as Parry's work shows, a single context rarely gives sufficient information for a second-language reader to guess the full meaning of the word in question. The proportion of partially correct guesses that Parry documents suggests that a clear sense of a word's defining features can only be reached through repeated encounters in diverse contexts.

A fourth problem with contextual guessing involves nonlinguistic background knowledge. Working with native speakers, Dubin and Olshtain point out that successful word guessing requires not only substantial textual support but considerable background knowledge (topic and cultural) as well. If this is true of native speakers, it must be all the more true of nonnatives. Yet, as Stein notes, many of the word-guessing exercises in our textbooks fail to take such background knowledge into account.

Finally, it is not clear that contextual guesswork always enhances word learning. It may depend on *how much* guesswork is involved. As we noted above, Coady (Chapter 1) observes that

> the very redundancy or richness of information in a given context which enables a reader to successfully guess an unknown word also predicts that that same reader is less likely to learn the word because he or she was able to comprehend the text without knowing the word.

A recent Dutch study (Mondria & Wit-de-Boer, 1989) concludes that there is an inverse relation between guessability and retainability.

Thus, it appears that heavy reliance on contextual guessing may not be the optimal learning strategy for nonnative speakers. There is some controversy about whether contextual guessing is the optimal approach for *first*-language learners (see Pressley, Levin, & McDaniel, 1987, vs. Sternberg, 1987). And even if first-language learners do rely mainly on contextual guesswork (which is an unproven assumption), there is good reason to think that second-language learners should not. A heavily top-down approach to reading and vocabulary building would invite a host of bottom-up problems.

On the other hand, going in the opposite direction and embracing a largely bottom-up approach would not be without problems of its own. First of all, trying to teach 40,000 or more words directly would take an enormous amount of instructional time, far more than most second-language learners or teachers have at their disposal. Second, focusing entirely on words in isolation would prevent learners from working on their reading skills and developing metacognitive monitoring skills. This would be an inefficient use of instructional time and would not help students learn how to build their vocabulary through reading. Third, learning words in isolation tends to emphasize the most common meanings of those words and inhibits the ability of language users to interpret words in unusual ways according to particular contexts.

Thus, a more viable approach to second-language reading and word-guessing appears to be one in which learners employ both top-down and bottom-up processing in complementary fashion. Ideally, bottom-up processing should consist of rapid, automated activities such as graphemic identification, lexical access, and syntactic analysis. Top-down processing is a more strategic activity that can be done consciously and deliberately; it oversees the reading and guessing processes and helps ensure that they don't go off the track.

This division of labor carries with it a number of binary distinctions that seem to play an important role in reading and word-guessing. The major distinction is that between automated processing and attended (conscious, deliberate) processing. Automated processing is fast and efficient, putting relatively little strain on working memory, but it lacks flexibility. Attended processing is more strategic and adaptable, but it is slow and inefficient and puts more strain on working memory. Given human memory limitations, a certain amount of automated processing is highly desirable, indeed necessary. But given the complexity and unpredictability of human communication, taking the path of least resistance via automated processing can lead to misinterpretations; a certain amount of strategic monitoring and problem-solving in the form of attended processing is necessary, too.

The attended/automated distinction manifests itself in a number of subdistinctions discussed in this book. First, there is the distinction between "sense selection" and "sense creation" (Clark & Gerrig, 1983). Sense selection is the relatively automatic process of accessing common meanings of words from the reader's mental lexicon, while sense creation is a more effortful process of creating new meanings. As long as a writer intends common word-meanings, sense selection is the fastest, most efficient way to process text. But in cases where *un*common word meanings are intended, sense selection will only lead to misinterpretation. In Haynes and Baker's study, words like *cuts, approximations,* and *bandaging* appearing in a medical text gave both L1 and L2 readers considerable difficulty, because they were being used in unconventional ways. If these readers had been more sensitive to context—which included definitions and other forms of lexical familiarization—they most likely would have seen the need to engage in sense creation.

Second, there is the closely related phenomenon of cognate recognition. As Holmes and Ramos note, the natural inclination of students learning a cognate language is to look for cognate words. Recognizing a word as cognate immediately activates in a beginning-to-intermediate learner rich associations from the lexicon of his or her native language (a form of sense selection). This process is a relatively effortless and automatic one, hence its universal occurrence among second-language learners. But, of course, it leads to problems in the case of false cognates. Holmes and Ramos show that, with suitable training, L2 learners can learn to be on the alert for false cognates, that is, to use more attended processing.

Third, there is the distinction between local and global context. Fine-grained case studies such as those presented in the Huckin and Bloch chapter indicate that L2 learners rely heavily on local context clues, clues located in the immediate vicinity of a target word. Indeed, it appears that learners use these local context clues naturally, without being told to do so (see also Haynes, Chern). To a significant extent, this strategy makes good sense. Using local clues puts less strain on short-term memory than using global clues. And local clues tend to be more reliable indicators of target word meaning than more global ones. For example, a recent dissertation by Duignan found that well-designed sample sentences, such as those used as dictionary examples, were more helpful as contexts for word guessing than were naturally occurring paragraphs (Duignan, 1990). But Stein's chapter illustrates many cases where single-sentence contexts like those found in ESL textbooks were misleading, and the chapters by Parry, Huckin and Bloch, Dubin and Olshtain, and Haynes and Baker suggest that global context clues are often needed to guard against textual misinterpretations. Thus, the natural and relatively automatic use of local clues should be encouraged, but learners should also be encouraged to use global clues. The effectiveness of such balanced processing is shown in the chapter by Holmes and Ramos, in Huckin and Jin (1987), and elsewhere.

A fourth way in which the automated vs. attended processing distinction manifests itself is in the difference between declarative and procedural vocabulary as discussed in the chapter by Robinson. Declarative vocabulary consists of words with relatively narrow, well-defined referents, while procedural vocabulary consists of more general words whose meaning has to be "negotiated" according to the context in which they are used. Of course, there is more of a continuum than a dichotomy here, since even declarative words vary in meaning from one context to another (see Clark & Gerrig, 1983; Smith & Medin, 1981; and Haynes and Baker, Chapter 7, this volume). But the point is that some words generally accommodate automatic lexical access while others require more conscious processing; as Robinson notes, *both* types of words are needed for fluent, accurate reading and word guessing.

IMPLICATIONS FOR PEDAGOGY

What does a thoroughly interactive conception of second-language reading and vocabulary acquisition, as depicted in the preceding chapters, indicate for second language teachers and students? What are the pedagogical implications that emerge from this book?

First of all, we think that teachers, course designers, and materials developers should try to devise interesting new ways to help learners develop automaticity in word-level processing. Rapid, accurate word-form recognition and lexical access appear to be essential, not only for fluency, but for top-down monitoring and contextual guesswork. Even spelling and pronunciation—long assumed to be important only for "active" uses of vocabulary (e.g., speaking and writing)—can be important in the "passive" recognition of words. Probably the most efficient way to develop word-recognition automaticity is through a well-planned program of direct instruction, with each word being given salient instructional focus (see Chapter 13) in a variety of contexts over time. In most educational settings it would be logistically impossible to teach more than three or four thousand words in this way, but, as Coady et al. (Chapter 11) point out, if these few thousand words are chosen according to general frequency of use in the language, they would include the vast majority of words appearing on any page of print. They would also include virtually all of the procedural vocabulary discussed by Robinson (Chapter 12).[2] Statistically based frequency lists (e.g., Francis & Kučera 1982, Carroll, Davies, & Richman, 1971) can be consulted for this purpose. Even learners studying a language for specific purposes (e.g., ESP, EAP) would benefit from mastering the high-frequency words of the language. As Robinson notes, the words that tend to give ESP learners most difficulty are not the low-frequency technical words but the relatively high-frequency non-technical words.

Attempts should be made to make this core vocabulary learning interesting and motivating to students. As discussed in Chapters 2 and 12, and in pedagogical books like Gairns and Redman's (1986), Morgan and Rinvolucri's (1986), and Nation's (1990), a variety of methods should be used, including keyword mnemonics, word families, puzzles, games, and other exercises. In schools where computers are readily available, computer-assisted instruction could be considered. As Coady et al. argue in Chapter 11, well-designed computer programs can be a convenient, enjoyable, and efficient way of drilling students on high-frequency vocabulary, giving them more autonomy and taking some of the burden off instructors.

Second, for less frequent vocabulary, students seem to need some instruction in using context clues, especially global clues. They need this instruction not only for cases where they do not recognize a word but also for routine top-down monitoring (or "metacognition"). The studies in this volume converge in their findings that, although second-language learners use *local* context clues naturally, they often do not use *global* clues at all. Instruction in the use of global clues would likely help learners improve both their word-guessing skills and their reading skills.

Thematic reading courses might make it easier for students to use global context clues, as suggested by Parry. Such courses would immerse the student in an ongoing context, just as many academic specialty courses do, and that context would presumably be available for word-guessing and reading comprehension. But it is not clear what the long-term effects of such richness of context would be. If there is an inverse relationship between guessability and long-term retention, as is suggested by Coady (Chapter 1) and by Mondria and Wit-de-Boer (1989), it may be that thematic courses have short-term benefits but long-term shortcomings. Also, the extent of interaction between background knowledge and vocabulary comprehension is still a controversial area of research. Clearly, these are empirical issues that need to be explored further.

Third, students seem to need instruction in how to use morphological analysis, syntactic structure, and procedural vocabulary. Sometimes the learners observed in the studies reported here misanalyzed words grammatically and then tried to "reconstruct" the sentence to make the misanalyzed word fit into it, with often infelicitous results. Traditional vocabulary-learning instruction has always included a morphology and syntax component, and it would appear that second language learners might well benefit from such instruction.

Finally, Brown's research with interactive video and Coady's studies of computer-assisted instruction suggest ways in which high technology can be used for instructional purposes. Brown, for example, noted that the video display created conceptual "gaps" in the learner's mind before the target words that served as labels for those gaps were presented in exercises. Her findings indicate that this gap-before-word sequence enhanced word learning. Although it remains to be seen whether these findings have general validity, they do serve to remind us that timing of input and immediacy of feedback are important instructional variables. Interactive video, self-paced CAI programs, and the new word-processing programs with their built-in spell checkers, style analyzers, dictionaries, and thesauri could all be used in various ways for instructional purposes.

UNRESOLVED ISSUES

It is a commonplace of research projects that more questions are raised than are answered. Loyal to that tradition, the present volume offers the following as a sampler of issues that await further study:

1. *Coady's mystery:* How does contextual learning of words occur over time? How well do learners retain the words they have learned through guessing? We have a pretty good idea of how learners infer word meanings from

context, but we know little about how this translates into actual acquisition. It has been claimed (Mondria & Wit-de-Boer, 1989) that there is an inverse relationship between guessability and retainability, but this cannot be true in any absolute sense, as *some* degree of guessability is *necessary* for a word to be understood and retained in memory. Is there some optimal degree of guessability for words to be learned? We need more longitudinal studies like Parry's, going into even greater detail about the incremental nature of incidental vocabulary learning. And we need to figure out how to test for such incremental acquisition.

2. *Coady's paradox:* How much sight vocabulary is needed in order to do effective contextual guessing? This of course would vary from one text to another (see Barnett, 1989) and would depend on other variables as well, such as reading purpose, reading style, reading situation, etc. But if a great deal of automatic word recognition is needed to guess the meanings of other words, then we may have to do more direct vocabulary teaching than we currently do.

3. How can we teach vocabulary directly without ignoring the complex patterns of meaning relationships that characterize a complete and fully formed lexicon? One of the arguments for learning from context is that it gives students a richer sense of a word's appropriate usage, collocational relationships, variations in meaning, etc. Is it possible to provide such information through direct instruction? And if so, would students find it palatable?

4. How important is repetition? Is successful learning a function of type of attention rather than sheer volume of repetition, as Nation (1990) claims? Proponents of incidental learning of vocabulary usually argue that learners need at least 10–12 exposures to a word over time in order to retain the word. But this does not take into account the sorts of saliency factors discussed by Brown and alluded to by Nation. Such factors might well have a major influence on contextual learning.

5. Does vocabulary learning work best when conceptual activation occurs *before* word presentation (as Brown's study seems to suggest)? Coady's observation about rich semantic contexts giving learners less reason to pay attention to word forms would seem to argue against this notion. That is, if a concept is activated by the context, why would a learner need to pay attention to the form of the word? Perhaps there is a difference between visual conceptual activation and verbal conceptual activation.

6. How does the internal structure of the second-language learner's lexicon change over time? As Coady notes in Chapter 1, most researchers on bilingualism subscribe to the view that the L2 learner's lexicon is, at first, part of his or her L1 lexicon but then gradually becomes differentiated from it. But we know little about the actual details of this development. Since this has major implications for pedagogy (e.g., Should learners be

immersed in the foreign language or allowed access to the native language?), more research on bilingual development is badly needed. One problem will be how to detect incremental acquisition of vocabulary over time.

7. What kinds of texts should be used for reading? Simplified? Authentic? If learners need to be able to recognize most words of a text automatically in order to use contextual guesswork on the remaining few, simplified texts would likely facilitate this process. But using simplified texts in class could impede learners when they try to deal with authentic texts on their own.

WHAT KIND OF RESEARCH?

In attempting to find answers to the questions just raised, researchers may want to use techniques that have already been used and found helpful, including:

- Longitudinal case studies like Parry's.
- Longitudinal experimental studies like those of Coady et al.
- Fine-grained process studies, like those done by Huckin and Bloch (this volume), Hosenfeld, and others. Such studies could include eye-movement tracking like that used in studies of L1 reading (e.g., Rayner & Pollatsek, 1989; Carpenter & Just, 1987).
- Nonsense words, as illustrated in the Haynes and Chern chapters.
- Classroom observation, as illustrated in the Holmes & Ramos chapter.
- Linguistics-based text analysis, as in the Stein and Robinson chapters.
- Using native-speaker groups for comparison, as is done in the Dubin/ Olshtain and Haynes/Baker studies.
- Using interactive video (Brown, Chapter 13) and other new technologies (e.g., hypertext, online dictionaries, thesauri) to control and measure input.

To enhance the validity of their findings, researchers may find it desirable to use naturalistic tasks. In the studies described in this book, for example, students were asked to do a variety of things that are fairly common in academic settings, such as:

1. reading course materials and keeping a log of difficult words,
2. translating course readings,
3. underlining difficult words in a textbook and writing a recall summary,
4. writing a collaborative summary of a class reading,
5. studying vocabulary through computer-assisted instruction,
6. learning vocabulary in conjunction with information in diagrams or other illustrations.

Finally, researchers would do well, we think, to try to assemble converging evidence from multiple methods. Single methods tend to yield one-dimensional perspectives, which are simply inadequate for a subject as complex as second-language reading and vocabulary learning. A number of the studies in this book use multiple methods of investigation and analysis. More importantly, the book as a whole presents a variety of methods focused on the same basic topic and on the same basic set of questions:

> *What constitutes the process of guessing words from context?*
> *What is context in the first place?*
> *What kinds of context clues do learners naturally use, and what kinds need to be taught?*
> *What kinds of reading exercises can best help the learner develop expert guessing skills?*
> *What sorts of learner differences can we expect to find?*

We may not have provided definitive answers to these questions, but the fact that many of our findings converge gives us hope that we are at least on the right track.

REFERENCES

Barnett, M. A. (1989). *More than meets the eye: Foreign language reading: Theory and practice.* Englewood Cliffs, NJ: Prentice-Hall Regents.

Carpenter, P., & Just, M. (1987). *The psychology of reading and language comprehension.* Boston: Allyn and Bacon.

Carroll, J. B., Davies, P., & Richman, B. (1971). *The American Heritage word frequency book.* Boston: Houghton Mifflin.

Clark, H. H., & Gerrig, R. J. (1983). Understanding old words with new meanings. *Journal of Verbal Learning and Verbal Behavior, 22,* 591–608.

Duignan, M. A. M. (1990). *An investigation of second language vocabulary acquisition through reading.* Unpublished doctoral dissertation, State University of New York, Stony Brook.

Francis, N., & Kučera, H. (1982). *Frequency analysis of English usage: Lexicon and grammar.* Boston: Houghton-Mifflin.

Gairns, R., & Redman, S. (1986). *Working with words.* Cambridge, UK: Cambridge University Press.

Huckin, T., & Jin, Z.-D. (1987). Inferring word-meaning from context: A study in second-language acquisition. In F. Marshall (Ed.), *ESCOL '86.* Columbus, OH: Ohio State University, Department of Linguistics.

Laufer, B. (1988). The concept of 'synforms' (similar lexical forms) in vocabulary acquisition. *Language and Education, 2*(2), 113–134.

Miller, G. (1987). How school children learn words. In F. Marshall, A. Miller, & Z.-S. Shang (Eds.), *ESCOL '86.* (pp. 405–420). Columbus, OH: Ohio State University, Department of Linguistics.

Mondria, J., & Wit-de-Boer, M. (1989, September). Worden leren door raden? De invloed van context op het raden en outhouden van woorden [To learn words through guessing? The influence of context on the guessing and retention of words]. *Levende Talen,* pp. 497–500.

Morgan, J., & Rinvolucri, M. (1986). *Vocabulary.* Oxford: Oxford University Press.

Nagy, W. E., & Herman, P. A. (1987). Breadth and depth of vocabulary knowledge: Implications for acquisition and instruction. In M. G. McKeown & M. E. Curtis (Eds.), (1987). *The nature of vocabulary acquisition* (pp. 19–35). Hillsdale, NJ: Erlbaum.

Nation, P. (1990). *Teaching and learning vocabulary.* New York: Newbury House.

Pressley, M., Levin, J. R., & McDaniel, M. A. (1987). Remembering versus inferring what a word means: Mnemonic and contextual approaches. In M. G. McKeown & M. E. Curtis (Eds.), (1987). *The nature of vocabulary acquisition* (pp. 19–35). Hillsdale, NJ: Erlbaum.

Rayner, K., & Pollatsek, A. (1989). *The psychology of reading.* Englewood Cliffs, NJ: Prentice-Hall.

Shand, M. (1990). *Vocabulary acquisition: A provocative new direction.* Unpublished manuscript. [Author's address: Inter American University, San German, Puerto Rico 00753]

Smith, E., & Medin, D. (1981). *Categories and concepts.* Cambridge, MA: Harvard University Press.

Sternberg, R. J. (1987). Most vocabulary is learned from context. In M. G. McKeown & M. E. Curtis (Eds.), *The nature of vocabulary acquisition* (pp. 19–35). Hillsdale, NJ: Erlbaum.

ENDNOTES

1. This figure refers to the estimated reading vocabulary of the average high school graduate. Miller (1987) gives an estimate for the same reader of 80,000 words.

2. An interesting unpublished paper by Michael Shand (1990) describes research done by Johnson O'Connor half a century ago that provides evidence supporting Coady et al.'s viewpoint. According to Shand, O'Connor claims that, if we rank the words of a language according to "difficulty" (this being defined by how many speakers of that language know the word), we find that native speakers know virtually all words on that scale up to a certain, individually determined level. In other words, there is consistency in order of acquisition. And word frequency is probably the major component in word "difficulty."

Author Index

Subject Index

A

Access hypothesis, 27–28, 33
Active model of language learning, 47
Active vs. passive knowledge, *see* Productive vs, receptive knowledge
Affixes, 29, 32
Aptitude hypothesis, 27
Arabic readers, 51, 53–56, 63
Attended processing, 155
  processing resources for (cognitive capacity), 8–9, 13, 18, 178
Attended vocabulary learning from context strategies for, 17, 19, 80
Automated (vs. attended) processing, 219, 291
Automatic processing, 8–10, 16, 18, 45, 50, 174, 227
  of grammar, 261

B

Background knowledge, *see* World knowledge
Backward scanning, 140–141
Bottom up processing, 6, 9, 47–48, 50, 57–58, 60, 62–64, 155, 182–183, 289, 291

C

Causality and correlation, 45, 83–84
Chinese readers, 68–80, 83, 130, 136, 138–148, 156–169
  traditional literacy and risk-taking, 80
Classroom-based research, 96–98, 108
Cloze testing, 58, 63, 181–201
Cognate language, 174
Cognate vocabulary, 56, 86–108
Cognates, identifying, 88–89, 292
Cognitive model of contextual word guessing, 169–172, 177
Cognitive psychology, 26

Cognitive style, 84
Communicative competence
  dimensions of, 233
  discourse, 252–256
  grammatical, 243–244, 248–250
  sociolinguistic, 246–248, 254
  strategic, 244, 250–252
Computer-assisted instruction, 220–225, 227–228, 293–294
  individualization of, 227–228
  motivation of, 227–228
  selection of content vs. task, 228
Concept gapping, 263, 265, 275, 278–281, 284–285
  for noun, verb and adjective, 280
Conceptual activation, 295; *see also* Lexical access, Concept gapping
  time for, 50, 59
Conceptual definition, checklist, 210–211
Conceptual relevance (definition), 207–208
Confidence ratings, 139
Confounding variable, 84
Consciousness, 169; *see also* Attended processing
Construction of meaning, 47–48; *see also* Sense creation
Containment (hyponymy), 207–208
Context clues, 50, 68–80
  backward vs. forward clues, 71–72, 74–77, 79, 83–84
  global vs. local clues, 52–55, 60, 62–63, 71–79, 81, 153, 161, 165, 172, 173, 178, 202, 292, 294
  guessing from, 18–19, 47, 67–129, 153–178, 181–211
    multiple guesses, 166
  inexplicitness of natural language, 213
  insufficient clues for guessing, 55, 166–167, 182, 205